Falling in love gives you no time or pl
a deliberate act that can leave you breathl
is no rhyme, no sense, no time. There is
befuddles you. In the right time and place it can cause you to reach highest highs or the lowest of lows. Bad timing though for any romance can hurt you more than the love itself.

Reese has worked hard all her life to garner the satisfaction in the jobs and levels she has obtained. Landing the position of estate manager for the Cavindish family of England is exciting. A new country, a new challenge, and a new life. She packs up her life in Connecticut, kisses her daughter good bye and set's off on what she is sure will be the adventure of a lifetime...in its own time.

Lady Cavindish is shy, retiring, and a bit out of her league when the attractive confident blonde, Reese Paulson arrives on the scene to run their family estates for her brother the lord of the manor. Her admiration for Reese soon turns to hero worship and at some point to a love that neither expected. Their love however isn't what the Cavindish family name or property's needs, it is bad timing for everyone involved.

The love she feels for Lady Cavindish is totally unexpected and Reese soon realizes that her presence can only hinder the woman she has fallen for. She makes the excruciating decision for them both to move on, without her.

Finding a new love in Australia though proves that life has plans for us that we can only hope gives us what we need, can Reese move on from the woman she loves, or can she love the women she has moved on to. How can she forget Victoria, her first love?

Fate however brings them together time and time again, can it time their romance so they can have their happily ever after or is it determined to rip their hearts raw time and time again?

A Novel by **K'Anne Meinel**

TIMED ROMANCE

Also by K'Anne Meinel:

In Paperback:

SHIPS CompanionSHIP, FriendSHIP, RelationSHIP
Long Distance Romance
Children of Another Mother
Erotica
The Claim
Germanic
Bikini's Are Dangerous
The Complete Series
Malice Masterpieces
The First Five Books
Represented

In E-Book Format:

Short Stories

Fantasy
Wet & Wet Again
Family Night
Quickie ~ Against the Car
Quickie ~ Against the Wall
Quickie ~ Over the Couch
Mile High Club
Quickie ~ Under the Pier
Heel or Heal
Kiss
Family Night 2
Beach Dreams
Internet Dreamers
Snoggered
The Rockhound
Stolen
Agitated

Novellas

Bikini's are Dangerous
Kept
Ghostly Love
Bikini's are Dangerous 2
On the Parkway
Stable Affair
Sapphic Surfer
Bikini's are Dangerous 3
Bikini's are Dangerous 4
Bikini's are Dangerous 5
Mysterious Malice (Book 1)
Meticulous Malice (Book 2)
Mistaken Malice (Book 3)
Malicious Malice (Book 4)
Masterful Malice (Book 5)
Matrimonial Malice (Book 6)
Mourning Malice (Book 7)
Murderous Malice (Book 8)
Sapphic Cowgirl
Sapphic Cowboi

Novels

SHIPS CompanionSHIP, FriendSHIP, RelationSHIP
Erotica Volume 1
Long Distance Romance
Bikini's Are Dangerous
The Complete Series
Malice Masterpieces
The First Five Books
To Love a Shooting Star
Children of Another Mother
Germanic
The Claim
Represented

Videos

Biography of Books
Ships
Sapphic Surfer
Ghostly Love
Long Distance Romance
Germanic
Sensual Sapphic
Sapphic Cowgirl
Couples
Lie Next To Me
Sapphic Cowboi
Timed Romance

INTERVIEW FOR TIMED ROMANCE

Why the name TIMED ROMANCE? Many relationships are a matter of timing. Sometimes good, sometimes bad. In this case fate keeps casting these characters together and life keeps pulling them apart until they think they have the timing right. Lots of twists and turns and simply life getting in the way of their love and what they want. Really that is the point though, life is not simple, and it's a matter of a delicate balance of timing. If you meet someone at a particular time in your life they may or may not be important to you at that time and that may change later on, all due to timing.

Did you base your characters on anyone in particular? I have a mental image of someone that they remind me of and describe them for myself and my readers to picture them. Sometimes I use someone I've met, someone famous, an actress or model but the personality, the character themselves, that is usually pure fiction. Occasionally I will use a friend or acquaintance who doesn't realize they have become a part of my story.

Is any of the drama part of your own life? Yes to a degree we all have been a victim of bad timing. That first relationship or that first love, that one person we can't get out of mind and move on mentally from for a long time if ever. I have fond memories of my first love and I used that here to describe some of the feelings and situations they both might encounter.

Have you been to the places that you describe in your story? No, not yet. I made these up based on pictures, ideas, and my own imagination. Someday I hope to travel to the general locations that I described in the story, I wonder how accurate I was, but then the reader has their own interpretation of what I'm describing so whether you've been there or not you have a place in mind.

How long did you research the story? I started it a year ago and wrote about 75% of it before losing interest and putting it aside. I always knew approximately where the story was going but didn't touch it again until this spring (2013). It surprised even me though as the story changed from my original plan. The characters had changed from what they were originally going to do, perhaps I changed and as a result the story changed.

Do your stories always end up like you plan? No, almost never. I make general outlines, have an idea of where the story is going to go but my moods, watching a movie, reading a book, even a casual conversation can alter where the story is going, not on a whim but more as it takes on a life of its own.

You seem to be a very prolific writer, any comments? Yes, I'm writing continuously it seems but really I just get these spurts of creativity that I capitalize on when the mood strikes me. It may seem that I'm releasing several novels, novellas, or short stories at a time but sometimes I've been working on them or started them long ago and just so happened to finish them at the same time. I get writers block even though I have dozens of stories on my word processor at any given moment in various stages of completion. I wouldn't really call it 'writer's block' really, more like writers ennui; I just don't 'feel' like writing for a period of time. Perseverance, determination, and sometimes just sheer will power overcome that and at other times something or someone 'inspires' me to write and write and write!

You made a video of this book this time, what determines when you do make one or don't? Sometimes I see pictures that I need to help me develop the story. In this case because I hadn't traveled to the locations except in my mind it helped to write the story. In fact the video is designed to build expectation, anticipation of a Timed Romance. One of the last pictures in the video of the two women in the library inspired one of the last scenes in the book. Those who read it will recognize the similarities that I described.

What would you like the reader to take away from your story? That there is always hope, we all keep it in the back of our minds, in the depths of our heart and soul. Not every romance is destined to die or fade out but not every romance is meant to be found again either. Always remember the good times and try to think positively about the person you've loved (even if they DON'T deserve it! It makes you a better person and you know you learned something from the romance). There is a time and place for every love even if you can't see it at that moment.

K'Anne Meinel

TIMED ROMANCE

Published by:
Shadoe Publishing on CreateSpace

ISBN-13: 978-1483901978
ISBN-10: 1483901971

K'Anne Meinel is available for comments at KAnneMeinel@aim.com as well as on Facebook, Google +, or her blog @ http://kannemeinel.wordpress.com/ or on Twitter @ kannemeinelaim.com, or on her website @ www.kannemeinel.com if you would like to follow her to find out about stories and book's releases.

www.shadoepublishing.com

ShadoePublishing@gmail.com

PUBLISHER'S NOTE

This is a work of fiction. Names, characters, places, and incidents are the product of the author's imagination or are used fictitiously, and any resemblance to actual persons, living or dead, business establishments, events, or locales is entirely coincidental.

The publisher does not have any control over and does not assume any responsibility for author or third-party Web sites or their content.

CHAPTER 1

"I got it!" she practically shouted as she read the letter of acceptance and contracts that had arrived by special delivery.

"What did you get?" Gillian asked curious at the letter her mother was holding so excitedly.

"I got the job in England!" she was so excited she had to read the letter again. She unconsciously fingered the fine scripted and embossed letterhead.

Dear Ms. Paulson,

Pursuant to your application and resume as well as our conversations via the telephone and

Internet I am offering you the position of General Manager for our estates here in England.

Please reply by quickest route so that we may arrange your travel itinerary.

Enclosed are the copies of our contract with you, please fax at your earliest convenience.

Regards,
Lord Cavandish

Not the warmest of letters but then the English weren't known for being warm and cozy. She handed the letter to Gillian as she began to read over the five page contract that was enclosed. Everything that she and Lord Cavandish had agreed upon was spelled out in legalese and black and white. She was so excited!

"England eh? When did this come about?" Gillian asked curious.

"Oh, it's been going on for months it seems," she sighed in remembrance, thinking it was never going to happen. "I can't tell you how many phone calls, emails, and internet chats I had with this Lord Cavandish."

"Why did you apply there?"

Shrugging she smiled, "Because it's somewhere different. I can use my skills for something larger than this." Her arms took in the living room where they were standing.

"Congratulations Mom, I hope it makes you very happy," Gillian smiled as she took her mom in her arms for a big hug. "I'm so proud of you!"

Reese smiled as she looked at her daughter. A lot of hard work had come to this point, not that the job wasn't going to be hard work but she had slaved in rotten jobs for years to get her degree and prove that she could and would manage the positions she had been given. Her experience and her educational background had proved to be the right formula to obtain this position and now she felt her life could and would begin.

"Oh my God! I have to get a passport and a working visa or something," she remembered. "It takes weeks too!"

Gillian laughed at her mother; she was the most efficient woman she knew. If it was up to her the paperwork necessary wouldn't take weeks but it would be up to bureaucrats who knew nothing about Reese Paulson and her efficiency.

Reese had the fax sent within an hour with her signed copies of the contract after she thoroughly read it twice. It arrived in England in the middle of the night but would be on the desk of Lord Cavandish first thing in the morning. She went to the post office that afternoon to fill out the paperwork necessary to get her passport. She had her birth certificate and a passport photo taken at the local Walgreens already in hand so it could go out that same day. She brought home convenient sized boxes to pack the things that she wanted to go with her to her new home. Gillian helped her pack away the things she would be leaving over the next few weeks. They would go into storage indefinitely as Gillian had no room in the dorms and wouldn't have a place of her own for years.

By the time her passport showed up in only four weeks everything was taken care of for an extended stay in England. Her boxes of personal things were either in a shipping container on their way to England or in a storage facility in Concord. Gillian drove her to La Guardia and kissed her goodbye at the curb. Since she couldn't walk her to the plane these days post 9/11 they had said their good-byes the previous night enjoying their last night together.

"Take care baby girl," Reese said as she hugged her daughter one more 'last' time.

"You too Mom, enjoy yourself, keep warm!" she handed her a bag and said, "Don't open it until you're on the plane."

"Don't you remember they ask you if have accepted a bag or package from strangers?" they both shared a laugh, a last laugh. Reese stuffed the bag in her purse and kissed her daughter on the cheek before she headed into the terminal.

Gillian would keep Reese's old Corolla which was in excellent condition and Reese had signed over the 'pink' slip to her daughter as she returned to the dorms where she lived. Reese regretted leaving her daughter but they both understood that she needed to make her own life, she had goals, and she had dreams too. As the plane took off Reese looked down on New York and wondered when she would see this part of the world again. As she opened the bag her daughter had given her she started to laugh at the pair of wool socks that Gillian had given her to 'keep warm.' Everyone had this mental image of England as cold and foggy.

CHAPTER 2

A sign with the name Reese Paulson written on it gave her a clue as to the identity of the chauffeur that met her after customs. Smiling she walked up and said, "I'm Reese Paulson," to the startled man.

She is not what I expected at all was his first thought. The staff had speculated endlessly on the identity of the new General Manager that Lord Cavandish had engaged. That she was an American was already against her. That she must be good at what she did though was accepted, Lord Cavandish didn't suffer fools gladly, he hired only the best. But this? Had Lord Cavandish realized what she looked like?

Reese was 5'11" tall and a leggy blonde with short stylishly trimmed hair. The elegant cut of her hair only emphasized her strong cheekbones and pert little nose. Deeply black lashes framed incredibly dark hazel eyes with an intense look outlined by dark eyebrows. She could have been a model and had done it part time occasionally to supplement her income from time to time. She hated the 'meat market' as she referred to it and couldn't bear to do it too often so it had never become a career for her. Instead she had taken courses from NYU until she got her degree in Hotel Management with a minor in Estate Marketing which was not necessarily something people looked for in this day and age. She managed hotels for years before she had the degree and slowly moved up the chain of command in the various establishments that she worked. People were always surprised that this leggy blonde though had quite a head for business and marketing. They assumed with her good looks that she was a ditzy model and she astounded them with her performance. All her past employers would have welcomed her back in a heartbeat and it was this with her impressive resume that had gotten her the job at Cavandish House and its estates.

"Is this all your luggage?" Frank asked surprised.

Reese grinned. Her two bags would have filled the back of her Corolla they were so large but the chauffeur apparently had expected an entire cart full. "My other things are being shipped over," she told him and her voice even surprised him, it was warm and caressing, and would make most men weak at the knees.

He soon had the two bags efficiently packed into the back of a Rolls Royce limousine. Reese was impressed in spite of herself as she sat in the back seat. She would have sat up front with the driver but knew that the protocol must be followed in this instance. Her reputation must be established from the beginning. She knew her looks would be held against her until her work spoke for itself. She didn't want to start off on the wrong foot before she even started the job.

The drive from busy Heathrow airport north took hours. Reese enjoyed gawking at the sights of this first foray for her to a foreign country. She had read endless books on the area she was going to work in but it didn't prepare her for the sheer beauty once they left the highway. She would have been delightfully lost and was grateful the chauffeur knew where they were going. She even felt like the country was 'old' it was so settled. Many houses and building she saw had been there for years, some of them hundreds of years and she was thrilled to see them. She loved where she had lived in Connecticut but this was a whole different feeling. She was so excited. She tried not to look like a country bumpkin as she looked out the windows.

As they pulled down the driveway of the large estate she mentally prepared herself to meet the Lord of the Manor as it were. She had thoroughly researched Lord Cavandish and his family as much as she could find on him. He was a fairly private man and the details had been sketchy but from the news reports she read and the history of his forbearers she wasn't surprised that he was stereotypically English. She was surprised though that he met the car as they pulled up into the portico of the mansion.

"Ms. Paulson?" he inquired politely if somewhat stiffly as he put out his hand to help her from the car. He looked a bit alarmed as she unwound her long legs from the car and stood up beside him. She was only an inch or so below his own 6'1" height. He had never thought to inquire about what she looked like and hadn't paid attention when they Skyped, he was very surprised at her beauty and elegance; the internet hadn't done her justice, the camera not quite catching the beauty. It didn't match with the image he had in his mind of a short and efficient manager for his estates.

"Good Afternoon Lord Cavandish. I'm delighted to finally meet you in person," she said politely. She wondered if she should curtsy.

He bowed slightly from the waist as he shook her hand. He masked his surprise immediately thinking he should have never hired a woman despite her excellent references and resume. This simply wouldn't do. Stiffly he asked, "Was your trip satisfactory?"

Reese could read what was going through his mind. She had heard it all before, she had seen it countless times. Smiling slightly she nodded before adding, "Give me a chance before you decide."

His eyebrows shot up in genuine astonishment. Seeing the humor in her eyes he rose to the challenge and gave a hint of a grin in spite of himself. "Let's go in and get you settled," he invited.

She smiled; she had a foot in the door at least. He allowed her to walk in first. The house was Edwardian in appearance but had an H shape to it in honor of one of the Henry's that once ruled this country. Reese was delighted to see the thick ivy covering the red brick although the house itself was amazingly shabby with bricks and mortar missing beneath the prolific ivy covering. Many windows looked out on the courtyard as they entered. The entranceway took her breath away with the largest chandelier she had ever seen in her life. It badly needed cleaning she could see by faint cobwebs. A large grandfather clock ticked ominously in the entranceway, a beautiful staircase led upstairs, rich woods lined the large entranceway which had cobwebs and dust balls around the edges and in the corners. She wondered at that but could tell that Lord Cavandish was already distracted. He escorted her into the library and invited her to sit. Looking around the book lined shelves she enjoyed seeing the rich honey colored woodwork that must be a hundred years old its hue could only be reached through time. A fireplace burned at one end and she could see it didn't draw well.

"I was wondering how long you feel you might need to get oriented before you begin work?" he asked as he settled himself behind an immense desk that matched the bookshelves.

Reese didn't hesitate, "What would you like to get started with Lord Cavandish?" she asked. She wondered if this were a test.

Lord Cavandish's eyebrows almost disappeared he was so surprised. It had been his experience that American's didn't delve right into work. They usually were more laid back and informal. He warmed at his choice for this position, "When we are with family or alone you may call me Lord David, only in public must you call me Lord Cavandish," he informed her trying not to sound haughty and failing miserably.

Reese smiled briefly and waited for instructions.

"Your office is through there," he pointed to a set of doors off the library. "I am afraid I have been trying to do your job as well as mine and doing poorly. It is in quite disarray and I hope you are up to the challenge?"

Reese didn't answer and instead waited for instructions. This silence worked in her favor as Lord David was made uncomfortable. He wasn't sure why she wasn't asking questions, protesting at what he was telling her, or saying something.

"If you would like to have a tour?" he asked hesitantly.

Reese shook her head and instead asked, "Why don't I see what I have waiting for me?"

David was relieved to pass it on to her. His solicitor had kept up on things for quite some time after their last manager had been fired for embezzlement and it had been a mess for quite some time before and after that. A recommendation from an acquaintance had led him to this woman whom he hoped lived up to the promise that had been implied. He wasn't sure though that this model was the woman he had spoken with so many times over the telephone or internet, although he had to admit that seeing her seated in a chair via the internet really didn't or couldn't tell him about her height. He would wait to see if she could do the job. Gesturing he gave her leave.

Reese rose and crossed the incredibly plush carpet that she sank into. It nearly staggered her as she just walked through it. Opening the right hand double door she looked with delight on the smaller office that had obviously been in use for a lot of years and yet not so recently by the stacks of mail that sat on every available surface. Closing the door behind her she was appalled that an estate the size she knew Cavandish was would be in such disarray. Such disorganization would only lead to theft and laziness in the staff, and this was just at the home estate. She was tempted to run and have them take her back to the airport only to realize this would be the first of many challenges in her 'new' life. She took off her jacket and rolled up her sleeves. Sitting down at the desk she realized she couldn't even see over the first stack in the middle of the desk. Standing she began on the first letter.

CHAPTER 3

"Did the new estate manager arrive David?" a voice asked him as he worked at his own desk.

David looked up at his sister as she came into the library and smiled. "Yes, she is at work now," he replied.

"Already?" she asked surprised. "Doesn't she need to rest after that flight?"

David shrugged, he hadn't thought of that but then he was busy with his own work so that he would be free for the weekend. It was already late on Thursday and if he wanted to play this weekend he needed to catch up on his work. He didn't want to even think of the estate work that was grossly behind and besides, it was no longer his problem.

"David!" she exclaimed to get his already wandering attention.

Looking up in surprise at his little sister's tone he blinked a moment to clear his mind.

"Don't tell me you put that poor little woman to work right off?" she asked in alarm.

He shrugged looking puzzled. What did it matter if she was working already or not?

"David, she is probably exhausted by the trip, hasn't eaten, and intimidated by this house! You should have given her a day or two before introducing her to that mess in that room!" she said exasperated. She knew her brother. He couldn't wait to hand off that part of his job to someone who was willing to do the work. He had been willing to pay well to get it off his shoulders. Although he worked hard himself for the family's good, managing the estates was not his forte. It was why the last manager had been able to fool them for so long and steal tens of thousands of pounds.

"I'll arrange a tray to be brought to her. At least if we feed her she might not quit!" she said to her annoying and already mind wandering brother.

"Thank you Veronica, that would be kind," he murmured as he looked down on his spreadsheet.

Veronica walked back to the kitchens catching the staff there scattering as she came through the swinging door. She knew they didn't do any more than they had to unless the members of the family were watching. It had been like this for years already and she didn't know how to change it at this point. "Mrs. Gunderson, I'd like a tray for the new estate manager to be brought to her office?" she asked politely.

A robust and apple cheeked woman nodded immediately and took down a wooden tray and began preparing a plate from what was cooking on the stove. When it was finished she said to a maid there, "Take this to the office," but Veronica vetoed the idea and said, "I'll take it myself," much to the staff's surprise and the maid's evident relief.

Veronica knocked on the outside door to the estate office and heard a pleasant and very American voice say, "Come in?" She balanced the tray on one arm as she twisted the latch. Carefully she opened the door with her foot as she walked into the now lamp lit room. There wasn't a table that didn't have a pile of letters, magazines, and papers on it. She had no idea where to put the tray. She looked curiously at the estate manager that her brother had hired. Veronica was stunned, she hadn't expected this. Veronica cleared her throat to get her attention.

Reese looked up from a letter she was reading and nearly gasped at the amazing purple eyes staring back at her. Incredibly long black eyelashes framed the beautiful eyes. A small nose and ruby lips that begged to be kissed added to the enchanting face of the woman before her. The woman looked to be in her twenties and nearly Reese's own height. Her curly brown hair came past her shoulders and was badly in need of trimming. No makeup but an interesting face thought Reese as she looked at the woman bringing in the tray.

"I thought you might like a bit of refreshment?" Veronica asked.

Reese smiled and looking around realized there really wasn't anywhere for the tray to be put down except in front of her. Rising she was pleasantly surprised that the woman was only a couple of inches shorter than she. "Here I can take that," she reached for the tray.

"I've got it, where would you like it?" Veronica asked.

"Here is fine," she indicated the space that wasn't quite clear but lower than when she had arrived in the room. A pile of opened envelopes was piled next to the desk by her feet.

Veronica stepped carefully around the stacks around the desk and placed the tray dead center on the desk on top of the lower piles. "There you go, I hope you like it."

Reese smiled seeing a bit of sliced ham, sliced turkey, some vegetables, sliced bread, and something that looked like pudding as well as a glass of milk and something that looked like tea. "Thank you, that's very kind of you."

Veronica was surprised that Reese was even taller than her own 5'9" height. She had always felt too tall and yet this very pretty woman was even taller and not in the least self-conscious about it. She didn't have the bent or curved shoulders that people who hid their height did. She stood tall and proud as she held out her hand and said, "Hello, I'm Reese Paulson."

Veronica held out her own hand and shook Reese's answering, "I'm Veronica Cavandish."

Reese cocked her head as though she had just heard something different, "Cavandish as in Lady Cavandish?"

Veronica smiled and nodded used to the title, "Yes, but you can call me Lady Veronica when we are alone."

Reese smiled at the similarity of the instructions given her by both Lord David as well as Lady Veronica. Not used to titles she would however respect their wishes.

"Is there anything else you need?" Veronica asked as she looked around at the mess. This office was a little overwhelming, it had bad memories for her and she desperately wanted to leave.

"Actually, I'd like to meet the housekeeper if she is available?" Reese asked.

Veronica nodded and began a retreat, "I'll send her in, I'll give you a few minutes to enjoy your meal."

Reese didn't know why but she was certain Veronica was very uncomfortable, she hid it well though, and she wondered why. "It was nice to meet you Lady Veronica; I look forward to getting to know you." She didn't know if that was too forward, she didn't know the protocol but she figured why not.

Veronica nodded as she closed the door relieved to have escaped before she had a panic attack. She went in search of Mrs. Anderson, the sister of their cook Mrs. Gunderson. Both had been with the family for their entire lives. One had married a groom and the other the former butler.

Mrs. Anderson entered the estate manager's office with the air of someone who owned the place. Reese noted that out of the corner of her eye as she finished reading one of the many letters she had opened. She also noticed that the housekeeper looked around the room with distaste and paused at seeing the tray that Reese had hastily eaten from sitting on the floor amid the stacks. Reese quietly looked at her waiting for her to look back. Finally the woman looked up at the blonde, "You wanted to see me?" she asked haughtily.

Reese smiled. This woman was exactly as she expected a housekeeper in a British household to be. Tall, austere, gray haired, and very snobbish. "Yes, Mrs. Anderson I believe?" she waited for the woman to nod before continuing, "I wonder if you will show me about the house tomorrow?" she asked pleasantly, pleased to see the woman look startled. She had come for battle and Reese didn't give it to her.

"I believe Lord Cavandish was planning on showing you about the estate," she replied.

Reese smiled further, "I will be delighted to have him show me about, I'm sure as someone who was raised here he will have an excellent view of what he wants done but as someone else who was raised here and has worked here all her life your views are ones I would likc to hear as well."

The woman preened slightly at the compliment. This woman was not what she had expected at all. "Of course I will be happy to show you the house."

Reese nodded and then asked, "Could someone show me to my room later?" she looked at her watch which she had already altered to reflect the six hour time difference from home and asked, "In perhaps an hour or so?"

The woman nodded and then reached down for the tray, "Would you like anything else?" she indicated the food tray.

Reese shook her head, "No, that will be all; it was delicious, please thank the cook, and thank you."

Mrs. Anderson took her leave and carried the tray to the kitchen. Mrs. Gunderson looked at the tray anxiously and asked, "Well, did she yell at you?"

"No not at all," she said the surprise still in her voice. "She wasn't at all what I expected. She said the food was delicious and asked me to show her about the house tomorrow."

"Isn't Lord Cavandish going to do that?" her sister asked curiously.

She nodded but added, "Yes, but she said I would have a different view of things and she wanted to hear it from me."

"Well, that's sensible. Servants always see things differently than the owners. What she like?" None of them had seen her when she arrived and the driver hadn't told anyone anything.

"She is blonde and very pretty but I didn't see much, she is already diving into those piles in the office."

"She has her work cut out for her with that mess."

CHAPTER 4

A maid showed Reese to her room late that evening. She was exhausted but she was anxious to get back to the office and that mess as soon as possible. She needed a good night's sleep though if she was going to be at her best. There were months of backlogged paperwork and bills that needed going through. Reese was surprised that she was being housed not in the servant's quarters as she had supposed but near to where the family rooms would be or so the maid informed her. Reese was also a little put out that her bags had already been unpacked. The only one not unpacked was her overnighter bag and this perhaps because the key was in her pocket. She was relieved that no one had gone through this one at least.

The room was luxurious, as nice as some of the five star hotels she had been in over the years. The room was full of antiques and she admired the rich colors of them. Slipping out of her clothes she showered quickly and not bothering to dress for bed she sank into the satin lined bed naked, and was soon asleep, exhaustion taking over.

When she woke in the morning she was still tired from her trip and the time difference but she was determined to set to work as soon as possible. Checking the time she was pleased that she had slept seven hours at least and quickly dressed. Slipping out of the room she noted its location because she was sure to get lost once or twice in this huge house. She found her way downstairs and taking a guess she opened first one door to find a living room and then another door to find the dining room. Already she saw Lady Veronica at the table who looked up at her entrance.

"Ah Ms. Paulson, please join me," she called.

"Good Morning Lady Veronica," Reese replied as she entered the room.

"Do help yourself," she indicated the food on a side table, "We are informal in the morning. Did you sleep well?" she inquired solicitously.

"Yes actually I did, I think I was a bit exhausted." Reese smiled at the understatement as she made a plate for herself of mostly fruits and some toast. Pouring a bit of orange juice she hesitated as to where to sit until Veronica nodded to the chair across from her. Grateful she sat down.

"Yes, I can't believe David set you right to work. You have your work cut out for you in that mess."

Reese smiled, putting her napkin across her lap she began to eat. "Well, he did warn me that it had been quite some time since anyone had been engaged at this position."

"That's an understatement." Veronica smiled back. "Are you making any headway?"

"I've just started but I have some ideas and I will know more by the end of today I am sure."

Veronica let her eat in silence for a while before asking, "Do you ride?"

Reese looked up from where she had been concentrating on her food to find Veronica studying her. She grinned, "Yes, I do." Then deciding to tease her employer a bit she asked, "You wouldn't happen to have any Western saddles here do you?"

Veronica smiled and shook her head, "No, I'm afraid only English riding hereabouts."

Reese shrugged, "I learned on English but I have always preferred Western."

"We will have to go riding; it's the best way to see the estate."

Lord David walked in just then and heard the last of that statement, "Nonsense, my Range Rover will show her the estate quite well."

Reese smiled at the friendly debate the siblings soon launched in: The merits of a machine over a horse. It was apparent they were fond of each other by their comments to each other and the teasing they engaged in. She herself had no siblings and it was amusing to listen as she quickly ate her breakfast, she didn't want Lord David waiting on her.

She did however wait on Lord David, for quite a while as he sat and chatted not only with Lady Veronica but with Reese. "So what made you apply for this position in the first place?" he asked curious. She wondered if he even remembered their initial phone interview.

"I wanted a challenge," she answered realizing how much of a challenge he had really given her when she had seen the office. She could only imagine what other surprises were in store for her.

His eyes twinkled at the unintentional double entendre she had given him. "I'm certain you will find this position very...um challenging," and she could see the hint of a grin.

She grinned back at him thinking the English weren't so stuffy after all. Later as he drove them on the back roads of the estate which badly needed fixing and the four wheel drive of the Range Rover was fully engaged she was surprised to find him totally enjoying himself, like a little boy with a toy. She wondered if it wasn't for the noises that the Rover was making on its own would he be making 'truck' sounds from his mouth. He showed her the meadows that they rented out and explained some of the contracts they had with local farmers to use their land for crops or livestock. The land was quite extensive. Lord Cavandish explained that his great great great grandfather had been a knight and his son was given a lordship for service to the king. The land had actually come from his great great great grandmother's side and through marriage they had added to the initial acreage over the years. He himself had handled the estate at one time but due to illness and the death of his father's estate agent and the hiring of an unscrupulous agent they were now in the mess she had found.

Reese was curious what illness prevented him from handling the estate himself? He seemed fine and in fact he talked enthusiastically about going away next weekend to visit friends and enjoy himself. She didn't dare ask though as she felt it was none of her business and if he wanted her to know he would tell her.

Their entire morning was taken up with him driving about the district showing her the various properties that were part of the estate. He mentioned that the other properties she would be in charge of were farther afield and she would have to go to them at another time. The chauffeur could take her or she would have to learn to drive herself eventually.

That was one thing that bothered Reese, could she drive on the opposite side of the road with the steering wheel on the opposite side of the car? Once Lord David mentioned it though he became intrigued by the idea and asked, "Do you drive manual transmission?"

Reese hesitated and then nodded, "Yes, I learned quite young to drive stick shift."

"Good," he pulled to the side of the dirt road they were on, "Let's see." Then he got out and came around to open her door. Surprised Reese let him hand her out of the Rover and walked around to the right side of the vehicle. She got in and was pleasantly surprised that she didn't have to adjust the seat since they were similar in height. As they both strapped themselves in she hesitantly released the parking brake and began to work the clutch and the shifter. After one bumpy start she found she got the hang of it quickly. It wasn't the open road but even with the steering wheel on the right side she was doing okay. They met a shepherd with a flock of sheep streaming over the road and she sat there watching and grinning. You never saw that in Concord, Connecticut!

"Are you enjoying the scenery," Lord David asked as he watched his beautiful estate manager look out over the hills.

Startled she realized the sheep were gone and they could go, she grinned, "Yes actually, it's beautiful here. So peaceful." She let out the clutch as she began to give it gas.

Her answer pleased David. Some people found their country estates too remote but he and Veronica had always enjoyed the solitude and found comfort in it. As Reese drove them back to the house he pointed out the barns and explained the breeding program that Veronica had enacted. She loved her horses.

"Yes, she invited me to go riding," Reese commented as she admired the beautiful horses and some foals she could see.

"Oh do go, she will enjoy that. Only friends that come out and stay occasionally ride with her besides a few of the grooms and she misses company so," he encouraged her.

"You don't ride?" she asked as she pulled up in the back of the house near the garages.

He looked sad for a moment as he shook his head and said, "No, I can't anymore," and he left it at that.

Reese was curious but again sensed if he wanted her to know he would tell her. She thanked him for the tour and the driving opportunity and left to go in and get back to work only to run into Mrs. Anderson.

"Ah there you are Ms. Paulson, do you have time for our tour now?" she asked pleasantly.

Reese smiled, she didn't want to, she had tons of paperwork to get through but there was no time like the present and she answered, "Of course Mrs. Anderson, if you are ready I am as well."

Mrs. Anderson began with the downstairs. The section of the H shape of the house where they were now housed the library, the office, the kitchens, the family living room, and the family dining room. One wing of the H contained a large ballroom and another dining room for parties. Above this on the upper floors which were reached by a magnificent staircase were the guest bedrooms. Above that were old servant's quarters that were now used for storage. On the other wing of the H were the conservatory with a beautiful array of plants and birds in cages. Veronica loved her plants and animals Mrs. Anderson confided. Also on this side was the formal sitting room or living room where they entertained guests when they came to call. Above this, again reached by a matching magnificent staircase were more guest bedrooms and above this more servant quarters which were in use by the household servants who lived on the grounds.

The rooms were spacious and beautiful but everything was slightly tinged with neglect. They weren't filthy but neither were they clean. Everything could use a thorough dusting. Finally, as they concluded their tour by the back of the kitchens near the gardens which had vegetables for the household use as well as beautiful flowers that were placed in vases throughout the living area, Reese had to ask. "Mrs. Anderson, why is that I see dust on the chandeliers and throughout the house?"

Mrs. Anderson had waited for this question. In fact it was what she had thought this new manager would comment on first. She had been pleasantly surprised at the delight and wide eyed wonder on the beautiful blonde's face as they toured the mansion. She was a little stiff in her reply, "At first it was a revenge on that Mr. Huffington that worked here before. But then after his Lordship became ill, we realized that stirring up the dust exasperated his symptoms."

"His symptoms?" Reese asked in surprise. She could understand the servants wanting to get Mr. Huffington fired, he had after all been a terrible manager, but to not clean because of Lord David?

"Yes, the dust tends to make his Lordship ill and he has even had to go to bed for a long period of time as he gets it in his lungs and it triggers an episode," she explained patiently.

Reese didn't want this woman to know she had no idea what she was talking about but she found the state of the house to be unacceptable. She wondered what she could do about it.

As they entered the kitchen though she thought at least they could start here. Mrs. Anderson introduced her to her sister 'Milly' or Mrs. Gunderson, the cook. Milly was surprised when Reese held out her hand to shake. The upper crust servants didn't usually bother and she was impressed that there were no 'airs' about this American. "I have you to thank for that delicious dinner last night, thank you," Reese said pleasantly.

"Ah, that little bit was the least we could do," she smiled liking this pretty woman.

"Mrs. Gunderson, I wonder if you would like some help this week in your kitchen?" she started.

Both the sisters looked at her strangely. "Help?" repeated Milly.

Reese nodded, "Yes, we need to give the kitchen a thorough cleaning. I want everything spotless and those stainless steel utensils haven't had a shine on them in quite some time I can see. His Lordship doesn't come back here but I'll bet you want a polish on your kitchen. We need everything in clean and working order and I bet the maids who aren't doing the dusting and other polishing about the mansion could use the practice," she smiled her eyes were glittering at her cunning.

Milly chuckled. This was no sly miss. She had understood the situation quickly. Those lazy sluts hadn't done a bit of work in years and still they collected their full pay. Practice indeed! There was going to be a lot of complaints heard over the next few days and it served them right!

Reese wasted no time. Everyone that worked in the house was called to a meeting in the kitchen before dinner. She explained very precisely and thoroughly what she expected from the staff from now on. Yes, overt dusting and polishing in the mansion had been avoided for his Lordships sake, however each and every room in the mansion and this included the staff quarters was to be cleaned in the coming weeks. Everyone was to start here in the kitchens and as there were so many of them, it should only take a few hours. Reese noticed the exchanged looks on several faces. Anyone who didn't like the new agenda could seek employment elsewhere she told them. Furthermore, his Lordship was out of the house at certain times in the day. The rooms around his could be aired and cleaned when they knew he was to be gone. Then she remembered he was going to be gone next weekend and she was inspired to add that his rooms would be cleaned, aired, and painted next weekend while he was gone. She had added the painted part on impulse as she had seen his rooms needed updating.

Milly had been right, there were a lot of complaints once Reese went to have lunch with his Lordship and Lady Veronica. Lunch was late today as dinner was to be with guests and late as well. Reese had no plans of joining them with their guests so she worked in her office until late. She was making headway in the piles. By that evening her desk was at least recognizable as a desk.

It took about a week but by the time his Lordship was on his trip her office was straightened out and organized. She found under the clutter an antiquated fax machine as well as a ten year old computer. After looking at the files she backed up what she could use and erased everything else. She ordered a new desktop computer as well as a laptop. Since faxes could come in at any time she ordered another one of those although both computers could send them.

She did as she had warned and while his Lordship was away she had his rooms thoroughly cleaned top to bottom and painted. Wallpaper was repaired and replaced and the whole appearance of the rooms was clean and fresh. Already she had fired two maids who weren't working up to snuff and this served as a warning to anyone else that times were a changing.

Veronica marveled at the changes in the house. No more did rooms smell musty and old. Even her arboretum was swept and cleaned, the windows for the first time in years polished from both sides. Her plants loved the new and brighter windows and responded accordingly. Veronica was amazed at how fresh everything felt and in such a short time.

Reese wandered down to the stables one day before his Lordship left looking for the gardeners. She found them sitting in the back of the stables smoking and sharing drinks. She memorized each of the faces she saw there for future reference and asked Mrs. Anderson to ask all the gardeners to meet her after lunch in front of the house.

Reese was early for their meeting and looking about the place as the five gardeners showed up. She could tell by their attitudes that they weren't happy with her and were wary, their body language said a lot.

"Hello, which one of you is the lead or head gardener?" she asked pleasantly.

A large fellow, beefy in appearance raised his hand. She looked at him, no expression on her face. "Can you tell me why there are weeds in the gardens?" she asked.

He looked at her in surprise. From what he had heard from the household staff who were busy scrubbing the house from top to bottom he thought he was in for it. He shrugged not understanding where this was going.

"Sir, I asked you a question. Do you know the difference between weeds and flowers?"

"I certainly do ma'am!" he said annoyed.

"How long have you been head gardener here?" she asked.

"Twenty years ma'am."

"How long would you like to remain head gardener?"

He looked at her puzzled, "I don't understand the question?"

"Sir, I would think in the twenty years you have been gardener here that you and your staff would know that all the gardens need to be maintained all the time. The gardens leading up to the house are in adequate condition but the grounds are in terrible shape. The lawns are pitted, the roads in horrible shape, and there are weeds in the flower beds throughout the side yards. I even found a gazebo that is falling apart."

He started to bluster but she held up her hand to silence him as she watched the four other gardeners to see their reactions. "I shouldn't have to tell you how to do your job and I won't. I see evidence by the front yard that you have talent but somewhere along the line someone got lazy. This *cannot* and *will not* continue."

All five of the gardeners heard the tone in her voice and were sure they were about to be dismissed. "I want to see improvement immediately or I will want to know why. No longer will you be taking three hour lunches behind the stables. Cigarette's will not be thrown about on the grounds. I want the butts picked up immediately and not just the new ones but the year's accumulations that exists about this place. It's a filthy, disgusting habit, and one of these times someone is going to throw down a used cigarette at the wrong place at the wrong time and we are going to have a fire on our hands. Do I make myself understood?" She looked at each and every one of the five men before her and received nods. "Good, then I expect to see steady improvement over the next few day's gentlemen. I will let you get to your work."

Veronica was astounded one day as she rode one of her Thoroughbreds to see Reese on a bulldozer helping to grade one of the back roads filling in the washed out and rutted areas and smoothing out and grading it. Furthermore she saw evidence where rock had been laid to circumvent water cuts in the newly graded road. Grass was planted and watered and would soon spring up alongside these freshly cut and laid areas. Fences were mended and painted. Reese even arranged for a bricklayer to repair any lose or damaged bricks on the house having him pull back the ivy where necessary to look and repair the loose bricks and missing mortar.

His Lordship was only gone five days but he was absolutely astounded at the improvements he witnessed as he drove up the drive and saw his gardeners working hard at cutting back overhanging branches and using a shredder to make compost. As he saw the bricklayer repairing things high up on some scaffolding he was thrilled to see how beautiful the outside was becoming. As he entered the foyer the sun was shining through polished windows and for the first time he realized how brilliant the Waterford Crystal chandelier really was. He hadn't realized it could shine so brightly. As he entered his library he stopped dead realizing not only the windows had been washed but every shelf had been polished, his desk and other furniture as well. The carpets had been carefully cleaned and the floor polished as well. Not a speck of dust existed and even the old drapes had been replaced. He was thrilled!

That night at dinner he waited until Reese sat herself and calmly stated, "Ms. Paulson, it seems that you and the staff have been busy while I have been away."

Reese grinned and nodded, "We have some excellent workers and those that didn't work out are no longer with us."

"You fired some of the staff?" he asked raising an eyebrow wondering if perhaps she had gone beyond herself too soon.

"Certainly, if they didn't want to do their jobs I found someone who was willing to do them." Reese waited, wondering if he would be angry or pleased.

David wanted to smile but at the same time he thought she had over stepped her authority, but then again, he had given her that authority. He gave a tight little smile and nodded and wisely dropped the subject.

CHAPTER 5

"How is it?" Gillian asked her after her first week and a half.

Reese smiled into the phone. Emails were never quite the same to hearing her baby girl's voice. "It's a mess."

Gillian smiled; she could hear the excitement in her mother's voice, "In other words, you're loving it!"

Reese nodded before adding, "Yes, and this is just the home 'estate,' next I have to check the outlying properties and get them up to snuff."

"How much do they own?" Gillian inquired never having been around anyone who owned 'estates.'

"I have no idea but I will soon. I'm working on mapping it to have a better idea of where and when and such."

"Do they resent you?" Gillian recalled many times her mother's going into a hotel and kicking butt only to have everyone from the chamber maids to the management resent her.

"Yes, but then I have the full support of Lord Cavandish and his sister."

"What are they like?"

"He is tall, graying, and quiet. He has some 'illness' everyone refers to but doesn't talk about. She is fairly tall, mousy, but has the most amazing eyes and when she smiles WOW, but they don't DO anything it seems."

"Are you attracted to her? Is she gay?"

"Gillian! I'm here to WORK, not to hit on my boss!" the exasperation could clearly be heard in her voice.

"Well, you never know, you're due for some romance!" Gillian teased.

"Cripes, where do you get these ideas? I'm here to do a job and I will do it amazingly well," she said with all modesty.

"Have you gone into town, checked it out?"

"I just drove through it, no I haven't 'checked it out' but I will eventually. I have to begin buying supplies. These people have no concept of how to save a buck or in their case a pound."

"Well, they are paying you that outrageous salary to do it for them."

"Shhh, that's just between us okay, don't spread it around..."

"Hey Mom, I've got to get going."

"Okay baby, take care, I love you!"

"I love you too Mom, have fun," but she knew her mother would have fun regardless of what she said.

CHAPTER 6

"David, have you seen your rooms?" Veronica asked him later when they were alone.

"No I haven't been up, did she have those cleaned as well?" he asked surprised.

Veronica nodded and added, "Yes, the first day you left she insisted they be overhauled as she said. She said as long as you were gone they should air them out and clean them so the dust would settle before you got home."

"Did she do your rooms as well," he teased and then stopped immediately as her face shut down. "I'm sorry, I was just teasing."

She shrugged her shoulders, "It's okay, and no, she hasn't even seen my rooms." She turned to go.

David watched his sister and wondered for the umpteenth time how to bring her out of her self-imposed shell.

David was pleased when he saw what Reese had arranged for his rooms. It was incredible the difference and he wholeheartedly approved. It felt nicer to even be in those rooms and none of the dust bothered him in the least for a change. The freshness made him even *feel* better.

CHAPTER 7

Frank drove Reese to the first of the many outlying properties that the Cavandish family owned and managed. Some were within a distance that she could visit herself with the Rover that Lord David put at her disposal. But some like the one today called Cavandish Sounds were a day's drive across the countryside. Nothing prepared her for the beauty of the landside when they arrived. A tidal property the land was known for fishing and gaming and the Cavandish family rented it out for those who wished to stay in the old estate house and get away. Reese found it in worse repair than the home estate. She made endless lists of what she wanted fixed and cleaned. The housekeeper who had lived there for the last 50 years she retired and hired another that promised to get things in 'ship shape' in no time. In the few days that Reese spent there she was as good as her word as she worked the few maids to their weary bones. There were no gardeners attached to this estate and she was glad to find her new housekeeper had nephews willing and able to do the job. Mrs. Carlyle was a find.

Frank drove her home and she was glad she didn't have to do the driving herself. Her endless lists and thoughts would have kept her distracted. She was surprised when they found themselves in a violent thundershower on the way home and she could no longer read. Putting aside her work she looked out and watched the thunder and lightning through the torrential rain. "Will this slow us up?" she asked Frank, the first words either of them had spoken for hours.

"No ma'am, the road soon turns into the highway and we will take that over to Cavandish."

She nodded and subsided into quiet. It was a little unnerving never having anyone to talk to. As an 'upper' servant she was expected to associate only with the upper servants or the owners but as an employee she felt she must keep her distance. It was a lonely existence, self-imposed.

As they drove through the town of Cavandish she looked thoughtfully out at it. Although a lot different than towns in Connecticut the buildings were hundreds of years older, it still had the same feeling of the towns she had experienced in the states. She was determined to meet the 'locals' and go into town that weekend.

Since she had a Rover at her fingertips it wasn't like she had to ask permission to go out. Her personal time was her own. Lord David had made that very clear. She had worked for week's non-stop and deserved some well-earned time off. It was with that thought she drove herself to town. She was glad she went while the sun was still up or she would have become hopelessly lost. She enjoyed walking down some of the cobblestoned streets, peeking in the store fronts, listening to the English voices. She found a pub to eat dinner in and later a club that catered to dancing. Sitting there drinking she enjoyed people watching.

"Would you like to dance?" a petite brunette asked her hopefully.

Reese started in surprise. She had been so lost in her own thoughts she didn't realize a new face would have people wondering about her. "I'm sorry, what did you say?" she asked over the music.

The brunette smiled at her accent, "Would you like to dance?" she repeated.

Reese was surprised. She was quite sure this wasn't a gay bar with all the mixed couples dancing but then there were a few same sex couples on the floor as well. The brunette must have read her mind, "They don't segregate us here," she grinned.

Reese was further surprised and it must have showed on her face. Tossing off the scotch she had been nursing she nodded as the brunette drew her onto the dance floor. Not familiar with the tune now blasting from the speakers she quickly just rocked to the beat. The brunette seemed to like her moves and danced accordingly. Soon they were joined by others dancing with or around them including a couple of cute looking guys.

"Who is that?" Audrey asked Veronica where they sat in a booth out of the way.

Veronica peered past her to see to her surprise that Reese was out on the dance floor. She had noticed her at the bar earlier but other than having a drink she wasn't doing anything out of the ordinary. "That is our new estate manager," she told her friend.

"*That* is your estate manager?" Audrey gasped looking at the leggy blonde.

Veronica nodded seeing nothing out of the ordinary and puzzled at her friends reaction.

"Did you know she was gay when you hired her?" Audrey asked surprised.

"I didn't hire her, David did and no being gay wasn't part of her credentials I am sure," Veronica laughed at her friend. "Are you sure she is gay?" Audrey was always looking for new 'potentials.'

"She is dancing with Moira after all. Wow, she is something to look at. Can she possibly do the job?" Audrey used a double entendre to make her point as she checked out the woman.

"She actually is very competent, and a hard worker besides. She just came back from the Sounds and retired our housekeeper there."

"Geez, that woman has been with you all your life, she just waltzes in there and hires and fires?" Audrey was amazed. You just didn't do *that*.

Veronica nodded. She actually was admiring of Reese's ability to do her job so competently. She wished she had the 'moxy' to do things like that.

"Wow, beauty and brains. Did David hit on her?"

"No, you know he won't do that, and you know why," Veronica said sadly.

Audrey stopped her flippant talk immediately feeling contrite towards her friend. "So, are we on for tomorrow, going riding?" she changed the subject.

Reese danced only one dance with the brunette thanking her for asking but not giving her her number or getting hers. She felt she should be getting back home after her afternoon and evening out. She had found out several things about the town that she wanted to know and enjoyed herself.

Reese began going into town several times a week. Not only for work but for fun. She found a dojo on one of the side streets and began working out again. She loved the feeling of working up a good sweat and her instructor was pleased to take her on. She was quite advanced compared to his other students and Juan was thrilled when she inspired other students who watched her moves.

Veronica wondered where their manager disappeared to and thought perhaps she was now dating Moira the girl she had danced with that night. It didn't disturb her that their manager was gay; her friend Audrey was as well. She just wondered at the attraction to that petite brunette when Reese was so tall and blonde. She discovered though that Reese didn't always disappear into town. She found her in the room they designated their 'gymnasium' one night. Curious at the light coming from around the door and the beautiful music coming from the room Veronica was surprised to find Reese dancing alone in the room. She had some really incredible moves as Veronica watched and wondered from the doorway. She had never seen anyone except for professional dancer's rock out to music like this. The music started with classical and segued into a steady rock beat that Reese danced to. Her head and body moves in perfect synch with the beat of the music. Veronica watched for a full ten minutes before a tired and sweaty Reese finally collapsed laughing.

Clapping Veronica startled Reese who had no idea she had been observed. "That was incredible!" Veronica praised her.

Reese was embarrassed. She had started dancing years ago to keep in shape and kept it up along with her karate to keep in shape. Someone as tall as she was needed to stay in shape, any extra pounds tended to exaggerate on her frame. "I didn't realize anyone was there," she said to cover her embarrassment.

"Do you do this often?" Veronica walked into the room her perfect little sun dress making her appear angelic.

Reese nodded from where she watched her employer from the floor. Grabbing a towel she got up and began to blot the sweat from her arms and torso.

"Where did you learn to dance like that? Were you a dancer in New York?"

Reese smiled and shook her head, "I always wanted to learn classical dancing. After I began going to classes I added my own steps and compiled my own music to make it a work out. I enjoy dancing and I enjoy getting my work out."

"It's incredible. I wish I could dance like that!" Veronica enthused shyly.

"You could, I'm sure if you wanted to. Didn't you take dance classes as a child?" Reese was certain she had, didn't every member of the ton take dance classes?

"Of course but they certainly never turned into this!" She laughed imagining it.

Reese laughed with her certain they never had either. "It isn't hard; it just takes a bit of a 'free spirit' to go with the flow as it were."

"I've never been a free spirit in my life," Veronica laughed at the thought.

Reese was sure she never had either, "Ah, it's just a state of mind. You have to really want it if you let yourself go." She began to gather up her things turning off the CD player and putting the CD in a plastic sleeve.

"Could you teach me?" Veronica asked hesitantly.

Reese looked at her in surprise and then answered almost without thinking, "Sure, if you want," and then wondered if this was a mistake.

"Could we start tomorrow?" "Veronica enthused.

"Ah, tomorrow I go into town after work," Reese answered.

Veronica tried to hide her disappointment and failed miserably.

Reese could read her like a book. She felt sorry for this employer of hers; she was so shy and introverted. She rarely went out and usually just to the stables for her precious horses. Only a handful of times had Reese actually known her to go into town. "Would you like to come along?" she asked her impulsively.

"Come along where?"

"I go to a dojo a couple of times a week to work out," Reese told her with a twinkle in her eye.

"A dojo? That's where you go to?" Veronica was strangely relieved and knew no reason why.

"Yes, I need to stay in shape and it's a great stress reliever."

Veronica was amazed. As far as she could see Reese was in great shape but she had to admit she might be under a lot of stress with the mess she had found the estate to be in.

Watching the whirling dervish that their estate manager became in her karate clothes that looked strangely elegant on the tall blondes body Veronica was further amazed. Was there nothing this woman couldn't do that she set her mind to? As Veronica watched from the sidelines Reese countered and then made moves that on a lesser person would have looked ridiculous or at least hurt their partner seriously. The instructor, Juan barely was able to counter them she was so quick. His own attacks were effortlessly rebuffed.

"Reese, you're going to have to find an instructor better than I," he told her as she packed her robe into her gym bag.

She smiled, "You're doing fine for now Juan, you're just are out of practice," she teased.

"Out of practice? I'm fighting to survive you and you tell me I'm 'just' out of practice?" He laughed with her.

Veronica watched the effortless exchange that Reese had with the instructor, almost a flirtation but she could see the instructor admired her work. She had looked amazing and obviously had gotten a good work out by the sheen of sweat that beaded her body.

Reese noticed her boss watching and smiled at her, "Veronica, you should meet Juan," she said by way of introduction.

Juan turned to look curiously at Lady Cavandish. He had never met her but of course in a town this size knew who she was. Shaking her hand he asked, "Maybe I should be teaching you instead of your friend here who could teach me!"

"I think that's a wonderful idea!" Reese enthused encouraging Veronica. Maybe some self-confidence is what she needs she thought.

Veronica laughed in genuine amusement. Ladies didn't get sweaty like this and take karate classes, "I don't think I could be that coordinated."

"It doesn't take coordination initially really and if you want to learn to dance this will actually help," Reese told her earnestly.

Veronica was surprised and then thought 'why not?' She soon found herself signing up for some private lessons with Juan that would take place before his lessons with Reese. Reese promised to help her along with the dance lessons and Veronica was pleased.

CHAPTER 8

The next few weeks Reese spent her days coordinating things and implementing changes throughout the properties that the Cavandish estates comprised. Her evenings were spent teaching Veronica to dance or helping her with her karate moves. She was right that all Veronica needed was some confidence and she gained that rapidly as she improved. She had a natural rhythm and as Reese taught her some of the dances she added her own moves that Reese encouraged her to continue.

There were days and sometimes weeks that required Reese to be gone and Veronica took herself to the dojo to learn from Juan. Audrey accompanied her a couple of times and was amazed what her friend was putting herself through but pleased for her as well.

"What is this that I must ask before purchasing the feed for my horses?" Veronica asked as she entered Reese's office one day.

Reese was sitting at the desk working on a spreadsheet and looked up in surprise. Veronica avoided this office like the plague and although she had never asked she had often wondered at her new friend's reluctance to enter it. "You certainly don't need to ask anything Lady Veronica," she told her with a grin at the absurdity of that question.

"How many times must I tell you to call me Veronica when we are alone?" she asked her anger dissipating at the answer to her outraged question.

"I'm sorry; it's a sign of respect that is all.", Reese smiled at the outrage that was leaving the little wren's face.

"So what is going on with the feed for my horses?" Veronica returned to the topic that had brought her in high dungeon into this office that she hated.

"I've been buying it in larger quantities to save money. If there is a different feed, please let me know and I will research the costs to buy it in bulk to save us more money," Reese told her. Part of her duties had been to reduce those costs that had been outrageously high for far too long. Already Lord David had commented on how much she was saving his pocketbook.

CHAPTER 9

"No, not like that, here let me show you," Reese put her arms around Veronica from behind and showed her where her hands needed to go and how.

"Oh, I get it now," Veronica repeated the motion. It was a lot different doing it yourself than watching someone else do it.

"It's always different with each person," Reese encouraged her. Already Veronica had progressed beyond a white belt. She seemed to be a lady on a mission and the extra classes with Reese certainly helped her with Juan.

Veronica really admired Reese. She had been so helpful and supportive. They had become real friends and as Veronica didn't have many friends she cherished this friendship that had developed. Veronica hadn't ever known a woman to be so competent and able to take care of not only herself but things around her, so in control of her own life and destiny.

"So you were saying that your parents bought you your first horse?" Reese encouraged her taking them back to their previous conversation.

"Oh yes, she was a little mare but perky as all get out. She helped me to win my very first blue ribbon and trophy." Veronica's eyes sparkled as she remembered.

"That must have been exciting."

Veronica dropped her hands and stood straight up, "Yes, she was the first of four different horses that I helped to train and win with."

"What happened to them?" Reese asked as she executed some moves that were far advanced of what Veronica had ever done.

She looked like a ballet dancer the way she moved and counter moved to imaginary foes, thought Veronica. Her workouts always started before Veronica even got there no matter how early she arrived Reese was there first and if not working on karate then at least dancing to music. Music that many times Veronica had never heard or thought of. Reese introduced her to many singers and genre's that Veronica found herself enjoying and would never have found any other way. Reese could talk about them too, she really knew things. Veronica found herself Googling many of the things they talked about so she didn't sound like such a dunce. "Oh, as I outgrew them, father sold or traded up for me. I still have the last horse, it cost him $100,000 pounds and he is still quite the spitfire."

Reese smiled. Far from being the mouse she had originally thought of her employer she was finding Veronica to be a woman of intelligence. She enjoyed talking to her and looked forward to their almost daily workouts together. There were times when Reese had to go on trips to the other properties to inspect, to order, to repair and even then they were in contact via the phone or even emails. David had brought her a phone so she was always available on her 'mobile.' Reese found this hilarious as they called them cell phones in the states and with their British accents hearing 'mobile' stressed out it sounded funny to her ears. She was learning to speak 'English' instead of 'American.'

"We need to go riding. You have been here for months and not once have I seen you on a horse. I thought you said you knew how to ride?" Veronica teased her, something she wouldn't have dared months ago.

Reese laughed; her boss had been surprised to see her on a bulldozer but complained that she didn't ride a horse? She would show her! "Ok, let's go get dressed and go ride before the sun sets."

Veronica was surprised; Reese had completely called her bluff. She was also pleased and said, "Ok, I'll meet you in the stables in say half an hour?"

"Half an hour? *Please*," she stressed the word, "It will only take me 15 minutes." She gathered up the few things she had in the workout area, turned off the radio, and as she headed for the door with her boss walking behind her added, "Race you?"

They giggled as they headed out the door and ran up the stairs. Their bedrooms were only a few doors apart and they both slammed into their rooms to quickly change. As Reese tossed off her work out clothes she thought about Veronica and the fact that in all the months she had worked on the estate she had never even seen the inside of her rooms. She felt Veronica was a very private person and wouldn't dream of invading her inner sanctum. She was soon dressed in jeans, a flannel shirt with the sleeves rolled up, and a pair of short boots with a modest heel.

Veronica changed in record time to jodhpurs, a tight little vest, and knee high boots as well as a velvet covered helmet. She thought about Reese as she pulled them on and realized she thought about Reese all the time now. She had become one of the best friends she had ever had.

As they both walked out of their rooms at almost the same time they both stopped to laugh at the other's attire. Veronica was dressed to ride English style and Reese was relaxed and totally Western.

Veronica phoned down to the stables as they walked down so that two horses could be readied for them. As they arrived the saddles were just being tightened. For Veronica was the very horse they had been talking about. Satin was a seventeen hands high horse of blue black who stood very proud and very arrogant. He gently nibbled at her sleeve as she mounted the block and got on his back. The other horse chosen for Reese was a gelding of equal height but a beautiful chestnut coat. He rolled his eyes as she approached the mounting block and she watched him closely.

"You didn't have a western saddle?" she asked to tease Veronica.

"Where, in a good English stable, would we keep a Western saddle?" Veronica replied sounding very upper crust with a hint of a grin knowing that Reese was joking with her.

"Well, you would think for guests and things...." Reese smiled as she fitted her boots into the stirrups.

As the groom handed her the reigns he looked at her cheekily. He had admired her for a while as she took control of things around the estate, this was the first time though that he had seen her in jeans and he liked the way the softness cupped her ass. He had been hoping she wouldn't use the mounting block and he could hoist her up into the saddle using it as a chance to grab that nice ass. Reese didn't realize he was even looking at her as she asked Veronica, "Well, where would you like to go?"

She followed Veronica as they went down the now well maintained driveway towards the back of the estate. They soon progressed from a walk to a canter. Reese was able to effortlessly keep up with her boss and Veronica wondered if she could manage jumps or an all-out gallop. She headed for a field she had in mind.

Reese thought they were having a rather sedate little ride as they ambled along. Even the canter wasn't that difficult to maintain. She held on with her knees and despite having no pommel to grab onto in case of emergencies she felt confident in her ability to ride. As Veronica increased their speed and headed for a hedgerow she realized what her boss had in mind and increased the pressure of her knees. They both took the first jump effortlessly and Veronica was pleased to see how well Reese was holding up. The second jump was a water jump and Reese's horse went ballistic. He first refused it and when she turned back for a second try he began to buck and twist.

Veronica was appalled at the horse's behavior. He was fishtailing doing everything in his power to buck her off and she was doing an admirable job of staying in the saddle. Veronica worried since Reese wasn't wearing a helmet that she would soon be thrown but she saw Reese smiling as she suddenly went, "Weee," and kicked the horse into a full out gallop back towards the stables. Taking the hedgerow again Veronica was convinced the horse was out of control and raced after her friend. As they both came to a nearly seated halt they were pulling on the reigns so hard Veronica realized that Reese was in total control of the horse and enjoying every minute of it.

"Are you okay?" she asked alarmed grabbing Reese's arm as they both sat on their mounts.

Reese smiled and answered, "Well, that was a little exciting wasn't it?"

Veronica was amazed. Reese had ridden that wild horse so well. She was barely panting from the effort even. Was there nothing that rattled this incredible woman?

Grooms hurried from the stable to take the horses halters and Reese swung her leg over to slide off her mount. Her legs nearly buckled but she managed to stay upright. She realized after the groom walked the horse away how closely Veronica was watching her. She grinned and said, "Well, we will have to do that again sometime."

Veronica shook her head. Calm, cool, and collected and she nearly collapsed getting off the horse. She was impressed.

CHAPTER 10

Reese had been gone two weeks touring the outlying properties. She was surprised to find David in her office when she returned. "Is there something I can help you find Lord David?" she asked from the doorway she had just walked through.

David looked up from the desk where he had been pouring over her ledgers. "How are you able to figure all this out so quickly?" he asked sincerely impressed.

Reese shrugged, "It all makes sense, everything has a pattern and I just needed to see it. Once we were organized it was easy."

"Amazing, you are a real find, do you know that?" he smiled, a genuine one.

"Thank you, I hope you're pleased with all my work." She was pleased.

"I am, I'd like you to arrange a party for all my family and friends. We haven't entertained in years and now that everything is looking and feeling so good, I'd like you to arrange it. Veronica has the list of whom to invite, I'd like you to work closely with her."

"Very well Lord David, I'd be delighted." Although arranging a party for them was the furthest thing from her mind.

Reese went in search of Veronica and found her in the conservatory watering her plants. She really had a green thumb and enjoyed cultivating many species of rare and tropical plants. Even when winter lashed the house with its cold, rainy, and sometimes snowy wetness the house smelled sweet from the flowers that Veronica grew in the greenhouse. It was part of her pride and joy. "It's beautiful," she said by way of greeting as Veronica carefully watered her Calla Lilies.

Veronica was startled but Reese's voice soothed her instead of alarmed her and she looked up with genuine pleasure at seeing her friend after all this time. "You're back!" she smiled.

Reese nodded as she looked around at the beautiful and rare plants, "Yes, and already hard at work. Your brother asked me to help you arrange a party." She looked back in time to see Veronica lose her pleased smile.

"Yes, David wants to have a grand party like the days of old." Her tone suggested she would rather have had teeth pulled.

"Days of old?" Reese asked wondering if it was going to be a theme party or a costume party.

"Yes, my parents used to entertain quite frequently. David wants the opportunity to show off the estate now that you've made it look so grand and before he isn't able to anymore." She looked sadder if that were possible.

"What do you mean 'isn't able to anymore?'" Reese finally asked. They had alluded to this type of thing for a long time.

Veronica looked up to see if Reese was kidding but seeing that she was not she said, "David has a rare form of multiple sclerosis and it's advancing rapidly."

Reese shook her head in surprise, "Has he seen someone?"

Veronica nodded, "Specialists, some of the best in England."

"He doesn't appear to be affected yet," Reese stated.

"It's because of the form he has. It will affect him eventually and quite suddenly and then he will be confined to a wheelchair and eventually die." She said this sadly but more matter of fact.

Reese stared at her friend aghast. She had never suspected. Veronica looked up to see the shock on the cool blonde's face. "Is there anything I can do?" she thought to ask.

Veronica shrugged. She had known for a long time and come to grips with it. "I think you doing your job is all we can ask."

Reese nodded not sure what else to say. But then Veronica wasn't finished. "It's one of the many reasons for this party, before his symptoms become evident. His memory is already affected. He is losing his sight. It's why he refuses to marry and have an heir; he is leaving that up to me!" She said that last part with such vehemence that Reese wondered at it.

"Why won't he have an heir?" she asked confused.

"He refuses to pass on his 'defective' genetics as he calls them," she said sadly.

Reese couldn't believe they were having this conversation about her active boss. She realized suddenly that all his trips to go 'play' could very well have been doctor's appointments. His reasons for hiring not just because of the mess but his inability to concentrate on the intricate or mundane matters of the estate anymore. A lot had been hidden here and apparently a lot more was to be hidden. All in the name of 'appearances.'

"Well, then let's make this a party to be remembered okay?" she tried to sound cheerful but sobered as she watched Veronica's face.

CHAPTER 11

Over the next two months as they planned and got ready for the party Reese learned much more about the Cavandish family than she thought possible. Veronica confided in her a lot more these days since opening up about David. She had been genuinely surprised that Reese hadn't known. During the course of sending out invitations, writing the addresses by hand, discussing who would be invited, etc. Reese learned details that she felt were none of her business. Since the death of their parents who had been considerably older than the two siblings, they had their children late in life, the two had become really close, but it was only after a chance remark about the 'incident' that they had become almost inseparable with David keeping Veronica home and both of them becoming homebodies. David still maintained his apartment in London and this was one property that Reese hadn't been expected to maintain for the estate. He hadn't been to it in seven years, not since the 'incident.'

It took the second month after the invitation acceptances began to arrive before Veronica finally confided to a degree what the 'incident' had been. Apparently the previous manager's brother had raped her in the office that Reese now used as her office. The manager had pulled the drunken man off of her but not before he had pierced her hymen. At twenty one Veronica had still been a virgin and while outgoing and having such potential, all of that was cut off and she had been allowed to leave college and stay at home to hide. Reese's heart went out to her. At twenty eight, Veronica was badly in need of some help and Reese wanted to help her and told her so.

"Oh, don't you see, you have helped! The karate has made me feel so empowered already!" Veronica enthused.

Reese thought she should have seen a therapist. Someone qualified to help in these situations.

"No, a Cavandish certainly could not see a psychiatrist. It wouldn't be allowed," Veronica informed her loftily.

"Allowed? That's ridiculous; you need to talk to someone!"

"I'm talking to you. My friend Audrey knows too. I think a few of my other friends as well although we don't talk about it."

Reese shook her head. Veronica had no clue what she meant by real help. She was a frightened little mouse and the trauma of the rape had scarred her for life.

"What happened to the man who did this to you?"

Veronica looked uncomfortable. "I don't really know, I think David arranged for him to be put away somewhere."

"Weren't the police called?" Reese said aghast at what had happened to her friend.

Shaking her head Veronica began to squirm, "It's why the manager was allowed to stay for so long. He used it to blackmail my brother before David finally had enough and fired him."

Reese couldn't believe what she was hearing. This woman had been raped. Not only raped but then her brother and she blackmailed by the very man who had pulled the rapist off of her and was his brother to boot. No one had been prosecuted or tried. Instead this woman endured her own private hell. Reese wanted to help but knew that just suggesting a psychiatrist wouldn't work.

CHAPTER 12

It was the Friday before the party and Reese, Veronica, and Audrey were all down at the dance club or pub which it really was in town. Audrey had hit on Reese numerous times and Reese just laughed it off each and every time. Audrey still wasn't certain whether Reese was gay or not. She flirted with guys in the bar but something, perhaps that Moira had danced with her that one time, said to Audrey that she might or could possibly be gay. Perhaps she was a bi-sexual. Reese had danced with women or men, whoever asked her and as she hadn't singled out either for favoritism Audrey still wondered and speculated. She had asked Veronica numerous times but she didn't know and she certainly couldn't ask her employee and friend that question.

Veronica watched as Reese danced on the floor. She was in a group of people, mostly younger than she was but she didn't look out of place except for her distinctive height. All she could do was admire how coordinated she looked. Reese had tried numerous times to get Veronica out on the floor and to teach her at the house but she felt so uncomfortable that she refused each and every time.

"Who is that?" Bert asked as he came up to Audrey.

"Who is who?" she asked looking around wondering who he was talking about.

"That blonde that you were sitting with?"

Audrey looked at him speculatively, "Interested?"

"Yes, but I'm going to need a ladder," he laughed.

She looked at his short 5'5" frame and joined in his laughter. Veronica watched the interplay and silently waited.

Finally Bert realized she was at the table and said, "Oh hello Veronica, how are you?"

She smiled and answered, "I'm fine, how are you?"

"Great, hey I'll be there next weekend for your party. It's been quite a while since you and your brother held a party hasn't it?"

Veronica nodded and said, "Yes, I think since my parents were alive if you don't count the horse shows."

"Do you still have that horse, Satin was his name?" he asked.

Veronica was pleased that he remembered, nodding yes enthusiastically she answered, "Yes, I rode him just the other day!"

"I was sure glad when you 'retired' him. He was unbeatable!" he smiled flirtatiously.

Veronica immediately withdrew as he leaned towards her. "It's too bad he was a gelding or I would have bred him for the foals that he would have sired."

"It would have been an unbeatable horse if you got the right mare!" he enthused.

They talked horses for a while much to Audrey's amusement but at no time did Veronica indicate any interest in him although he did try to flirt with her. She had his full attention until Reese walked up.

"Oh that was fun," she gasped as she reached for her drink.

"Reese, I'd like to introduce you to Bert Sommers, Bert this is Veronica's estate manager Reese Paulson." Audrey did the introductions.

Reese gave him a staggering smile and put out her hand to shake his. "Estate manager eh?" he said trying to put some sense into his empty mind.

"Yes," she answered looking a little bit puzzled.

Veronica smirked at his reaction. Audrey was amused.

"Would you like to dance?" he asked to cover up his stunned reaction.

Just then the music stopped as the DJ took a break and then put on piped music which no one would or could dance to. She smiled and said, "Perhaps another time?"

"Yes, perhaps another time," he repeated feeling like a fool. "I'll see you girls, have a nice night," as he hurried away.

Reese turned to the other two women and asked, "What was that about?"

Veronica and Audrey just started laughing. Here Bert had thought himself so cool and suave and Reese had floored him just by showing up.

CHAPTER 13

Car after car kept showing up at the door, dropping its passengers and then the valets took them to be parked elsewhere. Veronica hadn't done this in years and felt out of practice as David stood beside her greeting their guests. Everyone was exclaiming over the beautiful house. Once the last of their guests were greeted they began to mingle and for Veronica this was another trial. She watched as Reese effortlessly spoke with guest after guest. Eventually she drifted over to where a group was talking with the American.

"You've done wonderful work David tells me. Perhaps I should have you take a look at my husband's estate," Lady Emerson was saying.

Reese smiled, "Ah, my work is quite cut out for me here right now."

"You're not trying to steal our excellent manager are you Lady Emerson?" Veronica felt bold enough to ask.

Reese turned as Veronica joined their group smiling at the beautiful gown she had convinced her friend to wear. "I'm sure she meant it as a compliment."

"Lady Emerson is known for her acquisition of the best and as we have the best estate manager around, I'm sure it was not only a compliment but a genuine offer," Veronica smiled at Lady Emerson who laughed at what was acknowledged to be the truth.

"What kind of estate do you have?" Reese asked Lady Emerson curiously.

"Oh, some cattle ranch in the outback he won in a game of cards. I'm sure it's dry and dusty and going to drain our pocketbook," she said in disgust.

"Then you've never seen it?" Reese asked.

"Oh no, I have no desire to travel to Australia," she said as though Reese should have known.

"I hear it's beautiful and from the pictures I've seen it seems an incredible place and so different," Reese enthused.

"From what I've seen of the pictures of America it's different as well," she answered and this led to an extensive question and answer session about America as though Reese were an authority on all things American.

"Well, that was a smashing success," David told his sister and estate manager the next morning.

"I really enjoyed myself," Veronica told her brother with a smile. "I've got three people coming to go riding!"

David smiled at his sister. She had been coming out of her shell and while yesterday had tried her it had also proven to her that she had nothing to hide or fear. The house was in good order for the first time in years and they owed it all to the hard work of Reese.

"I received numerous compliments on your work," he informed Reese, "I'm quite pleased."

"Well thank you Lord David, I hope it continues," she smiled a little distracted. She had a subject she needed to broach with him but couldn't with Veronica there.

"Lady Emerson tried to steal her away yesterday," Veronica told her brother mischievously.

"Oh really?" David said drolly. "Whatever for?"

"That ranch or something that he won in that infamous card game down in Australia. She is certain it's going to ruin them."

David laughed. He knew anything that Emerson touched turned to gold, eventually. "He will do fine if he can keep her nose out of his books," he laughed again.

Veronica began to tell about the people who were coming riding with her in the next few days. Two of them were from the circuit that she knew from competitions and one was a new lady that had recently moved to town. She wasn't sure how she had been invited and hadn't wanted to be rude and ask.

"Oh, I invited her. Her name is Doctor Ana Sinclair, I met her in town and thought it would be neighborly to invite her," Reese told them looking down at her plate and eating a little quicker.

"That was nice of you, she is a really pleasant person," Veronica told her as Reese looked up with a expression in her eye.

"Yes, it doesn't hurt to get to know the locals. What kind of doctor is she?" David inquired.

Reese looked at Veronica hoping he was addressing her with that question and was relieved to see he was as she answered. "I really am not sure, we didn't discuss it but she is riding later today with me, maybe I will find out then." She turned to ask Reese but just then Mrs. Gunderson walked in and asked, "Ms. Paulson, may I speak with you?"

Reese was never so relieved having sensed that Veronica was going to ask her what kind of doctor that Ana was. Saved by the bell as it were.

CHAPTER 14

Ana was a regular visitor to the estate and became one of Veronica's closest friends and confidants. After a month as Reese showed David the books and they went over the expenditures he wondered at an insurance payment for 'psychiatric' treatment and wondered who on their insurance plan was seeing a psychiatrist.

Reese looked extremely uncomfortable as she confessed, "I authorized this payment Lord David."

"Well, who is it for?" he asked perplexed. They had an excellent program for all of the staff and the itemized statement showed the usual doctor checkups but this one he was surprised at the amount and the frequency so suddenly.

Reese took a deep breath. She had overstepped her authority and knew it. She had wanted to be honest and above board about it but hadn't had a chance to really explain it to her employer. This is it, I'm going to be fired, she thought. "It's for Lady Veronica," she said quietly.

"What? When has Veronica seen a psychiatrist?" he asked surprised.

"Almost every day. She rides with her. Doctor Ana Sinclair is a psychiatrist I hired to help your sister." Reese looked directly into Lord David's eyes as she told him.

"You what? Without her knowledge?" He asked incredulous at her audacity.

"Yes sir, I did. Your sister and I have become good friends and quite close. She confided in me her reason for her fears of my office and what occurred there. I felt she needed help in overcoming those fears and others that have been affecting her life. I know I overstepped my authority, but I wanted to help my friend and my employer," Reese finished waiting for the explosion she knew would come.

David was speechless. Of all the underhanded tactics...and he had seen a few with their previous manager, and then he stopped himself. He realized over the months that Reese had worked here how much she had changed things for the better. His sister was going out at night, sometimes to that karate class, sometimes to the pub, but she was going out which was the whole point. The change could only be for the better. He thought about what he could say at this point and he thought about what he couldn't say. "Your right, you have exceeded your authority. However, I can see that you and my sister have become friends and for that I am grateful. She would never have gone to see a doctor about this and I hope she isn't angry when she realizes that Ana is 'working' when they go out as friends. It may really hurt her. She has so few friends you know that she really trusts."

Reese could see that. She sensed it long ago. She also noticed at the party how much people enjoyed Veronica. She knew a lot about horses, had been very active in the circuit, and people from all walks wanted to talk to her. She was too close mouthed on too many occasions when her expertise and knowledge really could carry her through.

"Reese, I am happy that you have become her friend. I hope this lasts a long time. I won't be around to take care of Veronica forever and she will need friends like you," David confided.

Reese felt very uncomfortable at that moment. Lord David and she had never had this type of relationship. He had liked her work and was pleased with it; he admired how hard she worked and the results. They had never been very personal and she had accepted and actually welcomed it.

David could see her discomfort and despite it he continued, "If you ever need to talk to me about my sister, please feel free. I don't want you making decisions like this again without my permission. Do we agree on that?"

Reese nodded wanting desperately to get out of his office with her books. He let her go.

CHAPTER 15

It was gradual but the change in Veronica was there to see. Her karate classes seemed to empower her as well. Ana encouraged her to work with Reese who gladly showed her more advanced moves as she learned. She also showed her some basic dance moves incorporated with the waltzes and other dances she had learned as a child. Although she wasn't ready to do that in public she enjoyed learning the 'feel' of the music as Reese called it.

Thursday nights Veronica and David could be found watching television together in the family room. There were several 'American' shows that they watched together. Occasionally Reese joined them but she either worked or read a book on her own so she didn't invade their 'family' time although they assured her she was welcome at any time. It usually started with American sitcom, "Friends," and then on to one other sitcom before the hospital drama show "ER" came on.

Reese had been there a full year when the storyline on ER began to introduce a lesbian romance between a psychiatrist and the chief doctor of the ER. Veronica at first felt distinctly uncomfortable by the story line. She knew that Dr. Ana was a psychiatrist now, after all they were friends and she confided in her after all their months of friendship. She also knew that Ana had a wonderful husband and two beautiful kids. What made her uncomfortable though was that the doctor on ER reminded her slightly of Reese and made her wonder if Reese were a lesbian as Audrey had wondered for months. There was only a superficial resemblance after all; they were both blonde, tall, and beautiful women. She thought entirely too much about her friend and now she was thinking about her in a different and more unsettling manner.

As she analyzed her feelings about the situation she thought she was just thinking too much. Reese had never made any overtures towards her that would indicate that she felt other than friendship towards Veronica. For that matter Audrey had tried repeatedly but Reese shrugged those off as well. Veronica watched the story line on ER and found herself fascinated. She hadn't been involved in a romance in years and while the thought of a man touching her made her shudder the thought of the hugs she had shared with woman didn't bother her. Could she take that one step or many steps further? Should she?

Veronica was a healthy or rather a fairly healthy woman of twenty eight. She had needs and feelings just like anyone else her age. She regularly found herself wet by those needs and had no way to have an outlet. With her thoughts and emotions changing by the story lines she began to think about that part of her life, or rather the lack thereof. She began to do research on the internet. She hesitated and then entered into a chatroom for bi-sexual women and read the posts. As she became more enamored by the story line on ER, she also became bold enough to participate in the chats in the room. She started by asking women about toys. She was brave enough to buy her first. An imitation of a man's appendage that plugged into the wall was her first purchase. She figured that she would go through more batteries and having it plugged into the wall would save on that aspect. She was embarrassed and excited when the plain brown package arrived. Going up to her rooms that she locked herself inside of she wasn't sure what to do with it. Unpacking it she looked at it and was kind of offended by the sight. She knew though that she needed something and was willing to try. By the time she had it all set up she was fairly wet by the idea. It slid in easily but at the same time she felt very very full, very tight. Turning it on she felt nothing. It did *nothing* for her. She was very disappointed having expected some sort of stimulation instead of the uncomfortable feeling of it inside her vibrating around. She removed it and washed it, hiding it between her mattresses and then again in her safe. She knew no one came into her rooms and hadn't in years but she couldn't be certain and she didn't want to be embarrassed any more than she would be if anyone happened upon this toy.

Over the next few weeks she read up on the subject on the internet but could find no reason why she wasn't getting the orgasm it promised. She didn't know what she was doing wrong. She was aroused when she thought about it, she thrust it inside her wetness, but nothing ever happened. The thrusting felt good but not the good that an orgasm promised her from what she had read. She had never had one so what did she know?

She tried 'talking' about it with the anonymous strangers in the chat rooms she went into but was embarrassed to admit she knew nothing. She tried talking about it with Ana but didn't really know how to bring it up. It was frustrating her and she didn't know what to do about it. Girlfriends are supposed to be able to confide in one another. Could she talk about it with Audrey or Reese? She couldn't screw up her courage enough to even broach the subject. One of the strangers suggested she try a rabbit. Having never heard of one she asked what it was and was told to Google it. The variety and diversity of the sex toys that came up astounded her. She wasn't sure what to buy there and decided on the simplest and 'original' version of the toy. When it arrived she wasn't sure what the 'ears' of the rabbit were for. Reading up on it she realized all along that she never had stimulation on her clitoris before. She hadn't realized all these years where exactly her clit was. Yes, she had washed down there. She had felt herself down there, but she had never realized what the clit was for or what it did. She found with the rabbit that it buzzed at different levels on her clit with the shaft inserted inside and while she enjoyed the feelings nothing gave her an 'orgasm' as she supposed they would. She knew she was still missing something and didn't know how to achieve it.

CHAPTER 16

Reese was kickboxing in the gym in her preparation for helping Veronica with her karate. She was testing today to see if she could move up a belt and Reese wanted her confident enough so she was ready. It was nice to see some of the confidence that Veronica had achieved since she began taking the classes with Juan. If she was lucky today she could get a purple belt and Reese was pleased for her friend.

Veronica enjoyed watching Reese work out. She didn't wear the traditional karate outfit at home, instead wearing stretch clothes that did nothing to hide the muscular body. Her poise and grace were evident as she worked through moves she set in her own head. Juan had commented several times there were things he was learning from Reese. She worked out hard and many times she and Juan had demonstrated for the classes. Veronica enjoyed her own private classes and the show as she watched Reese. A particularly high kick had Reese lose her balance and as she lay there flat on her back she began to laugh at herself.

"Are you okay?" Veronica asked concerned as her friend lay on the floor laughing at herself.

Reese grinned as she rolled over to rise. "Yes, I was just clumsy there."

"I don't think I've ever seen you fall before," Veronica returned the grin as she watched Reese rise from the floor effortlessly and gracefully.

"Oh, I've taken my share believe me."

Reese began going through the simple exercises with Veronica and the room soon rang with the calls of, "kia," as they practiced. Soon Reese was moving into the more advanced moves as she led Veronica to what would be on her test later that night.

"Here, let me show you," Reese said as she came around Veronica and put her arms around her to show her where to hold her own arms.

Veronica could feel the warm and muscular body at her back and found she didn't mind. Reese had done this a hundred times in the months as Veronica learned karate. Today Veronica found herself realizing the perfume that Reese used smelled exquisite. She wondered if Reese put it on her neck and wrists as well as between her breasts. She was startled to think of her that way. It distracted her for just a moment and Reese said, "No, like this!" and moved Veronica's hands again. The touch felt warm and impersonal but not to Veronica's mind. She had to really concentrate to distract herself back to the karate lesson.

"There you go," Reese smiled at her friend. "I think you will ace Juan's test tonight!"

"Thanks to you," Veronica admired her friend.

"Well, if I didn't help you, Juan would. He is a good instructor."

"You should teach, you're so advanced, even Juan comments on it."

Reese shrugged, "I do it for myself, to keep myself in shape. I don't do it for the belts."

"What belt would you be?" Veronica asked curiously. Reese wore a black one but without the different tapes on the end designating what degree she was.

Reese shrugged again and said, "I have no idea; I stopped testing once I achieved black. Now it's about form and style, not about weapons or who I could compete against."

Veronica loved her attitude. She had helped others with Juan to show them technique and form. Many times Juan had used her to show more advanced techniques to inspire his students. She didn't teach and she really did know more than Juan so they sparred to keep physically fit.

That evening as Veronica held her new belt she was thrilled with how well she had done thanks to Reese and Juan. She shared in the joy with many other students, some younger, some older who also took the classes for various reasons. Although she had started with private lessons she had participated in the larger classes as she progressed and grew more confident. She still had her private classes with Reese but that was different from these. She along with the many other students who had come that evening were happy when Juan announced that Reese and he would be putting on a demonstration for their benefit.

"Don't hold back," Juan warned Reese with a grin. Several students smiled in anticipation of the bout that was to begin shortly, it was fascinating.

Reese grinned back at the smaller but more muscular man and said, "Bring it on Brit!"

He laughed at the standing joke between them. He was Portuguese but with his British accent she had teased him repeatedly about it. Her skill though was no laughing matter as she went on the attack. Their demonstration was soon a series of, "Ha's," and, "Kia's," as they each practiced their techniques on each other. They both began to sweat as they increased their speed and began to hold back less and less. Juan soon found himself flying across the mats. Angry but exhilarated as he hadn't seen it coming he tried and succeeded at flipping Reese. She looked up surprised as she landed at Veronica's feet.

"Are you okay?" Veronica asked concerned looking down at her friend.

Reese grinned and got up to confront Juan. Something about Veronica's face though swam through her head and she found herself distracted. Juan's well timed kick and her counter was off and she found herself going down with a crunch. Her counter from the sitting position was automatic and she was alarmed to realize she had broken something on Juan as he gasped from where he went down. She rolled to get up herself and realized she was in a lot of pain and it hurt to breathe. She walked to where Juan lay on the mats and unconsciously echoed what Veronica had said to her moments before, "Are you okay?"

Juan lay there stunned. He really hurt and was breathless. He had had bruises over the years of course but nothing like this. He too had heard the crunch as Reese's foot had connected with his ribs. He shook his head and tried to rise. Seeing his grimace of pain she quickly tried to stop him from rising only to grimace in her own pain. "Someone call an ambulance," she gasped.

Several people looked to see if she was kidding before someone grabbed a mobile phone and punched in the numbers.

"No one touches him, I think he has a broken rib," Reese cautioned the students who were crowding around. She herself was holding her right arm to her side tightly and breathing through her nose to lessen the pain.

"Reese, are you all right?" Veronica asked concerned watching her.

Reese looked at Veronica and realized it was the look in her amazing violet eyes that had distracted her earlier. It alarmed her for a moment before the sense of what Veronica had asked her penetrated her mind, she nodded and answered, "Yes, but I think I am going to have a hell of a bruise."

The emergency personnel were soon there and Juan was lifted onto a stretcher and taken out to an ambulance. Reese cleared the class and soon locked up for Juan. Veronica waited for her and asked, "Do you want to go to hospital to see Juan with me?"

Reese smiled a little. The Brits never said 'to the hospital' but 'to hospital' and that always bugged her. She nodded, "I think I should probably get this looked at," she indicated her side that she was still holding her arm down to.

Hours later Reese had her own verdict. One broken rib. She consoled herself that Juan had two broken and one cracked by her counter kick. He was laughing it off though as they were both taped up now. Reese had insisted on seeing him as soon as she was able.

"God Juan, I am sorry," she said when she saw him.

He grinned and grimaced as they finished helping him on with his Gi or karate robe. It was a good thing it had wide sleeves as his taped ribs would not have born a tight shirt. "No, don't be, your counter strike was beautiful and automatic. I wouldn't want to meet you in a dark alley somewhere."

Veronica looked on anxiously. She had been so worried about Reese when they told her she had broken a rib.

Reese smiled at her friend, "I locked up." She handed him his keys.

"Gawd, I'm not going to be able to demonstrate for weeks. I guess we made quite an impression on the kiddies tonight," he lamented.

"Is this going to affect your income?" she asked anxiously.

"Well, some are going to think twice before 'playing' around at karate but to be honest, word of mouth is going to bring in a lot of students." He grinned in anticipation.

Reese laughed at him and she and Veronica headed home together with Veronica driving.

"Can I help you?" Veronica asked anxiously seeing Reese favor her side as she headed up the staircase.

Reese shook her head as she thought over the evening, something she had done since the hospital on the ride home. She was grateful that Veronica had driven them.

David came out of the library, "What's going on?" he asked seeing Veronica hovering over Reese who was trying to walk slowly up the staircase.

Veronica turned and heard Reese's gasp as she herself tried to turn just as quickly. "Reese broke a rib," she informed her brother.

"How in the world did she do that?" he asked alarmed.

Veronica was the one that answered, "She got kicked in the ribs."

"By a horse?" he was confused, wasn't tonight the karate class? Then he realized Reese was still wearing her robe.

"No, by a well-aimed kick of our instructor," Veronica corrected.

"Your instructor kicked Reese?" he was incredulous imagining it.

Reese laughed, "Well, I did break two and a half of his ribs in return, it was only fair." She then grimaced because the laugh joggled her.

David stood there with his mouth ajar and Veronica said, "I'll tell you later," as she went to help Reese up the stairs.

"What can I do to help you?" Veronica asked as Reese and she entered her bedroom.

Reese shook her head again, "You can send in one of the maids to help me off with my clothes."

"Nonsense, just tell me what to do!" Veronica was taking charge and Reese was surprised, this was a side of Veronica that they rarely ever saw.

"Help me off with my Gi," she instructed.

Veronica helped her untie and then carefully slide her arms out of the robe. Underneath were the drawstring of her trousers and a sports bra.

Reese looked down at the sports bra in consternation. There was no way she would be able to get this off with her rib in the condition it was in. She was hot and sweaty and needed to sponge herself off. Showers were out for a couple of days at least as the tape on her ribs would wash off.

Veronica must have surmised the same as she said, "We will have to cut it."

Reese looked at her in alarm but conceded that was what they would have to do. "There is a pair of scissors in my top drawer," she nodded with her head.

Veronica opened the antique dresser and found the scissors. She went to the back of the bra and deftly cut it at the seam. Reese felt awkward at that moment with trying to hold the scrap of material to her bosom in front of her boss. Given the odd look in Veronica's eyes earlier that she hoped she had imagined she felt very uncomfortable. Looking down she thought she could at least remove her karate bottoms herself without help but could she manage to pull her underwear off? She certainly wasn't going to ask Veronica.

"Thank you," she said as she walked into the bathroom away from her employer.

Veronica watched as the naked back of her tall friend walked away from her. She realized she was staring at the expanse of skin exposed by the scissors as she also admired the firm round buttocks in the karate trousers as Reese walked into the bathroom. Turning suddenly she returned the scissors to the dresser and was surprised to see a sex toy hidden under a pair of underwear, covering it back up she closed the drawer. She looked at the pictures Reese had on her dresser of a girl in various stages of growth. Veronica assumed it was Reese as it looked so much like her but the last picture was of two women and one of them was definitely Reese, she wondered who the other woman or girl was in the picture. Sitting in one of the posh chairs positioned around the room she waited as she heard Reese turn on the water in the bathroom.

Reese got the drawstring undone and lowered the trousers no problem. The underwear proved a little tight and awkward because she couldn't bend normally with her rib hurting so. She finally got onto the toilet and used her free arm to remove them. Turning on the water she turned on the shower to wash around the taped area and remove the sweat from her body. She looked in the mirror and shook her head at the tape area. She had never gotten hurt like this. She was pleased with herself though that she had acted automatically with her counter strike. She could only imagine how Juan was feeling right now given the extent of her own pain. Thinking about her own pain she realized she needed to take the meds that the doctor had given her at the hospital. Blotting the water from her body as best she could she had to lift the robe from the back of the door twice before it fell into her hands. She could only get it over one shoulder though and the pain was too much to loop it over the other. Amazing how not being able to move around a rib affected everything.

As Reese opened the door she was surprised to see Veronica sitting in one of the chairs in her room. She tried to hide the naked half of her body by turning slightly and saying, "I can't cover that side."

Veronica rose and helped put the robe over the right side of Reese's body covering both her shoulder and arm which she still held to her side. She tried averting her eyes but couldn't help but see out of the corner of her eye the lush breast and firm body in front of her.

"Do you have the pills the doctor gave me?" Reese asked not noticing Veronica's blush.

"Yes, I have them in my purse," and Veronica went to fetch them.

Pouring out the required dosage Veronica went into the bathroom and filled a glass of water for Reese. Reese sat on the edge of the four poster bed and threw the pills in her mouth and grabbed the glass of water Veronica held out to swallow them. "God, I hope they work fast."

"Oh they do," Veronica assured her.

"Really? How would you know?" Reese asked curiously.

"I can't tell you how many times I've been thrown or bruised something when I was riding in competitions." Veronica smiled in remembrance.

Reese studied her remembering once again the look in her eyes earlier and wondering at it. She had to shrug it off though. It was inappropriate to speculate on it, Veronica was technically her boss, her employer, even if David had engaged her.

"Let's get you into bed," Veronica was all business.

"I think I'm going to sleep in my robe," Reese informed her.

"Good idea, the less you move around the better for that rib," Veronica told her as she helped pulled down the covers and Reese got into bed.

Whatever was in those pills did indeed work fast and Reese found herself getting sleepy almost immediately much to her relief. Veronica tucked her in and found herself watching as her friend was soon asleep. She examined her face in minute detail as she drank in the beauty of the woman before her.

CHAPTER 17

Reese took it easy over the next few days. She found she couldn't sit at her desk very long but she managed as best she could. She also found she needed naps frequently with the pain pills she was on. Veronica took her to her first check up and with the tapes removed the bruise around her broken rib looked vivid. Reese had allowed Veronica into the examination room with her and regretted it as she felt uncomfortable with her breast exposed. The doctor was one thing but her friend? That was awkward. She was wearing a hospital gown but the doctor had it aside as he gently probed to see the extent of her healing and damage.

Veronica found herself thinking about Reese all the time. She relished being able to take care of her as much as Reese would allow her. Bringing her trays for her meals was the least she could do and Reese soon put an end to that as she came down to the dinner table. The other servants were equally solicitous but Veronica took special pains to see to Reese's comfort. Even fluffing up the pillows on the couch where she sat and read papers for the estate. David watched amused as his sister became a mother hen. Veronica didn't know why but she felt this special need to be with Reese as much as possible, to touch if she could, to smell her perfume, to talk to her about the most mundane things.

Veronica wanted to ask Reese about the toy she had seen in Reese's drawer. Her attempts with her own toys had frustrated her as she knew she was doing something wrong. She couldn't discuss this aspect of things with Ana but she did mention her attraction.

"Do you think you are attracted because she is hurt and in need of your help?" Ana asked as they rode sedately along. She enjoyed this aspect of her job. Reese had given her an assignment she had truly come to love. She was helping Lady Veronica with her problems and she got to ride every day.

"I think I began thinking about women months ago when I watched that show ER, you know that American program?" she looked about as she blushed, never making eye contact with Ana.

"Yes, I watch that program myself," Ana responded.

"I became interested in a story line in that show that made me question things about myself." Veronica watched the scenery.

"Which story line?" Ana asked.

"The one between a lesbian psychiatrist and the ER chief," she confided.

"You're interested in a lesbian romance?" Ana asked, her voice never betraying her own feelings on the subject to her patient.

"Don't worry, I didn't think of you as I did the psychiatrist on ER," she grinned to show that no offense was meant, "I only was surprised that the story caught my interest," Veronica added, and then, "I began to think about the two of them and I became aroused by it. It made me start to think of Reese in a whole new light."

"Is Reese a lesbian?" Ana asked.

Veronica shrugged her elegant shoulders, "I have no idea. She has never said. My friend Audrey is bi-sexual or so she claims and she has hit on Reese several times but Reese always shrugs it off but she doesn't pair up with anyone exclusively male or female when we all go out. I just don't know her preferences that way."

"So she has no idea of your feelings?"

Veronica shrugged again, "I don't think she does. I just know how I feel about her. It started with admiration for the work she had done. She is so competent. David is thrilled with how well things are being run. But then at some point she became a friend. She encouraged me to go see a psychiatrist when she heard what had happened to me," Veronica paused as it still hurt and Ana let the silence continue until Veronica started again, "I refused but then she introduced you to me and for that I am very grateful," Veronica looked at her friend and confidant and smiled, "She shows in so many ways that she cares and she does it so unselfishly. I cannot but help admire her. When I started having feelings about women I couldn't help but think of her."

"You don't have feelings for any other women do you?"

"No, not at all," Veronica shook her head, "You would think if I was to become a lesbian I would go after Audrey who is openly gay and who would probably show me what I need to know," she laughed at the understatement. She did know that Audrey would jump at the chance and not be discrete about it. "I just don't feel that way about anyone else. Reese though makes me want to touch her, to feel her, to know her intimately."

"You have never been with a woman, how do you know that is what you want?"

Veronica blushed, "I've been reading up on things on the internet and I realize I don't feel this way about men. Reese is the most admirable woman I know and I feel myself sexually attracted to her."

"Sexually?"

Veronica nodded, "Yes, I get aroused around her."

Ana nodded and let her patient talk. Veronica had come a long way since they began their sessions. The rape had been traumatic but the years of trauma had intensified her fears instead of letting them subside. She had wanted nothing to do with sex since. This was an unexpected development. Ana wasn't repulsed at all but she was surprised that Veronica had researched it and obviously been thinking a lot about it.

"Are you sure your feelings over what happened to you haven't soured you to the idea of being with a man, any man and that perhaps your taking those feelings and turning them into something else, transferring them to Reese?"

Veronica shook her head, "Even when I felt attraction to men before...before..." she couldn't or wouldn't say it, "I found that their interest in horses was more attractive than being intimate with them. It feels completely different when I think about Reese. I don't know if she can ever return the feelings but I can hope, I know if I never try to find out I will always wonder. Even if she refuses at least I will have tried. Perhaps then I might find someone who can return those feelings. I don't want a man, I know that now."

They talked through the rest of their ride and Veronica was relieved when it was over. She had blushed so much she felt her face was permanently red. An unbecoming trait in an English woman with white skin. It was a relief to talk to someone about it though and Ana didn't judge her.

A few days later Reese was watching the grooms unload a truck full of pallets into the stables. She had a clipboard to make sure the count was right. There was a lot more work since she had come to the estate but the monies spent were less and for that the estate prospered. She turned as Veronica rode up on Satin.

"Riding alone?" she asked her friend with a smile.

"Well, one of my riding companions had to work today and the other is a little too bruised to accommodate me," she grinned at Reese.

Reese grinned at her reference to the bruises that still remained on her sore side. She was up and walking though and she thought that was progress. The thought of riding a horse though made her shudder. She could barely stand the weekly trip to the doctor although now she was driving herself.

"Care to go for a walk?" Veronica offered and Reese nodded as she signed off on the trucker's paperwork and handed it to the man as he came up. Veronica handed Satin to one of the grooms as he walked up.

They walked out into one of the pastures. Some of the mares were munching on the graze as their foals gambled around them. The two of them laughed over their antics and fed them and petted them. Reese grimaced as she tried to hug one close and Veronica watched her with a look in her eye she wasn't aware of.

Reese caught Veronica watching her this time and wondered at it. Veronica averted her gaze as she looked around the pastures. "Wow it's a beautiful day," she commented.

Reese had to agree with her. All her friends had warned her about gloomy and foggy and wouldn't believe this incredible sunshine and heat! "My daughter is coming over in a few weeks," she commented.

"Your daughter?" she asked surprised.

Reese turned with a grin, "Yes, you knew I had a daughter didn't you?"

Veronica nodded and said, "Isn't she in boarding school?"

Reese shook her head, "No, she is in college."

"You have a daughter in college?" Veronica asked incredulous looking at the youthful beauty before her.

Reese nodded proud of her daughter and puzzled at Veronica's response.

"How old is she?"

Reese thought for only a second before she answered, "Twenty but she will be twenty-one by the end of the year."

"I can't believe you have a daughter that old. How old are you?" Veronica was curious.

"I am thirty-eight; I'll be thirty-nine right before Gillian's birthday."

Veronica started in surprise. She had assumed Reese was a lot younger than that and closer to her own twenty-eight, almost twenty nine years. "Her name is Gillian?"

Reese nodded, "Yes, she has been studying at NYU and has been talking about transferring abroad. I haven't seen her of course since I got here except on Skype and I'm looking forward to seeing her."

"Are you going to take some time off?" Veronica was curious.

Reese nodded. “I am owed a week’s vacation. I’m going down to London and she and I are going to do the town.”

“What about her father?”

Reese looked sad for a moment, “He was a one night stand and wanted nothing to do with either of us. I raised her alone.”

“Did he help you at least financially?”

Reese looked out over the pastures herself now to avoid looking into Veronica’s face. “No, he avoided that as well. I was in college and my parents looked after Gillian while I got my degree. Then when I worked I also took night courses for my masters. It took a lot of years but eventually I got everything I wanted and even more I didn’t know I wanted.” She grinned in remembrance.

“That must have been difficult. Your parents must be proud of you and what you’ve accomplished.”

“My parents died when Gillian was four in an accident. It was a terrible loss.” She was silent in those memories.

“I’m sorry, I didn’t mean to pry,” Veronica put her hand on Reese’s shoulder to comfort her.

Reese put her hand up and grasped Veronica’s, appreciating the gesture. “It’s okay, it’s long ago. I miss them. They and Gillian were all I had in the world.”

Veronica squeezed before removing her hand. “Have you ever wanted to marry?”

Reese smiled and looked at Veronica, “No, I found I had a driving need to succeed in what I wanted. Not that I haven’t dated but I find I’m usually too busy to maintain a relationship for long. Besides, what can someone else give me that I can’t give myself,” she laughed.

Veronica realized this was the moment she had been waiting for. “May I ask you something?”

Reese smiled, hadn’t she asked her a lot of ‘something’s’ but she nodded.

“How are you able to make a toy give you an orgasm,” and then Veronica blushed at her audacity and daring and turned slightly away but waited anyway.

Reese was stunned. This proper English lady was talking about toys? Where had that come from? She realized in that instant though that the scissors had been in her top drawer and that Veronica had probably seen what the drawer contained. She wanted to squirm but an honest question deserved an honest answer. Gulping she looked back out at the pasture and answered, "You learn what feels good and learn to manipulate the toy."

Veronica felt like the earth should open up and swallow her but she swallowed and asked, "What if that doesn't work?"

"Well, you have to learn yourself but perhaps someone can show you, I don't have all the answers but that's the best I can come up with." Reese wanted to get away from this conversation. She was good friends with Veronica at this point but they hadn't really talked about sex other than the rape and that only in veiled terms.

Veronica nodded and let the uncomfortable subject drop. Changing it to another subject made them both relieved. At least it was out there though she thought. Although the answer was unsatisfactory so was the sex that Veronica tried on herself.

CHAPTER 18

Reese had a marvelous time in London with Gillian as they played tourist. The double decker busses were a hoot. They saw the changing of the guards, Westminster, and even took a tour through Windsor Castle when they were open to the public.

"Mom, I'm transferring to Cambridge next year," Gillian informed her.

"You got in?" Reese said excitedly. If she was here in England she could see her a whole lot more often.

Gillian nodded pleased at how happy she had made her mother. They had missed each other so much. The emails, the phone calls, the internet chats were just not enough. Hugging each other was needed, talking face to face, a touch, a caress, these were all missed.

The week however sped by way too fast. Reese was crying as she dropped Gillian off at Heathrow and managed to get on the wrong freeway on the way back. Cursing the English with their wrong sided roads and wrong sided steering wheels it took her an extra hour to get on the roads north towards the Cavandish estate. She was looking forward to Gillian's move to England so they could see each other more often. Strangely she wished she could have introduced Veronica to her. She talked about Lord and Lady Cavandish so often that Gillian felt like she knew them.

Gillian had been naturally concerned about the rib that Reese broke but the bruises were very faint at that point and her maneuverability increased that it barely pained her anymore. Hearing how Veronica had taken care of her had endeared her to her daughter for all time.

Veronica had missed Reese very much. She was used to her being away on estate business of course but her daughter was a different factor. She was surprised that Reese didn't bring her up to the estate to show her around but Reese felt that it would have been an imposition and wanted to play tourist with her daughter. Veronica found herself thinking about Reese increasingly since their talk about toys and strangely if that were possible thinking more and more about them becoming intimate. She wished she could discuss it with Reese but didn't know how to broach the subject. It wasn't like she could ask Reese to 'take care of it' for her and teach her how to orgasm. The thought of being intimate with Reese though did arouse her. The stories she read on the internet frequently had her imagining Reese doing those things to her. She mentally shook herself, she felt like she was becoming obsessed. There was no basis for the attraction beyond her own fevered imagination. Reese had never indicated her own interest and Veronica didn't even know *if* she *was* a lesbian, and even if she *was* there was no guarantee she would be attracted to her.

Reese was gingerly working out the day after she returned. Her mobility was increasing and she carefully stretched some of the muscles she had been careful with since the accident. She wasn't careful enough and gasped as she felt the exact spot where she had broken the rib. Veronica heard her as she had just entered and was watching her minimized work out.

"Are you okay?" she asked as she hurried up.

Reese was clutching her side and grimacing, "Yeah," she gasped, "I'll be okay in a moment," as she tried to get her breath back.

"Can I help you?" she asked alarmed at the sweat that broke out on her friend's forehead.

Reese shook her head as she just breathed through her nose to minimize the pain she had caused herself. She opened her eyes to realize how close Veronica really was.

Veronica had been watching as the pain subsided from her friends face and felt the immediate attraction she felt for this woman. As Reese opened her eyes Veronica couldn't seem to help herself and she leaned in for a kiss.

Reese stood there stiffly as Veronica kissed her. She didn't respond in any way she was so surprised.

Veronica attempted to kiss with her lips open but Reese's lack of response was a little intimidating. She didn't step back right away and realized only when Reese didn't return the kiss that she had made a huge mistake. Taking a step back she spun away to walk out and Reese grabbed her arm to stop her.

"What was that about?" she asked in her surprise.

"I'm sorry," Veronica stammered, "I made a mistake, it won't happen again." She was horribly embarrassed and only wanted to escape but Reese holding firmly to her arm prevented it.

"Veronica, wait," she was still waiting for the pain to subside and holding onto Veronica's arm was causing her to stretch the very arm she needed at her side.

Veronica turned back only to realize the pain she was causing Reese and quickly hurried to her side to take her into her arms and lead her to a chair at the side of the room. "Come on, sit down. Relax!" she ordered.

Reese was in enough pain that she didn't resist. She calmed herself as the pain subsided; keeping her eyes closed to not only concentrate on the pain but to think over what had just happened. Finally though the silence had stretched out long enough for both of them.

"Do you want me to get your pain pills?" Veronica asked anxiously eager to help her.

Reese shook her head but opened her eyes to see the anxious expression on Veronica's face and the tender look in her amazing yes. This shook her to her core. Gulping she ignored the remaining pain and asked, "Veronica, *why* did you kiss me?"

Veronica was immediately uncomfortable. She wanted to spring up from her own seat and run out of the room. Instead she bravely looked at Reese and said, "I'm attracted to you."

"You are?" Reese asked surprised.

Veronica nodded but didn't run. Every instinct told her she should leave but something held her glued to the seat.

"But you're my boss, where could this possibly go?" Reese asked confused and really not knowing what to say.

"I don't know, I really don't." She shook her head to emphasize what she was saying, "I've found myself attracted to you for a long time," she looked directly into Reese's face.

Reese looked dumbfounded. She wasn't normally this obtuse. Someone like Audrey she knew how to handle, but Veronica was a lady, an English Lady! Maybe though she had read her wrong? No, that wasn't it; she had come to know her very well this last year. She wasn't gay. "Have you ever been with a woman?" she asked gently.

Veronica looked down at her hands that were folded in her lap and wanted to twist them around themselves. She shook her head.

"How do you know you're attracted to me?"

Veronica shrugged looking away in embarrassment. "How does anyone know they are attracted to another person? I think about you all the time. I get flushed when you are around me. I like you very much, much more than a friend. I want to touch you, to hold you, to kiss you..." she trailed off embarrassed.

Reese wasn't sure what to do. She had never let on that she was attracted to women or men despite Audrey's blatant attempts. She felt her personal life should never cross over to her professional life.

Veronica glanced up hopefully for a moment, "Is it possible that you might be attracted to me?" Then she quieted immediately because she hoped so much on the answer.

"Veronica, I can't think of you that way. You're my employer!" Reese answered almost automatically as she absorbed the implications of this and all it could impact her careful plans for her own future.

"And if I wasn't?" Veronica had to ask.

Here it was, she was going to be fired and over what? Her employer's interest in her? She didn't know the laws of Britain but she was sure there was a sexual harassment or something suit in there here. "Veronica, I'm not in a good position here. Your interest in me makes for an untenable position. If I returned the interest and it went sour, how long would I be employed here?" The anger in her voice was beginning to show.

"My interest in you is entirely personal. It has nothing to do with your professional work here." Veronica tried to separate it all out in her own mind.

Reese shook her head. There was no way this could turn out for the good or in her favor. "You could fire me if you didn't like the way a relationship such as this went," she pointed out.

"I would never do that. Your work has been exemplary. It speaks for itself. All I am asking is that you consider the possibility. Are you attracted to me?" she asked again hopefully.

Reese sighed. This was an unforeseen circumstance. But was it? She had begun her friendship with Veronica because she felt sorry for the little mouse. The woman she had come to know was a little spitfire and had overcome quite a few of her anxieties. She was an attractive woman that showed such promise, but Reese was older, she had different goals, different priorities. This could only end badly.

"Of course I am attracted to you, who wouldn't be. You're a lovely woman. I thought it was just friendship though." She knew she was being a coward using a double entendre and not admitting anything.

Veronica looked up not exactly sure how to take the compliment but sure that Reese was hedging. Something in her look told Veronica that there was more.

As Reese looked into Veronica's eyes she attempted to mask her own feelings but those incredible violet eyes were her defeat. They mirrored this poor tortured soul that she had felt so much for so long.

"May I kiss you?" Veronica asked hesitantly still unsure.

Reese sighed quietly and said, "Mmhm." She knew this was a bad idea.

They both leaned in and Reese soon realized that Veronica was inexperienced where kisses were concerned. As Veronica pulled back and asked, "Are you okay?" Reese nodded and leaned in to kiss Veronica properly. She pulled her closer and opened her mouth. Gently she kissed Veronica using her lips and then her tongue to her advantage. Veronica began to melt in her arms. Wrapping her own arms carefully around Reese she began to caress along her neck and back. When she went to hug her closer Reese winced as she pressed against the healing rib. Veronica pulled back immediately and asked in concern, "Did I hurt you?"

Reese smiled and looked deeply into Veronica's eyes. Those incredible eyes, she could get lost in them they were so beautiful. They were a mirror to this woman's soul. Reese put her hand up to Veronicas head to caress along the side of it and cup her cheek. Examining her whole face she gently asked, "Where do you want to go with this?"

Veronica was flustered. She hadn't completely thought that far ahead at least not at this moment. Naturally she wanted to eventually go to bed with Reese but she hadn't really thought that was ever a possibility, only a fantasy. "I want you," was all she simply said.

Reese wanted to groan at that answer. She rested her forehead on Veronica and closed her eyes, inhaling deeply she smelled her perfume and personal smell. It smelled so good. She wanted to continue but at the same time she wondered if she was up to it. Veronica was technically a lesbian virgin. She had a lot of issues. Reese would have to tread carefully through this landmine field. She sighed deeply. "We are going to have to go slow," she told Veronica.

"Why?" Veronica asked naively.

"Because you are my boss, because you have never been in a relationship like this, because I don't want you to get hurt, because I'm still on the mend..." she stopped seeing the stricken look on Veronica's face.

"You don't want me?" she misunderstood thinking Reese was putting up fences to stop this before it even began.

"Gawd, no I didn't mean that," she smiled into Veronica face cupping her face with her hands, "I do want you. This is going to take a little time though, you have to be patient, okay?" she told her gently.

Veronica smiled her beautiful smile that melted Reese's heart. She wanted her! Reese wanted her!

Their opportunity to continue the conversation ended. Reese heard footsteps and sat back in her chair releasing Veronica face. Veronica looked confused for a moment before she too heard the footsteps and looked up as Mrs. Gunderson walked into the room.

"Ms. Paulson, there's a call for you."

Reese got up and gave Veronica a cautionary look before leaving the gym.

They didn't get another chance to talk until late that evening. It was customary for Veronica to watch television on Thursday nights with David. She was distracted and fidgeting.

"Are you okay?" David finally asked.

Veronica nodded automatically as she looked up and answered, "Yes, why?"

"You seem, I don't know, like you have your mind elsewhere. ER is almost over and you haven't commented on it yet. Usually you say something..."

"Oh, I guess I'm just thinking about what I am going to do tomorrow."

This was so unlike Veronica that he watched her puzzled. She continued to be distracted and fidget until the program was over and then announced that she was going to bed.

"Good night," he called as she left the room.

CHAPTER 19

Veronica headed upstairs to her rooms and then stopped, thinking, she then detoured to Reese's room down the hall. Knocking on the door she heard, "Come in," and entered to find Reese typing away on her laptop computer wearing a camisole night blouse with her legs under her covers.

"Am I disturbing you?" she asked anxiously. She had wanted to see her for hours since they had been interrupted and dinner hadn't allowed a personal conversation but she knew she couldn't have found a reason before now.

"No, not at all, I'm just finishing up," Reese said not surprised that Veronica had come to see her.

Veronica quietly locked the door behind her before crossing the floor to the bed where Reese sat propped up against the headboard. She finished typing and closed the laptop putting it on the bedside table before turning her full attention on Veronica. She smiled at the shy woman who had been so bold that day. Gently she grabbed her hand and pulled her to a seat on the edge of the bed. She cupped her head and moved in to kiss her gently, "Hello," she whispered before she kissed Veronica on the lips.

She has such soft lips Veronica thought. She really knows how to kiss. It's so wonderful; it makes me feel so wonderful.

Wow, is she inexperienced. She doesn't know how to kiss at all. In a way it's exciting as I can be the one to teach her but at the same time Reese felt intimidated at being the one to initiate Veronica, to be her first. "Do you really want to do this?" she asked when they came up from that first kiss.

Veronica nodded and then thought to ask, "Have you changed your mind?"

Reese shook her head. "I want you to be sure," she emphasized.

Veronica looked deeply into Reese's eyes, "I am sure, I want you, I want you to teach me."

Reese sighed. She did want Veronica but was she the one to teach her? It wasn't like teaching her dance or karate moves. "This isn't like anything you have ever done before; you can't un-ring the bell. I don't want you to regret it."

Veronica nodded, "I know, I won't. I've thought about this for a long time. I want this."

Reese wasn't sure how to proceed really. She thought perhaps she wasn't the one that was ready for this. Veronica was a beautiful woman though. She was an adult. She wanted to do this, who was Reese to deny her. She leaned in to kiss her again showing her with her lips and tongue how to kiss properly. Veronica immediately imitated her and Reese was pleased at the response. Next Reese began to caress along her neck and shoulders getting her used to her touch. Veronica imitated this as well but took it one step further. Her hand began to caress into Reese's camisole night shirt. Already Reese's nipples were hard and when Veronica's fingers gently touched the left one with her fingertips Reese gasped at the feeling it caused. Veronica backed away for a moment to see if the gasp was pleasure or pain. She smiled slightly when she realized it was pleasure.

Reese slowly began to lean back on the bed pulling Veronica with her until she leaned against her carefully. She rested her weight not on Reese but on the left side of her being careful not to lean against her right side where the rib was mending. This freed her right hand to roam against Reese's body. The first touch of her breast made her bolder as she released the breast from the camisole exposing it to the elements. Reese arched slightly as her palm captured it in its warmth. Reese began to kiss along Veronica's jaw and down her neck. Her hands began to remove the vest she was wearing over a button down shirt. Veronica was momentarily distracted at having to move her arms one at a time to remove the vest and began to unbutton her own shirt. Reese pushed her hands aside as she took over the task. They exchanged an affectionate filled look before kissing again.

Veronica pushed the straps down on Reese's camisole exposing her chest and then the other breast. She felt her own breath coming harder. She had seen pictures of other woman's breasts of course but she had fantasized about *this* woman's. She kissed her way down from Reese's mouth, to her neck which Reese arched to let her reach it unimpeded. Slowly she kissed her way down to the erect nipples exposed to her mouth and fingers. She began to touch them and heard Reese's slight indrawn breath as she touched first one and then other with her warm and wet tongue.

This was getting away from her and she couldn't let it or Veronica would be left out in limbo. She began to unbutton the blouse which soon allowed her access to her bra and smooth stomach. Her hand gently brushed against her stomach and she was gratified to hear her indrawn breath at her touch. She pushed the blouse from those elegant shoulders and began kissing along their exposed length. Slowly she reached for the bra clasp only to realize that Veronica wore a push up bra that clasped in the front. She mentally cursed herself for her lack of finesse but then Veronica would never know. She soon had Veronica naked from the waist up. She enjoyed the view momentarily as she moved in for more kisses. Slowly she kissed along her jaw line and under her ear. She could hear Veronica's breath coming harder, it excited her and she knew she was already becoming wet in anticipation.

Veronica wanted to be naked but didn't know how to make her wishes known. Reese had cautioned her earlier to patience and she mentally schooled herself to try that. She loved the feel of what Reese was doing to her. She had never liked to have her breasts touched before but she was surprised how badly she wanted Reese to touch hers. She finally grasped one of Reese's hands to cup it and bring it to her breast. It ached. Reese made it feel wonderful with her touch, her thumb rubbing the tip. She was surprised at the corresponding feeling in her crotch.

Reese slowly rolled Veronica over onto her back so she could access her trousers button. She slowly unbuttoned her and zipped it down. It was as she was pulling them down that she took advantage of the moment to slip her camisole down over her own hips. It was then that Veronica realized that Reese wasn't wearing any underwear as she glimpsed the bit of hair at the V of her legs. Reese peeled Veronica's underwear down then as well. They were both naked and Veronica welcomed the feel of Reese as she gently lay on top of her being careful to favor her right side.

Veronica immediately began to caress that strong back she had glimpsed those weeks ago and wanted to touch then. That led down to Reese's buttocks and she cupped them gently as Reese moved against her in response to her caresses.

Reese felt her own lust rising and fast. Mentally she tampered it down concentrating on Veronica, knowing she wasn't ready for such passion. She had such a delicious body that Reese wanted to devour it all and immediately. She kept the thought in her head though how inexperienced Veronica really was. She was gentle and slow with her. She returned to kissing her sliding her leg slowly between Veronica's legs to gently rub between them. With her own hand that wasn't trapped between their bodies she began to caress down Veronica's body. She could feel Veronica's indrawn breath as she touched along her hip and her leg rubbed between them. She kissed along her jaw and down her neck again to begin an assault on her breasts. Gently she began to kiss and tongue first one and then the other coral colored tips. She could sense Veronica's response as she arched against her and grabbed at her body pulling Reese closer if that were possible. Slowly Reese began to move down her body removing her leg from between Veronica's as she reached between Veronica's legs to feel her wetness.

"I'm sorry," Veronica breathed embarrassed to find she wasn't that wet for a change. Usually she was soaked as she even thought about this incredible woman, but now when it counted she was nearly dry.

"Shhh, it's okay. It's your first time," Reese whispered in return. Her fingers found wetness but not very much. That was okay, there was a cure for that. Her upper torso began to move down Veronica's body as she kissed her way down across her stomach, tasting every inch of her. She tongued her way from her nipple to her belly button and she heard Veronica catch her breath. Reese's finger began to play with the wetness around the hole where it came from. No one had ever touched Veronica there that she could remember other than herself. She didn't think about her rapist, this was not the time for that. She was surprised at the sensation, totally different from what she had expected. Reese began to play with the hard little nub of flesh between her legs at the top of her V. This sensation too was totally different. Veronica didn't know what to expect from that. Reese went further down and her tongue began to play with Veronica's clit.

God that is so warm was her first thought as she felt Reese kiss her there. Her fingers went inside and Veronica could only think, that feels so different from a toy, smaller, less thick. She had to stop analyzing it and just feel. It felt so very good but again she felt nothing more from the sensations that Reese was engendering.

Reese swirled the clit around on her tongue wetting it thoroughly as her fingers delved in to seek the wetness she knew had to be hiding within. She searched for Veronica's G spot but despite knowing where it had to be she got no response from the woman under her. After a long while and plenty of caressing though she wasn't sure what she was doing wrong. Thrusting and playing weren't getting the responses that she expected and although she enjoyed playing with Veronica's body she could sense her frustration building.

"Give up," Veronica breathed after a long time, realizing that something was missing and not wanting Reese to continue.

Reese began to move up her body, her fingers remained and her thumb continued to play with Veronica's clit. She kissed her way up to the erect nipples that told their own story of Veronica's arousal. When she stopped to pay them homage Veronica sobbed, "I'm sorry," to her in her defeat.

Reese looked up to see the frustration on Veronica's face and murmured, "Shhh, it's okay, relax," as her fingers and thumb continued to play between the V of Veronica's legs. Her own body slightly grinding against Veronica's.

I've got to at least give her pleasure Veronica thought. When Reese rose enough to kiss her again on the lips Veronica gently rolled her on her back and duplicated everything that Reese had been doing to her. Reese let her hand fall back from between Veronica's legs as Veronica began kissing along her jawline and down her neck to her nipples. Reese groaned slightly when she enthusiastically began sucking on them. "Gently," she whispered as she increased the suction. Veronica's hand began moving down Reese's body and she hesitated only briefly before putting it between Reese's legs. The satiny feel of the hair down there was not unlike her own and she gently probed with her fingertips between the folds. She was surprised at how hard Reese's clit was and the wetness she found between her legs. Imitating what Reese had done to her and from what she had read on the internet she began to caress and feel with her fingertips fascinated and curious. She kissed her way down Reese's body stopping briefly to tongue her belly button as Reese arched towards her. She rose up to look between Reese's legs and thought, "Well, if I am a lesbian, this is what lesbian's do," before she took her first taste of Reese's clit. Reese's breath whooshed out since she had no idea she was even holding it. Veronica slowly inserted a finger and began to feel around surprised at how tight it felt in there. She pulled it out and began to play with the wetness as her tongue started licking around Reese's clit. She was surprised that she wasn't disgusted at the taste and instead was enjoying the response of Reese's body. Reese reached down and began playing with her own nipples in response to the stimulation that Veronica was providing on her clit. Controlling the when, she soon was orgasming from the stimulation. Veronica licked and played until Reese calmed and then began to kiss up her body using the opportunity to touch her all over and to get the cum off her tongue. Soon she was held in Reese's arms as her breathing returned to normal. She really loved the feel of Reese's strong arms around her, holding her.

They held each other for a very long time before Reese could tell that Veronica was becoming fidgety. She loosened her hold and let her lay back. Looking up at the ceiling she sighed deeply. Reese rose up on one arm and gently caressed along the length of Veronica's body. "Are you okay?" she asked her softly.

Veronica looked at her and Reese could see by the light in her room that she was disappointed or at least her eyes seemed sad. "I'm fine. How about you? Are you disappointed?" She seemed unsure of herself and hesitant.

Reese smiled, "I'm fine, you give good head."

Veronica's eyes widened at the crude jest and she shyly hid her head into Reese's shoulder as Reese chuckled. She mumbled, "I didn't cum."

Reese sensed this was the reason she was disappointed. "Not everyone cums each and every time." She wondered about Veronica's past prior to the rape and how it might be affecting her now.

"I've never cum," Veronica shook her head as she kept her face hid. "What is it like?"

"Never? As in you've never had an orgasm?" Reese asked trying not to sound shocked or incredulous.

Veronica shook her head and waited for the answer to her other question.

Reese assimilated the information and then, "It's a lovely melting feeling but it can also be intense. Sometimes you feel a thread of pleasure and you pursue that and it gives you the most delicious feeling. Occasionally my toes tingle and my lips go numb."

Veronica looked up at her hopefully. "What's wrong with me that I can't achieve that? I am twenty-eight, almost twenty-nine and I have never felt that."

Reese shrugged, "You have had a lot on your plate for the past few years; I'll bet if you talk to Ana about it she might have some insight on it."

"Oh no, I can't tell her about *this*!" Veronica exclaimed embarrassed.

Reese smiled, "Have you told her you were attracted to women?" she asked astutely.

Veronica nodded and thought about the past hour. She was more than attracted. She had enjoyed it immensely even if she hadn't achieved her ultimate goal of an orgasm.

"I personally think it will just take time. It's like riding a horse. You have to learn the feel of each one to be in 'rhythm' with it. You are going to be learning your body. It might take you time to learn to orgasm. I am no expert but I think that may be it. Let's face it, you have had a bad sexual experience that affected your whole life in so many ways that you are still trying to get over it and past it. Talk to Ana, I'm sure she can help," she encouraged.

Veronica thought over what Reese just said. It made sense and Ana had helped on a lot of things. She nodded as she considered it.

"Is it always like that?" she asked hesitantly unsure of the protocol. They were lying naked side by side and Reese was gently caressing her as they chatted.

"Is what like that?" Reese asked back as she looked down where her hand was caressing.

"Are orgasms always like the one you just had?" Then she got embarrassed at her daring and hid her face again.

Reese smiled enjoying the shyness of her new lover. "Sometimes it's like that, each time can be different. I can have three or four orgasms sometimes in a short time and each one is different."

Veronica lifted her head in surprise, "You have multiple orgasms?"

Reese nodded as she grinned.

"How do you do *that*?" Veronica asked amazed and impressed.

Reese chuckled at Veronica's interest; she wondered if she had awoken a sleeping nympho in the making, "It depends on my mood, the stimulation, the moment." She pulled Veronica's head down onto her shoulder and began caressing her hair back as she began to drift off to sleep.

Veronica lay there a long time as Reese's hand caressed her hair, it was a pleasant feeling and she remembered back to when her mother did that to put her to sleep as a child, slowly though Reese's hand stopped as she herself drifted off to sleep. Veronica wrapped her arm across Reese's torso below her breasts and snuggled up to sleep.

Reese woke about four a.m. to Veronica slipping out of bed. Sleepily she asked, "Where are you going?"

Veronica started at the voice, it was raspy and sleep filled, and very very sexy. She had tried to be so quiet to let Reese sleep. "I think I should go back to my own bed in case anyone sees me in the morning I should be coming out of my room."

Reese nodded. That made sense. They didn't want to broadcast that they were sleeping together.

Veronica leaned over after she got dressed and kissed Reese lingeringly. She liked kissing her and was amazed how different it was to kiss her. Even she could tell that Reese was a good kisser.

Reese wrapped her arms around her in a hug and said, "Sleep well," before turning over in the bed and going back to sleep.

Veronica snuck back to her own rooms. Silently closing and locking the door behind her she looked around at the dark room. Turning on a lamp she looked around again and realized how drab the room looked with its stacks of books, papers, and magazines and the curtains and drapes always drawn. She quickly undressed and got into her own bed but had trouble falling asleep as she thought over the night's activities reliving them in her own mind. She kept remembering the feel of Reese's hand on her naked hip and how she had hoped she would touch between her legs at that moment. How much she had enjoyed Reese's kisses and caresses. She had slept well in Reese's arms but her worry over being 'caught' had awoken her early enough to leave. She had trouble going back to sleep but she really didn't mind as she thought about everything over and over.

Reese didn't have as much trouble going back to sleep but once she woke in the morning she lay there a long time as she thought over what she had allowed to happen. Was she a fool to get involved with Veronica? She was so sweet. She had no idea the life she was getting into. It wasn't accepted in most societies and certainly not in the circles that Lady Veronica moved in. Dammit, why had she let herself get into this mess? She could see that the writing on the wall said that this would end in disaster. Veronica was her employer for Christ's sake! If she didn't end up dismissed from her position she was going to get her heart broke. She was 10 years older than Veronica, she should have never let it get this far. Veronica was still very messed up despite the work that Ana had done and how far she had come. Did Reese want that headache? And how was Lord David going to react when he found out? So much for taking it slow… Jesus, she was not looking forward to their future.

Reese avoided both of her employers most of the day. It was easy as she was inspecting a couple of the tenant's properties to see where repairs were necessary and if they were keeping them up. A few suggestions which weren't major and both the tenants and the estate manager were happy. One of the tenants gave her a bag of pears to take home to Mrs. Anderson for their table.

"Oh thank you, these look delicious," Mrs. Anderson said as she accepted the bag.

"They taste good too!" Reese smiled as she continued to bite into the big yellow pear she had sampled.

Mrs. Anderson chuckled; Reese looked like a little girl with the fruit dripping in her hand. She liked this woman. She was hard as nails where the estate was concerned but she had brought a prosperity that had been lacking. She got work out of everyone but it was for the greater good. Even the repairs in the house had been done in record time to please her and to keep Lord David's discomfort under control. She was utterly devoted to the Cavandish's and her friendship with Lady Veronica was well noticed. She didn't mind helping when it was necessary, she pitched in like everyone else. Hadn't she worked the bulldozer of all things to fill in the roads? The gardener's told how she had cut some of the trees back herself showing where she wanted the arches on the drive to begin. As a result everyone put in more of an effort because they knew she could and would do the jobs as well.

"Lady Veronica was looking for you," Mrs. Anderson told her.

"Oh really, do you know where she is now?"

"I believe she is out riding with Dr. Sinclair."

Reese nodded and was relieved. She didn't need to hide but at the same time she hoped Ana would help Veronica further.

CHAPTER 20

"You made love with Reese?" Ana was genuinely surprised.

Veronica looked straight ahead as she confessed to her therapist having realized long ago that she was much more than 'just' a friend. Nodding she continued, "And I enjoyed it very much."

"How does Reese feel about it?"

Veronica looked troubled, "She's worried about me."

"Worried? Why?"

"She thinks I have a lot of issues to work through with you."

Ana smiled. Reese was a smart woman although at the moment she wondered how smart she had been to get involved with Veronica on this level.

"She told me to talk about all this with you." Veronica squirmed a little in the saddle as they rode along feeling a little embarrassed but she needed to confide in someone and she knew it would go no further with Ana.

Well that was a good thing. Veronica was so young in so many ways. Reese's age and experience were well beyond Veronica's. She was a strong woman though and perhaps this 'admiration' that Veronica had for so long would help her in the long run. But sex could complicate things with the emotions that would become involved. "Were you ready for it? Did you want to?"

Veronica nodded emphatically still not looking directly at Ana. If she didn't see the expressions on her doctor's face she could tell her without the embarrassment. "I wanted her, I think I seduced her."

"You think? You don't know?"

Veronica shrugged, "I kissed her first and she made me explain why I did that. I confessed my attraction. We started to talk about it. Later I went to her bedroom and we kissed some more but it turned into so much more."

Ana could only imagine. She herself was happily married and didn't understand the attraction between two of the same sex but intellectually she could explain it.

"I think I disappointed her though," Veronica confessed.

"Disappointed her how?"

"I didn't orgasm," she was truly embarrassed now.

Ana wasn't surprised. With everything Veronica had been through and suppressed for so long she was lucky she felt desire, this had been a very damaged woman. Ana was surprised that she was pursuing Reese of all people. Reese was a strong and confident woman. She understood Veronica's admiration. That Reese had allowed her to become a sexual partner worried Ana a little. "It may just take time, are you prepared that it might never happen?"

"Reese said it might take time too!" she exclaimed ignoring the rest of the question.

Reese was a wise woman, maybe she sensed something about Veronica that Ana was missing. "How do you feel about that?"

Veronica shrugged her elegant shoulders, "I guess I will have to learn patience. I've waited this long, I can wait. I had hoped for something immediately though."

"It's different for everyone."

"That's what Reese said!" she enthused.

Reese had said a lot and that was to the good. Ana wanted to talk to her and yet couldn't really without breaking the doctor patient privilege. They talked for a while about Veronica's feelings and Ana felt it was a good session as they rode along over the hills with the fine horses.

CHAPTER 21

Veronica threw the little bag she had brought onto the bed as she continued on into the adjoining bathroom where she could hear the water running. Reese lay back in the tub reclining and enjoying the heat of the water. Veronica watched the long limbs for a while enjoying the sight as she watched the beautiful blonde. There wasn't an inch of fat on her. Athletic and toned were the words that came to mind. She must have made some noise despite the sound of the water pouring into the tub because suddenly Reese looked up. Sitting up she nearly poured water of the edge as she leaned forward to turn off the faucet.

"Hello," she said as the sound of water pouring into the tub stopped with an occasional drip from the faucet.

Veronica smiled not sure that she hadn't overstepped some imaginary bounds by just showing up again. She felt unsure but she had waited all day to see Reese again and couldn't wait another moment. "Hello," she responded.

Reese watched her watch her. She could see the interest and while flattered she wasn't sure if she was annoyed at the invasion of her privacy. "Want to join me?" she asked impulsively indicating the full tub of water.

Veronica grinned, "There doesn't seem to be a lot of room."

Reese pulled her legs back and said, "I'll make room," as she watched Veronica decide.

Veronica wasn't so sure there wasn't some kind of challenge in the invitation and she turned to begin pulling off her own clothes, at first shy about disrobing in front of Reese. When she was naked she walked back across the bathroom floor trying to be unselfconscious as Reese watched her. Reese had after all seen her naked the previous evening. Reese stopped with the loofah sponge when she saw Veronica return. Pulling her legs back again she reached to let some water out as Veronica stood beside, the tub.

"Come on, you have got to be getting cold," she said amused as she noted the erect nipples.

Veronica gingerly put in her foot and felt the overly hot water. As she climbed fully in and began to lower herself the water level rose rapidly and threatened to spill over. Soon though Reese closed the drain again and they both sat there facing each other with their legs pulled up to their chests and the water very near the level of the top, the overspill drain was still taking out water. Reese gently began to put her legs around Veronica on either side, slowly rubbing them along Veronica's sides, and then reached forward to pull Veronica's legs around her own body, when they were both settled Reese leaned back and said, "Ah that's better," as she watched Veronica through lowered eyelids.

Veronica reached for the loofah sponge on the side and began to apply it to her body. The most delicious scent came up from the foam and she inhaled it happily, "This is wonderful, what is it?"

"It's peach, I don't use soaps, it's a body wash," Reese said amused watching Lady Veronica prissily apply the sponge to her body.

When enough water had spilled out the overspill Reese leaned forward and took the sponge from Veronica. Her movements were slow so as not to cause Veronica alarm but not to create waves that would flow over the edge of the tub either. She gently began to wash everywhere Veronica had patted already smoothing the loofah over her body. Raising her breasts slightly to wash around them and under them touching them and watching Veronica from the corners of her eyes to see her reactions. She could tell that Veronica was nervous, unsure of herself but at the same time aroused and wanting, needing something. Slowly she finished the front and gently kissing the brunette she whispered, "Turn around," as she backed up to give her room. Veronica who was enjoying the sensations that Reese administered woke from her day dreams and slowly turned around so as not spill water out of the tub. It was difficult, the tub wasn't overly large and with the two of them there wasn't a lot of room. Finally with her back to Reese she halted and began to feel the sponge on her shoulders, her hair pulled aside, her neck, her back. Reese reached down to where she could reach her buttocks as well. When everything had been soaped she put the sponge aside and began applying water with her bare hands, smoothing over the spots repeatedly in her caresses. Leaning back slightly she pulled Veronica against her and wrapped her legs around her from behind she leaned forward slightly and began to remove the suds from her front as well, her caresses relaxing and arousing Veronica all at once. Veronica leaned against her in the tub and sighed deeply. This was the most sensual experience other than making love to Reese that she had ever experienced. Better than the stories she had read. Reese began to kiss along her exposed neck and shoulder tonguing and sucking slightly as she caressed and petted Veronica's breasts. Reese kept this up for a long while but finally whispered, "Let's get up." Veronica woke from her reverie as Reese pulled the plug and they both rose to get out of the tub. Reese grabbed a towel and handed one to Veronica. Veronica wondered if she had done something wrong as Reese quickly dried herself but then Reese took her towel from her and began to dry her water drenched body. She did it thoroughly and slowed down as she watched Veronica's response and it became arousing. Once dry Reese took her in her arms and the towels fell to the floor as Reese kissed her deeply and thoroughly. Slowly she danced Veronica into a circle and began backing her into the bedroom and towards the bed.

As Veronica's knees came in contact with the edge of the bed she began to sit back and then lay back as Reese covered her and began to caress everywhere she could reach. Not once did she stop kissing her. Veronica held on for dear life but once on her back began to return the fevered caresses. Tonight felt different to Veronica, she didn't know if she was more relaxed or if it was from what she had Googled that morning and learned or at least wanted to try out. She realized she couldn't just lay there and she moved towards Reese at every opportunity writhing under her and responding to the caresses. Her indrawn breathes were heard by both of them as Reese made love to her. She could tell tonight that she was wetter and while she still didn't feel 'it' she was enjoying what Reese was doing to her body. Feeling inside her, touching a spot that made Veronica feel marvelous, playing with her wetness and spreading it around her clit and slit. As Reese moved to get in a better position her foot hit the bag that Veronica had brought and she looked puzzled at it. "That's mine," Veronica whispered as she noticed where Reese's attention had wandered.

"What is it?" Reese asked.

Veronica looked away embarrassed to answer, "Toys," she said almost too quiet to hear.

Reese smiled at Veronica and reached for the bag. Opening the small bag she found two toys. A dildo that looked amazingly like a man's penis except it had a spot where a plug could go in and be attached to a wall outlet and the other one was a rabbit vibrator. Reese pulled this one out and turned it on pleased that the batteries were in it. She looked at Veronica who had been watching her and looking away repeatedly. "Do you want me to use this on you?"

Veronica squirmed in her embarrassment but nodded. She had read whatever she could find and found herself getting aroused at the thought of Reese using toys on her.

Reese was amused that the little 'mouse' had the guts to own these two toys much less use them. She could sense that her amusement though would upset Veronica. She already realized how much this could overwhelm her. She began to play with the wetness with the rabbit getting it thoroughly soaked as Veronica lay there waiting, anticipating, she didn't know what. When Reese began to insert it she tensed and Reese whispered, "Relax, enjoy the sensations." She tried; she really did but didn't know what she was seeking. Reese had it fully inserted before she turned on the 'ears' of the rabbit only and began to ply them around Veronica's clit. She got a reaction.

Veronica nearly reared up off the bed. It tickled so bad she couldn't lay still. Reese kept the vibrations low and this Veronica was better able to deal with, she relaxed a little. Reese began to rub the ears along the side of Veronica's clit watching her reactions as she hit various spots. Veronica felt wonderful but wondered where this might go. Using her lips on Veronica she distracted her from what was going on at the junction of her legs, using her body to rub, tease, and entice she hoped to distract her enough to get her to relax and forget about the 'destination' and enjoy 'the ride.' Reese thrust the dildo part in and out as she rubbed deeper into and around the clit watching as Veronica's nipples got harder and she got wetter. She kept this up for a very long time before Veronica finally said in defeat and self-recriminations, "Stop, give up." Reese immediately stopped, turning the ears off, and slowly pulled the dildo out. Veronica wanted to cry in frustration. She knew she was missing something. That had all felt wonderful but it led nowhere!

"Are you okay?" Reese asked concerned as she moved up her body and gently lay next to her touching her with the length of her own body.

Veronica nodded feeling humiliated and a failure. She wasn't getting 'it' and she didn't know what 'it' was. That feeling that Reese had mentioned the previous night, she had no idea of what it was or where it would be. Maybe she was frigid.

"Veronica," Reese said gently as she saw the myriad of emotions pass over her friends face. "Veronica," she repeated when she went ignored.

Veronica finally looked into Reese's face. God she was beautiful, she wanted to kiss her and instead reached out to cup the side of her face to touch that beauty.

"You need to stop trying so hard for an orgasm and just enjoy what I do to you. You will find that feeling eventually. You're thinking too much and you can't do that." She smiled. "It will come, pardon the pun. Just relax and enjoy."

Veronica wanted it so bad and had no idea how to get it but she couldn't let Reese off without having her own 'fun' or orgasm. She leaned up to kiss Reese and ask, "Can I use the toy on you?"

Reese smiled and leaned back inviting her to do what she wanted. Veronica looked at the smooth body which puckered slightly below her belly button from having been pregnant. She began by kissing her again and it felt so good, it felt so right to be kissing her. Reese wrapped her arms around her in response and encouragement. She kissed along her jaw line and down her neck. She began kissing and sucking on Reese's nipples when she reached there and Reese whispered, "Gently, lick, don't suck, not yet." She arched her body into Veronica though in response. Veronica's hand reached down across Reese's belly and reached between her legs and much to her surprise she found her hand soaked almost immediately. She played with that wetness and spread it around as Reese spread her legs farther to give her access. The hard nub of flesh that she hit she began to play with and Reese caught her breath and moaned deeply. This encouraged Veronica that she was doing something right.

Veronica grabbed the rabbit and gently began to insert it into the very wet hole. Turning on the dildo part she heard Reese whisper, "No, the ears," and grind suggestively against it. Veronica turned them on and began to ply them around the very hard clit that resembled a very tiny penis. Reese bucked against it and groaned louder in response. She reached down and showed Veronica how to move it against and around it. Then she took Veronica's free hand and put it on one of her nipples. It was an awkward position but Veronica was determined to please Reese.

The combination of the nipple stimulation and the vibrating rabbit ears on her clit were incredible. She wanted to control her orgasm but she let it go and Veronica was amazed as she bucked and cried little panting cries as she leaned into Veronica's body and let go. It went on and on and on. When Veronica thought it was over and began to turn off the ears and pull out Reese grabbed her hand and whispered, "Thrust," and trapped her hand as her hips thrust against the dildo. Veronica soon figured out the rhythm and Reese's hand fell away. She ceased playing with the nipple and Reese tugged at her and whispered, "Now suck," as Veronica moved up her lover's body and complied. Being fucked with the dildo and the hard sucking on her nipple had Reese going mindless in another series of orgasms as she thrust against Veronica her body ululating to a primeval rhythm that Veronica could only marvel at. The mindless little cries rose in volume and when Veronica pulled back from sucking on the nipple to watch she found her mouth captured with Reese's as she cried out her passion. Reese wrapped a leg around her and thrust mindlessly against her until she felt replete and slowly calmed her overheated body and went limp.

Veronica was amazed, she had never imagined this much passion. While she had watched things on the internet she thought they were all 'faked' and to see Reese mindless with her need blew her mind. Slowly she removed the rabbit and put it aside. Reese held her close though as her body calmed. Finally though she unwrapped herself from around Veronica and lay back with a sigh.

Reese hoped she hadn't frightened Veronica. She didn't know why but she suddenly had had to let go. It had been a long time since she had done that though and she guessed some of it was pent up. She'd enjoyed it immensely though. When she felt up to it she asked cautiously, "Did I hurt you?"

Veronica leaned up on her arm surprise, "No," she shook her head and asked, "Why would you?"

Reese looked up into her beautiful violet eyes, "Sometimes when you let go like that you don't know what you are doing exactly." She reached out and caressed Veronica's face and asked, "Did I frighten you?"

Veronica shook her head and looked down at Reese. She looked utterly replete, loose, and limber. She had never looked so...attractive. "How do you *do* that?" she wanted to know.

Reese smiled and caressed her, "It didn't just happen, you caused it. I was aroused and your touch and actions helped increase my arousal. It hasn't always been that way, and thank goodness it isn't always like that."

"Why thank goodness?"

Reese grinned, "Because I'd be exhausted if it happened like that every time."

Veronica wasn't so sure it was a bad thing but she accepted it as something else she would have to learn.

Reese arose from the bed slowly and rolled away from Veronica grabbing the toy which she smiled at.

Veronica was confused and thought she had done something wrong but then Reese got up and headed for the bathroom where she could hear the water going. She must be washing the toy. She returned wiping it dry on one of their towels and placed it back in the bag which she put on the nightstand before pulling the blanket down and inviting Veronica under it since they had made love on top of the bedspread. As Veronica cuddled up to Reese in sleep she had a lot to think about.

CHAPTER 22

That Friday Veronica went out with Audrey. They met at one of the few pubs they enjoyed and were known at where they wouldn't be hassled.

"Did you want to go dance or something?" Audrey asked. Veronica was looking off into space and had a little smile on her face. If Audrey didn't know better she would swear Veronica was in love or something she had been so distracted during dinner. "Veronica!" she practically yelled to get her attention.

"Mmmm?" Veronica looked at her taking a second to focus.

"What is wrong with you?" Audrey asked a little concerned. She had known her for so many years she knew every nuance on that face.

She shrugged, "Nothing, why?"

Audrey leaned forward a little and said, "You have been distracted through our entire meal. I've made all the conversation. I'd say you are decidedly inattentive."

"Oh I'm sorry, I didn't mean to be."

"What is up with you? Have you fallen in love?" she teased and then was immediately contrite as Veronica's face fell. "What did I say?"

"Nothing, ah, nothing. I should go," she went to look around to get the bill.

"Wait a moment, what is going on with you?" she grabbed Veronica's arm and asked again, "What is going on?"

Veronica debated about confiding in her friend. They had been friends since they were teenagers. Audrey was the one friend she could count on but she wasn't sure she could tell her about this. Even Ana she couldn't tell some of the details. She knew Audrey had been interested in Reese herself. To tell her they were intimate might jeopardize their friendship. Would she be betraying Reese if she confided in her best friend? She needed to tell someone though. After three wonderful nights together Reese had to go on a trip to some of the outlying properties and would be gone at least a week. If this hadn't already been planned Veronica would have thought that Reese was avoiding her. She was just so unsure and had no confidence, this was so new and she didn't know what to do.

Audrey watched the play of emotions on her friends face. She knew there was something up but she couldn't fathom what it could be.

"I'm just tired, I should go home," she hedged.

Audrey didn't let go of her arm. She waited for Veronica to look at her and raised an eyebrow waiting patiently for her to tell what was bothering her. The ploy worked. Not one to keep secrets from her best friend she finally capitulated.

"I, um, I am having," she looked around to see if anyone else could hear them, "I am having an," she leaned over to whisper, "Affair."

Audrey blinked in surprise and withdrew her hand. Never in all the years she had known Veronica had she dated except as friends and that in their teenage years. Since the trauma of her attack she had remained basically secluded at the estate. Who in the world could she be having an affair with? A groom? How had she overcome her fears? Then she remembered she had been seeing Dr. Sinclair for a while now. "With whom?" she asked as she couldn't think of whom it could be.

Veronica squirmed in her seat in embarrassment. Although Audrey had been attracted to Reese, not once had Reese indicated an interest in her. She hoped that this wouldn't ruin their friendship. She sighed and breathed, "Reese," hoping no one could over hear this conversation.

Audrey about died on the spot. A man she could accept but Reese? Holy shit! "I was right! She is gay!" she said aloud and then realized who they were talking about and why. "When did this start?" she asked incredulous.

"This week," Veronica confessed definitely further embarrassed.

"Oh my god," Audrey said thinking.

"Are you disgusted?" Veronica asked anxiously.

"Disgusted?" Audrey shook her head, "I'm impressed! Good for you! But Reese? How did that happen? Did she come on to you? Why aren't you out with her? Did you dismiss her?" She fired the questions rapidly at her friend, "Tell me *everything*!"

Veronica took a deep drink of her wine before she started. She was amused by her friend's enthusiasm. "No, she didn't come on to me, I kissed *her*, and we started talking. She's not here because she had to go on an inspection tour of the far properties. I would never dismiss her, she's too good at her job, and you know David adores her."

"What about you? Do you adore her?" Audrey had a hint of a grin.

Veronica smiled shyly, "Yes, I adore her. She's wonderful," she hesitated for a moment before adding, "I think I could even love her."

Audrey was stunned. An affair was one thing but loving her would be a problem in their circles. Veronica was expected to maintain a certain level of proper behavior. Audrey was allowed because she was bi and outrageous and fun and no one cared what she did anyway, she wasn't a 'Lady' as Veronica was. "How was it?" she asked curiously wondering how Veronica had dealt with the intimacy.

"It was wonderful. Reese was kind, and patient, and loving," she rhapsodized.

Audrey nearly rolled her eyes. Her friend was 'in love' with being 'in love' and as this was her first, ever; she had to be patient with her words, nauseating as they were. "How were you able to ah, um...?" she couldn't really ask.

Veronica grinned a little, "Reese taught me a lot but," here she lost her grin and looked sad, "I think I may have disappointed her a little."

"How did you disappoint her?" Veronica was one of her best friends and one of the kindest and fragile people she knew. She would stand up for her in any way she needed. She was all set to defend her if Reese had made her feel inadequate.

"By my inexperience," Veronica almost whispered ashamed.

"She is older than you; she must have had other partners to teach her. If she cares for you, she will teach you" Audrey said outraged.

"She does, she did, but I..." she gulped, "I didn't, you know... I didn't," she looked hopefully into Audrey's face.

Audrey thought for a moment before dawning comprehension hit her like a slap "You didn't orgasm?" and her voice got a little loud.

"Shhh," Veronica shushed her looking around but no one had noticed. She shook her head and made a funny face at her overly loud friend.

"Why didn't you?" then she thought, "Oh, she wasn't any good?"

Veronica felt outrage that Audrey would think it was Reese's fault, "No, it's not like that. She was great! She tried, over and over, but..." here she whispered again, "It's me..."

"Over and over? So this wasn't just a one night thing?" Audrey asked interested.

Veronica rolled her eyes at her renewed interest. "Yes, we have been together several times. I am not however telling you those details. I don't kiss and tell!" she smiled at her friend's look of disappointment, "Okay, I will tell you," and then chucked at her look of excitement, "That she is a great kisser!"

Audrey made an exaggerated groan, "And here I had hoped to experience that myself! How did you *do* it?"

Veronica laughed at her friend. Audrey was so outrageous. She was a good friend to have though. "Seriously though Audrey, I have something wrong with me. I can't..."

"Have you *ever*?" she asked curious realizing her dilemma. They had never talked about intimacies since they were teenagers giggling over boys. Now that she thought about it though Veronica had listened to her giggle over boys, not the other way around.

Veronica shook her head.

"Never, as in *never*? Not even by yourself?" she tried not to sound too stunned.

"I hadn't started with myself until a few months ago when I bought a toy," she confided.

Audrey, who had a boxful, was incredulous. She couldn't imagine never having had an orgasm. She had been orgasming probably since before puberty but just didn't realize what it was until she was a certain age. "What made you buy one?"

"Remember that American show ER?"

Audrey was surprised at the turn of the conversation and nodded dumbly.

"You know that psychiatrist on there that is gay?"

Audrey nodded and then gasped, "Don't tell me you're in love with Dr. Sinclair?"

Veronica shook her head and rolled her eyes, "No, I am not in love with Ana." She chuckled at the thought. "But it did get me thinking. All these years I haven't been attracted to men, any men. Why not a woman? And then I found myself getting wet over the thought," she blushed at saying that.

"When did you decide on Reese?" She was a little disappointed having wanted her for herself but fascinated at her friend's tale.

"Well, you know how much I've admired her and the work she has done over the past year. When she started teaching me karate and we became such good friends I realized my admiration had turned to attraction. When I realized I was fantasizing about women it became one woman. I never thought she might return the attraction, not in a million years!" She got a glow about her thinking of the beautiful woman she had been with.

"Wow Veronica. You reach high!" she teased.

"You think she's too classy for me?" she worried immediately. Reese was older and more experienced. She probably thought

Veronica a child and foolish besides. The worry was on her face immediately.

"No, I meant that Reese is quite a woman and lucky you for having gotten into her bed!"

"Yes, but I don't know if I will be able to keep her. I know she has to be disappointed in me and after seeing what she is capable of." Here she stopped to shake her head in disappointment in herself, "And the passion, holy shit!"

"She's very passionate?" Audrey asked carefully, enviously *wanting* to know *more* but hesitant knowing her friends penchant for keeping things quiet.

"Oh my God Audrey, I don't know that I will ever be like that. It's incredible to watch much less cause. She is incredible!" Veronica enthused as she remembered.

Audrey wanted to know more, *much* more. She also wanted to know this incredible passion! She calmed herself to ask, "And what does she say about your lack of orgasm?"

"She says I have to be patient. That it takes time and that I'm overcoming a lot. She and Ana both say I have to patient, but I've waited years to be with someone and I want so much!" She looked stricken.

"You talked about it with Dr. Sinclair before you talked about it with me?" Audrey pretended to be hurt.

Veronica smiled at her friend, "She's my therapist, of course I told her. She too said the trauma might cause a delay and I should be patient. But I thought that Reese would give me one right off! She knows what she is doing!"

Audrey thought a while, "Veronica, since you have never given yourself one, how can you expect Reese to give you one? Don't you think that's a lot of pressure to put on another person especially since your also combating the trauma you went through and those hang-up's?"

"But I don't know how to give myself one. I've read everything I could find and I don't know what I'm doing wrong!" She thought about what Audrey said though and had to agree that was too much to expect of anyone. "Maybe I will never have one!" she complained.

Audrey leaned over and patted her shoulder, "You'll have one and then you will be the one telling me how great things are! You just need to relax and be patient and learn what your body wants."

"That's what Reese and Ana both said," she answered annoyed. Everyone was telling her to relax and be patient. How long did she have to be patient though? She was nearly twenty-nine years old and had never had an orgasm!

Audrey smiled. If she realized how often she quoted Reese she would be annoyed. Her friend was definitely smitten. She hoped she only confided in Ana because the few other friends that Veronica had wouldn't understand. But then, thinking about it, Veronica would never tell anyone else.

Veronica went home fairly early that night. She didn't feel like dancing and she was missing Reese. After three nights together and one already without her she didn't know what to do with herself. She knew that Audrey was right, how could she expect Reese to give her an orgasm when she didn't know how to give herself one. She was home by 10 and as she entered her gloomy rooms she plugged in her phone only to have it go off. Who was calling her this late?

"Hello?"

"Hey pretty lady, I didn't wake you did I?" Reese's voice came over the mobile phone.

Veronica immediately brightened, thrilled to just hear from her. Yesterday she would have been too tired from travel probably to call. "No, I just got in from dinner with Audrey."

"You didn't go out to dance?" She knew that was something Audrey always tried to talk her into.

"No, I didn't feel like it tonight. I missed you." She put that out there to see Reese's response.

"I missed you too. I've thought about you a lot today." She sat on the bed where she always slept when she stayed at the Sounds. She had thought about Veronica, a lot over the past two days. Much more than she should.

"That's nice, I like hearing that. Good things I hope?"

"Of course," Reese answered wondering if she would always be bolstering this woman's ego and then felt immediately ashamed. She knew what Veronica was like before she got involved with her.

"I can't stop thinking about you and the things we did..." she trailed off embarrassed and then thought why am I embarrassed? No one can see me. I'm talking with the one person I did these things with.

"Do you regret them?" Reese was curious how she was handling the feelings and emotions of what they did.

"No, not at all. I just wish we had done more...before you left," she answered truthfully.

"Really? Like what?" Reese settled back to get comfortable. This conversation was just getting interesting.

"I don't know, I just wish more..." she hedged knowing she was blushing.

"More of the same or more different?"

"Both?"

Reese chuckled; she might have opened her up to a whole new world.

"I just wish I knew more or that we had done more and then I think about what we have done and I get excited and I want more. Just more of everything," she finished lamely hoping she was making herself understood.

"Well, I will be back in a week or so and then we can explore some more..." she smiled thinking of things she would like to try with Veronica as she was open to the suggestions.

"Like what?" Veronica asked anxiously and excitedly.

"Well, anything you can imagine I'm willing to try. I'm not really into pain so perhaps not spanking or any whips and chains paraphernalia," she teased.

Veronica was startled, she had never thought of those things but realizing Reese was teasing her she relaxed. Reese would never knowingly hurt her, she trusted her. It was part of the many reasons she wanted to be with her. "I'm sure we have a dungeon around here somewhere," she felt bold enough to tease back.

Reese chuckled delightedly. She always enjoyed laughter with her lovers; it added something to the formula. They talked a long while about things they 'might' want to try. Reese was intrigued that Veronica was doing 'research' on the internet and encouraged her to figure out things she might want to try. "Don't forget to delete your browsing history now and again in case someone else uses your computer," she teased but she was also serious.

This startled her but she felt it was sound advice, you never knew. Veronica had a lot of blushes that evening but she did make some of her ideas known. She was in the hazy need phase of their relationship, she was in love with love and Reese was the outlet of all her fantasies. Whether she deserved them or not, Veronica put Reese on a pedestal for all of them. She promised fulfillment on so many levels.

"Then you should 'practice' while I am gone," she was saying advising Veronica to play with herself.

"I don't like it by myself," she complained.

"No one does but sometimes that's how you learn what you like and besides it fulfills a need when you don't have the real thing," Reese advised.

Veronica thought it over and had to agree.

"Hey, I need to get some sleep. It's been a long day and I have another one tomorrow. I'll call you," she said as she undressed for bed.

Veronica wanted the conversation to go on forever but she thought it best not to upset Reese. She didn't want to anger her. "All right, sleep well, I sleep better next to you," she put in.

Reese smiled; she knew that they were both treading carefully because of the newness of this relationship. She had to handle Veronica with kid gloves, Veronica was so unsure because she had never had a relationship. "Just fantasize about us and that will help you," she kidded referring to their earlier conversation.

Veronica smiled, if she thought about them she would never sleep "I'm already fantasizing all the time."

"Then do something with it, who knows where it might lead... Got to go to sleep now, talk to you tomorrow."

"Good night Reese."

"Good night Veronica."

As she lay there in the strange bed at the Sounds she wondered where this would go. Veronica was so unsophisticated on so many levels. She enjoyed teaching her what her body could do but she could only do so much, it was ultimately up to Veronica. She had enjoyed the three nights they had been together but they were very one sided and she enjoyed an active bed partner. It would take time and they had all the time in the world so she too would have to be patient. It might be exciting to see Veronica come alive.

Veronica thought over the last week of her life. From making love with Reese to their conversations including the one with Audrey. She knew it was all up to her. Thinking about making love with Reese got her very wet. She could tell she was wet without even feeling down there. Getting out the rabbit she considered it and the possibilities. Curious she pulled off her clothes and began playing with the rabbit imagining it was Reese doing it to her. It got her very aroused. She was soon plunging the shaft in and out and when that wasn't enough she turned on the ears and began playing about her clit. It felt wonderful. She still didn't feel 'it' but she stressed about it less and enjoyed the sensations she did have. Before she allowed herself to get frustrated she pounded the hell out of herself and felt satisfied with that. Washing the toy carefully she put it away before crawling into bed and trying to sleep.

CHAPTER 23

"Have you ever tried bearing down?" Reese asked in their nightly conversations while she was gone.

Veronica had confessed what she had been doing the past nights while Reese was gone. "Bearing down?"

"Yes, squeeze your kegal muscles. Sometimes that tightness helps."

Not having ever heard of kegal muscles she didn't know how to answer. She didn't want to profess her ignorance. She already was convinced Reese thought her too naïve. "No, but maybe I should try it." Later when she surfed the net she looked into that information and realized some more things she had been doing wrong or just didn't know about. Did mothers impart this kind of information to their daughters? Or had she just been given no information? She did try it and was surprised that it felt so different. She hadn't realized she had those muscles at all but then everyone did according to the website. She worried though that after a week of trying that she could feel like she was peeing from the strain of trying.

"That's not pee," Reese informed her when she confessed.

"What is it?" she asked confused.

"That's probably ejaculation if it's not yellow."

"Ejaculation?" she thought only guys did that and the thought made her slightly ill.

"No, women do it too although not everyone knows they do it. Don't worry, you're coming along and learning about your body. You should be thrilled though, not many women can do it when they want to."

Strangely pleased at the backhanded compliment she endeavored to try more but then was annoyed when her period got in the way.

"You can still do things despite your period. It's messier but possible." Reese informed her. "Put a towel down though and be prepared that you might get more intense cramps. If it skeeves you out then don't bother, there is no rush." She was surprised how much 'practice' that Veronica was putting into this and how much she had confided without prompting.

Reese's one week had already stretched into 10 days and looked like it was going to go to two weeks. Some of the repairs she had authorized had gone sour and she needed to be there to enact the changes.

Veronica was feeling very lonely and a little depressed with her period. Moodiness was always part of her period. She slipped into Reese's room while she was gone and looked around remembering their pleasant nights. Impulsively she walked to the dresser to look over the pictures on it examining Reese's daughter and wondering about this person in her lover's life that she really knew nothing about. As she stood there she hesitated for a moment before opening the drawer she knew contained Reese's toys. She was shocked and dismayed to realize they weren't there. She pushed aside the things in the drawer to look for them and then put them back carefully and closed the drawer. Had she taken them with her? She must have.

Veronica left the room. She felt she had crossed some imaginary line. She had invaded Reese's privacy and it really was none of her business. But wasn't it? She played that game in her head over and over during a restless night. Her period intensified things to the point where she was being a little obsessive. She wanted to call Reese and ask her but at the same time how could she when she wasn't supposed to be in Reese's room? What if there was someone that Reese was seeing at the Sounds? Would she have told Veronica or kept it quiet so as not to hurt her feelings?

That night she was on pins and needles until Reese called her. She sounded tired and Veronica didn't want to bother her but finally Reese must have sensed something was wrong because she said, "Why are you being so quiet? Your period getting to you?"

Veronica grasped at this and answered, "Yes, it's cramping bad," and then felt bad as Reese expressed her concern and sympathy. When they rang off Veronica still wasn't any the wiser as to whether or not Reese had taken her toys with her.

The next five days were miserable for Veronica. She alleviated her cramps with a combination of ibuprofen and physical activity. Both prescribed by Reese that had proven to work wonders. She had been in misery for years and Reese had simplified it for her. Karate, horseback riding, and long walks helped the physical parts and the ibuprofen took care of the rest. The moodiness though she had to deal with on her own. The long walks made her think, perhaps too much. The karate took out her aggression and anger. Horseback riding gave her a freedom but not from her thoughts unfortunately.

Reese arrived home the first day that Veronica was over her period. Seeing her come through the door with her bag Veronica wanted to fly down the staircase and into her arms but restrained herself to being friendly and greeting her, “Welcome home.”

Reese smiled at her friend. She had missed her, more than she should have but talking to her daily had been nice. Thinking about her the rest of the time had made her very horny though and since she too had had her period she was glad that was over. She always got hornier after her period so now that she was home she was looking forward to Veronica sneaking into her room at night.

David came out of his library where he had been watching a television program, “How was your trip?” he asked jovially.

Reese smiled at him and said, “Well, things are in order now!”

He laughed. She had kept him up to date on the problems and he had given her full authorization to make any changes or repairs on all their properties but she still felt he should always be kept in the loop. He didn’t worry, she was doing an excellent job, she always kept the bottom line in mind, costs were minimal and progress maximum. “Did you get those Bronson Brothers to fix the fixes?” he grinned; he knew from having dealt with them himself that they were a handful.

“No actually, I served them with notice that we would be suing them for their shoddy work and hired their competitors. They showed up yesterday with a check, I have it here for you,” she handed him an envelope from her briefcase.

“You got money back from them?” he asked surprised.

Reese nodded, “I also pointed out to them that the area was small, when word got around how bad their work was they could kiss their ‘odd’ jobs goodbye. There is payment in full for what we paid them for.”

David was thrilled. Not many people had the guts to back up what they said they would do but this estate manager did. “Well, thank you very much. This is excellent news!” He handed her back the check and said, “I’m sure you know which account to deposit that in.”

Reese nodded; she was pleased that he was pleased. She was also tired, having driven a lot of miles today just to get home to Veronica.

Veronica had listened to their exchange with interest. She really wanted to pull Reese into a room and kiss her but instead said, “I’m sure you are tired from your trip. Would you like a tray for dinner? We have already eaten,” she gave Reese a look that was just between them.

Reese smiled and said, "Thank you Lady Veronica, that would be lovely. I have to take a decent shower. The water was off for four days up there!" She picked up her suitcase.

"Oh let one of the maids take that up," David said as he watched her.

"That's okay, I've got it," and she continued up the stairs leaving her briefcase on a chair.

Veronica picked up the briefcase and carried it to the office. Walking in took a certain amount of bravery but she realized from Ana that this was just a room. It wasn't because of this room that she had been raped. It didn't even look the same since Reese had taken it over. She deposited the case on Reese's desk and then went to the kitchen to arrange the tray.

Knocking on the door she waited to hear Reese call to her. Instead she didn't hear her at all. Slowly she opened it and realized Reese was in the shower and couldn't hear her. She put the tray on a small side table that had two chairs and made sure everything was still carefully covered to keep it warm. She returned to the door and closed and locked it. Sitting in a chair she waited for Reese to get out of the shower. She was just as surprised as Reese when she came out stark naked.

"Oh, sorry, I didn't realize you would be in here," she said as she turned and grabbed a towel.

"That's okay, I don't mind the view," Veronica grinned.

"Well it might not have been you and they at least would have knocked," she lightly chided.

"I did knock, you didn't answer and I brought you this," she indicated the tray of food.

"Oh good, I'm starving," Reese answered as she wrapped the towel around herself and sat at the table to uncover the meal. "Corned beef and cabbage?" she asked and wrinkled her nose.

"You don't like corned beef and cabbage?" Veronica asked surprised.

Reese shook her head and lifted the other covers to find a salad, some fruit, and other vegetables. She began to eat them. She tried a little of the corned beef but none of the cabbage. Finally she finished her meal with a large glass of milk. "Ah that's better," she sighed. Then she realized how quiet her meal had really been, "Is something wrong?" she asked Veronica looking at her curiously.

Shaking her head she said, "No, I thought a hungry woman should be able to eat in peace," she smiled, she had enjoyed just watching Reese, she had missed her a lot.

Reese rubbed her belly. "I haven't eaten since this morning and I rushed home to get here so I didn't stop."

"Do you want me to get you some more?"

Reese shook her head, "No, I'm fine. I just want to kick back for a while and relax after that long drive."

Veronica liked the sound of that and looked intrigued.

Reese got up and rewrapped the towel which had come loose during her meal. Going over to the television she picked up the remote and headed back to the bed. "Want to watch some television while I digest?" she asked.

Veronica didn't need to be asked twice. As Reese got in one side of the bed she kicked off her shoes and got in the other. Channel surfing she finally settled on the news and laid her head against Veronica's shoulder as they both reclined on the pillows. Veronica wanted to talk but strangely she didn't either. It still wasn't any of her business about Reese taking her toys with her on a trip and masturbating but Veronica felt strangely hurt and left out by the idea. When she finally screwed up her courage to talk to Reese she found she had drifted off to sleep. Gently she eased her down on the pillows and undressing she got under the blankets but not before she covered Reese with an extra blanket. Turning off the television from the remote she left that on the nightstand and cuddled up with Reese.

She was having the most delicious dream. Reese was home and she had about six hands, they were everywhere on her body, touching and caressing, tweaking and probing, making her wet with her delicious and naughty thoughts. As she came awake she realized Reese was indeed there and she was covering her body with kisses and her hands *were* everywhere! Veronica gave herself up to the moment and was glad she did so. As Reese went down on her and thrust inside of her she squeezed around her fingers and felt the pleasure she had been learning. Reese had been right; it was so good with someone to make love to. It wasn't the same by oneself but her 'practicing' had paid off and she felt a lot of pleasure from this even if she didn't have an orgasm. The wetness and her relaxation made her feel wonderful and when she began to return the favor she found herself getting very excited and aroused in different ways. As she began kissing Reese's nipples and playing with her clit with her fingers, Reese reached over and thrust inside her wetness again and Veronica groaned from the unexpected sensations this caused. "Your distracting me," she complained as she also panted from the feelings Reese aroused in her. Reese thrust harder and Veronica had to stop playing with Reese. She chuckled as she rubbed herself against Veronica.

"Let's try sixty-nine," she breathed to Veronica who although shocked was feeling so good she was a willing partner to whatever Reese suggested. Although she had expressed disgust at the idea in the past she now allowed herself to climb on top of Reese who quickly got her into position and began to 'distract' her some more. Reese however had exquisite control over her own body and the stimulation that Veronica was able to provide was enough that she was soon cumming underneath her and still able to play with Veronica who got a lot of enjoyment out of it. When finally Reese's orgasm had passed she continued to play with Veronica until Veronica whispered, "That's enough," and began to roll off of her.

Reese let her go, not wanting her frustration to stop her from enjoying what had been a pleasant way to wake up. Looking at the clock she realized it was already 5a.m. and as she had a full day after being gone for two weeks she had to start early. She also knew that Veronica needed to get back to her rooms before any of the staff saw her. She watched as Veronica got dressed quickly and giving her a kiss goodbye she headed out of Reese's rooms.

Reese often wondered what Veronica's rooms looked like. She had been in every one of the rooms in the H shaped house except for Veronica's. In over a year this was the one exception and she wondered why. Why did Veronica hide in them, what did she hide in them, was she ashamed? Reese soon got up and began to empty her bags. One of the maids could have done this for her but she preferred to put away her own things. Putting her toys back in the top drawer she realized she hadn't used them much while she was away but she was grateful she had had them when talks with Veronica had aroused her. She put her dirty clothes in a bag for the maid and put away the few clothes she hadn't used or had washed up at the Sounds. Dressing for her own day she was down in the dining room before everyone else and busy at work hours before David made an appearance.

David wasn't looking well these days. Reese hadn't asked but she had seen the insurance paperwork and the increased doctor's visits.

She wanted to ask him but felt it would be mentioned to her if he felt it was any of her business. Since he hadn't, she felt she couldn't. Later that day as she inspected some of the grounds she was surprised and pleased to see David walking about and he joined her for a stroll.

"The grounds are looking well-tended these days," he observed looking around as they walked along.

Reese nodded thrilled with how sharp everything looked, "The gardeners have been doing a wonderful job," she agreed.

"I think perhaps my estate manager is keeping on top of things. I have to say Reese I am pleased with your work thus far." David looked away as he gave her the compliment.

Reese who knew David didn't dole out compliments very often was pleased and astonished. "Lord David, I appreciate the opportunity. I am enjoying this position very much."

"I noticed you have become quite chummy with my sister," he said musingly.

For a moment Reese's heart stopped, did he know about their affair? But then he went on, "It's nice to see her making friends outside our circle. For too long she has been caught inside her shell. The karate has given her confidence I haven't seen in ages and introducing her to Dr. Sinclair was a masterstroke. You've far exceeded my expectations and I would like to thank you," he turned to look directly at her and Reese held her ground. "In your next pay envelope will be a small token of that appreciation. I want you to start taking on the flat in London as well as the other properties. Perhaps you might need an assistant soon. I know you refused before until you 'got the lay of the land' but I can see how much work you do in a day and I think it's time for someone to help you."

Reese couldn't agree more, she was overwhelmed some days with everything she had to do and keep track of, "I'll start looking immediately, and thank you for your confidence in me." She started to go thinking he dismissed her.

"Reese," his voice stopped her. "I don't know how much you know about my illness and I thank you for not prying. I do know however that I can no longer drive and Frank will have to take over that, that isn't a problem. I worry however though about other aspects of my duties as Lord Cavandish. Eventually you and I will have to work out something as I become more incapacitated. Already I can tell that certain things aren't working well in my brain," he said sadly.

"I'm sure we can work out something and there is always Lady Cavandish to help you," she assured him.

"My sister," he hesitated, "Has been fragile for a number of years. Since she met you though she has found someone to admire and look up to. I believe you have been a steadying influence on her. The change in her in the last year has been wonderful. Still, I know she isn't ready to assume some of the duties that she will have to eventually. Perhaps you can help her with that as well?"

"I'd be happy to. You're right, your sister has come a long way in the last year," how about the last month, she thought, "I'll do what I can to help you and her."

"Thank you, I know you will," he said effectively dismissing her.

Reese thought over Lord David's conversation and previous ones as well. She knew that Veronica would eventually need to produce an heir for their holdings. It was how things were done here. That and a few other things meant that Veronica needed to come completely out of her shell to take the reins. She had no idea how to achieve that though.

CHAPTER 24

"Um, I'd like to shop," Veronica began the conversation looking decidedly uncomfortable.

They were sitting side by side on the bed and watching a television program. Reese was already feeling tired and knew she would soon be able to go to sleep. "Where would you like to shop?" she asked more interested in talking to Veronica than anything on the television.

"Um, on the internet," she gestured to the laptop that Reese kept on the nightstand so she could work in bed if she wanted to and frequently did.

Reese looked at her and how uncomfortable she was, shopping on the internet shouldn't make her this uncomfortable. "What for?" she asked.

Veronica looked around and said quietly, "Toys," before blushing and looking defiantly away.

Reese wanted to laugh, she really did but at the same time she was interested in what Veronica was looking for. "What kind of toys exactly?" They had discussed toys over the phone where Veronica could talk without getting too embarrassed.

Bravely Veronica said, "I'd like to buy us a strap on."

"Really?" Now Reese was surprised.

Veronica finally looked at her to see if she was joking around and was surprised to see how intrigued Reese was. She nodded and then continued whispering, "I've been fantasizing about riding you," her bravery ended there and she desperately wanted to leave or at least stop the conversation she had begun. She began to swing herself off the bed in preparation for leaving only to have Reese pull her back and down on the bed.

Looking down into her lover's face Reese smiled and said, "I need to hear these fantasies. I can't make them come true if you don't share them with me."

Veronica wanted to squirm away but Reese was too strong for her. "I find it embarrassing what I think about when you are not around, what I want to do, what I want you to do to me, what I want to try. It gets me so wet and bothered," she whispered frantically.

"In the privacy of our bedroom you can ask or tell me anything and should," Reese advised.

"I want to but this is all so new to me," Veronica almost sobbed.

"It's new to me too, with you. I want to share everything you want to do, anything you want to do. Don't shut me out." With that she leaned down and kissed her very hard and deep. Leaving her slightly breathless she rolled off the bed and went to her dresser.

Veronica leaned up confused and wondering. She watched as Reese leaned down to her bottom drawer and pulled out a bag about as big as her two hands. Unzipping it she pulled out a double headed red flexible dildo and showed it to Veronica with an amused look.

"This might do the trick," she informed her astonished lover.

Veronica looked intrigued and asked, "How does it work?"

Reese smiled and said, "Don't worry, I will show you," as she approached the bed and got in putting the dildo aside she began kissing and caressing Veronica until she was mindless with need and want. Reese's own excitement had built as she thought about Veronica and her responses; her own body was taunt with that need as well. Slowly she inserted one end of the dildo into her wet body and laying back she said; "Climb on," to Veronica.

"How deep should I go?" Veronica asked anxiously, she was so unsure of herself but she wanted this, she had asked for it.

"As deep as you are comfortable, don't hurt yourself or impale yourself," Reese answered her voice thick with passion. She wanted to take the dildo and thrust it in and out but was willing to watch and wait for her lover to catch up which would ultimately be more thrilling and fulfilling.

Veronica slowly impaled herself on the double head; amazingly she felt it slide completely in until she was against Reese. Looking into Reese's remarkable passion glazed eyes she said, "Now what?"

Reese gently raised her hips slightly, suggestively, and said, "Now you ride me."

Veronica began to rock back and forth feeling out the rhythm. She was soon thrusting downward and closing her eyes to the sensations she had never experienced before. Reese reached up to play with her breasts and to caress her, enjoying watching her and the expressions that changed on her face. Her own excitement was building. She reached between them and began playing with both of their erect clits. Veronica stopped her rhythm momentarily at the new sensation but continued to ride her lover. Reese lost herself in the moment and watching Veronica above her began to allow her orgasm to build. She could feel the sensations and squeezing sent her into a paroxysm of convulsions. Grabbing Veronica's hips she thrust over and over into her lover who tried to maintain her own rhythm but was so fascinated by watching Reese cum that she just held on. Squeezing down on the shaft she too felt incredible sensations but nothing like she could see Reese was experiencing as she rose up and grabbed Veronica to her body in a tight body hug. Veronica loved it when Reese lost control like this and her only regret was that she hadn't experienced it herself.

Slowly she came down from her orgasm and lay back releasing Veronica from the tight hug. Squeezing to control the shaft she began thrusting upward into Veronica's body. It was difficult since it was slick with her own juices but she liked the delighted surprise on Veronica's face. Playing with her clit at the same time she could tell Veronica was closer than she had ever been before. Reese could tell the exact moment Veronica gave up in frustration too. "Relax, let it happen," she whispered.

"I can't," she sobbed as she collapsed above her and then on her.

Reese held her as she came down from the little high she had gotten. "You were so close baby; you just need to be patient."

"I'm so tired of being patient," she quietly said. She pulled herself up enough to remove the shaft from inside her. It came out in a squishy sound it was slick with her own juices. She lay next to Reese still being held by her.

"I think you need to follow those sensations and think of nothing else but the sensations. Your mind is what is betraying you, not your body." Reese indicated the wetness on the shaft that was still sticking up between her own legs.

"That looks obscene," she mentioned looking at the wet shaft.

Reese smiled, "Maybe but we had a good time," her voice was still a little passion filled and Veronica noticed it.

Veronica reached out and grabbed the wet shaft wrapping her fingers around it and thrusting a little. She noticed Reese arched slightly to take it. She got a better grip and thrust a little harder pulling it back to thrust again. Reese gasped a little looking intensely at her. She began to thrust a little more and then a little faster watching the response in her lover. As her nipples hardened Reese closed her eyes and groaned. Soon Veronica rose up enough to get a better angle as she kept thrusting. Reese arched and spread her legs feeling the rising sensations again and again. She was crying out slightly closing her mouth against the really loud cries of appreciation for what her lover was doing to her body. "Use your fingers instead of the shaft," she finally gasped.

Veronica pulled the shaft out and quickly thrust two fingers inside doing the same things thrusting but bending her fingers inside. Reese soon went over the edge and Veronica was amazed the amount of wetness that soon creamed her fingers. She found she was thrilled that she had caused this in her lover. She continued thrusting and playing until Reese arched and then gasped, "Enough," and her body went limp. Veronica spread the wetness between her lover's legs on her clit and then discretely wiped her fingers on the bed before taking Reese in her arms and kissing her deeply. Reese showed her so much of what she herself could achieve if she could just get beyond that point.

CHAPTER 25

Over the next few months they tried regularly. Reese was thrilled she was there when Veronica had each of her little victories. Her first certified orgasm, tiny as it was, was joyously accepted by both of them. They built from there. Surprised at first at the sensation Veronica learned to grasp at that tiny bit of sensation. Veronica soon became as passionate and loud as Reese. Reese had to caution her to be more discrete as she sent her lover looks at the dinner table or when they were out together, even in the stable.

"You can't touch me like that," she admonished her one day as they unsaddled their horses.

"Why not, I love you and I want to show you!" Veronica pouted prettily.

"I love you too Veronica," Reese said quietly, it was the first time either of them had admitted it although they had shown each other in so many ways. She watched and waited for Veronica to realize it too.

Her lovely violet eyes widened slightly, "You love me?"

Reese nodded and looking around she took Veronica into her arms, "Yes, very much!" She pulled her tight against her own body.

"Oh God, I've waited so long to hear you say that!" she sobbed into her neck snuggling close.

Reese could hear the grooms not that far away and gently released Veronica and set her back on her feet. "We have to be discrete or everyone will know we are lovers!"

"I don't care if everyone knows!" Veronica said stubbornly.

"I do!" Reese said sternly and finally what she was saying penetrated Veronica's mind.

"Your right, it would not look good if people knew would it?"

Reese nodded watching her cautiously. She was still so young in so many ways.

"I'm sorry, I'll behave better," she said with her crisp British accent.

Reese wanted to laugh but at the same time she didn't. Veronica was so young, so naive. It would harm her status if people knew they were lovers. Reese would certainly be terminated and she wanted to keep this job. Already Audrey and Ana knew and she wasn't thrilled about that. She remembered them going out one night with Audrey...

"So, you seduced my young friend here?" Audrey began. It was apparent she was a little jealous herself.

"Audrey!" Veronica snapped, "It wasn't like that and if anyone seduced anyone I started it!"

Audrey subsided and waited until Veronica went to the bathroom to warn Reese, "You better not hurt her!"

Reese looked at her. She knew her pretty well after their months of socializing. She also realized she was a little miffed that her blatant attempts to make passes at Reese had come to nothing. "I don't intend to hurt her, she's been hurt quite enough don't you think?"

"You're her first love affair, how can you help but hurt her? What kind of future can you offer her?"

"You're not asking me anything I haven't asked myself a hundred times already! I don't know the answers. For now, I'm here, I care for her, I will do my best to not hurt her but what about me, this can't end well for me either."

Apparently Audrey had never thought about Reese getting hurt. It wasn't a good position for her either as an employee. She could be sacked and she wondered if she could be prosecuted somehow. Veronica was well over the age of consent though and while naive she certainly was an adult. She nodded to indicate she understood and then asked, "Why her? Why not someone like...?"

Reese raised an eyebrow from where she was seated on the corner, "Someone like you? Someone more experienced?"

Audrey nodded.

"She's right, she seduced me. She gets under your skin and you can't seem to help yourself. I felt compassion for what she has gone through, I helped her get some confidence through karate, but her mind and her beauty attracted me and I didn't realize it until she made the first moves," Reese told her candidly.

Audrey understood but she still couldn't help wishing that this tall blonde had gone for her. Their discussion ended though as Veronica returned to the table.

As neither of them wanted to be away from the other for very long periods of time Veronica began to accompany Reese on her trips to their other properties for inspections. It truly gave Veronica an appreciation for how hard Reese worked for her and David as she watched her competently managing things. Reese encouraged Veronica to learn about her own properties and taught her the intricacies of her job. It was a revelation for Veronica to realize it wasn't that difficult but she loved spending time with Reese and learning from her.

Their sojourns did not go unnoticed as David commented one day as they were going over the books, "You're spending a lot of time with Veronica these days..." he left it hang there waiting for an explanation.

Reese felt immediately uncomfortable wondering if someone had realized what they had come to mean to each other and reported this to David. "I'm teaching your sister my job so that she can have a fuller understanding of your properties."

"I didn't think Veronica was interested in our properties?" he asked in surprise.

"Your sister is very capable of doing anything she sets her mind to. She can be a very determined woman," Reese said neutrally. She wanted to sing Veronica's praises to her brother but at the same time she was being cautious. "As you mentioned months ago she wasn't ready to assume all her duties and this is giving her confidence and knowledge she will eventually need. Besides, now I won't need to hire an assistant."

David considered what she said and nodded, she was right, it saved them the cost of hiring an assistant, gave his sister confidence, and she needed to know how to do these things. "Thank you for helping her," he said and dropped the subject.

CHAPTER 26

David wanted another get together with the neighbors. In his own mind he needed to see people while he was still well enough to do so. Already he was having difficulties in walking and a little speech impediment. He wanted people to see him before he started using a cane or ended up in a wheelchair. He wanted to be remembered as whole. He knew it was all inevitable, the doctors had given him only an approximate time-table. He also had other reasons that he didn't share with his sister or manager.

Reese didn't mind organizing these sorts of events. She was only surprised they didn't have more as she had thought they would before she took the job. She put a lot of the burden on Veronica's shoulders and was pleased when she rose to the occasion and did a splendid job. She also made sure David realized how much Veronica had done.

"Your sister has certainly bloomed since the last time we saw her," were several of the comments David heard that day as he socialized with his various guests.

"Yes she has hasn't she," he smiled realizing it himself. Her confidence was showing and he was proud of her.

"Veronica, have you met Oscar Wilkins?" he said introducing her.

Veronica smiled and held out her hand. A tall man with dark hair he was stereotypically English and had a nice mustache. His eyes were a dark shade of brown and while he had a pleasant face she couldn't help thinking he was a little too handsome. "How do you do?" she said pleasantly.

He raised her hand to his lips and kissed the back side. "How do you do Lady Cavandish?" he said warmly.

Veronica withdrew her hand slowly and reluctantly as she had been taught years ago but she really wanted to pull it back abruptly and wipe it on her dress.

"Oscar is Sir Oscar Wilkins of the Chesterbrook Wilkins," David told her to clarify who he was.

Veronica chatted for a while with Oscar mostly about horses which certainly proved to be a nice conversation for them both. She drifted away after a while to take care of her duties as hostess.

David leaned over and said, "Isn't she everything I said she was?"

"Certainly and more," Oscar smiled as he watched Lady Cavandish expertly handle the servants.

Reese watched David introduce Oscar and something brought up an antennae. She also watched Oscar as he talked to Veronica and then watched her as she made the rounds of the backyard where they were having their party. Reese was careful not to get anywhere near Veronica at the party sure that something would give their relationship away. All evening though she thought she noticed Oscar being particularly attentive especially through the buffet dinner and then the dancing. Veronica looked lovely and relaxed as she expertly executed the waltzes and other dances that the small orchestra played having been taught such social niceties as a child.

"Something the matter?" Audrey asked her.

"Hmmm?" Reese looked down at her friend startled.

Audrey laughed, "Is something the matter? You seem distracted."

"Do you know who that man is that is dancing with Veronica?" she asked trying to keep the jealousy out of her voice.

"Oh, that's Sir Oscar Wilkins. His family lives south of Cavandish. He is the first of his family to go into business and apparently he is doing well."

Reese deliberately looked away to see if there was anything she could help Veronica with. As official hostess she was doing splendidly but Reese helped in silent and non-obvious ways whenever possible to free up her time for her guests.

"Why, does it bother you?" Audrey asked with a look in her eye.

"What?" Reese turned her attention back to Audrey and realized what she had said, "No, not at all. I was just curious as I hadn't met him and he's been watching Veronica all day." That last part gave her away. If he was watching Veronica all day that meant Reese knew about it because she was watching him.

"It's not like the two of you can dance here together," Audrey observed dryly.

That brought Reese back down to earth. She was right. Nodding to acknowledge she understood the subtle rebuke she grabbed a glass of champagne and pretended to drink to distract herself.

Reese too though danced with some of the guests. As a very pretty blonde she was in demand but the crudities of the suggestions she had received had been a distinct annoyance. Because she was considered an 'upper crust' servant but a servant none the less she was treated differently as would say a guest or all the Lords and Ladies or Sirs and

Madams that attended. She didn't like it but accepted it as part of the English society that her employers moved in.

That night as she got ready for bed or rather that morning at this point she thought about what would eventually be expected of Veronica. She couldn't allow her own jealousies and love for Veronica to hold her back. She would be expected to marry and produce heirs. Reese was very aware of that. She would also be handling parties such as the one they had last night, she had already proven she was very capable of it. When Veronica snuck into her room that morning she just held her, in no mood for lovemaking. Her heart was sad for what she must eventually do; she recognized it on a subtle level.

CHAPTER 27

Over the coming weeks they had smaller, more intimate get-togethers which David encouraged. It allowed friends to come to the estate he loved and was so proud of. Reese had worked wonders and he gave her all the praise. She in turn pointed out the things Veronica was doing. It was beautiful to see Veronica coming out of her shell. People found her to be intelligent and funny. Her beauty began to show through too as they came to know her better. A recluse for years people were amazed that at nearly thirty she wasn't snapped up already. It didn't seem to bother her though. Many people that she had avoided for years began to come around, especially the horsy crowd she had so enjoyed. Oscar became a part of that crowd. Many was the time they had an impromptu gathering talking over shows and other events they would all attend. Reese made sure she stayed totally in the background or was absent so her presence wouldn't be noted. It was proper and was her place she thought.

"Why don't you like my new friends?" Veronica asked one day.

"I don't?" Reese asked surprised. She was working on a new project for the Sounds and her paperwork was spread out on her bed.

"You never participate in any of our conversations and a lot of times you just disappear."

Reese knew she had to tread carefully. Looking up she said, "Veronica, those are *your* friends, as they should be. I am just the hired help."

"You know your much more than that! I hate it when you demean yourself so," she returned angrily.

"To them though I am just the 'help' however prestigious you make it sound. I can't go over that barrier they set. And I won't. If you're not careful, you will give us away." She said it sternly and hoped Veronica got the nuances.

"I don't care if they find out!" she said angrily, "I love you and I want everyone to know."

Reese got up from where she was working and walked towards her girlfriend, "I care! Don't you see that all these so-called friends would abandon you in a minute if they thought you were having an affair with the 'help' much less with a woman? I won't let you do that to yourself much less to me! Knock it off and grow up!" She had never been this angry with Veronica and she was pleasantly surprised when the little mouse fought back.

"Who are you to tell me how to behave?" Veronica came back in her pearly British tones.

"I'm the woman who loves you and will help you despite your penchant for destroying yourself. If you give up the game not only will I be gone, dismissed, but you will become a pariah in your social circles and go back to the hermit you were!" she told her brutally.

"I was not a hermit!" she said spiritedly.

"What would you call it then?" Reese asked interested.

"I was hurt, I just avoided people..." she trailed off. She knew Reese was right but she wanted to lash out despite it.

"Veronica, I have something else I want to talk to you about..."

Veronica braced herself, it sounded ominous.

"I have been here for over a year and a half, in all that time I have never seen your rooms. Why is that?" Reese asked gently. She felt it was time.

Veronica looked immediately trapped. She had hoped this issue would never arise and Reese's straight forward candor while something she had always admired annoyed the hell out of her at this moment. "I don't know, I, I, ..." she finished lamely trying to hedge and feeling extremely uncomfortable.

"Is there something there that I shouldn't see?" she asked curiously.

Veronica mentally cringed. She looked around everywhere but not at the direct look that Reese was giving her. "It's just that I..." she started and left off.

Reese waited and then sighed. Veronica had come so far for so long and she still didn't have the guts to tell her certain things. She wondered about it but she had to let her have her privacy. She could have snuck into the rooms countless times but she valued the privacy and she wouldn't do that to her besides Veronica kept the doors locked at all times and she wasn't about to stoop to picking the lock. She turned to go back to her project.

Veronica reached out and grabbed her arm certain that she had lost Reese in some pertinent way. "Come with me, now," she told her bravely but inside she was quaking with fear. Even the maids hadn't been in her rooms in years.

Reese turned and followed her without a word making sure her hand dropped off her arm before they were outside of the room. She was certain the maids had guessed that Veronica spent too much time in her rooms already but she wasn't about to announce their relationship. She followed Veronica down the hall to her rooms.

Veronica unlocked and opened the door and stepped aside for Reese to enter. Reese walked in just enough for Veronica to shut the door behind her and switch on the light. She was astonished at the darkness of the room despite it being afternoon. The carpet was filthy and dark with a distinct path from where Veronica had walked. The wood floors under it were even darker. Stacked around the bed were piles of newspapers and magazines. The draperies and bed hangings were all a dark scarlet color that were ripped, worn, and stained. The whole room gave off a sinister and evil feeling. Reese took this all in at a glance and then headed for the nearest door. A closet with musty out of date clothing hung throughout it. The next door another closet with more up to date clothes but still an aura of dark and sinister. The third door opened to a bathroom that had seen better days. She turned to look at Veronica who was wringing her hands. "You can't enjoy living like this?" Reese asked astonished.

Veronica shook her head as she looked down at the floor. "I don't know how to change it," she said miserably and hopelessly, retreating back to the mouse that Reese had met in her first days here in the house.

"What would you like to change?" Reese asked cautiously as she was unsure of how to handle this. This wasn't like David's suite of rooms where dust could cause a reaction. This was filth, grime, and age. It was depressing with the drapes constantly drawn and the air of neglect. It was beyond depressing. Reese didn't know how to describe the aura of sinister depression that hung over the room. No wonder Veronica no longer spent very much time in here.

Veronica shrugged, "I just didn't want anyone to know..." she trailed off.

"Not to know," Reese mused aloud looking about the awful room. "When was the last time a maid came in here?" she asked.

"I think about eight years ago, maybe nine," Veronica answered cautiously.

Reese realized this was not a good thing. For Veronica's peace of mind alone this would have to change, it *needed* to change. "Have you ever discussed this with Ana?" she asked.

Veronica looked at her oddly, "With Ana? Why would I discuss it with Ana?"

Reese looked at her like she had lost her mind. This wasn't healthy. Why hadn't she cleaned something over the years? How did you cope with this? "How do the maids do your clothes and why haven't they been in here?" she asked incredulously.

Veronica hung her head in shame, "I've been too ashamed to let anyone in here obviously for years. It started because I didn't want anyone near me and the maids were told not to come in. I take my clothes to them and they leave them at the door."

Reese was angry; they could have at least cleaned the room. This neglect was disgusting and then she thought it was also understandable. As Lady of the Manor Veronica would be obeyed and once a precedence was set they would continue mindlessly until told otherwise, this though was unacceptable under any circumstances.

Veronica was watching her cautiously from under her eyelashes. Darting little glances that made Reese wonder if she was waiting to be chastised or something. Finally Reese asked, "Do you want it to remain like this?"

Veronica immediately shook her head, "I don't want them to know though either."

Reese took it that 'them' were the maids. "Just a minute then, we will clean this up ourselves," she told the surprised Veronica.

"But, but how....?" she asked wringing her hands feeling distinct anxiety.

Reese looked at her like she had lost her mind. "By good old fashioned hard work. You muck out horses stalls as though it were nothing, this is the same thing."

Veronica glanced around the room and had the good grace to blush. It did indeed look like a stall in the barn that had seen better days. Her horses lived better than she did.

Reese turned and went out the door feeling infinitely better when she had that awful and depressing room behind her. Veronica followed quickly worried that Reese had been grossed out or horrified. She followed as Reese headed downstairs to the kitchen and ignored the staff sitting around the table she went into the storeroom and started taking things she wanted or needed.

"Can I help you Ms. Paulson?" asked an instantly anxious and hovering Mrs. Anderson.

"Nope, found a project that needed my personal attention. I got it," she told the woman who hovered nearby looking on. Handing Veronica half of what she had grabbed she took the other half and walked out hearing the whispers of the staff behind her.

"They are going to know!" Veronica hissed at her in alarm.

"Of course they are to a degree but we will clean it up so they won't know how bad it was!" Reese hissed back.

Once inside the awful room she had Veronica gathering up newspapers and magazines and sorting them as she attacked the bathroom. She soon opened the windows to get out the chemical smell and was grateful when a breeze began soaring through them clearing the mustiness of the room. She could see Veronica was having trouble going through the piles and after a cursory cleaning in the bathroom over the surfaces she hosed it all down and was never more grateful for the drain that was in the center of the bathroom floor. She started at the ceiling and hosed the walls, the cabinets, and all the deeply dusty surfaces. Letting that drip and dry she entered the bedroom and began asking Veronica "Do you want all these magazines?"

Veronica looked a little helpless and shrugged.

"How about these newspapers, some of them are eight years old!?" She began to shove them in plastic bags until she had several bags full. Carrying them to the door she set them down inside in preparation of taking them out. Going to the windows she pulled down the shades ripping them from their sockets much to Veronica's horror.

"I need those!" she gasped.

"You need new ones and these are so yellowed and faded I'm surprised they aren't cracking from the sun." Next she began ripping the drapes from the rods they hung by. She loosened eight years or more of dust and the air was soon full of it causing them to sneeze and cough. Opening the windows she noted new mosquito netting would be necessary for the holes in the current screens. The room soon was flooded with late afternoon sunlight showing how much more shoddy the room had become. Stuffing everything in plastic garbage bags she soon had a row of them against the wall by the door. Next she attacked the bed hangings. "When was the last time you changed the bed sheets?" she asked as a horrified thought occurred to her. She had slept with this woman for months and if she was sleeping in a disgustingly dirty bed all this time...?

"Last Tuesday," Veronica answered wondering if Reese were angry with her and desperately hoping she wasn't. She couldn't tell by the determined look on Reese's face.

Pulling the hangings she soon loosened another ton of dust that fell on the fairly clean sheets and bedspread. Reese rolled these up and threw them in a couple of bags. Seeing that Veronica was still having trouble sorting through the magazines she began gathering them up into bags as well until she could see the floor around the bed. This desperately needed vacuuming. She could see the depth of the dust around where the stacks had been and it disgusted her to think of the spiders and dust mites that existed there. Going to the phone she called down to kitchen. Veronica hissed, "Don't!" but Reese was already speaking into the receiver.

"Mrs. Anderson could you have a couple of the houseboys," this still cracked her up as they were men, "Bring up two of our best vacuum cleaners to Lady Cavandish's room and take away a few bags to the dumpster? Thank you," she said into the receiver.

"They are going to see..." Veronica gasped looking around the dust filled room.

Reese grabbed a garbage bag and said, "Not if we hurry!" carrying the first of many bags into the hallway and leaving it for the houseboys. Veronica hurried to help her, the bags of magazines staggering her. They had just gotten the last of the bags containing garbage out of the room and the door shut when two of the houseboys brought up the electric vacuum cleaners and Reese directed them to take ALL of these bags down to a dumpster. They never even batted an eye as they both grasped a bag in each hand and turned to go down the hall and down the back stairs with them, the first of many trips.

Reese handed one of the vacuum cleaners to Veronica and wheeled the other one in while the houseboy's backs were turned. Plugging them in she directed Veronica to one side and they both began to vacuum. The bag less vacuums soon plugged up and filled and the two of them were constantly emptying them or stopping them to unclog the piping. They each filled a garbage bag with the dust and debris they were vacuuming up. Both of them were dusty and hot and looked awful. The room was filled with dust on everything but Reese was determined to get as much up as possible before she allowed the maids in here so as not to embarrass Veronica. The floor would need a thorough scrubbing and perhaps they would have to exchange the carpet for another it was so stained but at least the inches of dust and debris were no longer visible when she stopped. Taking the bags out she stacked them by the few bags left in the hall for the houseboys to take away. Next she opened the closet with the older clothing and asked, “Whose is this?”

“Some of it is my mothers and the rest I don’t know,” Veronica shrugged.

“Anything of value or sentimental value that you want to keep?” Reese asked and when Veronica shook her head she began taking armfuls of clothes off their hangers and stuffing them in bags. They had gone through a lot of bags. Veronica helped her take the clothes off the hangers and then they began on shoes and bags. Reese insisted they go through each of the bags and pockets to make sure nothing of value or identification was in them. Once this closet was cleaned out she had Veronica vacuum it while she called down to Mrs. Anderson again and asked her to have the houseboys come up again for more bags but that one of them should get a truck to take these to the local thrift shop. It was late in the day already and as dinner was late they could leave the bags in the truck overnight.

“Do you want to go through the other closet?” Reese asked as Veronica finished vacuuming.

“That is my closet and most of those clothes I want to keep,” she said indignantly.

“Well go through it and choose those you want to give away, there must be a bag or two worth that can go with these others,” she indicated the piles of bags right inside the door.

Sure enough Veronica had four bags full by the time the houseboys hauled the others that Reese slipped out the door. By then it was 7:30 and as dinner was at 8 and they had guests that evening both of them hurried to their separate bathrooms to shower and get cleaned up.

Veronica looked around the now cleaner bathroom and thought, why couldn’t I have done this? It had been so simple, all Reese had done essentially was hose it down! She knew though that it had just simply overwhelmed her to the point she felt useless and powerless. She showered and shaved and quickly dried herself off. The dust had settled into her pores she felt and she left the windows open to dry everything else. Her bedroom while stark without its hangings looked a lot better but the dust was still in the air and she hurried to get dressed and out of the room. She noted that the houseboys had removed all the bags, the evidence as it were of her depression and anxiety over the years. It was a relief to see it gone.

Reese was opening her door as Veronica hurried by and she gave her a huge smile. Looking around carefully Veronica took her into her arms and said, "Thank you for not judging me," and gave her a kiss.

Reese frowned at this public display of affection, anyone could have caught them but she understood. "Tomorrow we will rip those old wallpaper swathes off the walls and arrange for someone to come in and paint."

They turned to walk together to dinner. Lord and Lady Emerson were among the many guests that were to eat at the table which was long enough to seat 20 people. Some of them were shocked that Reese was included but David had told so many people about her wonderful work that others accepted it as a matter of course.

"You should see the brumby's and the dunnock's that they found in the latest roundup!" Lord Emerson was enthused and he nearly knocked his wine glass over as Reese cringed looking at the embroidered tablecloth.

"What are brumby's and dunnock's?" David asked as though he were interested.

"Why they are wild horses and cattle of course," he answered as though David should know.

Reese smiled, she knew David only was interested and then only occasionally in pedigreed stock.

"Are there a lot of them?"

"Why of course, the station is huge and we cannot find them all of course."

"You don't run sheep as well as well as the other stock? I'd heard there were huge sheep stations down in Australia," Veronica asked.

Reese stopped to listen to Lord Emerson. His enthusiasm was infectious.

"No, we run cattle and a few horses but I don't know why we don't run sheep. My manager assures me that the profits from rounding up the brumbies and dunnocks will far exceed the expense. They have roundups like this in the 'wild west'" he looked at Reese as though she were an expert and asked, "Have you ever seen these roundups?" Everyone turned to look at her with interest.

"I assure you they stopped having roundups years ago in Connecticut but they don't call them brumby's or dunnock's out west.

They are called mustangs and mavericks in the 'wild west' and there are fewer of them than in past years. Many of them are on private range but there are a few on public lands or in parks. I understand they are difficult to train once they are caught. The meat on the mavericks often tough and stringy."

This delighted Lord Emerson, he hadn't caught the Connecticut remark and considering her an expert launched into his favorite past time, talking about the station he had acquired years ago at a lucky turn of the cards. Lady Emerson rolled her eyes she was so bored with the subject.

After dinner Reese was enjoying a nice drink when Veronica approached her and asked drolly, "Going to saddle up and catch your own?"

Reese nearly choked at the joke. Veronica looked on in amusement as she covered up the coughing. "Maybe we should vacation down there and learn something about it for the estate," she teased referencing the many trips they had made to the outlying properties.

"Reese, Lord Emerson is interested in the plans you instigated at the tenants farms for the fallow fields," David said walking up with Lord Emerson.

"Yes, what did he wish to know?" Reese inquired immediately giving them her full attention despite a cough or two to get rid of the drink she had inhaled.

"Reese had to get rid of one of tenants because he refused to maximize the potential of our fields. The other tenants soon fell into line with Reese's direction. That practice of leaving a field fallow every three years is no more with us putting in hay or clover to replenish the land with nutrients," David explained to Lord Emerson.

"Were you a farmer in America?" he asked impressed.

Reese shook her head and smiled, "Actually no, I was a hotel manager but I had read something a long time ago about maximizing yields from fields and while the fallow idea had worked for generations it also wasted time and effort allowing weeds to take over a normally productive field. It can take years to get all the weed seed out of a field even with chemicals that we don't necessarily want on a field in the first place. Talking to some of the old timers we hit upon using the 'fallow' field method to our benefit and planting seed that would allow us to have hay to feed to our stock. The field isn't left unused then. Once the crop is in we turn the stock out into the fields whether it be cattle, horses, or sheep, and they fertilize it as well as grow fat on the gleanings."

Lord Emerson was very impressed with this woman. Not only was she model beautiful she also knew her stuff! "Young lady, if David hadn't already hired you, I would!" he flirted with her.

"Ah thank you Lord Emerson but I am very happy in my position here at Cavandish Estates." Reese smiled and could hear the catch in his breath.

"You've impressed many of our friends," David smiled as they all had a drink before retiring. The last of their guests had just left. It was well after midnight and they were all tired.

"I hope they enjoyed themselves," Reese said modestly. "I have an early morning, so if you two will excuse me?"

"Good Night Reese," they said in unison as she left the room.

"How did your evening with Oscar go?" David asked

"He has a new horse I'm going round to see tomorrow or the next day," Veronica enthused.

"You're seeing a lot of him these days?"

"No David, we are just friends and he loves horses as much as I do," she corrected him knowing where he was going with this line of questioning. She didn't want to marry and besides she didn't want a man. Her thoughts were already on Reese and joining her shortly in her bed, she couldn't of course go to her own since it was full of dust and debris.

"Well you could do a lot worse than marrying into that family and their properties adjoin our southern boundaries," he pointed out.

Veronica felt decidedly uncomfortable as she kissed her brothers cheek goodnight. She wanted to tell him she loved Reese but she agreed with Reese that they had to keep it a secret.

CHAPTER 28

The next day Reese pulled the loosening paper from the walls and they continued to stuff garbage bags full. Having the houseboys haul that away as well the room now looked bare and stark. Reese had called a painter to come out and discuss what they wanted the room to look like and he agreed to start that week, first painting and then papering the room so it would look fresh and bright. Veronica of course could not sleep in the room while this was all going on and Reese had the maids into the room moving her clothing and other things into another room. They looked around curiously but hadn't seen the debris and thought Reese was just remodeling like she had various other rooms over the years she had worked there. There had been talk of course about the amount of garbage hauled downstairs but no one wanted to incur the estate manager's wrath and they kept such talk to a minimum.

"Why did you have them move me so far away from you?" Veronica asked that night as she snuck into Reese's room.

Reese shook her head; she was getting tired of these childish tirades from Veronica. As she became more sexually confident she became more interesting but her childishness was still apparent. Taking her in her arms she answered, "I picked one of the prettiest rooms for you, I'm sorry if you didn't like it. It's not like I could put you up in here without raising eyebrows."

Veronica was immediately sorry, "I didn't realize you thought I'd like the room, your right, it is pretty."

Reese looked down at those amazing purple eyes and leaned down to kiss her. The knock on her door had them both startled. She pushed Veronica towards the bathroom and grabbing her robe she belted it around her as she answered her door. Making sure Veronica was hidden she opened it and was surprised to see David.

"Lord David?" she asked astonished.

"I'm sorry to bother you, have you seen my sister tonight? I went by her new room but she is not there."

Reese looked thoughtful for a moment buying some time, "Maybe she went down to the conservatory. I think those night blooming flowers she was pampering are due any day. Perhaps she is checking on them."

David nodded and said, "I'm sorry for the intrusion. You're probably right about the flowers. Thank you, good night." He turned and left.

Reese closed and locked her door and at the click of the lock Veronica came out of the bathroom.

"Night blooming flowers?" she asked amused.

Reese shrugged, "I didn't know what else to say. Get out of here and sneak down the servants stairs so if he does go there he can 'catch you' in there." Knowing how slow David could be especially as his illness progressed she added, "If you hurry you can beat him down there."

"I wanted to spend the night with you!" she pouted.

"You spend almost all your nights with me, go on now, I'll see you later or tomorrow," she practically shoved Veronica out of her bedroom.

What the hell am I going to do about that woman? Reese thought. Every day she loved her more. Watching her become the woman she had been destined to be was fascinating. Ana had complimented her on many occasions. Even David was thrilled with the apparent change in his mousy sister. Her confidence, her friends, her abilities had all increased in the last year. Reese was thrilled for her but she was also noticing how clingy she was becoming and wanting to be 'out' to her family and friends. Reese couldn't allow this. She saw what direction that Lord David was heading. Although she didn't particularly care for Oscar she could see he would make an excellent husband for Veronica. They had a lot in common and Veronica enjoyed him as a friend already. Reese had always thought best friends made the best mates. She didn't know how to end what had become a very enjoyable affair. It wasn't just an affair, she was fooling herself and she knew that. She also knew sadly that it couldn't go anywhere.

As they drove the Rover on one of the many back roads of the estate Reese was pleased as Veronica gently touched her neck and shoulders with her fingertips. It was an enjoyable sensation and caused goose bumps, desire, and need to build inside of her. It promised that later they would wrap themselves around each other and make love until each of them had an incredible orgasm. Reese always told Veronica that it wasn't the destination that counted but the road to the destination that was so enjoyable. "Stop it," she hissed. Anyone could see them or come upon them.

"No one is going to see us," Veronica teased. Leaning closer she whispered, "Why don't we stop and spread a blanket and get naked?" She enjoyed talking a little racy which she knew would excite Reese to recklessness.

As they drove over a rise though they came upon a drover with a herd of sheep and Reese braked gently to let them cross the road. "You see, you never know what is around a corner or over a hill!"

That night David asked her into his library. "Reese, I'm concerned about Veronica and how things are going with Oscar. I find him eminently suitable and he has officially asked to court her. He finds her compatible and would like to eventually marry her."

Reese's heart was in her throat and she quickly cleared it. "I'm sure Lord Wilkins would be an excellent candidate for her hand. I think though that she is still sorting out things from her past. He seems to be a good friend and they both enjoy each other's company. I'm sure if he goes slow things will change for them and perhaps what you both desire will happen," she said carefully. Her heart was beating a mile a minute and breaking but she remained professional.

"She doesn't confide her feelings with you?" he asked surprised, they seemed so close!

Of course she did but only regarding how much *she* loved *her*! "I would never betray a confidence," she said in a tone that had David apologizing.

"Of course you don't, I don't expect you to! I'm very sorry."

"Lady Veronica just needs time and patience," she left it at that although how many times had she told that very thing to Veronica herself.

Reese knew it was time to move on. Veronica would never let her go though and with Reese gone from the scene it would forever change the dynamics of their friendship, their love. She would feel betrayed and Reese hoped that David would be able to direct that betrayal into the marriage he so desired. The Cavandish family needed an heir and only Veronica could supply it. Reese hoped that Oscar would be gentle with the damaged woman, she couldn't ask him of course but she prayed she was doing the right thing. She couldn't help think though, what about love? David hadn't mentioned that Oscar loved her, only that he found her 'eminently suitable.'

Weeks later while she was making her plans an extraordinary opportunity arose.

They were all devastated to hear of the death of Lord Emerson from one of his many trips to Australia to see those damnably fascinating dunnocks he was gored to death by one of them. Lady Emerson was devastated and wanted to sell off the station that she had been sick of hearing about only to find it wasn't as profitable or easy to sell as she had thought. Its immense size and dynamics made it a property that might take years to sell. Stuck with it she had a team of accountants go and asses the property only to find that the manager had been stealing her husband blind. Prosecuting him she was left with an unprofitable station that would drain her resources unless it was put on the block and with no buyers she was in a quandary. She could turn it over to the government but at a tremendous loss.

Seeing the estate manager for Cavandish properties in the village a month after the funeral for Lord Emerson she approached Reese and begged her to come see her the following week. Reese agreed puzzled at the request. She was astonished when Lady Emerson offered her the job of manager at the vast section in Australia. She left with her mind reeling at not only the incredible and profitable offer she had received but with a sense of relief for having found an answer to her own problem. She thought over all of the particulars for a few days but knew that ultimately she couldn't pass up the challenge or the insane amount of money that had been offered. Already she was well on her way to one of her many goals. She couldn't let Veronica interfere with those goals or so she told herself despite knowing that she would be breaking both their hearts.

CHAPTER 28

"Mom, I am on my way!" Gillian enthused over the phone.

Reese's heart sank again. Another problem that was getting in her way. "Ah Gillian, I can't wait to see you!" she told her daughter but didn't tell her about the terrific job offer she had been given.

Gillian had agreed to do her graduate work at Cambridge and she was excited. Reese had been lost in her own work for so long and in Veronica that she had nearly forgotten that Gillian had applied for and was planning on attending Cambridge. Reese had been impressed and pleased for her but she had her own things to do.

"Why can't I go with you to meet her?" Veronica whined as Reese packed her bag to go pick Gillian up at the airport.

"Because we are getting her settled in a strange country at a strange school and I don't want her uncomfortable with my 'boss' being there," she tried to reason with Veronica.

Veronica was moody and pmsing. She wanted to be a part of every aspect of Reese's life and as a result was smothering her. It only made some of Reese's decisions easier. Veronica had sensed on some level that Reese was pulling away and it only made her cling more.

"I can just pretend to be there to help," she told her lover as they had the conversation in her new room which had turned out gorgeous.

Reese had arranged for silk striped wallpaper to be hung and the result was a classy covering that made the room look infinitely better. Painting underneath and on the ceiling had really cleaned and brightened the room. Washing the windows, repairing and replacing the screens, and re-waxing the wooden floors, borders, and wainscoting had helped immeasurably. New hangings in lighter colors gave the whole room a fresh look. It smelled better, it was the room of a lady and Veronica was grateful for Reese's taste and insistence on cleaning it up. It gave off such a positive aura that she couldn't help but feel better when she was in it. It only made her love Reese more for her kindness and consideration.

"Veronica, I love you but you cannot come with me this time," she was adamant. She knew Veronica wouldn't be able to hide her feelings and around her astute daughter it would be suicide. Gillian would pick it up in a moment, she was one savvy kid.

They argued about it for a while and Reese finally went to get her case and get on the road to London where she was picking her daughter up before beginning the drive to Cambridge. She didn't like that they had fought before she left and she wasn't surprised that Veronica called her several times on the drive which only annoyed her more. Once she picked up Gillian though she didn't answer the phone when it read 'Veronica' on the caller I.D.

Reese was thrilled to spend time with her daughter again. Already several boxes had been shipped over and should be in her rooms that she had rented with the grant she had received to study abroad. Reese was impressed by the woman she had become.

"Why are you so quiet Mom?" Gillian asked as they took up the last of her cases.

Reese had been lost in thought and she had hoped to have this conversation sooner rather than later. "I have some news for you that you aren't going to like," she told her daughter.

"What is it?"

"Let's get this stuff up there before I go into it," she said as she carried her share.

Reese looked around the little flat or apartment and thought how quaint it was. England was full of these old time buildings that had been converted into little apartments.

"So what is it," Gillian asked as she sighed and sat down with her feet up.

"I'm leaving Cavandish Estates," she told her daughter.

"Why?" she knew how much her mother had loved the job that she had for the last couple years. It had been a challenge from the start and she seemed happy.

"I got an astonishing offer from someone else and I want to pursue it. It's just that you moved here to be closer to me and I'm going away..." she felt awful about that.

"What's the offer and where?" Gillian asked.

Reese told her about Lord and Lady Emerson and the station in Australia. Gillian was thrilled for her mother. It was an incredible offer and right up her alley. It sucked, the timing of it, but Gillian was going to be immersed in her studies for the next couple of years anyway.

"Mom, good for you! What do the Cavandish's think about it?" she knew how close they had become.

"I haven't told them yet, I wanted to tell you first."

"You're chicken aren't you?" Gillian said amused.

Reese nodded and then threw a pillow at her astute daughter.

They began to unpack boxes and the little apartment took on a normal appearance in no time. They talked over their dreams and aspirations together as they unpacked and really bonded. Reese was pleased with the results and the next two days were spent exploring the town where her daughter would be living the next two years. They both enjoyed their time together knowing it was limited now.

On her way back to Cavandish, Reese stopped and accepted the offer from Lady Emerson and signed the contracts. The sign on bonus alone was staggering and Reese felt a little guilty accepting it but let the number of zeroes console her as she deposited it on her way home. Home, she had been here nearly two years. She had accomplished a lot and she would be sorry to leave. She was well on her way to many of her goals. She would be sorry to hurt Veronica but she had no choice. She had no right to Veronica's life and she wouldn't allow the love that she felt interfere with things Veronica needed to accomplish. At thirty she had a lot to do yet and Reese was forty, she had things she needed to do as well.

She stopped in the village for dinner and was pleased to run into Audrey.

"Hello stranger, haven't seen you since that last dinner party," Audrey smiled.

"Hi Audrey, how have you been?" she greeted her.

"I'm good, want to join me for bangers and dick?" she asked knowing Reese's propensity for laughter over these two particular dishes. They meant different things in America and she knew that Audrey loved teasing her over the differences.

"God you're disgusting," she teased back as she joined her at her table.

They caught up on each other's lives as they waited for their dinner to arrive and Audrey was pleased for her friend about her daughter moving to England and getting into Cambridge. Audrey had begun seeing a nice broker from London who vacationed in the area; he was attractive, well hung, and rich so she was happy.

As they ate their dinner Reese casually mentioned, "I'm resigning my post at Cavandish."

Audrey nearly choked on the mouthful of food she had just shoveled in. Quickly drinking her wine she swallowed as quickly as she could. "You are what?" she croaked.

"I'm quitting my job," she informed her friend as she watched to see if she needed the Heimlich maneuver.

"Why would you do that?" she asked astonished.

Reese looked at Audrey sadly, "It's time. I need to move on."

Audrey studied her for a moment and then asked the question they both knew she would, "What about Veronica?"

Reese looked devastated for a moment before hardening herself and answering, "I know, I love her so but really, what can I do?" she pleaded with Audrey to understand, "We all knew this could never go anywhere or last."

"She is going to be crushed," Audrey stated the obvious. She was angry for what would happen to Veronica.

"I wish I could avoid that but what can I do? She has to grow up and I was never more than a part of her life. She has some definite 'duties' to fulfill. David is getting steadily worse. He is occasionally walking with a cane now. She needs to step up to the plate and take on those duties. I've prepared her as much as I can. I know you will be there for her. Can you understand why I am doing this?"

Audrey did understand. Reese had never been in a good position. Perhaps in a few years it would have been different. But then if it wasn't for Reese Veronica wouldn't have come this far. She knew very well that Veronica had a destiny that didn't include Reese at all. This opportunity was something Reese needed to grasp.

"Promise me you will be there for her," Reese grabbed her hand and squeezed hoping to convey her feelings.

"I'll always be her friend, I always have," Audrey told her and they both remembered that Audrey had been there the last time their friend was devastated.

"One more thing?" Reese asked.

Audrey nodded not knowing what Reese would ask.

"Don't tell her where I've gone, *ever*," she stressed.

"You're not going to tell her?" Audrey asked surprised.

Reese shook her head as she answered, "I'm going to tell her I'm leaving but I don't want her to follow me. It would kill David to find out about us and I don't want her creating a scandal that would harm her. She has become clingy recently and you and I both know that is not a good sign."

Audrey nodded. The way Veronica talked about Reese was somewhat alarming and more than once Audrey had been jealous of the feelings that Veronica had for Reese wishing she had the love and attention of the beautiful blonde. Reese had been exactly what Veronica had needed at this time in her life and she was correct when she said she had to move on. Veronica would never willingly give her up.

Reese had one more stop to make and as it was early enough but after office hours she stopped by Ana's home instead of her office. Standing by her gate she told her the decision she had made to leave not only Cavandish Estates but Veronica.

"Reese, do you realize what this will do to her?" Ana asked gently.

Reese wanted to cry but she nodded, "I know, but it's an opportunity that I can't pass up and she needs to move on to the next phase in her life without me. I can't keep her, I never could. I always knew I was just a part in her life but not her life. She won't understand that of course but I need to go. She needs to mature without me."

Ana agreed. Reese had always known. Ana had worried for a time that she didn't see things clearly but was glad to know this wise woman had Veronica's interests at heart, had always been there for Veronica, looking out for her best interests. She had known she was only a small part of Veronica's life and was bowing out as gracefully as she could, Ana agreed to keep the secret of her eventual destination. She was glad that Audrey was aware of the situation as well. Veronica would need the support of her friends when her best friend, her lover, and what she considered the love her life left her soon. Ana would at least have a heads up on the emotional state that would soon be coming her way in her patient and friend.

Reese arrived home and parked the Rover only to have the door wrenched open and a very enthusiastic Veronica in her arms. Pushing her away angrily she hissed, "Have you gone mad? Anyone could see us," she looked around but it was so dark only the lights in the parking area were visible.

"I missed you!" Veronica pouted but Reese was not amused.

"I'll talk to you later!" she said angrily and reached for her bag.

"Reese, didn't you miss me?" she said in a little girl's voice and this annoyed Reese all the more.

"Of course I did, you know that, but you're making a spectacle of yourself and this is certainly not the time or place to discuss it!" She turned with the bag and headed into a side door to the house with Veronica trailing behind her feeling chastised.

Veronica had waited anxiously all afternoon. She was still annoyed that Reese hadn't taken her along to meet her daughter. Reese was probably right though that she might give herself away. Already she found it harder and harder to hide her feelings for the beautiful blonde. She wanted to shout to the world that Reese was hers! She couldn't wait to see her, to touch her, to be with her. She had to change her panty liner thinking about her. Her rebuke though angered her.

Reese handed her bag to a maid to take to her room as she went into the living room where David was watching television. Veronica went to sit beside him as he looked up.

"Ah Reese, your daughter all settled in?" he asked jovially.

Reese smiled at the mention of Gillian, "Yes, and she has a beautiful little apartment. She is looking forward to her studies."

"Must be an amazing girl with a mother such as yourself," he smiled and complimented her.

"Thank you, she is. Could I talk to you in your study Lord David?" she asked him formally.

Surprised he nodded and began to rise from the sofa using a cane to stand and for balance. Veronica tried to get Reese's attention and Reese deliberately ignored her. They walked slowly into the library.

Sitting painfully behind the desk he waited for her to begin as she closed and locked the door. Sitting across from him she handed him a typed letter she had prepared before she left, she had carried it with her afraid that Veronica might find it in her office. Her stomach was full of butterflies as he read the letter.

"You're sure of this?" he asked when he had finished.

Reese nodded.

"We will be sorry to lose you," he told her honestly. "But you must train the next manager," he told her.

"I already have," she knew he would impose the clause that was in her contract with him.

"You have?" he asked astonished and looked around as though to see this person.

Reese nodded as she relaxed back in her own chair totally in control of the situation, "Yes, your sister Veronica. I've been training her for months," she informed him.

"That's why she has been going with you? I thought she just wanted to get away and see our properties. I never realized you were training her to manage them as you do. Did you know you would be resigning that long ago?" he asked astonished with her statement.

Reese quickly shook her head, "No sir, I didn't, but an opportunity has arisen that I am going to pursue and Veronica knows most of the job. I know she will learn quickly those few things she hasn't experienced. She is quite competent," she informed David.

"This is an astonishing turn of events," he mused. Then thinking it over he realized she was right. Veronica was perfect for the position. It should be a member of the family taking over. She had set things in motion and all Veronica needed to do was keep the ball rolling. Then he said something that told Reese he wasn't unaware of things happening in the house as they had assumed, "It is time she turned her attention to other forms of 'entertainment,'" he said looking deeply into her eyes.

Reese wouldn't acknowledge or deny that statement other than to nod in agreement. They had been discrete. No one needed to know the details. They discussed many aspects of her position and things he needed to be aware of. He agreed not to tell his sister about the date of her departure nor the destination. He knew his sister would be devastated by the 'defection' of her close friend as she would see it but it was time she turned her attention not only to the estate she would one day inherit but her duties as Lady of the Manor.

Reese left the meeting surprisingly relieved. She wasn't surprised when Veronica slipped into her room later and to distract her from asking too much she made love to her tenderly and sweetly and then again swiftly and intensely. Their mutual orgasms found them both crying out into each other's mouths to muffle the enjoyment that they found in each other's bodies. Reese was sorry she wouldn't see more of the woman that Veronica had become and would become in the following years. She loved her so much and this was breaking her heart.

CHAPTER 29

In the following weeks Reese made sure everything was in order, filed, and neat for when she left. She discretely packed up her belongings and sent them off to be shipped to Australia. Veronica in her love filled eyes didn't notice the absence of personal items and knick knacks from Reese's room as she left what was on her dresser to be packed in her bags when the time came. As the time came to tell her Reese didn't have the heart to warn her and left it until the night before she was to leave. Veronica found her packing her final bag and said, "You're going on another trip?"

Since Reese had just come from a final inspection with Veronica to the outlying properties she couldn't even lie and use that as an excuse. As she put in the final items she zipped the bag and put it by the door with her other larger bags. In the morning she would just have one more bag to pack with the nightclothes she was wearing now and her toiletries and she would be ready to go. She had laid her traveling clothes out for tomorrow. Nodding in answer to Veronica's question she approached her and grabbed her hands holding her close.

Veronica had a sense of foreboding but tamped the feeling down as Reese began to kiss her oh so sweetly. The kiss deepened and they both felt the desire and attraction that built within them. Reese made sweet love to her as a goodbye gift using her body and natural techniques on her that left her breathless and loving. Her own orgasm was bittersweet as she knew this would be the last. She wore out Veronica with her enthusiasm and she was there for the first time into the morning. Normally she had snuck out before the servants could catch her.

"Why didn't you wake me?" she gasped as she realized the time.

Reese knew why, she had watched her sleep for hours thinking about the last two years with her. Even though she had had past relationships she had *never* been anyone's first. She had *never* met someone like Veronica in her entire life. She had *never* loved anyone like this. She had *never* broken anyone's heart like she was about to, as hers was breaking. "I wanted you to be here in the morning for once," she told her caressing her hair back. She snuggled into her neck smelling the scent of the woman she loved so much. Her own heart was already cracking with what she must do now. Sitting up she hardened herself to do what she must. "Veronica, I have something to tell you."

Veronica felt that sense of foreboding again. It was stronger now and those ominous words weren't helping any. She wanted to escape but was held captive by the beautiful woman she loved so much.

"I'm leaving this morning. Frank is driving me to Heathrow," she stopped to let the words sink in.

"Where are you going? When will you back?" she asked as though she were going to the Sounds for the weekend.

Reese shook her head, she was being too vague. She needed to be honest and direct or as honest as she was prepared to be. "I'm leaving, *for good,"* she told her watching as the comprehension dawned in her beautiful purple eyes.

"What do you mean for good?" Veronica was panicking inside already.

"I've accepted another position and I'm flying out today to go to it." Reese looked directly into those eyes.

"But why, why do you have to leave? I thought you were happy here? I thought you loved me?" The tears began to well up in those amazing eyes.

"It's time Veronica. I was happy here. I do love you. I got this amazing offer and I have to go." It sounded lame to her ears.

"Where are you going?" She sounded like a puppy to Reese, whining and hurt.

"Bangkok," she told her having rehearsed part of this in her head over and over so it sounded believable.

"What will you be doing?" she asked incredulous.

"Managing a hotel." That part at least was feasible given her background.

"But *why*, why are you leaving me, I love you!" She started to sob and her voice was rising.

This was the part that Reese had anticipated and cringed inside at. "Veronica, we both knew this would come someday. I have no future here as your lover. I love you but I can't stay here." She didn't tell her she had to get away from her. She was becoming too dependent on Reese and her love. She was becoming too clingy. Rather than embarrass both of them she was trying to be gentle.

"Then I will come with you. Give me an hour and I'll be all packed." She jumped out of the bed buck naked and Reese appreciated the view she knew would be burned in her brain from that moment.

"No, your place is here and I don't want you to come. The scandal would never die down. Maybe in a few months you could come visit," she cringed inside at her cowardice at giving her hope that would die when she couldn't find her.

"You don't want me to come with you now?" she asked confused.

"Not right now. It would be too obvious." Reese rose from the bed naked as well and started to go into the bathroom to shower before she dressed.

Veronica followed her. "Reese, don't you love me anymore?"

Reese turned and they nearly collided, "Of course I love you, I will always love you but don't you see? I have no future here. I have goals. I have things I have to accomplish. I didn't intend to fall in love with you. I can't stay here forever."

"Why not?" she whined and knew that Reese would hate it. "Why didn't you tell me sooner?"

Sighing deeply she attempted to take Veronica in her arms and felt the stiffness of her body against her own, "Because of this exact reason. I didn't want you to nag me to stay; I didn't want you dwelling on it for days." I didn't want to hurt any more than I had to she kept to herself.

"Nag?" she took offense at the word pulling herself up to her full height and pulling the British cloak of nobility around her to a degree which was difficult to do stark naked.

"Okay, bad choice of words but I couldn't let you talk me out of leaving..."

"Could I have changed your mind?" Veronica asked hopefully grasping at straws.

Reese shook her head. She had to get out of here. She let her arms drop and turned on the shower she gasped at the cold as it warmed quickly and began to wash. Veronica watched her sadly as she admired that body she knew so well. The taunt flesh, the erect nipples, the beauty of it took her breath away time and again. She couldn't believe she was leaving! She couldn't allow it but then sanely she realized she was becoming obsessed. What could she do to prevent it? Neither of them were children. She was hurt, more hurt than she could imagine. For a second she thought of something dramatic or drastic that would keep Reese there beside her and then realized that wouldn't work either as it would only upset both of them. Besides she was past the days where suicide was an option. Reese had helped her to become strong; Ana had contributed to her well-being. David and Audrey had always been there for her. She didn't realize how long she had stood watching her lover and lost in her frantic thoughts until Reese was finishing her shower and drying off. She dried her bottles as well and slipped them into a bag that she had ready there. Brushing her teeth she dried the toothpaste tube and slipped that in as well. Putting the brush in its case it joined the others. Opening the medicine chest Veronica saw that was empty as well. Reese had been well prepared for this exodus.

Reese saw the devastation on her lovers face as she watched her momentarily in the mirror. She dried her hair with a towel and then running a comb quickly through it to style it she dropped that into the bag as well. She hardened her heart and carrying her bag she headed into the bedroom to begin dressing.

"Don't leave me," Veronica said simply as she stood there still naked.

Reese looked up as she pulled on her underwear and then her socks. Grabbing her bra she continued to dress as she watched but didn't answer Veronica.

"You can't leave me," she whined as the tears rolled down her cheeks unchecked.

Reese's heart was broken. She knew this was going to be hard but she refused to cry. "I have to, don't you see..." she tried reasoning with Veronica but knew that was a mistake.

"No you don't, I'll go away with you. We can live at the Sounds together; we can live in the apartment in London. No one will care if we are a couple there. I love you, please don't leave me," she begged.

Reese continued to dress methodically and ignored the tearing in her chest. When she was fully dressed she grabbed her nightclothes and toiletries bag and stuffed them in her traveling case. Looking around the room a final time she waited for Veronica to begin dressing as she stood there naked.

It was as Reese looked around that Veronica realized how much of the knick knacks were gone. She was crushed that Reese had been planning this for a long time and hadn't told her. "Please, I beg you, don't leave me."

Reese closed her eyes it hurt so much. She had known this would be hard. She had gone over the conversation a hundred times in her head. It was harder in reality. She didn't want an argument. She knew that Veronica couldn't and wouldn't accept anything she said anyway. She leaned over and picked up her cases slinging her bag over her shoulder. She grabbed a coat from the back of her chair and put it over her arm. As she reached for the door handle Veronica grabbed her arm nearly making her drop her bag.

"Don't go..." she pleaded the tears streaming down her cheeks.

"I have to," she said quietly as she died inside. Hardening her features to keep from crying she quickly opened the door and walked out.

Veronica would have immediately followed her but she suddenly realized she was naked and quickly closed the door. She sprinted to her clothes and began to dress hurriedly.

Reese quickly walked down the stairs knowing she only had a few extra minutes while Veronica dressed. Seeing Frank walking from the kitchens she called, "Ready to go?"

He nodded and met her at the bottom step, he tried to take her cases but she said, "No, I've got them, let's go!" and headed for the front door.

David came to the door of the dining room and nodded as Reese hurried past. He looked up the stairs but saw nothing. They had talked for days privately and discretely. There was nothing more to say. They had said their good-byes and while he would miss this incredibly competent woman he knew it was time for her to go. His sister would get over her obsession and infatuation with her.

Reese was pleasantly surprised as she and Frank put her cases in the trunk how many employees were there to see her off. She was only grateful that British standoffishness prevailed or she would have never gotten out of there before Veronica made an appearance. She settled with a direct look and wave to each of them as she nodded and got quickly into the back of the Rolls Royce. Frank drove them away just as Veronica sprinted from the house. "Wait," she shouted but Frank didn't hear her as Reese asked him at that exact moment to turn up the radio. She had seen Veronica out of the corner of her eye. Veronica could only watch as they drove away, tears streaming down her beautiful face. The employees quickly turned away to give her privacy.

Veronica returned to the house and then with a thought pivoted to head to the garages. David came out of the house and said, "No car is available to you."

She turned to him and seeing the expression on his face realized he knew quite a bit more than he had ever let on, "I've got to go after her..." she pleaded.

"No you don't," he told her.

"I love her, don't you understand?" she pleaded harder.

"Yes, actually I do know. That's why she left," he answered.

She looked at him amazed and the reality of what he said made her shoulders sag and she began to sob in defeat. She couldn't make the woman she loved stay and running after her was the sign of a desperate woman. She *was* desperate though, she had never loved anyone as she had Reese. "I thought she loved me," she cried as David pulled her uncomfortably into his arms.

"I know, I know. She did love you, that is why she knew she had to leave," he consoled her.

Veronica cried for half an hour on the stoop of their home. She cried for the woman who had loved her and left, she cried for the woman she had lost in both herself and in her life, she cried because she couldn't have what she wanted. Finally David was able to get her inside the house. He was concerned with the amount of grief she was showing. It was as though someone had died. Perhaps something had died though.

Veronica was quiet the rest of the day. She snuck off to a computer to check on the flights to Bangkok and found one she could follow Reese on but she had no idea what hotel she was working at or what flight she was on. There were many hotels in Bangkok she found when she looked. She needed to find her; she tried calling her mobile phone only to find it was already disconnected. She felt lost and hopeless.

CHAPTER 30

Reese cried discretely all the way to London. She hadn't eaten that morning and wished she could have a drink but knew that was a bad idea with the long flight she had ahead of her. Frank dropped her at the international counter and her bags were soon checked. She thanked him and wiped away her tears discretely. He smiled wishing he could say more, all of the staff had been shocked when Lord David had informed them the previous night of the departure of their estate manager. At first they thought she had been terminated for some unknown reason but he had told them she was leaving them for greener pastures. Despite her stern countenance she had been fair and they had all come to respect her. She would be missed and they had all discussed the possible new manager that would be engaged.

Reese sat in the lounge as she waited for her flight to be announced. She hated the way she had left Veronica but knew of no other way to have handled it. She was devastated having never had a love like this before in her life. She wished Veronica well and wished she could have done some things differently. She rose and headed for a pay phone.

"Hello?" Gillian answered her cell.

"Hey my darling girl, I'm at the airport and wanted to say goodbye one more time," Reese smiled for the first time in hours.

"Mom, you have talked to me every day for weeks. I'll be okay. I'll come down at break if I can manage it." She felt her mother was becoming a bit overprotective.

"We will be more than half a world away from each other. I'm sorry about the timing of this," she told her for the umpteenth time.

"It's okay, I'm a big girl. We will see each other in a few months!"

Just then the call came across the loudspeakers and Gillian could hear it. "You have to go Mom, I love you!" she told her.

"I love you too baby, take care!" Reese told her sadly. "Bye," she hung up.

This was a sad day all around. Finally on the same island as her daughter and she was flying across a couple of continents to go work in a country she knew only a little about. She was also leaving a woman she had loved very much but couldn't stay with.

Reese sat in her first class seat and looked out the window remembering hundreds of memories involving Veronica. Her insides were turned out and writhing. It didn't help that she had eaten nothing today.

"Could I get you something Ms. Paulson?" the stewardess asked solicitously.

Reese looked up at her and the woman took an unconscious step backwards at the devastation she saw on her passenger's face. She looked like she might cry at any time but her eyes looked haunted more than teary. Reese wanted a drink but on an empty stomach knew this would be a mistake. "When is the meal being served?" she asked quietly.

"Not for a couple of hours, could I get you some crackers or chips to tide you over?" She looked ill and the stewardess wondered if she should be alarmed.

Reese nodded and said, "Crackers please and perhaps some white soda?"

"Certainly, coming right up," she hurried away to get her them but commented to one of the other stewardesses her concern that Ms. Paulson in first class looked ill.

Reese munched on the salt crackers and sipped at the white soda until both were gone. They helped the ache in her stomach a little but her heart was hurting more and choking her. There were too many hours to think and she seriously thought about getting drunk to alleviate the thoughts that swirled around in her head. She knew though that flying drunk would be a mistake and make her sick, arriving in Sydney drunk would make a great impression on whoever met her. She suffered in silence, or tried to.

"Are you ill?"

Reese looked up at a passenger from across the aisle. She hadn't noticed him sitting there as she was so self-absorbed. The flight certainly wasn't full so there were a lot of empty seats. "Excuse me?" she asked not sure that he had spoken to her.

He smiled; man was she beautiful despite the look in her eyes and face at the moment. "Are you ill?"

Reese studied him for a moment absorbing the unfamiliar English accent before the sense of his words penetrated her brain. Shaking her head she played with the ice in her glass trying to look out the window again.

"May I join you?" he tried again.

Reese turned back and said quietly, "I would prefer to be alone, thank you."

Ah, a hard nut to crack he thought smiling to himself. She might *like* playing hard to get. "Are you running away?" he asked amused.

She frowned at him and the question. "Running away from what?"

"An unhappy love affair? Your lover? I don't see a ring so surely not a husband?" he teased attempting to get a smile out of the blonde.

The accuracy of his questions hit her like a blow but only she knew it. She ignored the questions and the man and turned back to the window.

"So tell me why you are heading to Australia? New start? Vacation? Hiding? I myself am going on business. I handle trade goods between the Aborigines and import them into England," he said self-importantly.

Reese tried to ignore him and was becoming annoyed. She just wanted to be left alone. Her thoughts and life were her own. She was free and independent or was she? When had Veronica become her whole world? When had the mousy little English woman become more important than her goals? When had she wormed her way into her heart? She had been touched and in love but never like this. It had hurt when she broke up with people over the years but not like this woman. She was ashamed at the way she left it. She had left so many unanswered questions for herself and for Veronica. Knowing things that Veronica didn't perhaps she could have explained her reasoning. Perhaps they could have worked around the obstacles. No, it was best she left. Veronica had a purpose and goals she didn't even know about that must be fulfilled. If Reese had stayed she would never have fulfilled some of them. She should have children; she should take on her family obligations. She would probably marry now that Reese was out of the picture. Reese thought about someone else making love to Veronica someday and her heart tore a little more.

"Maybe we could go out when we get to Sydney?" the man asked hopefully totally oblivious to her pain and misery.

"I'm sorry, that won't be possible. Please, if you would, I would like to be left alone."

"I'm just making conversation. This is a long and boring flight," he said sure of his charm.

Reese ignored him again as the stewardess returned, "Would you like to order your meal now?" she asked.

Reese nodded and being handed a first class menu soon ordered the English Pot Roast. Funny how she couldn't escape England despite having been in the air for a few hours. She was going to what had essentially been an English colony. Perhaps she should have looked in Bangkok for a job after all. She should be looking forward to the new challenges that her job would offer but instead she could only think of the face of Veronica as she told her she was leaving.

Eating a meal helped some of the emptiness inside her but only on a certain level. She asked for a drink and then had a second one. The fuzziness had a nice effect on her brain and she thought about sleeping. The bad thing about drinking is it also relaxed her to the point where she began to become horny. That led right back to thoughts of Veronica. A vicious cycle and one for which she was paying dearly. She thought about having another drink but kept herself from making that mistake.

"Why don't we become better acquainted?" the man across the aisle tried again after all she *was* quite attractive.

Reese looked at him for a moment and briefly thought about taking him up on his offer. Sex with a stranger would certainly take care of the physical needs for a moment but she had a hell of a lot of self-respect and knew she would always regret it. She shook her head at him and hoped he would leave her alone. Instead she leaned back in her comfortable seat and closed her eyes hoping for sleep to come. She dozed on and off for the rest of the flight totally lost in her thoughts until they landed.

In Sydney she quickly went through customs and looked around for a sign or something that would indicate that someone had come from the station to pick her up. They knew she was coming Lady Emerson had assured her. As passengers filtered out of the terminal though she realized she probably had to make her own arrangements. Knowing the station was over a thousand miles away she certainly wasn't going to rent a car. Going to one of the counters of the smaller and local airlines she asked about getting a flight to Wahbaing Station.

"Where?" the girl behind the counter asked unsure about her American accent which had a hint of British to it after having lived there for the past couple of years.

Reese pulled a folder from her bag and pulled out a map which showed Australia and the proximity of Wahbaing Station. She showed it to the girl.

"We don't go there," the girl told her popping some bubble gum.

Reese looked at her in annoyance. "Do you know where I can hire a plane to get me there?" she asked pleasantly her American accent never more evident with the broad twangs of Australia around her.

"You could try them over there," the girl pointed to another counter further down. Reese thanked her with a glare and pushed her luggage to the other counter.

"Could you possibly help me?" she asked the man behind the counter.

"Yes Ma'am how may I help you?" he asked professionally.

"I'm looking for a flight near or to Wahbaing Station," she told him waiting for him to ask where it was like the girl had.

"Ah, you want to go north west then. We don't have any direct flights of course but we do have a plane you can catch a ride with that takes mail to that area three times a week," he told her helpfully.

"Is it possible to catch that ride today?" Reese asked alarmed not wanting to waste any more time after the long flight she had just taken.

"Actually it might be possible to catch it this afternoon. Let me check with the pilot and see if he has room. Is this all your baggage?" he looked at the two cases she was rolling along with the bag over her shoulder. She nodded as he picked up the phone. In quick-fire Australian that she didn't totally get but a word here and there he talked to someone who answered the phone. As he hung up he gave her a huge smile and said, "Jack is willing to give you a lift if you don't mind a few stops on the way."

Reese returned the smile and his faltered as the beauty of the blonde before him became evident. "Oh thank you," she said relieved. "How much will I owe for this?" she began to get out her purse.

"Oh, you don't pay us; you will have to pay Jack. Here he comes now," he indicated a scruffy looking man that was walking towards their counter from a back door.

"This 'er," he asked as he pointed with his thumb at Reese.

She resented being called 'er' immediately but swallowed her annoyance as she turned with a pleasant smile and held out her hand. "Jack?"

He look surprised at the model before him, "*You're* going out to Wahbaing Station? You got friends there?" he reluctantly shook her hand.

She shook her head not wanting to give out more information than what was necessary since she was essentially going into the back of beyond with a strange man.

He shrugged; it wasn't any of his business why she was going there. "It'll cost you a few hundred quid," he told her.

She nodded and pulled out some English pounds which she handed him. He looked surprised at the British currency but knew here in Australia it was as good as the Australian money and pocketed it. "May I have a receipt for that please?" Reese asked knowing she might antagonize him by asking for it.

He asked the clerk for a piece of paper and laboriously wrote out a receipt for the 'flight' before handing it to Reese. "Can I help you with your bags?" he asked surprising her.

She accepted and he took the two she had been rolling along. Thanking the clerk for his help she slipped him a five pound note as she followed along behind Jack. She was pleasantly surprised when he led her to a private hanger where a small jet stood which he proceeded to throw her bags into. She wasn't thrilled to have her bags handled that way but figured she might not get a ride if she protested. He helped her up into the plane before following her in and closing the hatch.

"Sit there," he indicated the co-pilots seat and she strapped herself in looking around at the various and confusing array of instruments and wondered what did what. He soon did his checklist and put on a set of earphones. He handed her a set as well which she put on.

They began to taxi out to a different set of runways than what she had come in on. She could hear him giving information to what she supposed was the tower and them being given clearance to take off. The plane was so much smaller than the commercial jets she had ridden in for years and she was alarmed as her stomach lurched when they took off. She loved it though in short order as she could see a lot more of the countryside as they flew along. Jack didn't say anything but within an hour they were making a descent and he casually mentioned, "Mail stop," before they landed with a slight bump. He got up and opened the hatch and threw a couple of bags to some men that had arrived in a Rover. They handed him a bag in return and he closed the hatch and got back into the pilot's seat.

They did this many times and Reese stopped counting after the sixth time. Her stomach didn't like the abrupt take offs but she was enjoying the different landscapes they were flying over. Finally though they began circling for another landing and she resigned herself to the stomach lurch when Jack commented, "This is Wahbaing Station," which had her looking down at the ground as they circled. She couldn't see the house and nothing but rolling hills but she saw a dirt cloud that indicated someone was coming to meet the plane. Once they landed and came to a stop Jack indicated she should go first as he grabbed her luggage and the mail bags.

"What is this?" a tall and stocky man asked Jack as he looked past the blonde getting off the plane.

"This is a passenger that asked to come to Wahbaing Station," Jack grinned.

"We aren't expecting guests, just the new manag..." his voice trailed off as he got a good look at the 'passenger.'

"Hello, I'm Reese Paulson," the tall blonde held out her hand in greeting as she got off the last step.

"You're the new station manager?" the man said incredulously. "We weren't expecting a sheila!"

Familiar as she was with some of the different English twangs even Reese knew that sheila was a term for female. She didn't like it but then she knew there would be some resistance to her coming here and being a woman to manage a cattle station in the outback. Lady Emerson had complete faith in her and had given her a free reign; she would do what was necessary. She smiled at the man which staggered him with its sheer beauty, even after traveling for so many hours and with a bare minimum of makeup she was still an incredibly lovely woman. "I'm sorry; I thought Lady Emerson had made that clear."

He shook his head to clear it and was angry all at once. "Let's get you to the station house, unless you want to leave with Jack 'ere?" he asked hopefully.

Reese shook her head and grabbed one of her cases that Jack placed on the ground and headed for the Rover she placed it in the back. Her satin blend blouse and twill slacks seemed out of place here in the dusty outback but then she had known where she was coming and had stacks of jeans packed and ready.

The man came over with her other case and the mail bags and threw them into the back. As Reese climbed into the passenger seat she waved to Jack who threw her a cocky grin and salute as he closed the hatch in preparation for taking off. Reese looked around as the man drove fast through the rough terrain. The deep ruts of the road had her grabbing at the seat belt and the handle above the door but she never said a word as she looked around her. It was very dry and dusty and brown was her thought as she looked around. She didn't see any cattle on the hills though and wondered why. She already wondered if Lady Emerson's faith in her was misplaced. What did she know about cattle ranching?

"You manage a station before?" the man asked as they hit a straight away.

Reese shook her head, "No, an estate," she managed before they hit another series of ruts from water run off or what she thought could have formed these foot wide crevices in the dirt road.

He was surprised at her American accent but didn't comment on it. Lord Emerson had been an eccentric and Lord Gregorson before him. The place hadn't been run right in decades. The woman was going to have to be a magician to make it pay much less improve it. He only stayed on because he had been born out here and couldn't imagine living elsewhere. The food was good and the pay okay but he didn't know anything else and didn't want to go anywhere.

As he pulled through another series of curves around hills they saw their first glimpse of the home station which was nestled in a large valley with the gently rolling hills surrounding it. Reese's first thought as she saw it was 'The Thorn Birds' and the mansion in the movie but that soon changed as her second thought was 'what a dump' as she noted how dilapidated the place was with hanging shutters that a good wind would knock off and apparently had in several instances. Many of the windows were boarded over. Even the fences and gates were in a sad state of neglect and were falling down all over the immense home yard. The barns seemed to be in fairly good condition but that was the outside appearance. The air of neglect though seemed to permeate the entire place as the man pulled up in front of the mansion which stood out like a sore thumb in this landscape. Reese turned to him with a smile and said, "Thank you so much for the ride, what is your name?"

The man seemed surprised that she didn't know but answered, "Me name's Greg," but made it sound like Grog.

Reese nodded and asked, "And what is your position here on the station?"

"I'm just an employee, you might call me a cowboy like you American's have," he grinned.

Reese returned the grin, "Well, that remains to be seen, I haven't seen any cows."

"They be out in the hills near the creeks this time of year," he told her and she nodded to indicate she had heard as her attention returned to the house they were in front of. Several people had come outside and stood on the wide verandah. They were the first real Aborigines that Reese had ever seen although in Sydney she was certain some of the people she had mistaken for blacks were actually Aborigines. She opened the door of the Rover and hopped out reaching for one of her suitcases.

Greg got out and pulled the other one out setting it on the ground. He looked up and said, "Sheila, this is the new station manager," and then reached for the bags of mail. Reese thought at first he was calling her a sheila again before she realized the woman he had addressed stood in the group before her.

The tallest of the Aborigines looked at the model before her and never changed an expression. Inside she was thinking that she had seen this woman before somewhere, probably in some fashion magazine. Her short blonde and impeccably cut hair flowed in the evening breeze; she wore no hat, her outfit while nice was out of place here in the outback. Separating herself from the group that had come out in curiosity she came down the steps with her hand out, "Hello, I'm Sheila Robertson, the housekeeper here at Wahbaing Station."

Reese smiled and stunned the woman as she grasped her hand wholeheartedly, "Hello, I'm Reese Paulson."

It had been Sheila's experience that white Anglo's especially ones of apparent Aryan background shied away from touching a black woman but this one didn't. Her accent though wasn't British or Australian. She looked Norwegian but that wasn't the accent either. Sheila was surprised that the woman topped her own above average height by two inches at least.

Reese studied Sheila realizing she wasn't a true Aborigine but somewhere in her background had to be a white as she didn't have the classical wide nose or was as dark as her companions. She was a very striking woman in her own right. Her eyes were black which surprised Reese in their intensity.

"The new manager's a sheila," Greg informed the group grinning at their surprise. Never in the history of the station had this happened. He picked up her two cases and effortlessly carried them into the house

Sheila only looked at him with a calm face never changing expression. Turning back to Reese she said, "Come we should get you out of the sun, even the evening sun can be hard on the features. Do you have a hat?" she asked.

Reese shook her head, "I knew I would have to purchase several things when I came here. Perhaps you can advise me on what I will need?"

Sheila was surprised. Most people in power demanded and didn't ask. Perhaps having a 'sheila' for a boss might not be so bad after all. The present owner was a woman too after the death of her husband, a horrible tragedy that.

Reese walked into the most beautiful house she had ever seen in her life. A stark contrast with the outside dilapidated look she was thrilled that the house was kept up so nicely. Inside the front doors which contained colored glass was a large foyer with tiles. Rich mahogany woods lined every inch along the walls that also contained portraits of past owners or so the discrete plaques at the bottom of each told them. Off to the right of the foyer was the piano room with large glass display cases showing off a variety of knick knacks. A large fireplace dominated the room on the east side. Large windows that had the shades partially drawn lined the room bringing in plenty of lights but a huge chandelier dominated the wood lined ceiling. The room led off to the study with book lined shelves covering every bit of wall between the large windows. Across the hallway from the study was the dining room with room to seat eighteen. Back at the front of the house was a large parlor with prissy seating for guests. Reese far preferred the piano room with its warmth and briq a braq. Sheila finished the tour of the downstairs by taking her to the back of the house where a huge set of kitchens dominated it. Asked why the kitchens were so large Reese was told it was to feed the vast army that worked on the station at various times depending on the season.

Sheila took her upstairs and showed her the master bedrooms. There were two of them, one for the master and one for the madam. Reese had her luggage taken to the second bedroom when she discovered it in the master bedroom. That would be reserved for important guests or Lady Emerson should she ever decide to visit. There were six other bedrooms all in rich fabrics and beautiful antique furniture.

"I suppose all of this is original to whoever first built this house?" Reese asked appreciating the simple beauty before her.

Sheila nodded, "My great great grandfather built this place," she confirmed not only what Reese had asked but her thought that Sheila wasn't pure aborigine.

"If your family helped build this place then why..." Reese trailed off her question knowing it was indiscreet of her to ask.

Sheila didn't seem to mind, "We were on the wrong side of the blanket," she grinned, referring to a common practice with the early whites who took Aborigine wives and had children with them, sometimes not bothering to marry them. Their white or legitimate children often inheriting the land that they knew nothing about.

Sheila was very surprised at the attitude of this American. She wasn't what any of them had expected. First of all she was a woman, very beautiful yes, but for a woman to manage a station of this size was going to be some accomplishment. She didn't hold a superior attitude from what Sheila could see. She asked questions, made astute observations, and appreciated what she had seen. No arrogance and for that Sheila was grateful, it would make getting along much easier.

Reese was pleased with what she had seen thus far. The house was well kept up and beautiful. "Have you been housekeeper long?" she asked Sheila sure it was because of her work that it was so well maintained.

"Practically all my life. Me da got me a job as a maid as a youngster and at eighteen I got the job of housekeeper," Sheila told her proudly.

Reese looked at her assessingly. There was no way to guess the age of the woman before her. She could be any age within a 20 year span. She had a timeless beauty that was impossible to peg. "Then we owe you for the beauty in this house, it's been well maintained," she told the housekeeper.

Sheila appreciated the compliment. She took pride in her work and enjoyed the beauty around her. The house had been her pride and joy for as long as she could remember. She only wished she could do more about the outside but that was where her authority ended. Perhaps now with the new manager....

"Are you hungry? Of course you are, that trip is a long one," she said as she led Reese back downstairs to the dining room.

"The trip from Sydney or London?" Reese asked amused. Both had been long and tiring and she was dragging not only from the trip but from her emotional upheaval.

"I'll imagine the trip from London since I've never been there. Went to Sydney once but that was by car and I imagine it was equally long by airplane with Jack flying you," she answered amused as well.

Reese entered the dining room to realize only one place was set. "Isn't anyone going to eat with me?" she asked surprised.

Sheila studied her for a moment to see if she was serious. Didn't she realize the hierarchy in employees? "No ma'am," she told her.

Reese shook her head, "Where are you going to eat?" she asked.

Sheila was startled but her face never changed, "In the kitchen where I always eat," she told her wondering where this was going.

"If you don't mind, I'd like to eat with you. This is fine if we are entertaining guests or if Lady Emerson were to come here but I prefer the simplicity of the kitchen if that's okay with you?" Reese asked.

Sheila was astounded. Gathering the plates and silverware she began to take them off of the table. Reese quickly gathered the glasses and the napkins and place settings. She followed Sheila into the kitchen where several of the people from the verandah were already sitting around the large kitchen table in various stages of eating. The men immediately stood as Reese followed Sheila into the kitchen.

"Sit, sit, don't let me interrupt your meal," she told them and then wondered if they all spoke English as they stared at her.

"Ms. Paulson is joining us," Sheila told them with a hint of a smile as she placed the plate at the end of the long table. Reese put the place setting down and helped Sheila arrange the utensils before Sheila brought a chair from along the wall. Reese sat down and returned the friendly stares. There were people here that ranged in age from at least 70 down to toddlers. They couldn't all possibly work here she thought.

Sheila sat down at the corner next to Reese and handed her a tureen of stew. Reese ladled it onto her plate and helped herself to biscuits. Watching the others she saw they were astounded that she was eating with them.

"Would you like wine or ale?" Sheila asked as she indicated the bottle and the pitcher farther down the table.

"Do you have water or milk?" Reese asked.

Sheila never indicated the surprise that was passing through her head as she reached for a pitcher further down the table. The sides were lined with sweat marks as the condensation trickled down its side. She poured into Reese's wine glass filling it full of rich and frothy milk. Reese's eyes met hers in amusement as she noticed the others were horrified.

The meal was fairly quiet as the others had no idea why she had joined them. Reese enjoyed the meal, it was delicious and she wondered if Sheila was the cook as well as the housekeeper. If so, she had been trained well. She finally felt full after her harrowing last twenty-four hours and with it came the sleepiness. "I'm going to go to bed," she announced as she saw the sun had actually set. As she got up she was pleasantly surprised to see the men all hastily stand out of respect and she nodded to them all as she wished them, "Good night," before heading out of the kitchen for the stairs.

"What was that about," one of the men asked Sheila once they heard her on the stairs.

"She ate with us," Sheila shrugged as though it was no big deal but they all knew it *was* a big deal.

They all exchanged glances. This was unheard of. She was the station manager. She was up there with the owners. She was a woman!

CHAPTER 31

The astonishment continued to grow as Reese met the various employees. She was proven wrong as everyone who lived on the station apparently worked there in some capacity. There was an aborigine village in back of the house down a few hundred yards away on the creek. When Reese first saw it as she was being shown about by a cousin of Sheila's her first thought was abject poverty. Then she realized they were all pretty much wearing trappings of Western clothing but chose instead to live in these huts. The barns proved to be in good condition and the few boards and tiles that needed replacing were attended to as soon as Reese noted it. Going over the books Reese was surprised the place wasn't more profitable and then determined that the last two owners had kept the place merely as a hobby and the last couple of decades had set a precedence she was going to have to change.

Meeting the range men she was met with incredulous stares and outright hostility at her ability to manage the station. Reese watched several of the men as they worked around the home yard and choosing an old man who had been around forever she began to ask his advice. First he was flattered at her attention and then he admired that she had the guts to admit when she didn't know something. He began to help and advise her.

One of the first things Reese coordinated was the ordering of supplies. They were shipped in by lorry or in American words by truck and she found a great disparity in what had been done in the past and what she now wanted to implement. She began buying in bulk where she could and sought out new suppliers. The telephone poles she had noted on her way in through the hills kept them in contact with the world and her computer was soon busy finding her information from suppliers to how to milk a cow. She sent reports to Lady Emerson who she suspected didn't care in the least as long as it didn't cost her any more money and perhaps at a later date she could sell the property. Reese intended that she get the maximum for her husband's win.

Reese noticed there was a lot of lying around and jawing done about the place. A distinct lack of work was what she noted. Ordering gallons of paint she soon cajoled and ordered those she saw sitting around to paint first the house and then the barns and then finally the outer buildings. A lot of complaints could be heard but she silenced them when she told the complainers they could leave the station any time they didn't want to work. She herself could be seen in her 'off' time planting rose bushes and other plants in the now defunct gardens on the east side of the house.

The air of neglect around the home paddock was soon an era of the past as she had even youngsters as young as eight painting the fences that she had the men repairing at a record rate. Buying in bulk they soon had piles of building materials around the place that were used in various capacities. No more would she allow the fences and gates to lie as though a good wind would blow them down. Even some of the oldsters who had earned retirement she asked if they cared to pull weeds. The home paddock began to take on the air of a tidy and beautiful place to live. Everyone was taking pride in their work for the first time in a long time.

One of the first problems that arose was when it was time for their 'roundup' and stray cowboys began to come onto the station in search of work. Many had been there before and were astonished at the change to the home paddock. It now looked prosperous and shiny and in many cases new. Word had it on the roads that the new manager was a woman and a looker besides. Until they experienced it themselves the men at first thought the rumors were a joke. Reese's competence and no nonsense approach though won several of them over.

"I won't take orders from no sheila!" one cowboy complained.

Reese walked up to him and said, "Then you won't be working here! Get off the station!"

He thought he had her, using his brute strength in the past he said, "You and whose army?"

Reese flattened him quicker than he could wink. Using karate she had him on his back and rolled him over into the dust face first. Holding his arm high up on his back she threatened to break it whispering menacingly but clearly, "Get off my station before I break your fucking arm!" she told him.

The silence in the gathered men was alarming. No one had ever heard her swear much less seen her move. The man she had downed was twice her size and towered her by several inches despite her own height. He was helpless though as she let his face churn in the dust beneath him. Her obvious use of moves they hadn't expected showed she was certainly able to handle the man. Sheila who happened to be there watched her with her glittering black eyes thoughtfully.

"Okay, okay, I'll go!" he said through clenched teeth.

Reese released him to let him get up and turned to the others, "Anyone else have a problem?"

Something in Sheila's eyes told Reese she shouldn't have turned her back on her antagonist and she crouched suddenly as he swung at her from behind. His blow never landed and instead he swung around in a circle. Instinctively she reacted and before he realized it he had a broken jaw and several broken ribs. Reese looked down at her would be attacker and said, "Now that was stupid!" Looking up at the others she said, "Take this pile of shit to the nearest doctor and dump him off. If the constable wants to talk to me I'll be out riding." With that she went to the nearest horse and mounted up.

Reese liked the Australian saddles much more than the English ones she had become used to. They were like a cross between Western and English saddles and allowed a working cowboy to do his work in comfort. She rode towards the mustering grounds and hailed her foreman. One of the Aborigines he smiled when he saw her approaching. Sheila had advised her on hats and she wore one with the snaps up and the chin strap tight under her chin. Her only sign of frivolity was that it was a bright red color. The employees had grinned when they saw it but Sheila had smiled when she advised Reese on what kind of hat to get, she hadn't said what color. Reese had the same hat in a pretty blue color as well.

Her boots were the high leather ones she had worn in England when riding with Veronica. They went to her knees and protected her when she rode through the brush or in case a snake might decide to bite. Having been advised that five of the most deadly snakes in the world resided in Australia she thought she should keep these boots and wondered if she should wear higher ones. She settled on chaps. Long gone was the fashion plate days as she settled into wearing jeans daily and cowboy shirts which she frequently stripped off to wear just her spaghetti strapped muscle shirts. The tan she acquired from the Australian sun only enhanced her blonde beauty. Her hair was nearly white despite her wearing her hats. It was longer too as she couldn't get it cut as frequently or as stylishly as she once had.

"How goes the count?" she asked Peter.

He grinned, she was the best boss they had had here in a long time and he adored her. Sheila had sung her praises for months and the entire Aborigine community was 100% behind her. It was only the whites who occasionally resented her not only for being a woman but for her lack of knowledge. "The count she goes up, she goes down," he laughed.

Reese laughed with him. They were getting rid of a lot of the older stuff based on the recommendation of Barney the older stockman she had befriended. She looked around and exchanged a wave and smile with the old man who was watching the proceedings from a buggy instead of the back of a horse. His rheumatism bothered him too much to manage to get into the saddle these days and he told Reese someday he would be back with these 'youngsters' in the saddle. She had found the buggy in back of one of the barns and along with a couple of the men put it back into working order for the older man who appreciated her consideration for his age and rheumatism.

"Is it possible to bring in more of the brumbies and dunnocks?" she asked.

Peter looked at her in surprise, "There is a man we could hire that does that, few of them men we got know how to track them," he told her.

"Fine, hire him. I want a clean sweep of the station," Reese told him.

"The entire station?" he asked alarmed.

Reese grinned, "Should keep him busy for months." She knew how big the station was now that she had been here for months. The rainy season was due and she was getting rid of all the older and more dangerous steers and cows. She wanted young stuff that although hard to manage would at least have more of a chance to survive in this environment. She also wanted all the bulls off the station as they were dangerous and she wanted to bring in new stock for a breeding program. Having remembered what she learned working for Lord Cavandish and listening to not only his stockmen but the other 'gentlemen farmers' she knew a lot more than anyone would give her credit for.

The dust cloud around the valley where they were holding this herd was enough to choke you and Reese put on her bandanna. She had a slew of these too now thanks to Sheila's advice. They were becoming good friends and the woman of a culture that Reese had no concept of and the woman of culture who had studied and gone to college one would think had nothing in common and instead found each other fascinating and knowledgeable. They were learning a lot from each other and both enjoyed the mutually respectful friendship that had formed.

Reese rode on to the hills above the mustering ground and out of the dust cloud and looked out at the vast land she was coming to love. It was so huge and the lands that the Cavandish Estates encompassed could have gone inside this many times over. You could ride for days in either direction and still be on the station. It boggled the mind. There were several micro-climates that Reese had discovered as she rode around by horse and when possible in the Rover. She looked over at a dust cloud west of the ground and determined someone was bringing in more cattle. Branding, shots, and in some cases castration and butchering would be the result. The count was important if they were going to continue this operation. Already she had spent thousands of pounds on the improvements around the place.

She looked south and could see where a well was even now being drilled. They needed as much water as possible as there was no guarantee that the reservoir would fill from the rainy season. They needed to keep as much water on the land as possible to keep the graze for the stock. The wild cattle or dunnocks couldn't be allowed to continue to roam; they spread disease and ate badly needed grass. They also tore up fences and as in the case of Lord Emerson killed men. The wild horses too or brumbies were a menace and she had heard that some station owners were shooting them on sight. Although she found them beautiful she felt capturing them and selling them might be the better answer. She knew Mustangs had been rounded up for years and either given away or sold. She wouldn't sell them to the dog food companies, she shuddered at that thought.

CHAPTER 32

She had been there for months when one day the mail came and she was surprised to receive several invitations to other stations. The traveling cowboys or stockmen had spread tales of the new station manager far and wide. If the tales sounded a little far-fetched the other owners and managers would determine that themselves. Already the tale of her breaking the jaw and ribs of one insubordinate stockman had been exaggerated. His stay in hospital though told its own tale. They were curious of course and the fact that she was supposedly striking made many of them anxious to meet her. Now that roundup or mustering was over they had time before the busy rainy season to socialize.

Reese realized these stations were many days distant from their own and she couldn't 'just' ride the Rover over. She was expected to fly in and stay a couple of days for the parties. She knew she had the clothes to fit into any society but strangely she didn't want to go. Their station didn't own a plane and the problem was solved when the owners included in their invitations an offer to 'pick her up' with their own planes. She was trapped and knew she couldn't turn the offers down. She prepared herself for a busy few weeks.

Rick Jamieson almost died when Greg opened the door and a leggy tanned blonde got out of the Rover. Having been told the new station manager over at Wahbaing Station was a woman and an attractive woman he had been curious of course, who wouldn't be, but the reality of it staggered him. She gathered her overnight bag and swung it effortlessly over her shoulder as she walked towards the plane on their runway. "Hello, I'm Reese Paulson," she held out her hand to Rick.

He shook it automatically not sure where his brain was but knowing he would drool if he wasn't careful. "Rick Jamieson," he squeaked out.

"Oh, you own Shangri-La," she smiled remembering the invitation.

"Yes, my family has owned it for over a hundred years," he smiled thinking, *wow.*

"Shall we be off?" she asked as she waved to Greg who was watching Jamieson with amused eyes.

Rick helped her into the plane admiring the long legs that showed beneath the white dress she was wearing. She tucked her bag behind her seat before putting on the shoulder and waist belt. Rick handed her a set of earphones and she carefully placed them on as well and they were ready to be off. He checked his gauges and did his pre-flight before letting out the levers and they were soon off. Reese realized this plane was a lot less complicated than the jet she had arrived in. There were fewer gadgets and gages to confuse her and she could watch and observe what Rick did, it didn't look difficult.

Reese talked with Rick about his station and he was delighted and amazed at her knowledge. He was surprised to find she had sold off all of their older cattle, steers, bulls, and cows. She explained they were bringing in several bulls of a higher quality breed.

"We breed those as well, would you be interested in buying some bulls?" he asked.

Reese smiled and all thoughts left his head again, "I wish I had known one of our neighbors had them instead of sending away five-hundred miles for what we needed. They are on their way and should arrive by next week," she told him. "If we need more though it's nice that you are a bit closer" she smiled but they both laughed, closer still involved a bit of travel.

She even had an amazing voice he thought. She was really going to put their small society on its ear. Woman were going to be jealous of her good looks, and men were going to make themselves go crazy. When they find she has a good mind too they are going to be astonished. If I weren't married....he thought.

They landed on a small black airstrip. The tarmac made it a much smoother landing than the dirt airstrip at Wahbaing Station. A Hummer was parked at the end of the strip and after carefully parking the plane under an immense hanger and tying it down they got into the oversized SUV and were soon on their way. It was a brisk ten minute drive and they were soon pulling up in front of a long ranch style house. It didn't have the elegance or prestige of Wahbaing Station but it had its own simplistic beauty with vines crawling up each of the columns supporting the wide porch where people were gathered.

There was silence as Rick let her out of the Hummer. Soon murmurs could be heard as Reese walked with him up to the porch. A small oriental woman freed herself from the group and came up to Reese with her hand outstretched, "I'm Maddy Jamieson, Rick's wife."

Reese shook her hand and smiled. Several men went week at the knees. "Let me show you to your room to freshen up," Maddy told her and led her past the staring groups and into the house.

They passed into a long hallway and through a kitchen to another hallway at the back of the house where she was led into a green carpeted bedroom. Dumping Reese's case on the bed Rick touched his hat and backed out of the room. Reese went to the mirror hanging over the dresser and finger combed her hair as Maddy watched.

"You're certainly not what anyone out here was expecting," she understated.

Reese grinned, "I know, I've surprised everyone all my life." The twinkle in her eyes though warmed Maddy's heart. She too had always surprised people. They didn't know what to do with her oriental features.

Taking Reese's arm in hers she said, "Come on, let's shock them," as she led her back out to the porch.

Reese did shock people time and again. First of all that she was an American, secondly that she was an attractive woman with a brain, thirdly that she was running Wahbaing Station and competently from what people said. The list went on and on. Several single station owners made overt passes at her but she laughed them off and still managed to charm them.

She did have to lock her bedroom door she found as one drunken man tried to sneak in her room that evening. Apparently the story about the stockman she had put in hospital was true and this was proven when she sent the drunk staggering into the wall across the hall from her room and knocked him out. "I'm sorry, I just wanted to get him to leave," she cringed as the story came out. Everyone joined in on the laughing over this hilarious story. They had tales to tell about this amazing woman.

Overhearing the men talking about the expected flooding Reese listened. Unless they talked to her or asked a direct question she found this to be the best policy. It was still a very male oriented society out here and her presence wasn't always appreciated.

Rick had a bulldozer he wasn't using and Maddy told her about it as she showed off their home paddock. Reese offered to buy it on the spot. Maddy had been surprised of course and when Rick offered to teach one of her men to operate it Reese thanked him but said, "I'll do it," and that was the end of that. He said he would have it trucked over to her station the following week. She told him she would have a check ready and waiting.

Reese definitely made an impression and most of it favorably to those she met at the party. She was due back at another party the following week. The next month she seemed to go from one party to the next before the rainy season stopped a lot of the trips. Instead she was then kept busy dealing with the floods and the stock that got stuck in them. Seeing sheep washed down the creek that was now a river surprised her.

"Damn herders upstream must be trespassing again," she heard one of the stockmen mutter. They sat there on their horses in the rain with the slickers as they watched the level of the creek.

Reese returned to the house worse for wear and soaked. She was cold to the bone and felt like when she was back in Connecticut with the cold and snow. Sheila helped her off with the slicker but Reese refused to take anything else off but her boots before she headed up the stairs. Sheila walked in the bathroom with a stack of towels and dry clothes as Reese stood in the shower and let the steamy water sluice off her tired body. Sheila couldn't help but stare. The shirts that Reese wore were well defined by the tan marks where they ended on her shoulders but the rest of her body was not only perfectly formed but whiter than white. Sheila hastily averted her stare as she indicated the clothes and towels and said, "Here, these are dry," before she quickly got out of the bathroom.

CHAPTER 33

That night the dreams started for her again. Sheila cursed her Aborigine background sometimes. She had premonitions all her life. She had known that the new manager would be a woman and had even dreamed about the blonde except for the face, which had always been vague and unformed. That was why she had felt she had seen Reese before when she met her. Now the dreams were unsettling because they told her things that would eventually cause her great unhappiness. Who was she though to try and change her fate?

As spring began to come into the normally dusty area they lived in Reese was astonished at the transformation that the rains had wrought. Not only had they cut deeply into the earth and caused a lot of damage they had brought the plants to life. Previously dead areas were now lush with their growth that hastily grew and sent off buds and seeds before the hot summer sun would kill it. Reese enjoyed the beauty as she worked with her stockmen. The previous year's bulls had done their job well and the crop of calves was enormous. The new bulls were introduced at various sections of the station to take advantage of the now fertile cows and start their cycle all over again for next year.

Ryan McCormick had been engaged to find dunnocks and brumbies and had brought in several herds of both. He split the profits with Reese and was satisfied with his share. She was thrilled to be getting these pests off the station. Beautiful as they were, they were a nuisance. Every few days stockmen brought in small herds from all over the station that Ryan had found. Time and again the men expressed astonishment that he was finding animals where none should be or could survive. If Reese wasn't certain that they were trucking the animals off the station themselves she would swear he was using the same animals over and over again. They kept some of the better looking cows themselves as well a few of the horses that proved trainable. Steers, bulls, and un-trainable horses had to go. Reese wasn't running a charity and some hard decisions had to be made despite their beauty. Ryan was thrilled with the check she handed him when he came in on one of his few excursions back to civilization before heading back out to find her the wild animals.

Reese was having fun with her new toy the bulldozer. They began repairing the immediate roads around the home paddock before moving out further and even filling in the uneven landing strip. They were getting more visitors these days now that Reese had met quite a few of the surrounding neighbors. It wasn't the good food that brought them they all knew but they were grateful that Reese didn't seem to favor anyone in particular. Planes of all different sizes and shapes now flew onto their landing strip, some more welcome than others. Reese enjoyed listening to most of them but there were always a few that were condescending because she was a beautiful woman and couldn't possibly know how to manage a station much less one of this size. She had already been there nine months, she had been surprised how quickly it went, there was so much work to do and she was doing fine.

She got the men to begin lining some of the more important ditches and roadways with rocks to control the runoff in the next rainy season. They still got occasional showers which made her ask why they planted nothing in this area. The 'it's too hot' answer didn't satisfy her and she was delighted when one of her suitors finally gave her the information she was seeking and they were soon experimenting with their own crops. Crops that seemed to flourish in the heat or grow rapidly enough in a shorter period of time, with the internet Reese found herself studying nights to learn everything she could to make these crops profitable for the station.

A ride with several of their stockmen to the northern boundaries of the station answered the question where the sheep had floated down the river from. Reese met with several of the drovers or sheep herders and spent several hours talking with them. She understood when her stockmen stayed away on principle but she saw no reason why cattlemen and sheepmen couldn't get along. There was room for both and she knew there were stations that ran both. The animals didn't eat the same things and it could be profitable. One of the herders by the name of Johnny promised to come and see her at the station when she mentioned her plan to buy sheep and run them on certain parts of the station.

CHAPTER 34

Reese was walking out one night admiring the sounds of the digeroos that the Aborigines played. She loved the sound which she knew many people didn't. It was wild; it was exotic, and so very foreign from anything she had grown up in Connecticut expecting. How had that little girl come to this?

"Enjoying the night?" Sheila asked from where she was standing watching the blonde.

Reese should have known, never was she really alone on this ranch. There was always someone watching, human or animal. The few nights she had camped out with the stockmen she listened to their stories about dingoes, or wild dogs and had shuddered when she saw one for the first time. Their howls at twilight were eerie but still beautiful despite the menace they posed. She loved the flocks of wild cockatoo's and wild parrots she had seen, they were as prolific as pigeons had been in New York or London. She smiled at the beautiful woman and said, "Yes, it's so beautiful here, you're very lucky to have been born here."

Sheila shrugged; it wasn't like she had had a choice. "One never appreciates what they have until they don't have it anymore."

Reese had to concede she was probably right and for a second Veronica passed her thoughts. As always the shaft that pierced her heart hurt her again. There hadn't been a day in the last nine months that she hadn't thought about Veronica. She needed to move on. She had heard from Lady Emerson that Veronica had married Oscar Wilkins which was what she expected. It didn't hurt any less though.

Sheila watched her with knowing eyes. The devastation that was on her face when she arrived had faded as she tanned from the sun. The agony in her eyes though hadn't gone and while she often wondered at it she would never impose on their friendship to ask about it. She moved a little closer to say, "It won't be long and the nights will be too hot to walk out like this."

Reese couldn't imagine it. It was so lush and beautiful right now. She had arrived when everything was dead and dry. Now the creeks ran full and the grass grew long. Her cattle grew fat on it. Things were looking a lot better than when she had arrived. "I look forward to seeing every season," she smiled down at the striking Aborigine barely able to make out her features in the firelight that the Aborigines danced around. She watched them silently for a while.

"Each season is different and yet the same," Sheila said mysteriously as she watched the Anglo.

"I imagine one could say that about everyplace. The land here is so different."

"Some say God put the leftovers here in Australia," Sheila commented.

"Or maybe God started here in Australia and decided to try something different elsewhere. Maybe we should be looking for Eden instead of the leftovers," she smiled again at her philosophical statement.

Sheila turned to her and asked, "Do you believe in God?"

Reese turned to look down at her and noted the fine features. She was a beautiful woman in her own right. "Yes, I believe there is a God. A higher power as it were. I don't believe in organized religion though so I probably wouldn't be welcome in any so called church. How about you, do you believe in God?" she turned her head to the side as she asked the question of her friend.

Sheila found the way she turned her head to be endearing, "Yes, I believe in a higher power. I think though I am more spiritual than religious. I have heard from priests, I have heard from shamans. I think between the two I have a belief that is good for my soul. I know he tells me often enough."

"He tells you?" Reese asked surprised.

Sheila nodded looking at her intensely as she drew ever closer wondering if Reese was even aware of it as she stalked her. "God gave me the ability to see things. He frequently shows me things for my soul."

"You are clairvoyant?" Reese asked in no way shocked, instead she sounded intrigued.

Sheila nodded. "He told me you would come here."

"Anything else?" she asked.

Sheila nodded again as she looked deeply into Reese's eyes. "Yes, many things. Some of which I cannot tell you because you might try to change your fate."

Reese felt herself drowning in the black eyes. She gasped just before Sheila kissed her. Reese found herself kissing her back almost desperately. She held on for dear life as she took Sheila in her arms. A normally passionate woman she had denied herself for so long in penance for what she had done to Veronica. Not that she really had the inclination or the opportunity before. She pushed thoughts of Veronica away as she kissed this beautiful woman in her arms.

She is a very good kisser thought Sheila as she enjoyed herself. The feel of the tall blonde against her was welcome and she enjoyed that as well. The caresses through her shirt weren't enough as the kiss deepened. Sheila wanted to take her here and now but knew this wasn't the right time and definitely not the right place and reluctantly pulled back.

Reese held onto her like a life preserver. Where had that come from? She was panting as she leaned her forehead against Sheila's. She found herself beginning to cry and Sheila held her as she comforted her. "Shh, it's okay, shhh, babé it's okay," Sheila crooned. Reese swallowed hard to stop the sobs that wanted to break out. She had cried almost nightly for the first few months she had been here. Enough was enough. She had to move on. This wonderful woman seemed to understand though and Reese just let herself be held as they stood there beyond the firelight. No one seemed to see them as they stood off to one side. Reese finally swallowed and pulled herself together and then she just stared in astonishment at the beautiful dusky woman before her.

Sheila couldn't help but grin. It was hard when you knew what was going to happen not to become non-challant about it. It was totally different when you were surprised by it. Reese was definitely surprised. Sheila never was.

Slowly she released Reese and whispered, "Come," before heading back towards the house. Reese shook herself and followed wondering where this would lead.

CHAPTER 35

Veronica was devastated. This was worse than when her parents had died. Was this worse than the after effects of the rape? She wasn't sure; she just knew she was mourning. She couldn't follow Reese, she couldn't find her. She was not in Bangkok she had already had an investigator find out for her. What she didn't know was that David had also paid him and instructed him not to find Reese elsewhere.

First David and then Audrey consoled her but she was inconsolable. She loved and hated Reese by turns. She went around numb for weeks. David finally insisted she help him 'manage' the properties since he couldn't find a manager to replace Reese. She found solace in doing the books and did the work Reese had taught her almost automatically. Her only interest these days was her horses. Oscar could help her with that interest but she was oblivious to his courting. She had no idea that was what he was doing.

Only to Ana could she pour out her heartache. She understood. She listened regardless of what Veronica told her. She didn't judge or try to convince her otherwise as David did. Audrey was so self-absorbed that she couldn't comprehend the love that Veronica still felt for Reese. In all actuality though Audrey was jealous that such love existed and cursed Reese silently with the secret she had sworn her to. She wanted a happily ever after for her friend and couldn't give her it.

David seemed to take a more active role in the management of their estates but in all actuality he left it up to Veronica. He advised, he directed, but she made most of the decisions whether she was aware of it or not. As he led her she didn't realize how much of an active role he was playing in her life until she found herself engaged to Oscar. She began to come out of her fog as the plans were made for their lavish wedding but by then it was too late, the invitations had been sent, she couldn't back out without causing them extreme embarrassment. She began to have panic attacks at the thought of actually going to bed with Oscar. Audrey tried to help her but Veronica was freaking out. As the invitations were already sent and already all the plans laid she couldn't seem to find a way to back out of her fate. She didn't realize that her fate had been manipulated by those around her. How had it come to this?

Oscar hadn't even kissed her and as the wedding day approached she found herself more and more frightened at what she had gotten herself into. She felt trapped. Even at the wedding she went through the motions mechanically, automatically. The perfunctionary kiss at the ceremony was no more than she would expect from even her brother. The thought of what this night would bring was bringing on her fears and anxiety. She looked an ethereal bride to everyone as she stood there accepting the congratulations. She looked at Audrey who was her maid of honor with fear and Audrey could do nothing but stand by her.

That night as they got ready for bed Veronica didn't know what to do, what to say to Oscar. How could she tell him that she couldn't go through with this farce of a marriage? He couldn't touch her? How were they going to have children as they were expected to if she didn't let him touch her in that way? She shuddered with distaste at the thought. Why had Reese left her to this?

"Are you coming to bed?" Oscar asked as he watched her sit in fear in the sitting room of their suite. They were at the Savoy for the beginning of their honeymoon. After a long day of the wedding and the reception Oscar was tired.

Veronica shook her head. How could she go into that bed with him and do what was expected of a woman? How could she let him?

"What's wrong Veronica?" he asked as he came to sit on the couch with her. He noticed her slightly cringe and pull away. It angered him.

"I can't, I can't do what you expect me to do," she told him glancing at him and quickly looking down.

"What do you think I expect," he said with amusement.

"To let you fuck me," she told him crudely not knowing how else to put it. It certainly wasn't making love. She didn't love him. Reese had taught her what love and making love were.

He was surprised that the little mouse he had married could use such language. He looked at her contemplating what she meant. Legally he could do almost anything he wanted but in this day and age he didn't want the hassle. There were other more willing females to be had by just asking. She was his wife though and while he didn't love her she at least owed him an explanation. "So why don't you want me to fuck you?" he answered just as crudely which seemed to shock her.

"I can't..." she stammered visibly cringing at the thought.

"Why can't you?" he persisted.

"The thought of a man touching me that way just..." she closed her eyes at the images that had happened ten years ago.

"Just a man?" he asked astutely.

"Anyone," she quickly lied instinctively knowing no one must ever know about Reese.

"May I ask why?" he asked waiting for her answer.

"I was raped ten years ago, the thought of anyone touching me...." she got out fearfully.

It explained a lot. Why this woman was unspoken for all these years. Well, he hadn't married her for her body. He looked her over and thought he had horses that were more desirable. It was her land and horses that had attracted him in the first place. That she was a fairly decent conversationalist had led him to believe that marriage to her wouldn't be too bad. "So, why didn't you say anything before the wedding?" he demanded angrily.

"I couldn't..." she stammered, "I just couldn't and things rolled along I just couldn't..." she finished lamely.

"This is a hell of a situation you'vc put us in!" he told her definitely annoyed.

"I know, I know, if you want to annul the marriage, I will certainly understand it," she told him relieved at getting that out.

"There will be no annulment and no divorce, ever! Do you understand me?" he thundered.

No one yelled at Veronica and she cringed at the volume much more than at the words. Nodding mutely she shivered.

"Christ, our family has never had a divorce or an annulment and I'll be damned if I am the first. I won't be made a laughingstock either." He looked over Veronica with distaste. The thought of raping *that* didn't appeal in the slightest and he did feel a little sorry for her and what had happened all those years ago. She should get over it though. "I'm going to bed, I don't want anyone and I mean anyone to know that we aren't fucking each other's brains out. Do you understand me?" he stood over her to emphasize his words. Once she nodded he went to the bedroom and slammed the door.

She jumped as she heard the door slam and grabbing a throw from the back of the couch she curled up in the blanket and her traveling dress that she was still wearing and tried to sleep. The tears she shed made it difficult. She had shed a lot of them over the last six months. Reese, why did *you* leave *me*?

CHAPTER 36

Their married life got off to a bad start but Oscar was enjoying himself. He had a cutie over in Cutsbourough as well as another one in London. They frequently used the London flat to entertain and here at least Veronica was useful. She knew all the right people and Oscar liked that. It reflected well on him. He could brag that his family was now part of Cavandish House. His own name while a good one wasn't nearly as prestigious as theirs. He had married up. He liked living on Cavandish Estates and enjoying the fruits of someone else's labor. Incorporating his own properties into Cavandish Estates took almost no effort and even if Veronica was the one managing it all he didn't care. Although he had been successful in business or so everyone thought it was really from having eavesdropped on other's conversations that he had been so astute and successful. He didn't bother to pursue other business opportunities now that he had the brass ring, what was the point when the Cavandish Estates could support him in the lifestyle he felt he was entitled to?

After a few months though people began to ask when they would be having children and this began to bother him. He came home one day from a particularly bad game of polo where one of the fellow players had bragged about getting his wife pregnant on their wedding night and he realized he hadn't even had any relations with his own wife! How in the hell were they going to have children if they didn't have sex?

The suite that Veronica and he had moved into after the wedding was on the opposite side of the house from her brothers. They had complete privacy and separate bedrooms with a sitting room between them. He sat and waited for his wife as they would make an appearance at dinner and he knew she would come to change. Veronica was surprised he was ready and waiting for her as she hurried in from the office where she had been managing the books.

"I'll be ready in a minute," she called to him as she hurried to her bedroom. She was surprised when he followed her.

"I want to talk to you," he said ominously.

Veronica always treated him cordially and friendly. She didn't want hostilities between them. She wanted the friendship they had before their marriage but that had all changed on their wedding night. She looked up at him but not with the fear she had on their wedding night. Being home and remembering who she was had erased that fear.

"About what?" she asked wearily. This marriage was not what she had wanted or expected and the amount of work it engineered adding his estates and workload to her own was exhausting.

"I want to know how the hell you expect us to have children if you continue this 'poor little rape girl' routine?" he asked brutally.

Veronica was astonished with the question and how he had worded it. It was disgusting and implying she was faking her feelings was demeaning, but then that was what he had planned. She became angry. "Have you ever heard of invitro-fertilization?" she asked.

"You expect me to fuck a cup?" he asked incredulously.

She stared him down and she knew the minute his anger had gone too far. As he approached her she reacted instinctively. She would never be a victim again thanks to Reese and Juan. She was in a set stance when he raised his hand to strike her and he was soon on the floor yelping.

"What the hell?" he shrieked at her as she backed away watching him warily.

"Don't you ever raise your hand to me again!" she told him in a vicious voice.

He looked at her amazed, he had never seen her look like this much less sound like that. Rolling to get on his feet his face scrunched up in its anger. He started towards her again, she waited for him to make the move, once he raised his hand he found himself slammed against the wall, he bounced off a door jamb and found himself on his butt. He stared at her in astonishment having never expected this of the mouse.

"I warned you, next time I'll break it," she warned.

He slowly got to his feet and straightened out his clothes before walking silently from her room. Veronica quickly changed her clothes so she could go down to dinner. Inside she was quaking in fear for what she had done, her fingers shook in response, but mentally she was telling herself he had deserved it.

CHAPTER 37

Their behavior to each other was so cordial it set your teeth on edge David thought as he watched his sister and her husband. He knew they couldn't possibly love each other. There was none of the warmth he had seen even with Reese. The friendship they had before the marriage was even gone. He wondered when it had all gone so very wrong. He had just wanted his sister healthy and happy and in a normal relationship. He was never so relieved when dinner was over and he could use his walking sticks to go into the family room to watch television. Even this though he could not enjoy as Oscar began to talk about the latest horse he had seen that he wanted to buy. He must have felt it was up to David to buy it the way he talked. David had absolutely no interest in horses. "You should discuss this with Veronica," he subtly suggested but to no avail.

The tension between the two lovebirds increased over the coming weeks. Finally Oscar waited for her again to 'discuss' their future. When Veronica entered the suite she had a terrible sense of de-ja-vu and worried that they were going to have a repeat of their previous fight.

"I want to talk to you," Oscar blustered in the annoying way he had developed.

"So talk, I need to change for dinner," she informed him.

"I want you to go to see a Dr. Klein over in Westchester. He will perform the invitro, I have already donated," he informed her as though the whole thing had been decided.

Veronica stared at him dumbfounded. They had a casual conversation said in the heat of anger and she was expected to spread her legs for a strange doctor to pour her husband's sperm into her womb? The very thought was repugnant. Rather than fight about it though she nodded briefly and went into her room. She thought about it a lot over the next few days and realized if she ever wanted a child this would be the only way. Swallowing her distaste over the entire subject she found Dr. Klein and made an appointment in Westchester.

A nurse who couldn't care less about the answers to all the questions that Veronica answered took the details. Dr. Klein was a nice little man who Veronica felt comfortable with. He explained exactly what the procedure would involve. He also cautioned her about the possibility of multiples with this procedure. He was thorough and knowledgeable and he made her relax. She listened attentively and in her mind she was comparing it to what she had done on her stud farm. It was all very clinical and modern. She couldn't help but wonder why she was going through with it but then realized there was no other choice if she wanted children.

They figured out her most 'fertile' times and scheduled an appointment for the next time to implant her husband's sperm. She recoiled at the idea but swallowed the distaste that arose from the notion. Why was she here? Where had her life gone so terribly wrong? As she lay on the table after the examination she wondered these thoughts and many more. Her life was one big drudge. Reese had made the management of the properties seem so much fun always looking forward to the next big adventure. Challenges never threw her instead she met them head on. Reese....she had been Veronica's last bit of happiness in a lifetime of unhappiness. Veronica still cried when she thought of the loss of the one person she had loved other than her brother in her whole life. Yes she adored Audrey but loved, not like what she had felt for Reese. Would she ever see her again? Love another like she had loved Reese? She still 'practiced' when the need grew too great and it was always Reese that she dreamed of to make her cum, but it wasn't the same by any stretch of the imagination. Damn her, why did *she* leave *me*?

Lying on the table after the procedure Veronica couldn't help but think over her life and compare it. She thought a lot these days, she couldn't help it. She thought about what this child would look like, what it would mean. She already realized that it would not only be Oscar's heir but David's as well. David's decision to never marry and sire his own heirs she understood. What she hated was that she had become the sacrificial lamb. She wondered if Reese had been aware of her brother's plans for her. Of course she had! It was why she had left! That was the only thing that now made sense. Veronica almost got up off the table where she lay when she realized this but then lay back as she had been instructed to 'relax' a word she had come to hate. Reese had loved her, she was certain of that. The need to achieve her 'goals' had been a made up story in Veronica's best interests. She wondered if David had 'told' Reese of his plans. No, that wasn't his style. He would have subtly hinted at what he wanted and Reese being as astute as she was would have figured things out and done what was best for them. Veronica would never have let her go. She hated the way the last few weeks had been. She had sensed something was wrong. She had clung. Reese had been right to leave her so abruptly or Veronica would have found a way to keep her there. She had disappeared so well that the private investigator had not been able to locate her in Bangkok. Veronica often wondered if she had gone back to America. She didn't want to be found and Veronica had to learn to live with that.

CHAPTER 38

Veronica took it easy over the next couple weeks until they could determine if she was pregnant. She didn't give up her daily rides and this annoyed Oscar no end. He wanted the stables to himself feeling as a man he was more knowledgeable than her. She kept her knowledge to herself knowing she knew more than he could hope to. She also found herself feeling spiteful towards him and wanting to show him up which she did occasionally, always when he was sounding off about something to someone with his 'superior' knowledge. Lady Cavandish or rather Lady Wilkins as she was now known was a knowledgeable woman regarding horseflesh and the upcoming foals she had from her stud farm would fetch high prices. Oscar had to content himself with the feeling of being associated with something so important if not an actual part of it to a degree. Those less knowledgeable bought his superiority routine. Others merely put up with the annoying man because they wished to get to know Veronica better.

The first implantation was not successful and Veronica tried not to get her hopes up as she went through the procedure again and then again. When the pregnancy test came up blue she wanted to scream it to the heavens but instead made an appointment to be 'formally' tested. When those results came back positive as well she was over the moon. She was pregnant! She wanted to share it with everyone. At the same time the doctor cautioned her to wait until she was at least three months along. Veronica began to glow immediately, at least mentally and then physically. Her attitude about everything began to change. She understood how Reese had gotten satisfaction out of her work now and made it fun. She had been happy and now Veronica understood so much more.

"What is up with you these days?" Audrey asked one day as they met for lunch.

Veronica shrugged and then smiled, "I'm just feeling better these days. I've gotten out of that funk I was in for so long."

"Are things better with Oscar?" Audrey asked amazed.

Veronica's face clouded at the mention of her husband, "No, he's still a pig, but he doesn't matter. I've just decided that I should be happy, and I'm working at it for me."

Audrey suspected there was more but she wasn't going to rain on her friend's parade. She glowed. She *seemed* happier, and if it was pretend for now perhaps later it would be for real. She wanted to ask her if she had put Reese behind her but knowing how painful that subject was she just didn't dare. She briefly wondered if Veronica had met someone else but then who could that be? She enjoyed her lunch immensely with her friend, much more so than she had in ages.

CHAPTER 39

As they entered Reese's room she found herself practically thrown up against a wall. Her karate instincts wanted her to fight back but instead the balled up passion inside of her exploded. She instead grabbed Sheila and pulled her close, both fighting to get each other's clothes off before Sheila roughly plunged her fingers inside her welcoming body. There was no finesse, there was no tenderness, there was just raw need and both of them welcomed it. It was a little pain filled, but at the same time the intensity took both of their breaths away, and they both needed it. As Reese jerked against her time and again she couldn't help but briefly compare it to the tenderness she had known with Veronica. Sheila saw the shadow cross her eyes and distracted her by taking her again. The sheer need that they both had, Sheila to possess, Reese to be possessed proved that they were well matched. By the time they made it to the bed they were both sweaty and had cum several times.

"How did you know?" Reese gasped as they lay side by side in the sheets.

Sheila turned towards her and smiled, a perfect whiteness against the coppery color of her skin. In fact she draped herself across Reese for the color contrast that appealed to her so. She felt the need again begin inside her and wondered if something had come over her that she had to possess this white woman. "Are you asking how did I know you needed that or how did I know you were into women?"

Reese chuckled, she was feeling so relaxed and so replete and yet a madness was building inside of her again and she didn't even try to tamp it down. "Both?" she answered.

"I sensed it, nothing less would do for us this time. And I figured out when every male within a hundred kilometers hit on you and if you didn't hit back you must be a woman's woman. You were flattered, you even flirted back to a degree to pick their brains, but no sexual chemistry, none. I've enjoyed our friendship but you were always careful to not get too close, not indicate an interest, and yet I knew."

"Your sixth sense?" Reese asked still not entirely convinced of Sheila's intuitive powers.

"You could call it that. My dreams told me we would be together and it would be good. Who am I to change the fates?"

Reese laughed at her but at the same time she believed her. She knew there was more to life than what she could see. Sheila did have amazing perception. If she was dreaming their fate then who was Reese to change it. A small part of her let Veronica go at that moment and she was happy about it. She rolled herself on top of Sheila and they made fierce and intense love to each other until quite early in the morning.

Sheila watched the blonde beauty sleep. It is so unfair that life brought her into my sphere and I *cannot* keep her. I am just a part of her passage. I am her healing balm. Her soul was so tortured when she got here. She shut that part of herself off for so long. I am going to hurt so badly when she goes. I have her for now though, she's mine as I am hers.

CHAPTER 40

As their second year on the station came to a close Reese could look about the place and feel pride in what they had accomplished. They now had superior cattle as well as horses being bred and producing and more recently she had allowed flocks of sheep in their northern paddocks. Her attempts to fence off as much of the place as possible while met with resistance initially provided jobs when before they had people loafing about all the time. She never could abide people being paid to do nothing. She felt she was missing something though yet. It would come to her eventually but she still couldn't put her finger on it yet. Sheila would say she was developing her sixth sense. She didn't know if that were so but she knew something else was on her horizon.

She looked at how well maintained the home paddock was and was proud. She herself had wielded a shovel, a rake, and a hammer from time to time. Even the 'shacks' that the Aborigine villagers lived in were cleaner now, they still had chickens pecking about under their huts but the huts were painted and some had beautiful trim. Reese had made sure they had boards to improve their homes and it was with a sense of pride that they painted them beautiful colors using every color of the rainbow. Reese loved to walk down there now, many times accompanied by Sheila, her good friend. No one suspected that the housekeeper and the station manager at Wahbaing Station were lovers. They kept it discrete and if occasionally their eyes met only they knew what they were thinking.

Reese hadn't been to the 'city' in two years. Her hair was a lot longer now and suited her tall blonde looks. Despite wearing her funny hats as Sheila called them she was tanned very dark by the blazing sun that shone most of the year here. Reese had come to love this land and many of the other station owners and managers were amazed that this 'city' girl from the America's had adapted so quickly and so well. Reese could ride, she could manage, and she could even shoot now thanks to the stockmen who patiently taught her. She didn't mind sweating and getting dirty and would try almost any job on the station that a man would do. As a result she was hated, loved, respected, and her every command was followed. She had proven she could stand up for herself and any man who didn't like it soon found his walking papers. The fact that she had sent one man to the hospital wasn't discounted. Her legend was growing and many loved her for it. She was also sought after by every single man in the region. While friendly and outgoing she didn't allow liberties and a rumor began that she had a broken heart back in England. Reese suspected Sheila of planting that one.

The haunting beauty of the outback and its immense dimensions did not frighten Reese. She thrived on it. Sheila taught her to respect Australia and its mysticism's. The Aborigines appreciated her interest into their culture and while she wasn't included in all their events she sat by their fires often enough that she was accepted. Many was the time that the manager was sought and found in the village with children climbing all over her lap and the contrast between their dark skins and her white skin was remarked on. Aborigine children had blonde hair that turned dark later in life and the blonde against her white blonde was interesting to see. While some of the stockmen didn't approve of associating with the 'coloreds' as some of them put it Reese didn't even see it. She enjoyed the children; she enjoyed the elders and their stories, their wisdom couldn't be discounted and she learned a lot from just listening.

Reese spent an almost equal amount of time in the campfires of her stockmen and their wives. She had converted one of the empty stockmen's houses into a kind of meeting place where they could all sit and relax, enjoy a beer or two, she even managed to find a pool table, a jukebox, and pinball games as well as a few arcade games that they all enjoyed. The 'colored' stockmen were welcome but rarely did they bring their wives. The white stockmen were expected to bring their families and their wives. Reese made it clear that drunkenness and coarse language were not acceptable under any circumstances and that a family atmosphere was what she wanted promoted. It brought a sense of camaraderie that had been lacking before in this male dominated society. The single men found they enjoyed seeing the children playing around the place and it gave everyone an alternative to sitting in the bunkhouses and just watching the television. When Australia managed to go to the World Cup Reese even imported a large screen television and put it outside with chairs lined up like a movie theater and they all watched the football games together until Australia lost. Then Reese arranged for movies to be sent in and anyone who wanted could watch them under the Southern Cross. There was nothing like the feel of watching a movie in the outdoors under that big sky. When weather forced them to put the television inside it was never quite the same and they all looked forward to better weather.

CHAPTER 41

Hey Mom,

I did it. I'm going to graduate from Cambridge with my master's in English Literature and History! Can you come?

Gillian

The email was short and sweet and not unexpected. Reese wasn't sure she wanted to leave. Was she hiding here at the Wahbaing Station? Perhaps. She loved it here and was happy. Sheila made her happy. Sheila often cautioned her though not to get too attached citing her ability to see the future and that someday Reese would have to go. Reese hated that. She immediately made a call to get a plane out of here at the appropriate time and then bought tickets from Sydney to London. Sheila encouraged her to go.

"Is this the end that you have been warning me about?" Reese asked as they lay in each other's arms.

Sheila shook her head, "No, that's not for a while, you still have things to do here."

Reese smiled pleased and relieved that it wasn't over yet. She had faith in Sheila's abilities, she couldn't help that she didn't want to believe her sometimes.

"No, you're not going to see her," Sheila watched as Reese's mind and expression changed momentarily. The shadow crossed her eyes ever so briefly.

Reese looked at her startled. "Gillian?" she asked puzzled for a moment.

Sheila looked at her exasperated. "No, and you know who I am talking about. Don't you think I know she was your love? Don't you think I read you like a book? I am not jealous of who you have loved. It helps to make who you are. I'm just telling you that on this trip you won't see her."

Reese looked at her startled. "Why won't you and I be forever?" she asked instead. Sheila was so good for her, so good to her.

"We are meant for now, for a time. We are not meant forever. Your love is meant for another for all time. She will come back someday, but not this trip, not even the next. You must be patient," Sheila told her wisely.

Reese was startled. How many times had she told Veronica that she 'must be patient' and now Reese was the one that must be patient? She didn't want to be patient. She wanted her life to be set but she knew that Sheila knew a lot more than she did.

The reverse trip from the station to Sydney wasn't so bad this time. The mail plane took her direct as she had been his last pick up. "Going to London?" he asked cordially and Reese launched enthusiastically into an account of her daughter she was so proud of. Not many people knew she had a daughter much less a full grown one graduating with an impressive master's degree from college and from such a prestigious school as Cambridge. The mail carrier would spread the word though while she was gone.

The long flight to London seemed even longer this time but not really. This time she didn't have the intense sorrow accompanying her. Sheila had healed a lot of that for her. She thought a lot about Sheila but she also thought a lot about Veronica as well since she was heading towards her. She respected what Sheila had told her that she wouldn't see Veronica this trip but at the same time she wondered what it would hurt. It had been two years...

As she landed at Heathrow she headed through customs and then went to a car rental counter. She was staying at a modest hotel near Cambridge so she could watch her daughter graduate. She also had meetings with a couple of suppliers that were based here in London with offices out of Sydney as well. Lady Emerson of course was a big priority to meet with for 'tea' and go over the financials at the station which was showing a profit despite the large expenditures that Reese had insisted on. The vague idea that she had had that there was more she could do to make the station pay was still stewing around in her brain.

"Hey baby girl," Reese enveloped Gillian in a big bear hug.

"Mom!" Gillian returned the hug just as hard. Pulling back slightly her eyes opened wide. "Well look at you! Holy cow! What happened down under?" she pulled her mother in from the hallway of her apartment building into her small flat.

Reese looked down at her attire as though she was wearing something wrong having no idea what Gillian was talking about. She looked back up puzzled to her daughter's amusement.

Gillian reached out and yanked the long hair that she was now sporting and said, "I don't think I remember ever seeing you with hair this long goldilocks," she teased, "And look at this tan," she held her own pasty white arm against her mothers and the contrast was remarkable.

Reese grinned, "I do live near the tropics you know," she laughed in relief.

"The look is totally different though. You look younger than you did the last time I saw you!"

Reese was pleased by the compliment. "So what's the plan?" she asked

Gillian launched into the details of her graduation which was much more formal than in the states. Plus the fact that she was graduating with honors and a master's set her apart from anyone with a bachelor's degree. Reese sat back and enjoyed looking at her daughter after two years apart. She loved her so. It was amazing to hear an 'American' accent after years of Australian and British ones. Even some of the slang was welcome. There was a bit of British influence in her daughter's voice though now after two years of studying with other British students. Reese had missed her daughter very much and sat gazing at the youth before her amazed that she was this old, she remembered her as a little girl just growing up and now she was an adult with a Master's degree from Cambridge!

The ceremony was set for the following day and Reese stood there proudly with hundreds of other proud parents and relatives of graduates. The costumes while similar to those in the States made the ceremony seem different. Reese realized it was the British accents during the speeches that made it so, not the actual ceremony. She loved the pomp and circumstances. She cheered when her daughter's name was called and as she was one of the few many people exchanged shocked glances at the beautiful blonde but Reese was so proud she had to let loose. She set precedence as several other parents after her did the same.

Gillian approached her mother with a man at her side. "Mom, I'd like you to meet Steffan Cantwell. Steffan, this is my mother Reese Paulson," she said proudly.

Steffan stared at the woman before him. She was almost as tall as he was but her looks were what astonished him. He had seen pictures of course but the reality of the model sleek woman before him blew his mind. He had always thought Gillian's mother attractive in the pictures he saw with her perfect coif but with the longer hair and the tan, wow. She looked only a few years older than Gillian!

Reese shook his hand totally oblivious to his thoughts but not his looks. He was a tall handsome man and must be the Steffan that Gillian had occasionally mentioned in their phone calls and emails. If he was meeting her now at this moment he must be important. Standing next to her pretty daughter she couldn't help but think they made an attractive couple. He was tall, dark, and handsome and when he smiled two dimples showed up on his cheeks that made him look adorable and dangerous. She fully approved of her daughter's choice, looks wise. She hoped she had time to get to know him.

They went out to dinner to celebrate her daughter's achievement. She found Steffan to be ever the British aristocrat. He was actually Sir Steffan Cantwell she found out and wondered if he was related to the Cantwells near to where she had worked. During the course of dinner it came out that they owned property up there so yes, he was. His father was still alive and hale and hearty so he wouldn't inherit the title or the estates for some years to come but he was studying for his doctorate and wanted to be a pediatrician so he wasn't worried. Reese found him funny and charming.

Reese wasn't what Steffan had expected at all. Not only was she beautiful she had an amazing mind. He had appreciated it in her daughter but he was astonished at her accomplishments and what she was doing she made sound fun even if it was a tremendous amount of work. Looking at her daughter he saw the same bone structure but not the incredible blonde looks. Gillian while very lovely had a more subtle look compared to the striking good looks of her model mother. He felt he preferred the comfortable looks of Gillian and would be intimidated by her mother.

"Are you going to visit the Cavandish Estates?" Gillian asked while Steffan excused himself to use the bathroom.

Reese frowned slightly and shook her head.

"Why not? I thought you loved it there?" Gillian had always wondered at the almost abrupt departure but had believed that the job in Australia was bigger and better.

"I did but that's in my past. I've moved on and I am sure they have as well."

Gillian thought it prudent to change the subject. "So you're happy there?"

Reese got a spark in her eye as she thought about Australia. The first six months or so had been brutal as she threw herself into her work to forget her heartache and to make something of the place. Sheila was a bonus she hadn't considered. "Yes, I love it there and I enjoy the constant challenges."

"Have you met someone?" Gillian asked gently. She had noticed the change in her mother on the phone in the last eighteen months or so but had thought it was the job.

Reese hesitated and then nodded but told her nothing.

"I got the impression you were hurt when you left here and now you seem almost glowing."

Reese grinned; Sheila had helped a lot, first by friendship, and then by loving her.

Gillian had always respected her mother's privacy. She rarely had brought anyone home when she was growing up and for that she was grateful to a degree. She wanted her mother happy but her goals had always been paramount. She had wanted to retire when she attained certain ones. Changing the subject which apparently her mother wasn't going to elaborate on was par for the course, "So have you enough now to retire?"

Reese nodded and almost as if on cue handed her daughter a card.

Gillian looked blankly at the card and before opening it she asked, "You do?"

Reese grinned and nodded again. "Yes, sometime last year I got there."

"Then why don't you retire as you planned?" her daughter asked incredulous. Her first goal had been to be worth a million dollars so she could retire and never work again. If she had achieved that goal then she had no reason to keep working.

"I am having too much fun doing something I love, so I keep going. Aren't you going to open that?" she asked to change the subject indicating the card.

Steffan came back to the table just as Gillian gasped at the check amount in the card. "Mom, you can't afford this..." she trailed off as the tears welled up in her eyes and she leaned over to give her mother a hug.

"Yes baby I can. I hope it helps you start out in your job. How goes the look?" she asked.

"I already have several interviews lined up in the next weeks," she told her mother proudly.

"Here or in the States?" she asked.

Gillian exchanged a look with Steffan before answering, "Here and in Europe, I thought I'd stay around. There really is no reason for me to go back to the States right now."

Reese caught the look and it confirmed how important this young man was to her daughter. She asked her later when she was dropping her off at her flat how important he was.

"Steffan wants to finish in about 2 years and then we will be discussing marriage. Meanwhile I'm going to work with my degrees and see where it takes me. Thank you so much for the check Mom, it will be a buffer until I get a job," she hugged her again.

"Well, be sure to let me know when I need to buy a killer 'mother of the bride' dress." Reese exchanged a delighted smile with her daughter at the thought.

CHAPTER 42

Over the next few days Reese had several meetings in and around London. She hesitated and then decided it was cowardice and called Audrey.

"Hello?" Audrey frowned at her caller identification not recognizing the London number.

"Audrey, it's Reese," she said quietly waiting for her reaction.

"Reese?! Oh, this is marvelous. Are you in England?" she asked excitedly.

Reese smiled at her enthusiasm, "Yes, I'm in London actually. I was hoping to have dinner with you while I'm here. I'm driving up to Lady Emerson's estate for a meeting tomorrow for tea, would you be able to meet me afterwards?"

"I'd love to, where would you like to eat?"

They discussed the details and rang off. Reese looked forward to seeing her old friend. She wished she could call Veronica as well but thought it prudent not to.

"Ah Reese, there you are!" Lady Emerson held out her hand to welcome her.

Reese smiled. She liked this old bird and the freedom she had given her with the job in Australia. She didn't interfere and she certainly didn't complain at the money that Reese had spent.

"You look marvelous," she told her admiring the blonde beauty. She herself had looked this good in her youth but Reese not only looked attractive, she looked healthy. If this is what Australia did for your health she was going to have to visit.

They talked over all the details of the station, repeating a lot of what had been in reports and phone conversations as well as emails. Hearing it in person though gave Lady Emerson a better feeling for the place. Reese had a book of photographs to share with the lady as well and enjoyed explaining the stories behind the snapshots of various places and activities on the place. Lady Emerson loved it; it would give her a lot to talk about and show with her compatriots in the coming months.

"Lady Emerson, I've had an idea for making even more money out at the station if you are interested in hearing my rough idea's?" Reese ventured.

"Oh do tell, you are doing a wonderful job. The sheep were an excellent addition and the projections on the wool production and mutton are a pleasant surprise, I hope that investment works out for us," she complimented and encouraged.

"I'd like to add some bungalows, another bunkhouse, and begin to allow people to take vacations at the station as a sort of working vacation on a real station. Kind of like the cowboys in America where you can go rope and ride and see the country on a real working ranch. We would have several levels of vacations to offer with and without families. The bungalows would be for families. The bunkhouse for singles. We would let those more affluent guests stay in the ranch house, those bedrooms are going to waste anyway." She waited to let the elderly woman absorb all she had just suggested not wanting to oversell the idea.

"What a novel idea! Do you think there would be a market for it? How would you get them there?" she asked.

"I'd like to buy a small used plane. I would of course learn to fly it and perhaps one or two other employees. It could be used to bring in our guests, as well as supplies, and a few other uses. We are just too far out there to wait for trucks and vehicles to bring in these things anymore. A plane would be more convenient and certainly faster."

"You would learn to fly it yourself?" she asked astonished and then the glitter in her eye turned to a twinkle, "I don't know why I am surprised, you're an amazing woman. You know my solicitor objected to employing you in the capacity of a station manager and you've proven him wrong! I love holding that over at him at our monthly meetings!" she smiled, "You go right ahead and do exactly what you've told me. Get the cost breakdowns and idea's to me as soon as you can and I'll make sure the funds are available to you. We will make those old fuddy duddy's turn on their ear!" she laughed in genuine amusement at the thought. They had been too conservative when her husband was alive and even more so for his widow. She had shocked them with her placement of a woman as manager of the station in Australia, much less the fact that she was an American! This idea would really upset them and she looked forward to the battle of wills, because she was right and would win.

Reese gave her an initial outline of her thoughts and ideas that she had already been compiling. The thought had come to her when she was checking into her hotel and she saw the stand containing brochures of things to do around the city. It reminded her of bed and breakfast lodgings and then she thought of dude ranches in the Wild West. She wasn't the first to think of doing this in Australia but she thought with Sheila's excellent taste and housekeeping abilities they could be one of the best.

"This is very exciting," Lady Emerson said enthusiastically. "I may have to come down there myself. The pictures you have sent are very beautiful. Is it as harsh as I have been led to believe?"

Reese sat back and thought for a moment. "Harsh? It had been hard, hot, dry, and dusty at varying degrees, wet, cold, and miserable, beautiful and ugly all at once. Harsh is too simple a word. I am not a poet or a woman of great words but it is an experience that is very personal for each person. Some hate it immediately and others come to love it." Her eyes sparkled for the beautiful land.

Lady Emerson studied her manager as she spoke of the strange land that was Australia. "You are one of those that have come to love it aren't you?" she asked.

Reese nodded, "There are times when I could hate it but overall it's been an adventure and I really believe I have made a difference or it has changed me."

Lady Emerson noted the changes from two years ago. The polished and ever so proper American had let her hair grow longer, her white skin tan, she looked sculpted and chiseled. She had been strikingly beautiful before and now she was ethereal, breathtaking, but in some ways even more approachable in her beauty. It had softened her and yet hardened her. Lady Emerson was hard pressed to find the words. "You have changed a lot since you worked for the Cavandish Estate. Did you go see them while you were here?" Her own estate was only forty-five minutes away.

Reese shook her head, "There wasn't a lot of time and I'm meeting with friends later for dinner and returning back to London to spend the rest of my short stay with my daughter before returning."

"You heard Lady Wilkins had a son?" Lady Emerson asked cordially.

It took a few moments for Reese to realize that she meant Veronica. "Really, is he healthy?"

Lady Emerson nodded enthusiastically, she adored her own grandchildren. "Yes, I went to the christening a few months ago. She's already talking about having another."

Reese's heart was in her throat but she swallowed it enough to change the subject and bring their meeting to a close. She had gotten what she wanted, permission to add to the station the bunkhouse, the plane, the bungalows. She didn't need to hear the 'local' gossip.

As Reese drove herself away she was tempted to head for Cavandish Estates. It was in the same general direction but she knew it would cause her nothing but heartbreak. She was to meet Audrey for dinner anyway. If she wanted to know anything about Veronica, she would be the one to ask.

Audrey stood up and gawked at her friend. The changes everyone had noted astounded her. Reese looked at ease and content. She was a lot different sight than Veronica. Audrey wondered if she had gotten over their affair that much sooner. "Wow, look at you!" she kissed her on both cheeks.

Reese smiled. She had thought about having a decent haircut while she was here but knowing how much Sheila liked running her hands through her hair and how much she enjoyed that herself she had decided to leave it. "It's so nice to see you after all this time," she returned.

They sat down and ordered their dinner and drinks. Not a lot had changed in Audrey's world, a few more men, and a few more women, nothing out of the ordinary. She was fascinated though to hear what Reese had been doing. The pictures she had brought along were incredible. "Oh Veronica would love to see these!" she enthused before she realized what she had said.

An uncomfortable silence ensued between them as she looked at Reese in shock. The agony she saw in Reese's eyes at that moment told its own tale. Reese hadn't gotten over Veronica after all. She just was older and better able to hide it than Veronica. Audrey hadn't seen Reese the day she left but Veronica had told her an awful tale about how cold Reese had been and how she had begged her to stay. Audrey felt awful for bringing it up, she hadn't meant to but the three of them had been good friends and partied so often together it was inevitable that she mention her.

Reese finally broke the silence and asked quietly, "How is she?"

"She was really shook up when you did a goner," Audrey said quietly.

Reese looked down and mumbled, "I didn't know how to do it, any way I did it was going to be bad for both of us," she defended herself.

Audrey nodded. "She went around like a corpse for months in a stupor barely able to function. David got her to start managing things you had taught her but then somehow he also had Oscar get engaged to her and then they married."

Reese looked at her and waited for her to continue. She needed to know.

"She was a beautiful bride. David made sure of that but I don't think she was really aware of what was going on. Oscar was a good friend and then something happened on their honeymoon and he came back bitter. They barely speak to each other and when they do it's nearly a snarl. Oscar has several girlfriends I think and that seems to relieve Veronica. She began to bloom though when she got pregnant and I still wonder about how that came about but she is *very* closed mouthed about her personal life now." She looked sadly at her friend. "I see her only occasionally now and then but when she talks about her son she just lights up, I think that's why she wants another one so quickly."

Reese looked near to tears thinking of all they had sacrificed for this. What she had sacrificed to give Veronica a life which apparently wasn't the fairytale she had hoped. Had she stayed would it have been any better? "I wish I could have explained, I would have liked to see her but I thought it would hurt more..." For her, for Veronica, which would hurt more? "Does she hate me now?" she couldn't help but ask.

Audrey shook her head, "I don't think so. She looked for you, she hired a private investigator but he didn't find you."

Reese looked puzzled, "It really wouldn't have been that hard to find out what flight I was on..."

"I think David interfered in that."

Reese nodded. All of this boiled down to David's desire to have an heir from the family for the estates. He had gotten what he wanted, but at what cost? Veronica needed a husband and a child and now apparently children. "I wish her well, I always have."

"What about you?" Audrey asked.

Reese shrugged, "I'm doing well. I love my job," and Sheila and yet there was something missing but only she knew that.

"Is there someone else?" Audrey said astutely. Reese tried to look away but Audrey recognized the look that had come into her eyes briefly. "What's she like?

Reese smiled momentarily, "She is kind and sweet and smart and funny. She's earthy and mystic." She couldn't help but think of Sheila in those terms.

"Do you love her?"

Reese nodded and then, "But it isn't the same at all. I think she knows it too. She is very astute that way and content with her lot in life."

"Are you staying there then?"

Reese nodded, "Yes, I've just gotten permission to start another project and it's very big. I'm excited at the idea and I have to stay to see it through." She began to tell Audrey all about her ideas.

Audrey wasn't surprised. Reese had always been a smart cookie and the idea had its merits. She was sure she would make a success of it with her background. She couldn't help but think that Veronica would have been proud of her and her success. She wished that she could tell her but of course knew she couldn't and wouldn't.

They parted after a couple of hours and shared a hug and a peck on the cheek. "Let me know if there is anything I can do although I'm sure I will never hear from you again," Reese told her sadly.

Audrey looked equally sad, "You gave up that right but then you knew that when you left."

Reese nodded, she *had* known, she *did* know.

CHAPTER 43

The flight back she concentrated on her proposal and the idea's she had come up with. Researching had proved to be the easiest part, she had tons of models to choose from and adapt to their own particular circumstances. When she arrived in Sydney she decided to stay a few days to look around the city and to pull her ideas together, possibly get a line on a plane, some lessons, and supplies. She was dining at her hotel when she heard, "Reese Paulson!" and looked around in surprise.

Smiling she got up to greet Rick and Maddy Jamieson, "Hello, what are you two doing in Sydney?" She exchanged a hug and a kiss with each of them, "Would you like to join me?"

The three of them sat down as Maddy said, "Oh we get out a few times a year to shop and see the sights. How about you, what are you doing off station?"

"I'm actually coming back from London, my daughter graduated from Cambridge with honors and a master's degree!" Reese told them proudly.

"Oh that's wonderful. You are so lucky to have a daughter!" Maddy teased it was well known that with their four sons they were 'practicing' on getting a daughter.

"She's a terrific young woman and she's got a wonderful boyfriend, he's studying to be a pediatrician. I may have to go back in a couple of years for their wedding."

"Well, you'll have that to look forward to," Maddy enthused. "How will you plan that from here?"

"I haven't the faintest idea but knowing my daughter she won't need her mother's help and I will only be needed to show up and be in the pictures. I raised a very independent girl there."

They talked for a while about weddings and parties they had all attended as they ordered and ate their excellent dinners.

"You're looking for a plane or a jet?" Rick asked when she told them that she had been authorized to buy.

"I think a plane originally so I can learn to fly it but eventually if this venture takes off," she grinned, "pardon the pun; I think I can convince Lady Emerson to buy a jet. What do you think a jet or a plane?"

"There are a lot of planes out there that you can get for a good price. A jet of course is going to be costly but it's so much quicker that it might be worth the cost eventually. Don't be worried about learning to fly either. I can teach you in our little plane and I know a few blokes that would be willing to teach a sheila such as yourself how to fly a jet!" he joked.

Reese grinned, "Yes but at what cost!?"

They all laughed because their bottom line was always what they were looking at.

"I heard you added sheep, how's that working?" Rick asked.

"Well, we had a few men putting lines in the dirt but I crossed them out and bashed some heads in, it's still a new venture but I am hoping to recoup our costs by next year with the wool check and the mutton we gather as well as the offspring." Reese launched into a knowledgeable discussion on sheep; it was obvious she had researched it thoroughly before she spent the station money.

Rick advised her on some contractors who would appreciate the work on the additions to the station. He also suggested she put in a pool which she thought an excellent idea and got out her notebook to add it to the list and rough in some notes about it.

"What? Were you going to let them swim in the pond out back of the barn?" he teased and Maddy laughed outright.

The previous summer Reese had been swimming in the pond and some snake had joined her. Her screams had been heard all over the home paddock and fortunately for her she had a swimsuit on so the men while appreciative of her physique had gotten no more than a good look and nothing more. Reese had laughed about it since with her various neighbors as news such as that traveled fast. She didn't like the water there anyway since it smelled like rotten eggs. A pool would definitely be at the top of the list.

CHAPTER 44

Reese got a ride home with Rick and Maddy and he promised to come at least twice a week to teach her how to fly. The little she had picked up on the way home had made it seem simple and easy as driving a car and Rick was a patient teacher. Maddy confessed she had never wanted to learn and sat in the back with their supplies and luggage. As she looked down on Wahbaing Station she felt she was coming home, but then she had felt that way as she drove up into England and near the Cavandish Estate. She watched the dust cloud that sprung up when their plane made their landing, a car had come from the home paddock.

Jeremiah, a cousin of Sheila's was at the wheel and he helped her with her luggage and the supplies she had purchased. She waved as Rick and Maddy took off again and then hopped into the driver's seat. "Good trip Misses?"

She smiled, "Yes Jeremiah, it was a good trip. Anything happen here while I was gone?"

He returned the smile, "No Misses, nothing new," and then laughed but then Jeremiah was always laughing. His strong white teeth were in stark contrast to his dark skin. It was when she was around someone such as Jeremiah who was pure Aborigine that she knew without a doubt that Sheila was a mix. Whoever her ancestor had been his bone structure had prevailed. She wasn't as dark as other Aborigine's either instead she could pass for white in some societies, although with a dark tan. For that matter Reese's own tan had been commented on time and again while in England and while she was dark, with her light Anglo skin she wasn't as dark as Sheila and certainly not as dark as a pure Aborigine.

As she pulled up in front of the house the usual crowd was already mulling about wondering who was there and she saw several smiles in greeting. Her eyes were drawn to the tall woman though; whose black eyes haunted her. They exchanged a smile as she grabbed one of her bags out of the Rover. As she walked up she waved at a few of the people who had begun to head for the Rover to unpack it for her.

"Hello Ms. Reese, welcome back!" Sheila said formally and smiled at her.

Reese wanted to pull the tall woman into her arms and give her a hug but the formality of the greeting reminded her that she was the station manager and as such was a representative of the owner. "Hello Sheila, everything okay here?" she asked.

Sheila nodded and then moved aside to open the door so Reese could pass with her bag. She dropped it at the bottom of the steps and headed into the office where several faxes and a stack of mail waited her. Sighing deeply she sat in her chair and went right to work. No point in waiting, it wouldn't get done without her.

"Hey babé" Sheila whispered making the name sound so endearing but with an almost French inflection as she slipped into her bed with her after everything and everyone was done for the night.

Reese turned towards her sleepily and pulled her into her embrace. She had been dozing for who knew how long waiting for her to join her. "God I missed you!" Reese said as she buried her nose into Sheila's neck to inhale the earthy scent of her. Sheila had never used perfume despite Reese buying her some for Christmas and Reese understood out here there was no need for such fripperies.

They both began to caress each other knowing what buttons to push after being together for over a year. It soon became heated and wild, almost a battle of wills as they both sought to please each other. Sometimes Reese worried at the almost violent state they both got into occasionally but had known after being apart for some time they needed this. She had never had a lover as wild or strong willed or passionate and Sheila brought something almost primitive out in herself. It bordered on the insane sometimes the wild and heated couplings they had. Sometimes it hurt and this pain too added fuel to their fires. It could also be very sweet and endearing but the intensity that they both sought seemed to bring out the wild and primitive side more often. They were both wildly passionate women and as rough as it got they both found they enjoyed the pleasure that pain could bring them. When they both lay there sated after an hour of sweet combat Reese leaned over and tenderly kissed her lover and said, "Thank you."

Sheila wasn't sure she could answer. This Anglo always seemed to take her breath away and make her do things that she would later feel ashamed for. Her tenderness though always made her love her more. She held her close as they both fell into an exhausted sleep.

Sheila was the first to wake as always well before sunrise. She had to be up to light the fires and to sneak out of the master bedroom where Reese slept. Hurrying into the bathroom she washed and then dressed. She looked down on the Anglo who slept oblivious to her surroundings and thought about her for a moment. She had no idea how much Sheila loved and adored her; she would *never* let her know.

CHAPTER 45

Over the next few weeks Reese gave any employees who wanted it extra work. They laid out where the new bunkhouse would go as well as the extra bungalows. Reese herself used the bulldozer to dig out the hole where a swimming pool could be put in. Rick's recommendations on contractors soon had the sounds of hammers and machinery heard throughout the home paddock as they enacted the changes that Reese wanted. Twice a week Reese was taking lessons on how to fly a plane and Jeremiah went along to learn as well.

It was during these lessons though that she saw views of the station that gave her more of an appreciation of the size of it. The animals in the home paddock soon learned to ignore the sound of the planes droning as they practiced take offs and landings. Rick mentioned an official from Sydney could give them their tests when next he came through this part of the territory but Reese chose instead to fly down there and take the tests with Jeremiah so they could buy their own plane sooner. Rick graciously offered to help her find a plane of their own and flew her around the territory to anyone who had one for sale. They were soon in possession of a six seater Cessna that Jeremiah promised to keep in peak condition. A small hangar was built at the end of their own small runway to house it.

Reese arranged for a photographer to come out and photograph the station at various times of the year for their brochures that she was working on as well as the buildings, the animals, and some of the more handsome stockmen. A good natured teasing went on when the men were finally chosen to pose for the pictures at various jobs around the station. Reese insisted on Sheila in one of the pictures only to have that backfire when her own picture was taken with her ridiculous red hat. She wanted natural pictures of the Aborigines and their now colorful village as well as scenes of quiet splendor around the station. It took months and hundreds of pictures to sort through but she had a brochure she was proud of when they were done.

Lady Emerson was their first guest. Reese had kept her apprised of all of their expenditures as well as the progress on all their buildings. She herself flew down to Sydney the night before Lady Emerson was due to fly her and some of her lawyers back with her. She welcomed Lady Emerson who seemed game to fly in the smaller plane but the prissy faced lawyers she could have dropped off somewhere between

Sydney and Wahbaing Station. Their endless questions and prying drove her crazy but she had to remember that they were looking out for the financial well-being of this sweet lady. Reese had spent a fortune on the improvements in the past and this new venture an additional fortune. They were naturally suspicious but the gleam in the old lady's eyes told Reese that she was enjoying herself. They didn't seem to appreciate her being dressed in jeans and a checkered shirt with her t-shirt visible underneath, they themselves looked uncomfortable in their expensive three piece suits in the heat of the sun. Reese remembered when she herself had dressed very differently as well.

They arrived late in the day and Reese expertly flew the Cessna over the station and showed them various points of interest before flying over the home paddock and then finally onto their own private airstrip. Jeremiah had painted the hangar and Reese noted with amusement that he had painted 'Wahbaing' on the roof of it. The lawyers hadn't really realized the massive size of the property their late client had left his wife and heirs, they were used to estates on English scale and not an Australian one and were impressed but still managed to get under her skin with their probing questions. There was a vast difference from seeing numbers on a statement and actually seeing the square miles that they owned that constituted Wahbaing Station.

Reese drove them to the house in the Rover which was a little cramped with Lady Emerson in the front seat and the three lawyers crammed into the back. Reese had chosen to only bring Lady Emerson's luggage in the far back and told the men she would have one of the stockmen bring their luggage later. They didn't look pleased with the arrangement.

Lady Emerson was thrilled with the beauty of the house and the room she was shown to by the striking housekeeper and Reese. She just loved everything that Reese showed her from the house, to the barns, to the gardens. She even turned on her lawyers one day and told them to stop complaining about the wasted 'space' on the station as Reese had explained that here in the outback it couldn't support the same number of animals per square foot that you could in England due to its lack of water. They had improved several areas with having drilled wells but they were a long way from anything like the 'old' country. Their snobbery over England versus the 'wastes' of Australia was hard for anyone to swallow.

Lady Emerson's stamp of approval put the balls in motion for advertising and sending out the brochures. Reese had thousands of them printed and literally sent them all over the world. Their emails and faxes as well as phone calls ensured a full house in all seasons. Sheila was busy training new staff to clean the bungalows and bunkhouse as well as the rooms in the house. She had a lot to choose from in her own extended family in the village as well as those who applied to work in the outback. Reese had to hire more stockmen to help show around their guests as well as the actual stockmen who still worked the animals on their station. It was a delightfully busy time for all of them and Reese was well satisfied with the responses they were getting. An executive for a web publishing company stayed with them in exchange for making them a website to be envied. The pictures and videos of Wahbaing Station captured the imaginations of people all over the world to have a vacation in the mysterious outback. Reese soon was able to budget a jet into their finances despite the objections of the lawyers and the expense. The end justified the means. It was quicker and more efficient and she secretly enjoyed learning the new machine despite the time it took from her other duties.

It wasn't all a bed of roses of course. Guests meant a lot of headaches in each season. From the rainy season when it frequently flooded and guests were confined to the home paddocks to the dry season when the heat had them squandering the air conditioning and complaining about the flies. Reese was also kept busy keeping them entertained and answering stupid questions. One that always amused her was, "What time do the dingoes come by?" If they only knew the rifle she kept on her saddle was not for show. Dingoes were shot on sight as a rule on this station. Any colonies found to exist were soon eradicated. They were a menace to the sheep as well as the cattle they were now breeding even though they were necessary to the balance of life far out in the outback often cleaning up dying or killed animals. Unfortunately they also killed animals and since they were breeding animals for profit this had to be prevented or stopped.

Hot summer winds too provided them with difficulties to complaining guests. Fires that swept across the acres were a definite cause of concern and excitement. They had to keep their people safe as well as the guests.

The inconsideration of the guests for the people who lived and worked there were another annoyance and their waste of electricity and water. It was a constant battle to stay ahead but at the same time after the second year of this great experiment Reese could look back on the wrinkles they had ironed out with pride. They had put in several solar panels throughout the property as well as large windmills to provide them with sources of electricity. She had imported a teacher and a doctor to improve the education and the medical facilities in the nearby town that sported two bars and an outpost but not much more. The station sponsored sports and athletic scholarships at the local school and encouraged its young people to get an education. Many grumbled at this idea, why would their young come back after experiencing the outside world but Reese felt it was a choice not a duty. Besides they had more applications for people to come and work than they knew what to do with and from all over the world. As a result they had an eclectic mix of people, some who might stay and some who couldn't adapt. The outback certainly wasn't for everyone, some loved it, some hated it, some just coped, and some went mad trying.

CHAPTER 46

Reese was midway through her fifth year on the station working out a way to buy several mobile homes in bulk for their sheep herders and drovers in the far reaches of the station when they received a guest from one of the resorts on the Great Barrier Reef. Elton Morris and his wife Patricia were an odd fit onto their 'dude' ranch but they enjoyed the oddities of the outback. It had become Reese's custom to take cocktails with their guests around the pool or in the rec hall that they had expanded to include dancing so as to get to know their guests. Some of the employees had joked she was, "Mr. Roarke," from Fantasy Island reruns that they got on the satellite television. Reese joked she was more like Tattoo...except for the height. She even could be heard saying, "The plane, the plane," when Jeremiah would fly in some new guests.

Elton and Patricia were most impressed with how well run the station was by Reese. The respect she received from the stockmen who for the most part were surly and different characters was astounding. One of the nastiest customers had been a stockman who Reese tied into and never hesitated to go toe to toe with over a procedure she wanted followed. The rumors about her reputation were repeated around the campfires nightly. When the rumors about her breaking some man's jaw were told as truth they weren't believed until it was witnessed that she could indeed hold her own against a grown man in a fight.

"Ms. Paulson, I wonder if you would be interested in a change of venue," Mr. Morris asked her one night as they sat around the moonlit waters of the pool. Floating in the water were votive candles placed in flowers. It was the little touches that impressed them all the most. Mr. and Mrs. Morris had had the rare treat of seeing the pictures that Reese had shared showing the before and after pictures of the last five years here on the ranch which they had enjoyed immensely and been suitably impressed over. It showed that Reese knew what she was doing, in anything that she set her mind to do.

"What did you have in mind?" Reese asked tiredly, having been up since four a.m. with a problematic horse. She could have left it to her stockmen but felt her presence and help kept their respect.

"My wife and I are looking for a manager for one of our resorts. I understand you were in the hotel business back in the States?"

Reese smiled at her guest. Many people seemed to be interested in her background but few realized beyond England that she had managed successfully some very important hotels in New York, Connecticut, and New Jersey. This man had done his homework if he had researched that far back. She nodded and added, "Yes, I was for many years as I got my degree and raised my daughter."

"Your daughter is here on the station with you?" Mrs. Morris asked curious having seen few if any white children except down by where the married stockmen lived.

"Oh no, she lives in England. She graduated from Cambridge a few years ago with her Masters and is working in a museum in London. I expect her to announce her engagement and wedding plans soon to a delightful man who will be getting his doctorate any day now," she couldn't help but brag a little. She was so proud of Gillian and missed her very much.

"You have a daughter with a Masters from Cambridge?" Mrs. Morris asked astounded and impressed.

Reese nodded. She knew the outback aged most people but she seemed to thrive by living there. She certainly didn't look old enough to have a daughter Gillian's age. She knew her job and loved what she did. Lady Emerson loved the reports she received and had sent several friends on vacations. They all raved at the property that Lady Emerson had inherited from her husband and the excellent manager who ran it. Strangely word had never reached the Cavandish estates or perhaps no one had put two and two together and realized who Reese was.

Both Mrs. and Mr. Morris reassessed the woman before them. They had thought she was a little young to be running this huge station and all it involved but they had been most impressed with the reports they had on her from people they had sent to stay here as well as what they looked into when they checked out her background. Someone had missed the daughter aspect though as well as the age of this amazing woman. Coming here though the reports hadn't lied. Reese did her job and she did it well with ease. She hired the right people to do their jobs and if they didn't do them she gave them a chance to do something else or leave. Most of them were happy in their jobs and liked their boss. Even the most chauvinistic man who worked for her took off his hat in her presence, they might not always like having a 'sheila' for a boss but she was fair, she was honest, and she'd do a day's work in their shoes if it was necessary as she had proven time and again.

Both of them explained what their resorts were about and Reese despite loving the outback was intrigued. She hadn't been off the station other than to fly guests to and from Sydney in years but then that was by choice. She loved it here and it showed in a myriad of ways from the gardens she herself had planted to the way guests were treated. It was five-star operation and that was why the Morris' wanted her to consider coming to work for them. By the time their vacation ended they were convinced she was the woman for the job and a vacation was arranged for Reese to visit.

Sheila never said a word as she watched her lover of the last four years pack a bag to take the jet up to Queensland. Jeremiah was excited because he would be flying it back and had never seen that part of Australia. The area they were flying to was well populated and a big tourist destination. Sheila knew even if she hadn't told Reese that their time was coming to an end. She had known approximately four years ago as it was foretold in her dreams. Although saddened and heartbreaking for her, she would not have changed her fate. Reese was destined for bigger things. She was also destined for love, just not Sheila's.

CHAPTER 47

Reese enjoyed herself immensely on the beach. If possible she became even browner from the sun and the sands. The outback had hot blistering winds that had browned and burned her skin at various times but the long blonde tresses had only blown whiter and the green of her hazel eyes was snapping with the brown flecks. She knew she was a beautiful woman and had been blessed but she had also fought her entire life for respect as people assumed beauty and no brains. This job offer would make her have to fight for it all over again. She wasn't sure she wanted to leave the station. She knew she loved Sheila but hadn't she been warned by the same that it was only for a time? She respected Sheila too much and she had been right too often not to know that her premonitions were usually correct. In some ways this job would be a lot easier than the one on the station. They were in a 'civilized' area of Australia and the headaches of working so far from a populated area would be eliminated but at the same time Reese would miss the quiet of the outback, the stillness, and the sounds that only the outback generated. She had a lot to think about when she went back.

Mr. and Mrs. Morris did everything in their power to make it a perfect vacation for their potential manager. Their investigation had revealed even more impressive information about the woman and they knew she would be an excellent addition to their resorts. They owned a series of them along the coast and she would start at one of them and eventually take over handling all of them. Something the Morris' did now themselves and they wanted a competent manager to do it *for* them. They were convinced that Reese would be the perfect person for the job. She knew people all over the world and look what she had done with the station. Even the reports regarding Cavandish Estates and the hotels in the States had them salivating over her working for them. They upped their original offer and sent contracts to Reese negotiating they hoped for a final contract.

"Hey Anglo, what are you thinking about so hard out here in the dark," Sheila's voice penetrated her consciousness as she stared out into the night.

"How did you see me in the dark?" Reese returned smiling at her lover.

"You glow in the dark you Anglos, and besides, I could smell that Jasmine perfume from a mile away," she smiled and Reese could see the perfect teeth in the dark.

"I do not glow, I'm very tan and I haven't put any on in days," she returned but didn't doubt that was exactly how Sheila had found her.

Sheila just stood there. She sensed the deep thoughts that had kept Reese from sleeping soundly since she had returned from the coast. The pictures she had taken and what she hadn't said about it convinced Sheila that her mind was made up but she just didn't know it. She wanted to put her arms around her Anglo and tell her whatever she decided she would love her forever. But after four years, no one suspected, no one knew they had been lovers. You never knew who was out in the dark and she wouldn't let anyone see them now.

Reese sighed. Sheila had been there for her a lot longer than anyone else she had ever known. How could she leave her? It was as though Sheila could read her mind, hadn't those black eyes always fascinated her, hadn't they always made her drown in them? She was so wise and knowing. Despite a lack of a formal education she was well read having read every book in their library as well as anything she could get her hands on but she was knowledgeable in ways that weren't in books and Reese had always been impressed, always treating her as an equal.

It was that mind reading skill that unnerved her tonight, "You should go, it's time," Sheila said quietly.

"How do you know it's time?" Reese asked and then mentally kicked herself. Of course she knew, she always knew, had always known.

Sheila just waited.

Reese sighed again, "Do you know when?" she asked.

"No, only you can decide that, but I sense it's soon," she said in her mystical way.

Reese knew she was probably right. The last offer from the Morris' had been incredible. She knew she wasn't likely to ever receive such an offer again from them or anyone else. She really didn't need the money but that was fantastic too. She had achieved her goals, why did she need to leave a job she not only loved, she enjoyed. Why did she need to leave a woman who had given her so much love?

"Yes, I love you but I have always known this was a timed love. Your time to leave is nearing, you have to decide when," Sheila practically whispered but her quiet voice was soothing to Reese's ears.

"How can I leave you?" Reese said almost taking her into her arms but Sheila stepped backwards and then disappeared.

"Ms. Paulson?" a voice called from out of the darkness and Reese turned to one of the stockmen.

"Yes? Over here," she called as she headed toward the disembodied voice she had heard.

"We have a problem with the herder in Waygang Paddock, the sheep are coming faster than he can handle and he called it in," he told her. Reese knew she wouldn't be getting any sleep tonight and followed him back to the barns. They took 4-wheelers and headed toward Waygang Paddock to help out the sheep herder. They would be relieved by another set of exhausted stockmen in the morning but Reese would only keep going for her day to start again. It was the time of year, it was her job, and she loved it despite the occasional sleepless nights. The really bad thing for her was that despite the fatigue, the hard work, the hassles, it gave her a lot of time to think...her thoughts that night were on the job offer, the station, but especially on Sheila...

CHAPTER 48

"Mom?" Gillian's voice came from thousands of miles away and Reese could picture her instantly in her mind as well as on the computer as they chatted this week.

"Hey baby girl, how are you?" Reese asked.

"Steffan and I just booked a flight to Sydney so we can come see the station!" she said excitedly.

Reese was just as excited. She had been trying to get her busy daughter and her equally busy boyfriend down for a vacation for years! "When are you coming?" she smiled into her camera.

"Two weeks!" Gillian told her seeing how pleased her mother had become at the news.

"Oh baby girl, you have just made my mother's day!" Reese told her. They still celebrated although in Australia and England it wasn't the same day on the calendar as in the States.

The next two weeks were frantic for Reese. She insisted that Sheila and her staff clean the house extra well. Sheila ignored her and kept it clean anyway. The barn staff though didn't fare as well as things got painted and freshened, stalls got mucked, and gardens got weeded. Everything was going to look it's best for her daughter's visit even though Reese had always had a high level of cleanliness for the home paddock anyway. She found things for everyone to do even if they had already been done. Even the inside of the jet was pristine and in spit and polish order when she flew to Sydney to get her daughter and boyfriend.

Reese waited beyond customs remembering her own first arrival. When she saw Gillian she felt her heart leap. She waited until she crossed half the distance to her before she herself headed into her daughter's arms and gave her a great big bear hug. "Oh Gillian, it's been too long baby girl!" She was equally pleased to see Steffan hovering and happy to see her. She escorted them into another part of the airport where their smaller jet waited.

"You fly this thing?" Gillian asked with a grin looking at the neat little plane.

Reese returned the smile and helped Steffan and Gillian with their luggage onto the plane. She then proceeded with her pre-check before entering the plane, settling in her daughter and boyfriend and doing her pre-flight.

Gillian watched curiously from the co-pilot's seat. Reese had offered to put her in the cabin but she wanted to be up front with her mom. "You really enjoy this?" she asked as she watched her.

Reese smiled as she finished a few more last minute details and the tower directed her to the strip they wanted her to take. They were soon in the air and heading northwest from Sydney toward Wahbaing Station. Reese pointed out features of interest and Steffan, once Reese told him he could, took off his seat belt to join them in the front and look out over Gillian's shoulder. The long flight seemed to take less time when they had things to look at and discuss, their lively chatter helped to pass the time.

As Reese came into the station she flew around a couple of times to show her daughter certain features that were better seen from the air before taking them into their landing strip. They had gotten authorization from Lady Emerson to have the strip blacktopped and the crew had finished just last week. It looked impressive and felt a lot better than the bumps and potholes of the dirt strip. Reese had the jet stowed in the hangar and their luggage was soon in the Rover. As she pointed out things on the drive to the home paddock she couldn't help but feel pride in the changes she had enacted since her arrival nearly five years ago. Gillian thought the changes in her mother were even more amazing.

Steffan and Gillian loved their visit to Wahbaing Station. The party that Reese threw and had invited everyone from hundreds of miles around was the largest they had ever had on the station. Everyone they met raved about her mother. Several guests were surprised to meet this full grown daughter of Reese's having not known she had one or not guessed her age. They were also surprised that Gillian wasn't nearly as beautiful as her mother and while pretty she didn't have the stunning factor that Reese exhibited unconsciously.

"Reese I need to talk to you if I may," Steffan asked with his crisp upper class British tones.

Reese smiled; she had anticipated this and was only surprised it took him a week to work up the nerve. She had suspected one of the many reasons her daughter and her boyfriend had made the long trip was because of this very reason. She didn't want to spoil it though so she waited patiently for him to harness in his courage.

"I'd like your permission to ask your daughter for her hand in marriage," he practically stammered.

Reese smiled even broader and took Steffan into her arms. The usually undemonstrative Englishman couldn't help but feel pleased at the gesture as she said, "Steffan, nothing would make me happier than to see you make my little girl happy. Do you love her?"

Steffan nodded getting a little emotional at the thought of Gillian.

"But do you like her?" Reese asked him as she pulled back to watch his face. She watched the puzzlement cross his face at her question.

"Yes, I love your daughter more than life itself," he told her passionately.

Reese shook her head and said, "I don't doubt you love her. But do you like her? It's important for a marriage to work to like the person you love, do you understand the difference?"

Steffan took a step back from her embrace as he pondered what she had just asked. Did he like Gillian? They had known each other for nearly five years. They had fallen in love after six months of being friends. He thought about all the many admirable qualities she had that would make her an excellent wife and then he thought about everything that she did that made her an equally admirable and excellent friend first and foremost. He smiled; it reached deeply into his baby blue eyes as he answered Reese. "Yes Ms. Paulson, I like your daughter very much. She is my best friend."

Reese loved the answer and took his hand in hers and said, "That's good because she is my whole world. I don't know what I would do if she was unhappy. It's best if your mate is your best friend first and foremost. Passion and its intensity fade, but a good friend? That can be a lifetime," she told him from her heart and from experience as she pushed away her own thoughts on the subject pertaining to herself.

Gillian watched as her boyfriend talked earnestly to her mother. It was important to her that they get along. Her best friend and her mother, they seemed to like each other. Although Reese hadn't lived close by in years they still talked often, sent emails, and corresponded regularly. The mass of pictures her mother had sent over the years didn't do this place justice. She could sense her mother's touch in hundreds of ways as she went about the place. The love and admiration that the employees and other station owners and managers had for her mother was an extension of that touch. She was well appreciated.

"Ms. Paulson, may I talk to you for a moment about your mother?" John Reid asked Gillian as she stood there watching her mother and Steffan.

She turned to him with surprise but she nodded.

"I can't seem to make any headway with your mother; I've tried for years to get her to take notice of me. Is there some special formula that it would take for her to go out with me?" he asked earnestly.

Gillian studied the man as he spoke and he was an attractive man. He was physically fit, a little older than her mother with a touch of gray. He owned his own station south of Wahbaing Station so he wasn't after her mother for money or manager abilities. There was something about him though that she knew her mother just wouldn't go out with him. She smiled and in that smile you could see her attractive mother, it transformed the pretty girl into a beautiful one and the man noticed it immediately. "My mother as you know is a unique individual, I don't seriously think her free spirit can be tamed. I'm sorry; I can't give you an insight as to why she wouldn't accept your suit. All I can advise is to remain her friend and be content with that."

He smiled ruefully. He had tried that tactic as well and while she respected him she never had accepted his invitations to make it something more. He regretted that all they would ever be is friends or acquaintances. She was the most beautiful and intelligent woman he had ever met and it was such a waste.

Sheila smiled from behind the column where she was bringing out more drinks. 'Free spirit' indeed! She had often wondered if Gillian knew her mother's preferences, she was a pretty savvy young woman, but Reese explained it was a situation where the conversation had just never come up and she certainly wasn't going to explain the facts of life to her grown daughter now. She probably knew but out of respect for her mother kept it to herself. Sheila had laughed when Reese insisted for the duration of Gillian's stay that there be no sleeping together. She didn't want Sheila 'accidentally' seen by her daughter coming or going from the second master bedroom across from the one she had installed her daughter and boyfriend in. Sheila knew that at the end of their stay that Reese would be so horny that she would more than make up for the abstinence they were both enforced to endure.

The party was declared a great success especially when Steffan got down on one knee in front of all the guests and proposed to his longtime girlfriend and she immediately accepted. Reese got out the champagne and many toasts were said to the delighted couple. She was so proud of her daughter and wished her every happiness.

All too soon the trip came to an end. As Reese drove them to the plane which Jeremiah was flying today for her she had some alone time as Steffan discretely made himself absent at the hangar. Gillian looked at her mother and thought about the changes she saw in her. It wasn't just the long hair that her mother now sported, it was a definite difference from the immaculately cut do she had for Gillian's entire life, it was now covered by that ridiculous Australian stockman's hat in red. It was her whole attitude. There was a sadness in her eyes that one had to look deep to find. She loved it here in the outback but there was just something...something that you just couldn't quite put your finger on, a vague shadow that haunted her eyes that hadn't been there in years past. She had noticed it on Reese's last trip to England too but here in the outback things seemed a lot more wide open.

"So when do you think your wedding will take place," Reese was asking, her arm around her daughter touching her for the last time until God knew when.

"We want a fairly quick one but that means in the next few months we are going to have to work very hard. He has a lot of people that just have to be invited and all the planning is going to drive me delightfully insane," Gillian grinned in anticipation. She wanted nothing more at this point than to be Dr. and Mrs. Steffan Cantwell. Someday they would be Lord and Lady Cantwell but as she adored her future in-laws that could wait.

"So it's going to be a fairly huge wedding?" Reese mused knowingly.

"Yes, I don't see how we can avoid that. Heir and all that," she added.

Reese nodded. "What can I do to help?"

"Don't take this wrong Mom but nothing. You're too far away and I know how much Lady Cantwell is going to love 'helping' me plan this. If you were closer I know you could help in so many ways but it's just not feasible." She smiled, "I hope you don't mind but Lady Cantwell is going to love advising this 'American' on the social graces and who and where of this wedding. She doesn't have a daughter and if you don't mind I'm going to give her this opportunity."

Reese smiled; she had never planned her daughter's wedding in her own mind. Perhaps she hadn't been a 'normal' mother that way. She herself had never had one and probably never would. She really didn't mind this stranger who was to become her daughter's mother-in-law helping her daughter have a dream wedding.

Gillian stopped as they walked along and turned to face her mother, "Mom, you did good here." She indicated herself, "I'm an independent woman who you taught to pursue her dreams and her own happiness. I've found a man to be my best friend, to walk beside me for the rest of my life. I'm so proud of Steffan I can't wait to be his Mrs. I'm okay Mom, you never have to worry about this chick," she pointed at herself with her thumb. "I want you to find your happiness now, I know you love it here but is it really your fate?" she asked.

Reese smiled at this amazing woman who was her daughter. Her talk of fate was something Sheila would have said. She loved Gillian more than life itself, there was nothing she wouldn't do for her. Only once had one other person occupied that portion of her heart and she pushed the thoughts of Veronica from her mind immediately, a practice she had been keeping up for four and half years. The shadow crossed her eyes however briefly and Gillian saw it before it was gone. "I do have a job offer that I'm considering," Reese told her having told no one about it before.

"Is it something worth pursuing?" Gillian asked wisely knowing certain criteria would have to be met before Reese would even consider it.

Reese smiled and nodded, "It's the most amazing offer, I think I may be on the verge of accepting it." She told Gillian almost all the details and Gillian was astounded not only at the money offered but that her mother had procrastinated in signing the contracts.

"*Go,* it's too good to pass up!" she encouraged her with a smile.

"Hey you two, we have a plane to catch in Sydney!" Steffan joked as they were flying in today so they could putz around the city for a couple of days before catching their international flight back to London.

Reese smiled before she cried. She pulled Gillian into a bear hug and squeezed, pleased when her daughter returned the gesture. Patting her on the butt she pushed her towards her impatient fiancée.

CHAPTER 49

Reese accepted the Morris offer that afternoon. She would have a few months before she had to actually be there. She tendered her resignation with Lady Emerson carefully wording it so that in no way it reflected badly on herself, the station, or her relationship with the lady.

"So it's done?" Sheila asked that night after they made mad passionate love. That was something she was going to miss. Nowhere had she ever met someone who was able to keep up with her and dish out as much as she had taken. Sheila had been amazed that this Anglo not only had captured her heart but been able to enjoy the violence that was kept carefully masked under the surface. She had learned to give it as well and Sheila wondered if she would ever be as compatible with anyone else again. It hadn't always been violent, there was genuine love and affection, and Reese had taught her tenderness she hadn't known she needed or existed within her.

Reese nodded thinking about the letters and contracts she had sent off that afternoon. She wasn't surprised that Sheila knew but she would have told her anyway. "Why don't you come with me? Your experience I'm sure would..." she cut off watching Sheila's facial expression change.

"I can never leave here, don't you know? This is my fate, you're going on to yours," she said mysteriously.

"Why can't you leave? I love you; I really don't want to leave you!" Reese said earnestly believing every word she was saying.

"I am meant to be here, always. I love you too. I always will. This however was our time. I always knew it was a limited time. I warned you of that many times over our years together. I can tell you this. There will be others. There will be a couple of others in the years to come but they will never occupy your heart like she does."

"What do you mean she does?" Reese had never discussed Veronica with Sheila feeling it was a breach of propriety or something.

"You don't think I know, you don't think I could tell there was a part of you I would never reach? You came here with such devastation in your eyes, in your heart. You threw yourself into a job you had no knowledge of in so many ways. You succeeded at everything you set out to do, except erasing her from your heart. I saw how conflicted you were when you went back to England for Gillian's graduation on whether you should see her again, that's why I tried to help by telling you not to. It wasn't the right time. I can tell you that someday you will have the opportunity to know this woman again but not the next time you go to England. Allow her to become the woman she was destined to be and although it pains your heart you did the right thing by leaving. You too needed this, she needed to grow," Sheila told her such wise and mystical things that Reese could only stare at her in amazement. She believed every word.

"What about you?" she asked in a small voice.

Sheila smiled, the white against her copper skin something that always fascinated Reese. "I will hurt for a while, perhaps in a small way for always. No, don't feel bad," she stopped Reese from talking by putting her first two fingers across her lips, "I always knew and I wouldn't change my fate for anything. I had you Anglo; I had you longer than any of these loves in your life. But I only had you for my time. My fate and yours are not the same. Yours lies in England but not for a while. Live your life as though tomorrow may never come and you will have lived," she advised as she removed her fingers and replaced them with her lips.

CHAPTER 50

Lady Emerson regretfully accepted her resignation, after all this time though she was surprised. She immediately began looking for a replacement and no one satisfied her when she interviewed them, she even interviewed some via that new-fangled Skype thing but no one satisfied her. Reese had some special quality, some special enthusiasm that they needed in an operation such as Wahbaing Station. Then she received a terrific offer for the complete operation and having consulted both her lawyers and Reese she accepted. A multi-national conglomeration would be taking it over and sending out a team of managers to learn the operation. Reese's only concern was for her friends and employees and the managers who would now be handling them. She was relieved that the managers chosen were from Australia and were eager to learn her methods. Sheila soon had them eating out her hand and Reese left her job feeling she had done the best she could for those she had left behind.

The night before she left she and Sheila made love for the last time. Despite the near violence that marked their passion throughout most of their relationship Reese insisted on making love to Sheila slowly and sweetly. She wanted this time to be memorable for both of them and while they both had had tender and incredible moments the intensity that came from their violent couplings had always alarmed Reese. It made her feel there was something wrong with her deep down that she felt she needed the physical combat with Sheila, the primitive couplings. While she made sweet love to Sheila who kept trying to turn it into one of their physical battles she held her and refused to allow it to get to that point. While she would later give in to her violent urges for now the sensitive and sweet love she made to Sheila almost changed her mind forever. Reese loved her so well and so much that this tender side nearly unnerved the Aboriginal woman's resolve to let her go.

Arriving on the Gold Coast in the jet that she had flown for the last time Reese was pleased to see a limousine meeting them on the private strip. Jeremiah helped stow the boxes and bags in the back with the limo driver as she gave him a hug and a kiss for the last time.

"We will miss you Misses," he sniffed audibly.

Reese smiled and said, "I will miss all of you Jeremiah. I've loved working with you all. You taught me so much."

They exchanged a final handshake before she got into the limo and was driven off to her destined job transforming herself back from the 'outback' jeans and shirt woman to the 'city' gal who dressed in slacks and suits.

CHAPTER 51

"We've been invited to Lady and Lord Cantwell's son's wedding, would you like to go?" Veronica asked Oscar at the dinner table hoping he wouldn't make a scene in front of David.

"Oh I say, I'm planning on going, will you two be there?" David put in, putting subtle pressure on his brother in law.

"When is it?" Oscar asked as he ate his dinner and glared at the maid who was attempting to keep his son from making a mess at the dining room table. Children should be fed in their nursery and not eat with adults he always said but Veronica insisted they be brought to the adult table to teach them manners.

"Next month," Veronica answered cautiously adjusting herself in her chair since she felt uncomfortable in more than one way.

"Isn't that about the time of the Wimbley's horse fair?" Oscar asked.

Veronica gritted her teeth, if Oscar bought one more damned horse she would ... "No I believe they are different weekends," she told him before turning to David and saying, "Can the children and I ride with you if you are going?"

David eyes showed amusement before Oscar could say, "I didn't say I wouldn't go..." he drank his glass of wine down so the servant could fill it.

That being settled the only conversation was the children and their maid helping them to eat. Veronica assisted when her daughter had enough and needed to be excused from the table using it as an excuse to leave herself. David watched her thoughtfully.

CHAPTER 52

Reese always said a job had a three month window for its learning curve. She walked into this job knowing how to do a lot of the tasks that the Morris' expected of their new general manager. What she didn't expect was the animosity that hit her almost immediately in this male dominated resort in the management team. Apparently it had been a family oriented structure for a long time and her coming in when it was expected that they would hire from within didn't go over very well. She experienced resistance at every level and it didn't make for a pleasant time.

"So why did you hire me then if not to make changes that would benefit your company?" she asked exasperated as Mr. Morris countermanded her orders for the umpteenth time. Other employees had gone whining to the husband and wife team and he continued to interfere. Mrs. Morris watched the confrontation that had been building between her husband and their new manager with a hidden smile thinking her husband wasn't going to be happy with the outcome. Not only was Reese in the right, she had a contract that her husband would not be happy in paying out if she quit for just cause or he fired her.

"I thought you could manage my hotel, I also thought eventually you would be taking over the resort and other properties that we own along the coast!" he shot back.

"Then let me do my job and quit interfering," she told him angrily. "You hired me because I am good at what I do and when your 'good ole boys' club gets their feelings hurt and comes to you to complain you side with them each and every time. Don't you think that undermines my authority? I am used to making the decisions and being responsible for them, total autonomy. You don't like my decisions then you discuss them with me, not countermanding them behind my back!"

Mr. Morris had the grace to look ashamed. He looked at his wife for her support but she was examining her manicure and he knew by the set on her face that she was amused and would be of no help to his cause. She had warned him that Reese wouldn't put up with his interference for long. The bitch of it was they were both right. Sighing deeply he made a final decision, "Okay, you have it, my full support.

I'm not going to let them come to me with their complaints anymore. I will refer them to you from now on."

"Fine, I want one more thing before I take over the whole resort though..." she left it trailing off.

"I'm traveling to England next week for my daughter's wedding; I will need you both here while I am gone. When I get back I want the two of you to take a month's vacation where you are not available to any employee here at the resort unless it is an emergency call from me," she sat back and waited for the explosion she figured would come.

Mrs. Morris looked up at her demand with delight on her face. She had been trying to get him to take a vacation forever but he always said they had the perfect vacation spot in their own properties so why bother?

Mr. Morris looked at his wife and knew he had lost any support of any argument from that angle and he thought of a few arguments he wanted to make. He studied his annoying General Manager for a few moments before asking, "What would that accomplish?"

"It would first of all get you out of my hair," she swept the blonde mane out of her way to emphasize her words, "Secondly it would put you absolutely out of their whining, complaints, and manipulations and me in total control. Thirdly it would give you a well-deserved vacation when the last one was to the station and you know you loved that," she gentled her demands by reminding him of a thoroughly enjoyable vacation that they had both talked about for a long time, it had also put Reese into their realm of employees.

She continued on a little more gently, she actually liked her boss, "Mr. Morris, you hired me because I'm good at what I do, let me do it. One month is not that much to ask. You want to enjoy yourself, not be constantly inundated with petty employees. It's time to clean house in many areas, you both know it and have been too soft hearted to do it. I'm an unknown factor. If I have the control that I need to do my job, I'll do it."

Reese walked back to her suite in the hotel with a sense of accomplishment. The time she had been here had been to get the lay of the land. She considered it time well spent. Despite the egotistical employees she had to contend with and the sexism that put her in a spot since she was the antithesis of what they expected in a General Manager she would make this job work. She had a contract that was in her favor if she decided to quit, but she wasn't going to do that. As she entered her suite she walked through the living room to her bedroom which she unlocked with her own key. No one else was allowed into her inner sanctum, she needed some privacy and while the maids could clean her living room, they only cleaned her bedroom and bathroom when she was there.

She removed her jacket and hung it over the back of a chair. It was a far cry from the years of casual shirts and jeans to wearing suits again but she enjoyed the change. She had her nails impeccably done again and had seriously considered cutting her hair for convenience but right now was enjoying the long golden curls. She had never had her hair this long before in her life and it quite changed the way she looked at herself. She knew she was still beautiful but it softened some of her features and gave her a more youthful appearance. She wore it up in a bun during the workday but right now she pulled the pins and let it flow down her back as she changed into a swimsuit and shorts. Putting on a toweling robe and flip flops she used the private elevator hotel elevator that only went to the upper floors where she lived and certain guests stayed and used a special key to go down to the employee entrance and walk across the sands to the beautiful aquamarine colored waters. Leaving the toweling robe, her shorts, and her flip flops on one of the chairs her hotel provided for its guests on this stretch of the beach she dove into the surf and began to do her daily routine of laps out to a far buoy and back. She was on her third lap when reality intruded in the form of her assistant.

"Ms. Paulson, there's an urgent phone call from England for you," Simone told her as she held out a portable phone and called to her from shore.

Reese rolled her eyes; there was an 'urgent' call almost every day from England these days. For someone who didn't have to help plan her daughter's wedding she was doing a lot of work for Gillian and for Lady Cantwell, remotely. She knew it was nerves with Gillian but Lady Cantwell, who she couldn't remember ever meeting was trying to include her into their 'family' since the poor dear had none of her own. It had offset the dynamics of the wedding and created a terrible imbalance in the church. Reese's suggestion that they elope had created chaos and when she finally got through to the uptight Lady Cantwell that she was joking she thought the poor woman had had a heart attack.

Reese walked out of the surf and Simone handed her the phone, "Hello?"

"Mom, I'm just calling to finalize some plans including your travel itinerary do you have some time?" Gillian asked.

Reese could hear the frazzle in her daughter's voice, "I'm sorry Gillian you just interrupted an important meeting," her eyes met Simone's and they both shared a grin.

"I can hear the surf in the background Mom," Gillian told her.

"I know, I'm outside with a client. Can I call you back later?" Reese hedged.

"Yes, but will you?" Gillian knew her mother very well and she was sure she was getting the brush off.

"As soon as I can baby girl, you take care now, bye!" she pushed the button to hang up the phone and handed it to Simone before grabbing her toweling robe and rubbing her face with it to get off some of the salt.

"Problems with the wedding?" Simone asked with a grin. Most of the calls from England these days were about Gillian's anticipated nuptials.

"Live and learn Simone, don't marry, elope!" Reese said exasperated. One of the many reasons she had never married, and the fact that no one had ever asked.

"She will be fine once you are there," Simone soothed. She watched her boss as she dried off her suntanned body. The two piece sports swim suit didn't cover much but then her boss had a good body to show off. All the men in the hotel thought so and after several firm rebuffs they were calling her the ice queen with her halo of blonde hair.

"I'm not so sure of that. I think it all stems from Lady Cantwell and the ripple effect of her nerves." She sighed, she would be there next week, and they would survive.

That night Reese looked out her ceiling to floor windows out over the beautiful ocean that it faced. She hadn't turned on her lights so she could see something of the water. Opening one of the patio doors she slid through it and allowed the cool night air to enter her apartments. One of the perks of living in the hotel was that her suite was one of the best and it overlooked this magnificent little harbor that had the barrier reef only a little ways off. She was often soothed to sleep at night by the waves hitting the beach. She was often awoken by the sound of people on the beach early. It was beautiful and she appreciated it.

Sometimes though she missed the outback and its silence, or rather the sounds that were unique to the station. She missed the people who had become her friends, she missed Sheila. She felt very lonely but shrugged it off with hard work.

Sitting up late nights and working on paperwork she was almost caught up on it all before she was due to leave on her vacation. She wanted the Morris' to have nothing to complain about on that end. She knew when she returned and they left that a lot of heads would roll. She had plans that would be implemented immediately and if they didn't like it that would just be too bad. The Morris' would have an efficiently run hotel and eventually the entire resort if she had to fire them to do it! She knew Mrs. Morris had run with the idea of a vacation as soon as she had left that meeting. If she played it right it might be longer than the one month she had asked for. She was eager to start if she could just get through her daughter's upcoming nuptials intact.

CHAPTER 53

As one of Steffan Cantwell many cousins escorted Reese to her seat in front of the church she heard whispers as they passed. It was inevitable since 99% of the church was packed with the Cantwell friends and families. Gillian of course had many friends who were in attendance but the amount was pathetically small compared to the endless mass of humanity represented by the Cantwells. Also the fact was that the bride's mother was incomparably beautiful, not well known, and lived in another country. It was a smorgasbord for the gossips. Many compared her daughter's beauty to her own, she had lived with that for a long time, didn't people realize how truly beautiful Gillian was in her own right, and to compare them wasn't fair to either of them. Reese had lost faith in her own looks a long time ago when it caused more problems than it helped.

As she walked on the young man's arm to her pew in the front she wished that her parents had lived to see this day. The huge wedding, the decorated church, the loving groomsman, her parents would have been so proud, they would have gotten the fairytale wedding that they had never seen for their own daughter. And Gillian, she would have made them so very happy, had done so up until their deaths. The one thing in Reese's life that she had never been regretful for was her amazing daughter. As she watched Steffan and his groomsmen come out she watched his face and could tell the exact moment he spotted Gillian as he lit up.

Gillian had asked her to walk her down the aisle but Reese had refused gently explaining to her daughter that it was her day, her moment and she didn't want the whispers and the untraditional request to mar it in any way. "You've got your own path to plow my darling girl, show them how proudly you go to this man who makes you so happy that you are willing to bind yourself to him for the rest of your life," she felt a little like Sheila with her sage advice, the mysticism to a degree. "I'm just your mother, I will always be there for you!" she told her happily and then laughed and added, "Do not make me a grandmother for at least five years!"

Gillian had understood. Her mother's arrival in England had caused all sorts of problems with Lady Cantwell who seemed to resent her beauty, her poise, her intelligence, and the fact that she had no escort. It unbalanced more than the seating arrangements. Reese took a few of her snipes but then gently reminded the woman that Gillian was *her* daughter and she was there for *her*. Whatever Gillian wanted was fine with her, it wasn't the 'Cantwell's' wedding but the Paulson-Cantwell wedding after all. The woman had sputtered but her husband quieted her. Reese had been immensely helpful despite being 1000's of miles away with her contacts and once there had immediately helped where she could. He found no fault in the woman and he too was soon under her charming spell.

When the minister indicated, Reese along with the rest of the assembled guests rose to the strains of the wedding march. She turned to watch her daughter walk proudly up the aisle. Reese was enchanted by the gown her daughter had chosen. A Vera Wang modern she looked elegant. How in the world had her darling little girl grown up into this beautiful woman? She felt the tears well up in her eyes as she watched her and only her.

Veronica gasped. She was holding little Clinton on her hip holding Vanessa's hand. Oscar stood beside them already a little drunk as he swayed there turning with the rest of the guests and being careful not to bump David who awkwardly stood on the outside at the aisle holding tightly to the back of the pew. Audrey stood on the other side of Veronica and heard her gasp quite audibly as she stared across the aisle at the blonde mother of the bride. Audrey was surprised at how the long hair made Reese look even more beautiful if that were possible. The ringlets only added to her youthful appearance and they appeared so natural. She had wondered when she received her own invitation if the bride were related to Reese, after all the name Paulson wasn't common in their circles. She now realized having never met Gillian that she must be Reese's daughter. What an odd coincidence, fate stepping in. Audrey watched the emotions flick across Veronica's face.

It had been five years. She would recognize that face, anywhere. It haunted her dreams, it entered her fantasies. She had changed though. Her hair was longer, much longer. How in the world had she gotten younger looking though? The dark tan made her look so healthy. Veronica felt immediately fat and gauche gazing at the woman who had taught her to love. Being eight month's pregnant though she was very large, in fact Oscar had wanted her to stay home with the children but she had refused the opportunity to go out socially. At that moment she put the name Gillian Paulson into its proper perspective realizing too for the first time that this must be Reese's daughter whom she had never met. She was marrying into the Cantwell family too, a prominent family of the ton who were distantly related to Oscar and hence the invitation. Veronica stared at her wishing she could somehow communicate with her. There would be ample opportunity later at the reception but she continued to stare, not even seeing the bride walk by. David tensed beside Oscar when he realized who the bride's mother was as well.

Reese never saw the group of people across the aisle staring at her so hard. David wondered if he would get a chance to talk to his brilliant ex estate manager, he had enjoyed their conversations. He also wondered at the relationship she had with his sister all those years ago and if it might prove awkward. He knew his sister had mourned her going; it had enabled him to maneuver her with Oscar into a marriage he knew she now regretted. Oscar stared at the somehow familiar woman through his blurry eyes, he knew her from somewhere and thought perhaps she was one of the many woman he had bedded over the years, if that were the case perhaps they could meet up again, she was very attractive after all. Veronica felt the anguish of unanswered questions, the baby moved a little painfully in her stomach and Clinton squirmed to get down. Audrey wondered at the emotions she saw flitting across Veronica's face.

Reese listened with such wonder at the beautiful words of the English ceremony. It was lovely. It was traditional. It was right. These two were being joined in a old-fashioned way. She wished fervently, and perhaps for the first time in years, prayed that her daughter would only know happiness. Steffan was a wonderful man and she respected him greatly.

Once they were married and introduced as Dr. and Mrs. Stephen and Gillian Cantwell the guests rose and cheered of all things. Reese had never heard a cheer in a church but she joined in the smiles as they all rose and the couple began to walk down the aisle. One of the groomsmen came to escort the mother of the bride and Lady and Lord Cantwell on the other side. Lady Cantwell was using a lace handkerchief to her best abilities, blubbering. Reese exchanged a sympathetic but amused glance with Lord Cantwell behind her head. Steffan must have inherited his sense of humor and for that Reese was relieved. Reese never saw the group that still stared so intently at her as she walked by.

In the receiving line Reese was introduced proudly time and again to the various people. As Gillian had been to many parties she was an accepted member to the family already. Reese found though that she knew many people from her time on the Cavandish Estate. Time and again people exclaimed in surprise not only at her altered appearance but that her daughter was Gillian. No one had made the connection.

Reese stiffened. David Cavandish was sitting in a wheelchair before her. Her glance confirmed that Veronica was nearby and the blood drained from her face momentarily. The man at her back weaving slightly must be Oscar. Oscar? He looked very old; time hadn't been kind to him. And there was Audrey! These children must be the much sought after heirs to Cavandish Estates. Veronica! God she looked hugely pregnant and by the propriety air of Oscar with his arm around her for balance he had done his wife proud. Reese took all this in a moment.

"Lord Cavandish! This is a surprise!" she said delightedly hiding her surprise that he was in a wheelchair but then that had been inevitable.

"Ms. Paulson, you are looking spectacular. Doesn't she look wonderful?" he turned to Veronica who just nodded stiffly beside him drinking in the beauty before her but not trusting herself to speak. Her eyes though said a lot. "Where are you working these days?"

"Oh, I've gone back into the hotel business," Reese said airily but as they were in the receiving line she left it at that keeping it short and sweet.

'Back?' thought Veronica, where had she been before? She certainly wasn't in Bangkok or any of the surrounding area's as she had been told. "Oscar, you remember Reese Paulson our estate manager from years ago?" she managed to squeak out.

Oscar put out his hand but didn't show any signs he recognized her through his bloodshot eyes.

Reese was drowning in those amazing violet eyes of Veronica's before she snapped out of it to look away, "Audrey, how lovely to see you again," Reese said as the line moved on. Veronica sent her one last look that promised they would have a conversation later.

"Still in Australia?" Audrey asked and then realized she was giving up the game. Veronica heard her and glanced back. It confirmed that Audrey had known where Reese was and it explained why Veronica hadn't been able to find her. Reese nodded and turned to the next person that her daughter was introducing her to.

The reception was right outside the estate church on the lawns to the beautiful estate house that the Cantwell's owned. As part of the estate as well as the town it was a short walk to where the tents were set up in a large mown field. Reese grabbed a flute of champagne from a passing waiter. She looked around for what she knew would be an uncomfortable confrontation. She wondered if she could make herself scarce but knew it was impossible with her being the mother of the bride. The pictures had been impossibly long but she had made a concerted effort to forget that Veronica was only yards away and waiting to talk to her. She thought happy thoughts and smiled for her daughter's sake.

"You look like your waiting for an executioner," Audrey whispered coming up beside her.

Reese turned with a laugh at her friend's sally. "I don't know what I am going to say to her. I've thought about running into her for years. I didn't expect her at my daughter's wedding obviously."

"How are you going to deal with it?" Audrey asked curious.

"I have no idea," Reese answered and for a woman used to handling crisis' and multi-tasking all day long this was an uncomfortable sensation. She saw Veronica hand her children off to her husband and begin to make her way towards them. Briefly she wondered how Veronica had handled the obvious intimacy that she had to of shared with her husband to get in that condition three times.

"Reese my dear! How are you?" Lady Emerson cooed loudly causing many people to turn to see who she was talking to.

Reese smiled in delight, she had always been fond of this little ole lady. "Lady Emerson, you look terrific. I'm doing well."

"I miss the station! It was such fun finding what you were going to do next. You drove my solicitor's mad with your idea's which always seemed to work out. They are relieved to have the station sold but I miss it and you! How's the hotel working out?"

Reese smiled and answered, "Fine," knowing that Veronica had come up and was getting an ear full.

"Do you ever see or hear from anyone from the station?" Lady Emerson must be getting hard of hearing she was so loud.

"Occasionally I get a note or an email but we have all moved on," she smiled.

"Reese had those stockmen eating out of the palms of her hands," she told the assembled group and Reese noted that David had wheeled up as well "Everyone adored her out there. You know she'd been managing that station of mine that Lord Emerson left me in Australia and won in card game?"

That explained why she had never been able to find her, she had been tucked deep away in the outback, the last place on Earth that she would have looked, thought Veronica.

"She did such a terrific job that I still hear from people who stayed there about the marvelous time they had on vacation there. She took a cattle ranch and turned it into what did you call it dear?" she turned from her audience back to Reese who stood there blushing.

"A dude ranch," Reese supplied her, her American accent never so apparent than at that moment.

"Yes, a dude ranch where everyone could experience ranch life to their heart's content. I myself went and loved it. Reese made it wonderful. She even flew the jet herself to get people there from Sydney," the woman was so enthused and delighted to regale her listeners with the tales she had repeated hundreds of times to all her friends. She totally forgot the agreement she had with Reese to never tell where she had been. "Do you still fly dear?" she asked Reese, not waiting for an answer as she turned back to her captive audience.

Reese sensed Veronica wanted to speak to her, desperately. David was watching the two of them as was Audrey but neither gave the other away. Reese was finally rescued by a harried Lady Cantwell who said, "We have one more picture dear," and pulled her away from her admirers. Reese was pleased to go as she heard Lady Emerson start talking about a cattle drive, something she had absolutely no personal knowledge of but didn't apparently care as she told stories about her station.

It wasn't until after the toasts were drunk and the dinner eaten that Reese found some time alone. The dancing would start in a while and she knew she couldn't avoid that either. Despite the tension she was causing within herself with Veronica's presence she was having a good time, she kept thinking; for her daughter's sake. She steadied herself in preparation for seeking out Veronica. She didn't get a chance as Lord Cantwell whiskered her off to 'meet' someone terribly important. Before she knew it, it was time for first dances, the bride and groom and his parents, Reese dancing with the best man in lieu of Gillian's father. Switching off to the father of the groom and then the groom himself and then mischievously dancing with her daughter who laughed delightedly.

"Mom, I love you!" Gillian smiled, her eyes suspiciously wet.

"That's good my darling girl because I love you too!" Reese smiled down at her daughter wondering where she had gotten those amazing dimples that her groom so obviously adored.

Veronica watched as Reese danced. The long golden locks swayed with her efforts. She looked incredible and Veronica felt miserable. She wanted answers though to her many questions and yet did she? They had both obviously moved on. When Reese began to dance with the bride the resemblance was apparent to all. They really looked nothing alike but yet there was a hint within the two beautiful women that could only be heredity. Veronica wished she could stop staring; already Oscar had slurred an insult about her watching the bride's mother.

It was late and Reese had danced with at least two dozen guests. She took a breather and another glass of champagne and sat down. She hadn't seen Veronica in a while and wondered with children in tow if she had left early. "Tired?" she heard gently in her ear and looked up to see a large stomach at eye level. Following it up she looked into those incredible purple eyes. She stood up immediately. Gesturing to a chair on the corner she said, "Join me?"

When Veronica was seated Reese couldn't help but notice how enormous she looked. How miserable she looked. Some women bloomed when they were pregnant, some got to looking tired and run down. Veronica obviously fell into the latter group. Reese had no idea how to begin their conversation.

"You've been in Australia all this time?" Veronica hesitantly began.

Reese nodded over the champagne glass she had just raised to her lips for fortification.

"Couldn't you have written, called, or talked to me in some way?" she asked quietly trying not to let her nerves get the better of her.

"No Veronica, I couldn't. A clean break was best for both of us. I still believe that."

"You left me without giving me a chance, you left me!" she said incredulous and despite trying not to let her emotions get involved she could feel her temper rising.

"I know I did. It was the only way. Things had changed, things had to change. I wasn't a part of your life that you needed. I couldn't be that part." Reese tried to explain and knew she was failing.

"You gave me no choice!"

Reese nodded, "I know, I didn't."

"I tried to find you but you lied to me didn't you?"

Reese nodded again.

"What else did you lie to me about?" she hissed, "Loving me?"

Reese felt like her heart was breaking again. Why hadn't she felt like this when she left Sheila? Had she known that she and Sheila were only 'temporary?' She was with Sheila for nearly five years and this woman only two, why did it feel so different? Shaking her head she said, "No, I never lied about that." She looked Veronica directly in the eyes trying to convey so much more. Suddenly she realized Sheila had been wrong, she wasn't supposed to of 'met' Veronica for two of her trips back to England but the third one, then she also realized she had canceled a trip because she was so eager to make the hotel job work so perhaps she had changed her own fate. She looked at Veronica drinking in the beauty of the woman who looked so tired, so worn, so uncomfortable.

Veronica looked down and sat there looking at a glass instead of back at Reese thinking over so many things.

"What was I supposed to think?" Veronica asked mournfully still feeling the pain that Reese had caused those years ago.

"That I loved you but couldn't stay," Reese said stupidly. She hadn't known what to say then and she really didn't know now.

"We could have worked things out..." she left off as Reese shook her head.

"No, you were at a different stage in your life than I was. There was no way I would stand in your way..."

"What do you mean 'stand in my way?'" she frowned looking at her curiously.

Reese felt very awkward. She didn't want to cause dissension between Veronica and David but she knew, instinctively knew that David had never explained her 'duty' to her. It wasn't Reese's place but at the same time she wanted Veronica to know the truth. "I couldn't give you what you needed." She quietly said.

Veronica looked at her as though she had gone mad, "I was happy with you. For the first time in my life, I was happy. Didn't you know that? Didn't you sense that?"

Reese knew, she sensed it, for she too had been very happy.

"What did I need?" Veronica asked.

"You needed *this*," and for the first time Reese touched her as she indicated her big billowing belly. "I could never have given you *this*. Oscar seemed to make you reasonably happy..." she stopped at the glare Veronica gave her.

"Reasonably happy? Do you know what my life is like with him? He's drunk most of the time. He spends money just to make himself 'feel better.' He sleeps with any woman who will let him. He's abusive, rude, uncultured..." she left off at the fury she saw on Reese's face.

"He's abusive? Why I'll...." she didn't know what she would do as she saw red before her eyes. Before she finished her sentence she got up to walk over to where he sat.

Veronica was alarmed. She had never seen Reese angry before in quite this way. Grabbing her arm she hissed, "Sit down!"

It took a second for Reese to realize the sense of Veronica's words and then she stared at her dumbly for a moment before complying. "He can't treat you that way!" she hissed.

Veronica's face softened as she realized Reese still cared, "He does and I don't let him get physical anymore," she thought of the incredulous look on his face when she downed him and nearly laughed, "Not since I floored him."

Reese cocked her head at the change in Veronica, she looked... amused, "You floored him?"

Veronica nodded and said, "Yes, he came at me to grab me and I reacted just like you taught me. It worked by the way," she couldn't help it and a snorting giggle escaped her control.

Reese felt immediately relieved. She calmed down. She grinned, "Well, at least some good came out of that!"

Veronica smiled and Reese's heart melted. It was so familiar it was etched in her brain. "You never went to Bangkok?"

Reese shook her head, "No, I had this terrific job offer and as it was so different from anything I had ever done, I tried it. I've been there up until a few months ago."

"I thought perhaps you had gone back to the States."

Reese shook her head, "I don't think I fit in there anymore but who knows what the future holds."

"What do you do now?"

"I'm managing a hotel for a resort. Eventually I will be managing the resort and then the rest of their properties as I get the hang of things."

"You are still in Australia?"

Reese nodded watching her carefully, examining her, memorizing each minute detail for future reference.

They chatted a little while longer and Reese asked, "You're managing the estate now?"

Veronica nodded and looked a little uncomfortable but then that could be because of her ballooning stomach. "When we got married I began to take over Oscar's estate as well. I don't know how I manage with all that and the children too but I just keep going, I don't have anything else..." she said sadly.

Reese didn't know what to say to that. She wanted to say, "I'll help you," but she knew she couldn't. Reese felt the awkward silence stretching and asked, "Tell me about your children?"

Veronica looked up and for the first time Reese saw something in her beautiful eyes. It was the first sign of happiness that Reese had seen, the first sign of life. She smiled and looked across the reception where Oscar sat with the two children who were playing on the chairs. "Clinton is our oldest, our beautiful boy. He is three. Then there is Vanessa who is two, she's a handful." She began to tell her all about her two 'babies' and what they had accomplished. Like every proud mama she thought they were child prodigies.

"When are you due?" Reese indicated her large belly.

Veronica looked down at her own mass and smiled nostalgically, it was one of the few things that made her happy these days, being pregnant, "Next month," she answered with a large smile and then looked up into Reese's stricken eyes.

Reese couldn't have given her that. She knew that David had been right. Veronica had needed these children. Although Oscar as a choice of her mate hadn't apparently worked out, at least she was getting the family Reese knew she had always wanted. They made her happy apparently.

Veronica wondered what Reese was thinking. At one time she would have asked at the look in her eyes. She seemed suddenly very sad.

"Can we go now?" Oscar suddenly stood there by the table with a sleepy child on each arm.

Veronica awkwardly got up from the table and tried to take one of them which Oscar gladly began to give her.

"Wait, I'll help," Reese offered. Veronica should not be picking up such heavy things at this stage, didn't he know that?

Oscar handed her the little boy and Reese settled him against her. It had been a while since she was around children and except for Sheila's various relatives she hadn't held one in years. He fit against her perfectly and wrapped his arms around her neck. He didn't seem to mind that she was a stranger and snuggled in to go to sleep. Reese looked over his head at Veronica who was staring in amazement. Following Oscar Reese headed with them towards the bride and groom for them to say their good-byes.

She looks like a natural with him, Veronica thought. He even superficially looks like her with the blonde hair. Clinton didn't just go to anyone and yet he had never hesitated. Did he instinctively know that Reese was a good person or what? For a moment Veronica fervently wished the children were Reese's too.

"Where'd you find him?" Gillian laughed at her mother. She couldn't remember ever seeing her mother hold a little child. With his blonde looks he could be hers she thought.

"Shhh, he's going to sleep," she indicated Veronica and said, "Gillian this is Lady Wilkins who used to be Lady Cavandish, and this is her husband Lord Wilkins and their delightful children," she indicated the little boy she was holding.

"It has been a pleasure but we really must be taking the children home," Oscar told Gillian and Reese was only amazed that he didn't slur the words as he stood there weaving.

Gillian and Steffan both said all the appropriate good-byes.

"I'm going to walk them out to their car," Reese said as she walked away with the couple.

Veronica kept pace with her despite her awkward gate. Reese held Clinton firmly and relished the feel of the small body against her. It brought back maternal feelings she had thought were long buried or dead. She couldn't remember feeling this way with any of the children from the station. Maybe it was because he was Veronica's, a part of hers that she could hold for a moment.

As they approached a long Rolls Royce, Reese was relieved to see a driver, knowing Oscar wouldn't be driving them. She was thrilled to see Frank get out of the driver's seat to help them get the children settled in their car seats. Oscar got in and was soon sitting comfortably in the back, he never offered to help his wife who awkwardly got into the back and sat facing the rear so she could roll down her window to talk to Reese before they left. Reese handed off the little boy reluctantly to his parents.

"Frank?" at her voice he looked at the long haired blonde who had accompanied his employers. His surprise was immediately apparent as his eyebrows raised into his cap.

"Ms. Paulson?" he exclaimed in surprised delight. He went to hug her and remembering his place held out a hand.

Reese ignored his hand and gave him a hug anyway, he appreciated it, and she smelled and looked so good. The long hair really changed her appearance. "It's good to see you ma'am," he got out.

"It's so good to see you too, say hello to everyone will you?"

"You won't be stopping by?"

She shook her head causing the long hair to dance, "I'm sorry, I just don't have the time. I'm leaving for London tomorrow and Sydney in two days."

"Well, it was good to see you anyway. I will tell everyone how well you are looking."

"It was good to see you Frank," she said with a kind smile.

Oscar leaned across his children and asked nastily, "Can we go now?"

Reese exchanged a quick glance with Frank as he hurried to get into the driver's seat, that glance told her Frank's opinion of Oscar. Reese looked at Veronica who looked back mournfully. They watched each other as the car pulled away saying not another word. A final wave was their last sight of each other.

Reese stood there looking long after the lights of the Rolls had faded. What if she had stayed? What if, what if, what if....

"Oh, hello Reese," she heard behind her and turned to see Audrey pushing David's wheelchair.

"Hello! I wish we had time to chat this evening, your leaving already?" she said with genuine regret.

"Yes, David is tired and as I came as his date I'm driving him back to Cavandish," Audrey smiled.

"Well, Lord David I do wish you well," Reese said with genuine affection. She didn't blame him for her what ifs. She had made her choices and she had to live with them. She wondered though, had he suspected the relationship was deeper between herself and his sister? Well, he had gotten his wish. He had heirs. She had done her 'duty' but his sister was unhappy, she wondered if he had thought of that eventuality.

They said their appropriate good-bye's and Reese headed back to the tent where the party was still in full swing and danced a few more dances but her heart wasn't in it. Pleading fatigue she eventually made her own excuses and headed up to her room. She was already packed and ready to go by the time her daughter and new son-in-law made a mid-morning appearance.

"You're going all ready?" Gillian asked regretfully.

Reese nodded, "Yes baby girl, I have to go. I only just started this job and I'm determined to make a success of it if it kills me. I have to get back."

They kissed each other goodbye and Reese stage whispered, "Don't make me a grandmother for at least five more years!" which had both of the newlyweds chuckling as she picked up her bags and headed out to her rental.

CHAPTER 54

Reese used her one free day to sight see, something she didn't do often enough. It cleared her mind but not her heart. She wished she might have her daughter, a friend, or someone (she tried not to think of Veronica) to see the sights with. Veronica though was heavily on her mind. She wished she could fix things for the 'mouse' that was no more. Veronica had grown into a strong woman and Reese hadn't been there to help her. Maybe that was why she was stronger now. Reese would never know she had given up the right to know.

It was as though she had conjured her though as the doorbell to her room rang that evening. Standing on the doorstep was a very pregnant Veronica.

"What in the world are you doing here?" Reese asked surprised.

Veronica smiled; she had been in and out all day looking for Reese while she had been out seeing the city. She had followed her up to London after 'visiting' the newlyweds one more time and pumping Gillian for information of her mother's whereabouts.

"Why do you want to know Lady Wilkins?" Gillian asked suspiciously.

"Oh, I'm going to be in London tomorrow and I thought if she hadn't left yet we might go to dinner. Has she left yet?" Veronica asked innocently knowing full well Reese hadn't left yet.

"No, I believe she leaves in two days," and proceeded to give her the hotel information.

"I'm doing a survey wondering if any hungry American's exist on this floor and could I take them to dinner?" Veronica's purple eyes danced having finally found her.

Reese smiled catching Veronica's spirit and said, "Well, statistically speaking with the time difference and all I should have eaten hours ago but no, this American hasn't and is starving, it's going to cost you a lot of money to feed me."

Veronica looked the thin blonde up and down and said, "You could use some feeding; a good wind would blow you away!"

Reese laughed and they went down to dinner in the hotel dining room. Reese was hungry and happy to see her friend. She hadn't been happy with the way they left things at the wedding and was thrilled to have a chance to talk some more. Reese ate a small steak, tons of vegetables, and Veronica ordered Reese's favorite Cabernet. After one small glass of her own Veronica made sure Reese's glass was never empty. Ordering another bottle for her room they adjourned to the couch in the suite and sat and chatted for hours.

Reese told her exciting and interesting stories about the outback in Australia and Veronica told her all about her children and managing both sets of estates. Reese gave her advice almost automatically and Veronica relished it. She just loved being with her again after all this time. It was so easy. The time passed and Reese had a bottle and a half all by herself. She was feeling so relaxed but she knew that Veronica was deliberately plying her with the wine. When Veronica started playing with the curly ends of Reese's hair she didn't mind. When Veronica leaned in closer as they were talking, Reese's voice faltered for only a moment before she let Veronica kiss her. It felt so right, it felt like coming home. Reese felt an immediate stab of desire. Her hands cupped Veronica's head as she held her close, smelling her unique smell and her wonderful perfume.

Veronica had planned this seduction. It had been on her mind since she left Reese at the wedding. She had been surprised at the lust she felt as she talked to Reese at the wedding and thought of her afterwards. At eight months pregnant she shouldn't be feeling this way but it had been so long since anyone had actually touched her. She couldn't use her toys inside of her at this stage and it wasn't the same with toys anyway, she needed the touch of another human being but not just *any* human being, *this one*. The *one* who had taught her and her body how to love.

Reese enjoyed the touch and the taste of Veronica. This was the woman she had craved for so long, thought about for so long, wanted to see, to taste, and to touch for an eternity. Veronica was hers, she had taught her, and at one time she had only been *with her*, she had been Reese's alone. That sense of belonging, of owning, of possession all swirled through her head as her tongue began its delicate dance with Veronica's. The first kiss blended into many as Veronica nearly climbed into her lap despite the big belly. Touching each other the caresses became fevered. Finally though Reese had to pull back, her conscience demanded it, her forehead against Veronica's own "I can't, we can't," she whispered.

"I want you, I still love you, please don't say no..." Veronica breathed.

"You're married Veronica," Reese tried to get some sense into her. It wasn't the wine, it wasn't the woman sitting on her straddling her, and it wasn't the pleading note in Veronica's voice that was weakening her she convinced herself. "This is wrong..."

"He's never touched me, I've never been with anyone else but you...." she kissed her again and said it against her lips.

Reese pulled back again and asked, "But you're pregnant...?" confused she looked deeply into those beautiful purple eyes and knew she was lost as she began to drown in them.

"Invitro fertilization, I'm still yours..." before she was kissing her again, desperately.

Reese capitulated and threw herself into the moment kissing Veronica hard and almost desperately in return. She fisted her hands into Veronica's hair to hold her head as she ravished her lips almost as though she were drinking after a long thirst. She began to remove the maternity blouse that Veronica was wearing caressing the bulging stomach that lay between them, kissing it tenderly. She reached up behind her to remove the maternity bra before the enlarged breasts fell into her face. She breathed the heady scent that was uniquely Veronica's mixed with her perfume. Memories assailed her as she remembered other times making love with this woman.

Veronica relished the moment when Reese stopped resisting her. She had thought of this woman almost daily for over five years. She was her 'dream' woman when she played with her toys, she was her fantasy woman, she was the only person who had ever made her feel so good inside and out. She had berated herself for missed opportunities while they were together, she had thought a million times of things she wanted to try that she had missed, she now had her before her and could actually touch her, could act out some of those fantasies. She couldn't get enough of touching her and with Reese fervently caressing her in return she felt fat and unattractive. For a moment she thought of stopping it, Reese must find her disgusting. When she made a move to stop her whispering, "Don't I'm too fat," Reese firmly pushed her hand away to caress her and say, "No, your beautiful, this is beautiful," and she caressed the bulging stomach and kissing again it making Veronica feel loved and cherished as only Reese could.

Reese rose from the couch pulling Veronica up, holding Veronica close she danced her into the bedroom where she laid her carefully on the bed. So caring, so careful. Veronica could only look at her with loving eyes anticipating how Reese would make her feel. Reese soon stripped her of the rest of her clothes and stripped the rest of her own off. Veronica admired the thin and muscular body with its deep dark tan; she smiled at the tan lines from obviously a bikini. She lay there feeling like a beached whale but Reese caressed her body so lovingly, so adoringly, she felt beautiful in those eyes. Reese kissed her way down her neck which arched to allow her access. She kissed across her chest and played with the engorged nipples which had Veronica moaning. She rubbed her extended belly and kissed over the mound amazed that a life was contained inside. Slowly she kissed down Veronica's body making sure she didn't miss an inch. She skipped between her legs and instead caressed and kissed along her legs, the sides, the hidden spots behind her knees. Veronica felt wonderful and only wished she could reach Reese's body as she bent over her own. "Relax," Reese whispered as Veronica tried to reciprocate in some way and they both smiled in remembrance. Veronica lay back and took it enjoying the sensations that were being provoked. She already knew she was very *very* wet and she eagerly anticipated Reese's touch, and when it came she nearly orgasmed instantly, instead she tamped it down, delaying it, prolonging the sensations and their time together.

Reese played with the wetness gently as she kissed her way up Veronica's legs before first kissing and lovingly tasting her clit. Veronica arched into her mouth having fantasized about this moment for years. Reese expertly worked her clit as her fingers slipped inside and petted her G spot. Veronica nearly rose off the bed from the sensation that provoked. She hadn't been able to do it to herself ever, her toys didn't hit it, and Reese's knowledgeable fingers made her feel fantastic. She couldn't look down and see but oh could she *feel*. Gently Reese plunged inside almost accidentally brushing the G spot with her fingers as she flicked and licked Veronica's clit over and over with her amazing tongue. Veronica's excitement grew until she was hoarsely panting little cries of her duress and in a shriek she came and came her body bucking under Reese's ministrations. Reese held her and played with her until her body quieted and then she rose up over her and began to rub their clits together. This new sensation made Veronica's eyes bulge open. She had thought about something like this before but Reese had never done it to her and she liked it, very much so. Reese ground against her to find her own release and Veronica could tell it wasn't giving her what she wanted or the satisfaction that would come from her own release.

"Sit on my face," she whispered hoarsely.

Reese looked at her in surprised amazement. She started to shake her head thinking that it would be too much for the hugely pregnant woman but her lust filled eyes told their own story.

"Please, sit on my face; I've fantasized about it for so long..." Veronica whispered almost desperately her fingers grasping unconsciously in her pleading.

Carefully Reese drew herself up and over the mound that was her stomach and straddled first her shoulders and looked down on her lover. Veronica raised her hands to cup Reese's buttocks and urge her up as her chin lowered. She could scent Reese's arousal and wanted desperately to taste her. She raised her head to meet the clit that was coming towards her mouth as Reese gently placed her crotch on her face. As Veronica got her first taste she felt ecstatic that she was finally making this particular fantasy come true. She felt almost trapped, totally subjugated but at the same time so powerful that she was making Reese feel so good. She looked up Reese's flat body and raised her hands feeling up that incredible body and playing with her nipples. Reese threw her head back and arched into her hands grinding down slightly on her mouth as it worked her clit and wetness. It felt so good and when one of the hands slipped between them and began to play with that wetness first outside and then in Reese thought she would collapse on Veronica and smother her. It felt so damn good! Veronica worked her and enjoyed the little pants of obvious arousal she heard from her partner. Reese ground down into that mouth and hand that was giving her so much pleasure. Her orgasm caught her by surprise. It didn't rise slowly out of her as she was expecting and instead just appeared and was jerked out of her. The effect was devastating and she caught herself as she held onto the headboard from falling and collapsing on Veronica's face. When she felt strong enough to get off she gently rose and settled herself next to her lover's body caressing her as she kissed gently along her shoulder in gratitude for how she was feeling. Veronica turned as best she could to have full access to Reese's body returning the caresses and kisses in the aftermath of both their orgasms.

The caresses continued, they had both missed each other too much, too long, and taking advantage of the moment was their only chance.

Apparently it wasn't over for either of them as the moment escalated for both of them. Each of them felt their arousal and started grinding and rocking against each other. Reese contorted herself around Veronica's bulging stomach but her longer torso accommodated it. They were both soon aroused to a fever pitch and although the orgasms weren't as intense as before they were mutual, within moments of each other, and completely satisfying. They lay there side by side breathing in the essence of each other, enjoying the closeness, the comfort. Reese couldn't seem to help herself from caressing Veronica's bulging stomach.

"Do you find it disgusting?" Veronica asked sleepily.

Reese shook her head immediately, "No, not at all. I'm in awe. It's just so amazing how a little person can grow inside of you and when you meet him or her to realize what you have created."

Veronica thought for a moment and then said bitterly, "It will be my last."

Reese looked up concerned and asked, "Why?"

"I don't like how Oscar treats me and the children. I've been able to shelter the children from most of his abuse but I can see its growing. I have to work out a way to get him to cease. He is very angry at this bargain we call a marriage." She looked down and then her glance flicked to Reese's, "I don't know why he is so angry. He's got all the prestige he wanted by marrying into my family. He has access to the finest horses our money can buy, and he buys more all the time. He has his little pieces on the side and I don't object, so why is he so angry?" she was truly puzzled.

"Maybe, he just wants you," Reese said quietly knowing that would be enough for her.

Veronica shrugged unconcerned. She despised the man she had once thought of as a friend. "He has become disgusting."

"Hey, let's not discuss your husband here," Reese turned her face to her and kissing her said, "We only have tonight together, let's enjoy the moment."

Veronica didn't need that reminder and surrendered herself to the moment concentrating on the feelings that Reese incited and only Reese had ever provoked.

Reese woke early in the morning despite having drunk an entire bottle of wine herself and getting very little sleep. She could feel Veronica's protruding stomach against her back and realized what had really woke her was the kick she could distinctly feel. She smiled remembering her own one and only pregnancy. It might have been horrible except for her parents and their loving support. Veronica only had David who didn't or couldn't understand that she was alone. Audrey was too self-absorbed to really deal with anything besides their friendship. Ana had helped but was hindered by their doctor patient relationship to a degree, she could listen, she could offer advice, but she couldn't make Veronica do anything. Ultimately it was up to Veronica and despite wanting to help her, having helped her in the past, only Veronica could make herself happy, whole, and whatever she wanted to be.

She lay there smiling remembering their evening together and then feeling sad that she had to leave today. She had already returned her car rental preferring to take a cab to Heathrow when she needed it. She wondered how difficult Veronica was going to make it. Logically she had to of known it was only this one night that they would be together. Reese remembered the end of their previous relationship and how that clingy feeling Veronica had caused had helped her to make the break wanting desperately to just get away on some levels. It had been one of the many excuses she used but ultimately it had driven her away. Why had she let Veronica seduce her last night? Remembering the woman she knew from over five years ago she knew this wouldn't be a good goodbye. She knew though what Veronica had been doing and let it happen because she too had wanted it.

Reese knew the moment Veronica's breathing signaled that she was waking up. She was wrapped so tightly against Reese almost as though she were afraid she would leave without waking her. Reese didn't mind because she wanted this closeness, she wanted this woman. Despite being a pain in her backside at times, she still loved her on so many levels. Levels that Sheila had never tread upon and that made Reese wonder what was wrong with her. Sheila had been a good partner, a loving woman and yet there was always something not completely there for either of them. They both knew it, Sheila perhaps more so than Reese but it was nothing that would keep them together forever. Something about Veronica drew Reese back even after all this time. Reese had been with Sheila nearly five years and Veronica nearly two and yet the draw was totally different. Was it the fact that she knew Veronica needed her, needed protection to a degree? Reese turned over to look upon the face, the one that she had thought about so often over the last five years. It had filled out considerably with her pregnancy but it was still the same endearing face she had fallen in love with. She sighed wondering if their parting today was going to be difficult.

Veronica watched Reese through half closed eyelids wondering what she was thinking about as she examined her face so closely. In the pre-dawn light it was difficult to see anything but Veronica didn't want to waste a moment of their limited time together. She had hoped they would end up in bed together when she made this difficult journey to see her but hadn't been sure it would work. She was so glad that it had. She loved this woman more than life itself. She was grateful for her teaching her the job, her abilities that she hadn't known existed, her confidence to defend herself, but most of all she was grateful for the love they had once shared. She only regretted that it had ended but now she at least understood a little better that Reese hadn't wanted to leave, had thought that Veronica needed more than she could offer. Perhaps she was right but Veronica sensed David's fine hand in this and wondered if her resentment towards the situation might change their relationship ultimately. She felt sorry for him but he had his precious heirs through her.

Reese must have sensed she was awake because she leaned down to kiss her and with her response began to passionately make her breathless once more. Not passing up this last opportunity to make love to each other they were both soon panting over each other and enjoying the bittersweet moments they had as they made love around the baby that Veronica was carrying. As they showered together Reese couldn't stop showing her how much she loved her body despite Veronica's feelings that she was bloated and unattractive. Reese brushed any protestations aside and assured Veronica that she was desirable.

Reese was surprised when it came time to leave that Veronica offered to drive her to Heathrow and drop her off. As it was not in the same direction that Veronica needed to go to get back to Cavandish Estates Reese assured her she could catch a cab. Veronica insisted saying, "It's the least I can do and besides it will give us a few more moments together," how could Reese resist this plea when she felt the same way?

CHAPTER 55

The flight was similar in many ways to the one she had taken over five years ago missing Veronica desperately. She had been surprised at how Veronica handled it, wishing her well but not saying anything that made Reese uncomfortable or the expected clingy. Reese thought about her the entire flight as she dozed in and out of consciousness from her lack of sleep.

Veronica had to pull over to the side of the road to cry her eyes out. She stopped several times on the journey back to stretch her legs and give the baby some exercise and to pee. She wondered if the multiple orgasms she had experienced were causing some of the cramps she was getting, they didn't increase so she crossed her fingers that she wasn't in premature labor. She too thought constantly about Reese. She thought she had handled their parting maturely and knew she had to of surprised Reese with her lack of 'poor me' attitude. Veronica realized she had grown up a lot recently, perhaps in just the last few days since seeing Reese once again after all this time. She loved her, she couldn't have her, and their interlude together would have to suffice for the memories she now shared with her. There had been no last minute pleas or requests to stay in contact. She knew now that Reese was working in Australia and that provided her some relief just knowing where she was and that she was okay. Seeing how healthy she was, how good she looked, and knowing she still desired her had also given her some of that relief. She made no plans for her future or theirs since there was no future for them. She had a child to produce and the three she would have to raise. Reese's future was her own and Veronica resigned herself to having no part of it.

CHAPTER 56

When Reese returned she was surprised that the Morris's were not only willing but able to give up the control that she had demanded prior to her vacation. She sensed Mrs. Morris had argued until Mr. Morris capitulated fully. She began to enact the changes she had wanted from the beginning. Within three months people were happier with things that she had done and she was promoted to running the entire resort. Within two years she was running all of the Morris properties up and down the coast and they were thrilled with her work. Mrs. Morris had finally gotten her husband 'retired' and enjoying their hard gotten gains the way they had planned and Mr. Morris had a more than a competent manager for their properties so he needn't worry about it anymore. Reese sold off a couple of their smaller less profitable properties and he couldn't be more thrilled with the dividends.

Reese knew that thinking about Veronica was a bad idea at most times. But especially bad when she was horny and had no outlet except for returning to her suite for toys. That did not appeal in any shape, manner, or form most of the time and was only a last resort. As she assured herself she was entering the bar and checking on the dance floor for the 'hotel' she tried to convince herself she was not scoping out the locals. She had been hit on so often since she moved here, but had never mixed business with pleasure since her last two near disasters, she had concentrated on business and had earned the nickname 'ice maiden' by her blonde good looks and lack of paramours. As almost 90% of the offers had come from men she didn't particularly care. She was dressed casually but classy enough that she could go to a business meeting if the need arose; you never knew who you might run into and have to discuss business details with. She also looked hot as the glances that were thrown her way attested to.

She looked through the bar and onto the dance floor. Many tourists gathered here to drink and dance the night away and since their 'club' now also opened out onto the beach it had become a popular night spot. She was pleased as this was one of the many changes she had enacted that had turned out for the better over the years she had been here. She made eye contact with a few women and even fewer men but passed them all by. One woman with dark hair caught her eye again and again. Superficially she looked like Veronica but Reese had learned to put Veronica out of her mind since their ill-advised but totally memorable one night stand. Although neither of them regretted it at the time, it had preyed on her mind on many levels for months and she still thought about her a lot. She had even looked up Sheila once to talk to her only to be told that she had moved to another village and resigned her post at the station. Reese sent her a letter but had never heard from her perhaps that was for the best. She had just decided this was a bad idea when a youthful voice asked at her shoulder, "Would you care to dance?"

Reese turned and was surprised that the woman with the dark hair was at her elbow looking up and asking her to dance. She had fine bones and looked a lot younger to Reese's eyes. Her hair was the only comparison that still reminded Reese of Veronica. She was more petite in an athletic sort of body. She appealed on so many levels but mainly that Reese hadn't been with anyone in years and wanted to be with someone tonight. Smiling brilliantly at the younger woman she stunned her momentarily as she answered, "Yes, I would." She let herself be taken by the hand as she was led onto the dance floor and started dancing to the beat. The woman soon moved in closer to synchronize their moves together. She was soon touching Reese's hips with her hands to coordinate their moves. Reese moved closer and they were soon kissing, gently at first, and still managing to dance to the rhythm of the music. When the woman who Reese still didn't even know her name began to kiss down Reese's long neck she hit a point that was always a trigger for Reese and she moaned. The woman pulled back a moment to look up deeply into Reese's eyes, they were soon kissing deeply and dancing to their own rhythm.

After a couple of dances Reese said, "Would you like to come to my room?" She was pleased and surprised when the woman nodded and taking her by the hand led her off the dance floor.

Reese never had picked someone up like this. If it wasn't for the fact that she was so horny, so lonely, and hadn't been with someone since Veronica years ago she might not have put herself in this situation. As they walked across the hotel lobby Reese dropped her hand, the woman looked over surprised but continued to accompany her to the private bank of elevators. Using her key Reese opened one and they both got in. The woman went to take her in her arms but Reese pointed at the cameras and shook her head. It didn't take long to get up to Reese's floor. Once inside the luxurious hotel room that was laid out like an apartment Reese took her in her arms and began to kiss her ardently. Kissing led to other delightful pleasures such as caressing and groping. Reese turned her about and began to undress her being firm and taking what she wanted from the woman who seemed to acquiesces to her demands and let Reese do whatever she wanted to her and her body. Reese took what she wanted, she gave pleasure as well, but it wasn't what she wanted…or rather whom.

Reese watched the woman sleep in her bed; she sat in a chair by the window. She felt awful. Never in her life had she had a one night stand. She didn't even know the woman's name. After the intimacies they had just shared she was ashamed of herself and what she had done. She was an attractive woman, she didn't need to pick up strangers in a bar and bring them home. She had been too lazy and too anxious to work on a relationship in a long time. This was not her style and the self-loathing she felt wasn't comfortable. She was berating herself mentally when she realized the woman who was sleeping so soundly in her bed had allowed herself to be put in this situation. Had allowed herself to be taken, and Reese had taken a lot. The violence she felt in herself, just below the surface had come out to a degree and not since Sheila had she allowed herself that forcefulness. With Veronica it had always had to be gentle because of her past and the fact that Reese loved her so much. With Sheila it had been wild and sometimes almost violent but they had both loved in their own ways. With this woman it had been anonymous and Reese had led the way, not allowing the woman to gentle the act as Reese took her again and again and then took her own pleasures against the woman's willing body. It had been a wrestling match that Reese enjoyed thoroughly but she had really given no thought to the woman she had pleasured. The woman's pleasure had just been to enhance Reese's own. She felt totally selfish and was disgusted with the way she had behaved. The woman slept in an exhausted sleep with her arms flung out in supplication. Reese watched her and wondered.

"Good Morning," the woman's voice came to her as Reese read the newspaper and drank her morning coffee.

Reese looked up and smiled, "Would you like something?" she indicated the breakfast spread she had ordered.

The woman looked relieved having expected something totally different in response apparently. She was dressed in the same outfit from the night before. "I should be going," she offered hesitantly, again waiting for some sign or something to be said.

Reese had no idea what to offer and instead nodded and got up to let her out of the hotel room.

The woman turned to her at the elevator and smiling said, "I had fun last night, thank you," before the doors closed.

Reese hadn't really said anything but then what could she really say? "Me too?" how lame would that have been. She was already embarrassed at her behavior and was only relieved that the woman had left before she really humiliated herself like asking, "And what was *your* name?"

Reese dismissed the incident as a moment in time. She avoided the bars unless she was there on business for the resort. Months went by where she dedicated herself to her work and took very little time off for herself. She went places of course on her time off and for work as some of it was required in a resort and properties this size. She regularly met with people who had services they wished to offer to the resort, the hotel, and their guests. She was frequently out to dinner on 'dates' with men or women who had an agenda. She was also commonly hit on by both sexes. She still refused all offers as diplomatically as possible. Her dedication to her work and her ethics hadn't gone unnoticed with the staff and certainly not with the Morris' as her pay had increased substantially over the years. She was set for life but she wondered sometimes why she still did this. She didn't have to work anymore; she had achieved her goals and certainly had enough to retire with. She knew though that for some reason she felt the desire to keep on working. She wondered though if she was going to end up alone or was she waiting for someone? Anyone who saw this attractive woman would have thought she had everything, they certainly would never have realized how lonely she really was.

CHAPTER 57

Reese was out on the Great Barrier Reef having finally succumbed to the owner of this chartered boat request after nearly two years. Jack was a nice guy; his daughters who also helped with the charters were equally nice. In fact, if rumors were true one of his daughters was gay and while Reese was definitely attracted to him she would not mix business with pleasure. Besides, she knew Jack was interested in her as well. It could be a horrible situation if she wasn't careful.

Sitting on the boat she was carefully baking her already bronze skin when a shadow interrupted the flow of sunrays. Shading her eyes she looked up into Jacks amused blue eyes.

"You can't come out here and not go snorkeling," he indicated the gear he was holding in both hands as he admired her bikini clad body. He had seen it before on the beach and been trying to get her on his boat forever but this was the first time she had agreed to come.

Reese rose from the deck effortlessly showing her grace and physically fit body unselfconsciously. Smiling she stunned Jack with its brilliance as she reached for one of the sets of fins and mask asking, "So, there aren't any sharks in this area?"

Jack laughed as though she had actually made a joke, "There are sharks all over the reef."

Reese hesitated for a moment but figured he knew what he was doing. He hadn't invited her out here to act as shark food. He showed her how to strap on the gear using it as an opportunity to lightly touch her. Reese recognized the effort but felt nothing from it. His daughters were staying on the boat as one of them watched them interact. As they slipped into the water she followed him as he began to show her the various spots. Diving down a little they came to area's with unbelievable beauty. She wondered if she should return with scuba gear to see even more of this incredible reef. It was absolutely astounding how the fish seemed to know they meant them no harm and were showing off for the two of them. Sure enough they saw different kinds of sharks that Jack pointed out to her but nothing that seemed threatening. She of course thought of Jaws but staying close to Jack she felt he at least would let her know if there was any danger. It was an amazing experience and she was surprised how quickly time flew. Between the sun and the water and despite her own physical fitness, a couple of hours and she was beat.

Lida helped her get her feet back on the boat as she climbed up the ladder and over the rail. She was a little unsteady and was grateful for the extra help although Lida held on a moment too long. Reese looked into her hazel eyes and recognized the attraction immediately, unconsciously returning the look into the now startled hazel eyes. She turned away as Gaby was there to help take her and her father's gear.

"Amazing isn't it?" he smiled.

Reese couldn't help but noticing how handsome Jack was but she just wasn't interested. She wished she were because he was an attractive specimen. She liked talking to him but other than as a friend she wasn't physically attracted to the man. It sure would make things easier if she were though. She grinned, "I think I should get scuba gear and come back."

He liked her enthusiasm, "We have the gear anytime you want to learn."

Gaby pulled up the anchor and Lida who was startled to realize that her admiration for Reese and her longing looks hadn't gone unnoticed stared at her in fascination. In fact after that one look they had just shared she would swear the woman her father had been after for years was gay or at least bi. Lida started the powerful engines and headed the boat expertly back into the bay where they docked.

Reese thanked her hosts and got into the car that was waiting to take her back to the resort. She had agreed to meet them all for dinner on her at the hotel. When she got back she took a long shower to get the salt off her bronzed skin and to add conditioner to her almost white blonde hair. By the time she toweled it mostly dry, brushed it out, reapplied her makeup and got dressed it was nearly time for dinner. She dressed in a nice little black dress and heels. Meeting Jack and his daughters at the dining room she was pleased to see that not only Jack approved of her appearance but Lida. She was also pleased to see they had dressed up a bit as well. Jack in a nice tan suit and both his daughters in dresses that flattered their well-toned bodies.

During the course of dinner, fish of course, they discussed other charters and scuba diving adventures they had been on. Jack was ten years older than Reese and his daughters ten years younger. Fraternal twins they still looked very similar although not identical. They were both well-educated and very interesting. Reese tried not to show undue interest in Lida who still managed not only to sit on Reese's other side but to casually touch her a few times just to see her jump. With Jack on her other side she devoted a lot of conversation to him to avoid this daughter who apparently had decided to pursue Reese under her father's very nose.

Reese had a hard time over the next few days. Jack wanted to start 'going out' together and a repeat of their day out only in the form of a scuba diving session. Lida was showing up at inopportune times and making a nuisance of herself at Reese's work. Using the excuse of her work being so busy Reese escaped to one of their properties further north. It didn't stop the phone calls from both Jack and Lida.

"Hello?" she didn't recognize the number on her cell.

"Hello Reese," Lida answered. She had hesitated to call sensing that Reese was feeling uncomfortable about the whole situation but yet so attracted to the stunning blonde she couldn't help herself.

"Hi Lida, how are you," she tried to be polite. This was amazingly awkward with both Jack and Lida pursuing her. She hadn't encouraged either of them and their one excursion seemed to of opened a Pandora's Box.

"I'm good, how are you?"

"Busy, work work work you know?" Reese smiled but was puzzled at this call.

"Ah, all work and no play make Jack a dull fellow," Lida riposted laughing.

It was the mention of Jack though that made Reese stiffen, was she amused at this situation? This was his daughter for God's sake. "Well, it is my job after all," Reese answered.

"When will you back?" she inquired hopefully. She had been fantasizing about Reese for a long time, almost as long as her father had and now having exchanged that look, she *knew*, she *felt* there could be so much more.

"I'm really not certain," Reese answered hesitantly. She didn't want to give this woman any hope. She couldn't and with Jack a part of the scenario, it was really not a viable relationship.

They chatted for a while longer and then Reese really did have to go. She had just rung off, handled some work, when Jack called and the conversation was very similar to the one she had just had with his daughter. On impulse and perhaps as a way to stop this before it got ugly or untenable Reese mentioned, "I just got off the phone with Lida."

Jack was surprised. He had just seen his daughter as she geared up a boat for one of their many charters. She must have been on the headset because he hadn't seen her on a phone. "What did she have to say?"

"Oh pretty much the same as you. I thought it was amusing that the both of you called. I appreciate it but I'm just very busy. You knew that though with trying to get me to go out on the boat for so long." She was trying to let him down easy. There was no way anything beyond a friendship was viable and she wouldn't let her attraction to Lida hurt him so she wouldn't even start that one.

He sighed, "Yes, I knew you were a busy one. Well, let me know when you're back. If you have time we could perhaps do something together, let's not let it take two years again." He knew though without her saying that there weren't reciprocal feelings. He had felt he was reaching with his attraction to her for so long but she was a beautiful woman and he liked her fine mind. He was a bit puzzled at Lida's involvement though.

Reese relaxed. He had gotten the slight innuendo of 'let's be friends' without her having to spell it out. They chatted for a few more minutes before ringing off. When the calls kept coming from Lida over the next few day's Reese let them go to voicemail and only returned them through voicemail letting her know she was just so very busy. It wasn't a lie, Reese was indeed very busy but she could have found time for the attractive woman if she had truly wanted. She regretted this course of action but felt she had no choice, it was too bad really, Lida was an attractive woman and Reese would have loved to pursue it if not for Jack.

CHAPTER 58

Reese hadn't had a vacation since her daughter's wedding. She was due over six weeks but knew being gone that long wasn't feasible all at one time despite her excellent assistants and managers that she had trained herself. Although she would have loved to have visited her daughter who had settled into married life astonishingly well, she wanted to see things she hadn't seen before, a real vacation. She knew she was fooling herself that she didn't want to go to England and be that near to Veronica. She couldn't afford a repeat of the last time they were together, it would destroy her soul. The one night 'stand' they had had taken months to get over the guilt and yet she knew she wouldn't have done things differently. She loved Veronica, perhaps would always love her but she couldn't have her, she had children and a husband and while it wasn't a good marriage, she *was* married. Reese felt that at least should have been sacred and she should honor it. Her children must come first and she wouldn't screw up any of that for her. Distance was the answer. She really couldn't be further away from England than Australia if she tried.

While in the north at some of the properties she made arrangements to be gone for at least two weeks of her vacation. She had excellent staff that she herself had picked and trained so she knew things would run smoothly without her being there constantly to attend to every detail herself. She admitted she was not going back to the main hotel and resort because Lida's phone messages had become more intense and revealing. Reese no longer answered her phone if it read Lida's number, a 'private' number, or a number she didn't recognize since Lida had begun to ring her from random or unknown numbers. Her patience was wearing thin and Reese could think of no other way to avoid her than to go on vacation. She returned for only one night, long enough to pack another set of suitcases and board a plane to New Zealand. She landed in Auckland and began her adventures there.

CHAPTER 59

The inn she was staying in was out of the way and had a private beach. The tours she had already gone on revealed that New Zealand was as unique as Australia. It was so different from anything she had ever seen and yet it reminded her in some places of California and what she had read of Italy. She enjoyed what she had seen and welcomed after the chaos of her intense job and then the tour to stay for a few days in this little inn that had been recommended to her. It was pricey but she could well afford it. The solitude was just what she needed. Her cell phone didn't work but she called the office every few days from a landline anyway to check up and so far nothing had come up that she couldn't handle from thousands of miles away.

"Hello," a pleasant voice greeted her as she lay on the sand on her towel and watched the waves that were mesmerizing her. It was really too chilly to be lying out but she had become so used to doing this almost daily back at the hotel that she was addicted to it. It had become her winding down relaxing time and it cleared her head for business, almost a meditation. Now she was using it as an excuse to decide whether to hike into the little village the inn was located outside of for dinner or eat at the inn. Not many major decisions on this vacation.

Reese shaded her eyes from the glare of the sun and looked up. She couldn't really see who was standing there but by the figure before her and the pleasant voice she guessed correctly that it was a woman, "Hello yourself," she answered.

"Ah, you're an American," the woman replied.

"Actually, I am," Reese laughed. She hadn't thought about it in a long time since she hadn't lived there in years but technically, yes she was an American. Not that she wasn't proud of it but she certainly had been living abroad a long time.

"May I join you?" the woman asked.

"Certainly," Reese said and made to move over and sit up on her towel where she had been lying face down.

"Oh, don't let me inconvenience you!" the woman exclaimed.

"That's all right, I should be getting up, and it's too chilly really to be lying here on the sand."

"That's how I knew you were a tourist. None of the locals would have been caught here with the tide coming in."

Reese looked out again at the water and sure enough she could see it was rising. She got up effortlessly and began to gather her few things into a beach bag. "Thanks for the warning," she told the woman who she could now see better without the sun behind her. She was worth seeing too. She was a few inches shorter than Reese with curly sand blonde hair that reached her shoulders. Reese couldn't tell if it was a perm or natural but it looked nice on the woman who looked back at her with warm brown eyes framed with a double set of eyelashes. She had a pleasant and pretty face with a fine almost too small nose and mouth. She smiled at Reese and that was what made her very pretty indeed. It transformed her pretty face into something so much more. Reese found herself almost staring. "Are you a local?" Reese asked.

The woman shook her head, "No, I'm an Aussie, here on vacation. And you? You're from America?" She asked politely. They began to make their way up the sandy path away from the slowly incoming tide. She was surprised when Reese shook her head.

"I'm from America but I live in Australia. I manage a hotel," she said matter of factly downplaying her actual role. She didn't need to brag, she knew her worth.

"Oh really, what part of Australia?" her companion asked as they hiked up the rather steep path together.

"I'm off of Queensland by The Great Barrier reef in a town called Mulumba," she answered wondering if the woman would have heard of it despite it being a tourist destination it was huge country after all. "Have you heard of it?"

The woman laughed, "I'm living in Mulumba Minor!"

The village outside of the town hadn't wanted to give up its name so one was called Mulumba Major and one Mulumba Minor, they were really the same town but run separately. A friendly rivalry existed between the two villages. Reese shook her head at how strange that was and how small the world. They chatted for a while as they climbed the steps from the beach which was now swamped with the incoming tide. Reese was grateful for she wasn't sure of the times here and might have been in trouble if not for the timely rescue by this woman.

"I'm Ariel Timmons," the woman said as they reached the top of the path and steps to the inn.

Reese held out her hand and shook the woman's as she said, "Reese Paulson."

They chatted a while and Reese was pleased when the woman invited her to join her and her friends who were also from Mulumba for dinner in the little village.

"Here she is now," Ariel told her friends as Reese walked into the pub where they were meeting. She had changed her clothes from the beach to something casual for dinner.

"Good Evening," Reese smiled at the group and Ariel quickly introduced her friends. Reese was pleased they were all about the same age as herself or just a few years younger, it meant they might have a few more things in common. There were four men and two other girls besides Ariel which meant Reese evened it off nicely.

Although a small village the pub was a happening place. The others were staying at a hotel at the far end from Reese's little inn. It was too commercial for Reese's tastes and as she lived in one like it she didn't want that for her vacation. She enjoyed talking to all of Ariel's friends and they compared notes of where they had been and what they had seen. They had been in New Zealand for a few days and Reese for over a week already. She had done the whole 'tourist' thing since she knew nothing or where anything was. One or two of Ariel's friends had been there before and were showing their friends around. They found it fascinating that she was brave enough to strike out on her own. A couple of them went and danced in the small corner where the 'dance floor' was with even a small live band. Their dinners arrived and the food was quite good. Reese found herself sitting between Ariel and a man called Igor.

Igor had made it plain that he was interested in her but she also made it clear she wasn't interested in anything but friendship. He concentrated on a girl on his other side named May and this allowed Reese to talk to Ariel.

She found that Ariel had been named after that Disney movie with a princess of the same name. Her parents had loved the movie, fell in love on a date to see it and consequently were convinced she was conceived when they bought the tape years later, hence the name Ariel. Reese laughed with her about the story. Ariel was a marketing manager for a small firm that coincidentally Reese did business with through the hotel. She didn't tell Ariel this yet not wanting to brag.

They had a wonderful time. All of them dancing after dinner and having a good time. Since it was a good sized group it was nice when a few of them paired off that there were still others who kept up a lively conversation. Although most of her evening Reese talked with Ariel she also talked with May and several of the others. It was quite late before she said she had to be going. Ariel said she needed to clear her head from the many beers she had consumed and if Reese didn't mind she would walk with her a ways.

"I enjoyed your friends," Reese's head indicated the pub they had just left as they walked along the street back towards her inn.

"They're good mates," Ariel smiled.

They walked in silence for a moment and after the noises from the pub had receded it was very quiet indeed.

"How long are you staying?" Ariel finally asked.

Reese shrugged, "I have no definite plans. That was the plan when I came here for vacation. I could go anywhere; see anything, on a whim."

Ariel smiled, "We will be pulling out in a day or so."

Reese nodded not knowing what to respond really as they walked along. It had turned chilly with a fog rolling in. She had packed for this and was now dressed in jeans and a sweater which she had removed in the pub and was grateful for now.

"Reese, may I ask you something?" Ariel asked.

Reese stopped, they were almost to the inn and Ariel had only asked to walk part of the way. She nodded looking inquiringly at Ariel.

"Are you gay?" Ariel asked bluntly.

Reese's eyes widened slightly at the suddenness of the question but nodded, "Yes, I am. Why do you ask?"

Ariel looked up at the beautiful blonde and said, "Because I am too and I wondered if you would be interested in getting to know one another." She held her breath slightly. Talking with Reese this evening she had found her fascinating. Although she was probably one of the most beautiful women Ariel had ever met she was also very intelligent and this she found even more fascinating than her face.

Reese was surprised. She hadn't caught that vibe at all, but then she hadn't been looking for it. She had met a group of interesting people from an area of Australia she had been living in and since they had a lot in common had looked forward to making their acquaintance, nothing more. This had come out of nowhere.

Ariel hesitated sure that Reese was going to turn her down. She wasn't usually this bold but had figured, I'm on vacation, what the hell, give it chance. Reese hadn't done anything 'gay' that would give her away but she also hadn't done anything indicating an interest in any of the guys. Ariel figured it was worth a shot. If she turned her down, then so be it. Nothing ventured, nothing gained.

Reese thought it over quickly and nodded, "I'd like that," she answered.

Ariel blinked surprised and pleased all at once. She smiled hesitantly. "Maybe we could seal that with a kiss?" she grinned teasingly.

Reese didn't hesitate and moved in to lightly take Ariel's face in cold hands and hold it as she kissed the welcoming lips. Reese realized Ariel knew how to kiss well as she returned it gently. When they both pulled back by mutual consent they shared a look into each other's eyes under the street lamp before turning and walking the rest of the way towards the inn as though nothing had happened.

They talked about what they might do the next day and agreed to meet for breakfast. "Good night Reese," Ariel said as she left the blonde at the gate of the inn.

"Good night Ariel," Reese smiled as she turned and went in. This had been an unexpected turn of events she thought as she walked up the steps and went in. She looked back at the door to see that Ariel had watched her walk inside and she waved as she turned to go up the stairs to her room closing the door behind her.

CHAPTER 60

The next few days proved to be very interesting as the group of them went sightseeing together. A few of them paired off occasionally including Ariel and Reese but not for long and not so it was noticeable. They went hiking on the hills and along the beaches finding odd little coves and sights that few saw. Reese had wanted to go to the southern tip of New Zealand to Bluff on South Island or even further to Slope Point or some of the offshore islands. A few of the others were interested and of course Ariel offered to travel with her. Four of them set off together, Reese, Ariel, May and a guy called Guy who was obviously interested in May. They traveled by bus and then hiked the last kilometers to take photos of each other standing by the signs that told everyone this was the southernmost point of New Zealand except for the offshore islands. It was also one of the oldest European settlements in the country from 1823 or so.

They all had a blast. Since they were traveling together they had to get hotel rooms and May and Guy decided to take one and Reese and Ariel the other. As each room had double beds no one thought any of the wiser of it. Ariel and Reese had been taking this relationship slowly. Other than getting to know each other and that first kiss they hadn't been physical and Reese felt strangely relieved this time. Thinking over past mistakes she realized that women tended to move too fast and she really wanted to get to know this one slowly. Ariel seemed in no hurry either and they both enjoyed talking and getting to know each other's interests and likes.

That night as they took turns getting ready for bed Reese realized she would have to wear pajamas for the first time in ages and was grateful she had packed some since you never knew what you would need on a trip. When she came out of the bathroom in satin pants and a spaghetti strapped matching blouse she at least felt covered. Ariel admired it as she went by to get herself ready for bed. Reese had taken the bed nearest the bathroom but sat in a chair looking out the window at what she could see despite the dark. She heard Ariel come out of the bathroom and come up behind her.

Putting her hands gently on her shoulders she asked her quietly, "What are you looking at?"

Reese looked up at her and smiled hearing her breath catch as she answered, "Nothing, just thinking..."

"What are you thinking about?" she returned the smile and started gently rubbing Reese's exposed shoulders.

It felt wonderful and it was relaxing, "I was thinking I'd like to come back to this country and hike those beautiful Southern Alps. There was so much I didn't see while I was here."

Ariel leaned down and kissed along the elegant line of Reese's shoulder. She answered quietly, "Maybe we could do that together."

Reese turned so she could kiss Ariel. She had been thinking about that too. It was gentle and sweet and oh so nice to share. The first touch of their tongues felt good too. As they pulled back by mutual consent they shared grins and Ariel sat in the chair facing Reese so they could talk.

They talked about things they would have liked to see, what they would still like to do in the few days they had left. Reese would be going back a week before Ariel and her friends and they both promised to see each other once they were back. They had exchanged cell phone numbers and knew how to get in contact with the other. They talked quite late finding out how much they had in common. Finally though they rose and gave each other a hug and another kiss before getting into their separate beds. They fell asleep still chatting.

Their last day together the whole group went on a horse ride together on the beach and had a bonfire. People always assumed New Zealand was warm but since they were so far south they were really nearer to the South Pole than any other country and it was cold! Sitting around sharing beer and conversation they all had a great time. No one found it odd as Reese and Ariel snuggled up together. Returning at dusk with their horses Ariel admired Reese's riding skills and she explained about running the station years ago. Ariel was finding herself very attracted to this woman of varying interests. She had done so much and seemed so nonchalant about it. That she was talented was obvious but Ariel found herself wondering if perhaps she wasn't smart enough or sophisticated enough for this woman.

Reese was sad to be leaving the group and especially Ariel as she made her way back by herself north to Auckland. Although they both were definitely attracted they hadn't addressed the physical side of their relationship despite being together for a week and a half. Ariel wouldn't be back in Australia for another week and would be missed but Reese had to get back to work. She sensed something was bothering Ariel and although she didn't know her as much as she would have liked to yet she wondered what it was. She hoped it wasn't because they hadn't gone to bed together yet but didn't have a chance to ask her before she left.

CHAPTER 61

She returned to her well run resorts. The few problems that had arisen had been handled expertly by her staff. She was really pleased that there wasn't a mess to handle when she returned. There were many messages from Lila which annoyed her. There were a couple from Jack and on impulse she returned his call.

"Hi Jack, its Reese," she smiled into the phone he had just answered.

"Reese! Where have you been?" he sounded like he was laughing.

"Oh, I took a vacation," she answered airily.

"Did you go to England to visit your daughter?" he knew about Gillian from their conversations.

"No, I went to New Zealand to see the sights."

"New Zealand! You should have asked me, I'm an expert guide!" he laughed again.

"Ah well, sometimes going alone is the best way to find things and do things. I had a wonderful time," she thought about meeting Ariel and her friends. "I met some people and we started traveling together a little. It was fun."

"Would you care to go to dinner tonight and tell me about it?"

Reese hesitated. She didn't want to lead him on but she still wanted to retain his friendship. He must have sensed her hesitancy because he added, "I could bring the girls," as though that would entice her. At the mention of his daughters, one of whom seemed obsessed with her it made her not want to go even more. Instead she said, "Jack, I'd love to see *you*. Would you like to meet me for dinner here in the hotel? A nice relaxed dinner, nothing fancy?"

Jack brightened at the prospect. "Sounds great, see you at eight?"

Reese nodded as she answered, "See you in the south lounge at eight," before she rang off. She called down to the manager in the south lounge and requested a table for two in the middle of the restaurant. She didn't want Jack assuming it was an intimate dinner for two.

Reese was chatting with the bartender when Jack arrived. They had both dressed nicely but casually. She smiled as he walked up and accepted a kiss on the cheek.

"Hey pretty lady," he greeted her.

"Hey yourself!" she smiled. "How's the charter business?"

"Pretty good, how's the hotel business?" he returned her smile taking on a teasing note.

"I don't know I've just gotten back," she turned to the bartender and said, "I'll have that red wine," and turning to Jack asked, "What would you like?"

Jack accepted some of the red wine that Reese had been discussing with the bartender, a nice fruity little red that was made right here in Australia.

They sat at a nice little table right in the middle of the restaurant as per Reese's instructions. They chatted for a while and Reese told about what she had seen and done and Jack talked about the charters he had been doing. Finally though he had to ask, "So, where is *this* going?"

Reese knew immediately what he meant. She had been prepared for this all evening and while tense about it hadn't had the courage to just bring it up herself. She didn't want to hurt the guy but she had to let him down gently. She smiled, "I like you Jack," she shook her head slightly as she looked down a moment and then directly into his eyes, "But only as a friend." She didn't want to explain further, she shouldn't have to.

He looked briefly annoyed and then asked, "Was it something I did or said?"

She shook her head, "No, really it wasn't. It's me, it really is me. I like you a lot and if I were inclined to get into such a relationship you would be a great choice, but I'm not and I'm sorry," she reached out to touch his hand which he clasped immediately.

"Inclined?" he looked puzzled.

Reese sighed. She would have to be blunt. "Jack, I guess you didn't realize that I'm gay," she looked at him directly and saw the shock in his eyes. "I didn't mean to lead you on in any way. I thought at first that you understood I just wanted to be friends..."

"I thought friends first and then perhaps more later," he still looked a little puzzled or perhaps stunned.

"I'm sorry, can we still be friends or is this a deal breaker?" She looked sadly at the attractive man.

He smiled, "How could I be angry at such a beautiful woman wanting to be my friend. Besides, no one would believe that a woman such as yourself is gay." He laughed, "All my friends will assume..." he laughed again and Reese joined him. He was such a nice guy.

"I'm so relieved. Once I realized where you were going I just wasn't sure how you would react."

He shrugged philosophically, still holding her hand he leaned over and pulling the back of it to his lips he said, "Ah, a good friend is always an added bonus."

They shared a laugh.

"Hey, maybe I should hook you up with my daughter..." he started to joke but left off at the odd look that came over her face. "What's wrong?"

"Ah, Jack, Lila has become a bit of a problem," Reese felt uncomfortable.

"You and she haven't...?" he asked a little concerned as he let go of her hand.

Reese shook her head immediately, "No, absolutely not. I wouldn't do that to you and to be honest she was pursuing me a little too ardently for my taste."

"Is she bothering you?" he asked concerned.

Reese shrugged her shoulders and looking at him a little embarrassed said, "Well, let's just say for every one of your messages, there were three to four of hers..."

He did a rapid calculation in his head and his eyes opened wide as she nodded. "I'll tell her you aren't interested."

She smiled, relieved, "Thank you Jack, I hope I haven't made a mess of things here."

They shared a nice dinner together as friends.

CHAPTER 62

Reese was working diligently at her desk when Simone stuck her head in and said, "Ms. Paulson?" when she looked up at the intrusion surprised that she hadn't called on the intercom Simone continued, "There is a Ms. Timmons from Alistar Marketing Firm to see you? She said you told her she wouldn't need an appointment." Simone gave her a look that said she had no idea what this was about.

Reese stared at her for a full five seconds before she realized why the name sounded familiar. Grinning conspiratorially she said, "please, send her in," as she saved the work she was doing and turned from her computer in time to see Ariel in a beautiful business suit come through her door. Simone closed it discretely behind her.

"Hello," Ariel said with a huge grin.

Reese smiled back and got up from her desk to envelope her friend in a hug, "Wow, it's great to see you, why didn't you call and tell me you were back?"

"I wanted to surprise you and here I am the one surprised!" she smiled as she returned the bear hug.

Reese pulled back just enough to ask, "Why are you surprised?"

"You told me you 'managed' the hotel. You didn't tell me you were the General Manager of the resort much less all the resorts that the Morris Family owned!" she said in a teasing note.

"Well, I just didn't want to brag," Reese grinned and let her arms drop indicating that Ariel should sit on the couch.

Ariel looked around Reese's elegant office. It was all done in rich tones of red. Leather couches and chairs with inlaid buttons complemented the red on the wood paneling lining the walls. A blue banker's lamp was on the mahogany desk its surface polished to the point of glare. A complimentary blue area rug sat under the desk in a rectangle. One wall was lined with shelves showcasing books and odd little trinkets peculiar to The Great Barrier Reef. The overall appearance of the room was elegant and sophisticated, just like Reese herself. "This is nice, this is really nice," she commented.

Reese was so happy to see Ariel. She had thought about her frequently since she had returned and hoped she would hear from her soon. Her appearance was even better. "So, Alistar Marketing?" she asked with a grin.

"I had to say something when I got through the dragon to the other dragon outside your door!" she laughed.

Reese grinned. Not many people could get through to just 'see' her without an appointment. It was really clever of Ariel to have thought that one up.

"Besides, if I had your account, I wouldn't just be in a small firm anymore!" she laughed imagining it.

"I'm so glad you're here! Can I get you anything?" she indicated the bar in the corner made of a globe of the world.

"No, I'm fine. I was wondering what you were doing for dinner tonight?" Ariel grinned realizing how nicely and expensively Reese was dressed, a bit of a departure from the shorts and casual blouses she had been in previously.

"Absolutely nothing," she made a mental note to cancel the business meeting she had planned, "I'm at your convenience."

Ariel raised an eyebrow at her wording, "Good, where would you like to go?"

Reese shook her head, "Anywhere but here, I live here so I don't want to eat at home."

Ariel frowned, "You live here?" she looked around the office as though looking for a bed.

Reese grinned, "No, I live on one of the upper floors of the east tower. But yes, I live in the hotel. It's convenient and I'm always on hand in the event of an emergency."

"Isn't that a bit confining?"

Reese shrugged, "Yes and no. I've devoted myself to this job for the last couple of years and I've made a success of it. There is always something though that needs my attention. I have great staff but still I like to be kept abreast of important things and be on hand if we have important guests or something..."

"So do you get time off for good behavior?" she asked sarcastically, Ariel's Australian accent made that sound really amusing.

Reese laughed, "I get time off any time I want pretty much, I just don't always take it."

They decided to meet up later in front of the hotel and agreed to dress casual. Ariel wouldn't tell her where she was going but told her to look for a red convertible that she would pick her up in.

Reese laughed when she saw the little Miata that Ariel was sitting in as she came down the steps of the hotel. With her height she felt she was getting into a sardine can but she was game.

Ariel took her to a sea food restaurant. What else? They enjoyed a sampler between them trying some of the specialties and sharing the platter. Reese liked that as sometimes there were things she wanted to try but didn't want as a whole meal.

Ariel told her about the rest of her vacation which strangely had been kind of boring once Reese had left. Her friends had teased her about the leggy blonde American but Ariel had kept mum about their relationship. She reached out at one point and Reese held her hand squeezing reassuredly letting her know without words that she was still interested.

They decided to walk off their excellent dinner on the beach. Holding hands they enjoyed the sunset behind them as they looked out over the waters. Reese always felt disoriented as the sun set in the west and the ocean was to the east. The colors over the water though were incredibly romantic. Reese wanted desperately to kiss Ariel but not being sure how she felt about public displays of affection wasn't going to make a fool of herself. She finally invited Ariel up to her apartment to show her the view as it got too dark too quickly to see much on the beach except by the street lamps as they had walked pretty far down the beach.

Ariel was amazed at the size of her rooms and the view must be incredible in the morning when the sun came up. Right now it was too dark to see beyond the street lamps far below them from the balcony. The lights from those lamps didn't even reach this high. Occasional voices could be heard in the night air but not too many unless they were raised in a shout. The huge bay of windows was impressive. They shared a bottle of wine on the balcony as they chatted about this and that. Reese finally though had enough of waiting and leaned over asking, "Do you mind if I kiss you?"

Ariel grinned at the question, "God I hope I don't mind, I've been waiting for the opportunity all evening," she leaned forward to meet Reese in the middle.

It was a nice kiss, not too pushy but sort of experimental as they both learned each other's lips again. Neither touched each other except by their lips and this too was interesting. Finally they pulled back by mutual consent and looked into each other's eyes grinning.

"So," Ariel was the first to speak, "Where is this going?" she asked, she had to know. She already felt intimidated by this woman and her surroundings. She found Reese to be intelligent and classy but *this* apartment, *this* job, *this* woman was way beyond her league. She wanted to know, she wanted to get out before she got hurt with her expectations.

Reese smiled which had the effect of numbing Ariel's mind for a moment and distracting her. The words were amazingly similar to Jacks from the other night. She leaned forward and took Ariel's hands in her own, they were very cold and she warmed them between her own. "I think this is going slowly and steadily towards a friendship that could possibly be more."

Ariel found that vague and still wondered. She didn't want to invest her feelings and emotions in something that she really couldn't have.

Reese continued, "I like that we are taking this slow. I've gone too fast a few times and I seem to get burnt when that happens. I like you Ariel, a lot. I don't want to lose out on getting to know you. I don't want sex to get in the way of a relationship. Is that okay?" she looked worriedly into Ariel's eyes which seemed to clear up as Reese explained.

Ariel was relieved. She thought perhaps that Reese was playing with her and that had concerned her. "I don't mind going slow either. Too often women jump in with both feet. I've seen friends practically move in together overnight and I don't want that. I like you too. I am enjoying getting to know you. We can wait on the sex as we date okay?"

Reese grinned in agreement. As long as they both understood where this was going neither should get hurt.

CHAPTER 63

They took it slow over the next few weeks as they dated and explored each other getting to know each other in ways neither had expected. They were right; sex would have gotten in the way.

Ariel learned about Reese and her relationships before and after Veronica. Ariel soon realized that Veronica was the one that Reese regretted the most. She could tell when Reese spoke about her that there was genuine love and sadness there; there was a catch in her voice that changed it, softened it.

Reese learned that Ariel was a few years younger than herself and had a few serious relationships but nothing that had lasted beyond a few years. Reese also learned that Ariel had lost one woman to cancer and another to a car accident.

"I nearly died in that same car accident," Ariel told her with tears in her eyes as she shared.

Reese got up from the couch where she was sitting and took Ariel in her arms. "Shhh, you're here now, you're here for a reason. I am so sorry about her death. I really am." She rubbed Ariel's arms as she comforted her.

"After losing Bonnie to cancer it took me a long time to trust Reba and then we had such a short time together before the accident," Ariel began to sob.

Reese held her as she let it all come out. She felt uncomfortable but she had shared her own anguish about Veronica, could she do anything less for Ariel?

Ariel felt like a fool but they both needed to know about each other's past. She was wiped out when she finished her crying jag. Reese was one of the kindest women she had ever met. They had both commiserated and were well on their way to becoming best friends. She enjoyed this woman and could feel herself falling hard and fast despite their 'slow' courtship. She wondered though how to introduce the subject of sex again. They kissed, they hugged, they touched but there was some invisible wall that neither of them went beyond and she wanted to tear it down. Now wasn't the time of course, she was vulnerable and Reese had been so kind.

"It's late," Reese began and Ariel took it as a hint that she should go.

Ariel got up immediately out of Reese's arms. "I should go."

Reese looked startled and stood up as well "No, that's not what I meant." She grabbed Ariel's hand as she reached for her purse, "I want you to stay." She looked sadly at the curly blonde.

Ariel looked up at Reese trying to interpret her thoughts, "What do you mean?"

"I'm not asking for sex," she grinned to hide the awkward moment that had arisen, "I just thought we could hold each other and have breakfast together for a change. You're feeling down and I don't want you driving when you're upset."

Ariel was strangely relieved and yet, *not*. She liked that Reese was concerned enough for her welfare though to offer. "I don't have anything to wear and your clothes," she looked up and down at the statuesque blonde, "Won't fit me!" she grinned.

Reese laughed, "Well, I can certainly lend you some ill-fitting clothes to sleep in and you can get up early enough to wear these," she indicated the outfit Ariel was now wearing, "And go home and change before going into your office."

Ariel liked the idea and they sat down again. They changed the subject from their exes and began talking about their careers. Ariel was amazed how much and how far Reese had come. People all over wanted to do business with the resorts that Reese managed so effortlessly. When Ariel had mentioned her name in conversation people knew her from all over it seemed. She was very respected and admired.

Reese really enjoyed talking to Ariel. Her marketing ideas were amazing and she had had a couple of her managers send some business her way. She herself couldn't do it without possibly offending Ariel or giving her an unwanted spotlight but she could make suggestions to help her firm and her career subtly. She made sure that Ariel knew about it so it wasn't underhanded in any way so there would be no misunderstandings between them.

That night Reese set Ariel up in the guest room which had never been used in the years that Reese had lived in this suite. She handed her a set of pajamas that she of course swam in being shorter. Reese laughed when she saw Ariel dressed in them. She was sitting in the living room finishing some paperwork when Ariel came out of the bedroom.

She shrugged her shoulders and said, "Well, I tried," but she couldn't help the laughter that bubbled up.

Ariel joined her in the laughter, "You don't wear these do you?"

Cocking her head slightly and narrowing her eyes Reese asked, "How did you know?"

"The price tag was still tucked in the shirt," Ariel chuckled.

"Busted, no I rarely wear anything to bed," Reese confessed.

Ariel nearly groaned at the image that conjured up, to hide it she made a joke, "Good to know," they shared a laugh and then, "Well, I just wanted to say goodnight before I turned in," she stood there awkwardly holding up the satin pants that swamped her.

Reese rose from the desk where she had been working while Ariel changed. She leaned down and kissed Ariel as she put her arms around her. Ariel returned the kiss wholeheartedly. "This is silly, why don't you sleep with me, then at least we can chat until we fall asleep?"

Ariel looked up at the beautiful blonde wanting her but not knowing when the appropriate time would come to suggest they consummate their relationship. "I can restrain myself if you can," she grinned.

Reese held her close as she looked into her pretty eyes. Something about eyes always captivated her like they were endless pools to the soul. "Come on, let's go," she said releasing her and turning off the desk lamp she put her arm around the smaller blonde and led her to her bedroom.

Ariel stood and looked around the bedroom at the knick knacks and pictures that Reese had on her dresser and tables as Reese changed her clothes in the bathroom. She realized the wedding pictures had to be of Reese's daughter Gillian who only bore a superficial resemblance to her mother and didn't in any way match the beauty that Reese had. There were many pictures of Gillian at various ages with and without Reese in them. It was interesting to see a younger Reese but to Ariel's discerning eye she looked best right now at this age.

Reese slid her arms around Ariel from behind as she looked at her pictures, "She's beautiful isn't she?" she indicated all the pictures of Gillian.

"Not as beautiful as her mother," Ariel turned in her arms to capture her in her own.

Reese looked down on her and was captivated by the beauty she held in her arms, she leaned down to kiss her. It was then that they both realized that they were in pajamas and only a thin layer of satin separated their bodies from each other. The kiss rapidly became heated. Reese finally pulled back enough to say, "Are you ready for this?"

Strangely Ariel wasn't. After talking about her exes tonight and their deaths this seemed the wrong time. She shook her head, "I'm sorry."

"No, baby, don't be. It should be romantic and right," Reese rushed to assure her.

"Thank you for understanding," Ariel was relieved. She wanted Reese, she didn't doubt that but she just wasn't ready, not yet, not tonight.

"Come on, I've got meetings tomorrow and I'm sure your plate is just as full, let's get some sleep," she urged her to the queen sized bed.

As they both got in Reese leaned over and turned off the lights from her side of the bed. Flicking another switch the drapes across the bedroom windows opened to the full moon. Reese leaned her head on Ariel's shoulder and said, "Romantic isn't it?"

Ariel had to agree, it was beautiful. She reached out to caress Reese's face as she turned for a kiss, "It's beautiful," but she didn't mean the moon.

The sweetness of the kiss was nearly Reese's undoing. She too wanted to consummate their relationship but sensed it just wasn't quite the right time, not yet, not tonight.

They fell asleep holding hands. Ariel woke a couple times during the night with Reese cuddled up to her back unconsciously and gently caressing a hip, across her stomach, and once with her arm draped across her chest. Reese woke up in the morning with Ariel glued to her back with her arm draped across her stomach and her breath tickling her ear. It made her want her but she also wanted it to be right.

CHAPTER 64

That 'right' came a week later. The two of them decided on a night on the town. Reese arranged for one of the hotel limousines to be available for them. They both dressed up and met at Ariel's little bungalow. A cute little house that was a throwback to the 50's 'after war' construction. Reese thought it was adorable. Ariel only liked it because it was convenient to both her work and the beach. It was outrageous rent with all the bungalows so near to the beach but it suited her and she didn't need much. Two small bedrooms with a kitchen and a dining room as well as a really small 'parlor' and an upstairs that could be used as a bedroom but instead was used as storage. The limo took them club hopping and they had a blast. They started at a club where they enjoyed the music of the 80's and danced until both of them were sweaty. Then they went to a 50's diner, a take-off on the American trend to keep everything Elvis. They both enjoyed it as they ate hamburgers and shakes before hitting a few more clubs. They both were hit on by both men and women but they laughed it off as they went clubbing. Having the limo available to them they needn't worry about drinking too much. The after-hours clubs started after the regular clubs closed. Both of them were off the next two days so they didn't worry about over indulging. Neither really drank a lot but they both felt good and had a marvelous time dancing and singing together. Reese couldn't remember the last time she had let herself go, perhaps once or twice on the station when Sheila's cousins tried to get her to dance an aborigine dance or two. They met up with a few of the friends that Reese had met on vacation and they were pleased to see the two of them together. Another woman was with them that Reese knew she had met before but as she wasn't introduced to her she had that vague 'I know you from somewhere' feeling. She dismissed it as she met so many people in her line of work, the woman probably worked for her. It didn't help that the woman kept sending her strange looks.

They finally went back to Ariel's in the early morning and the limousine dropped them off. Ariel gave Reese a 'good morning/night' kiss and that was all it took to enflame both of them. They were both so relaxed from their night of drinking and dancing, pleasantly tired, and both of them had wanted this for weeks. It was the 'right' time. They were soon pulling each other's clothes off of their bodies to get at the more 'interesting' parts and caressing and kissing their way to ecstasy. Reese was pleased to find that Ariel gave as well as received and she was soon panting from the release. Ariel was thrilled that the beautiful woman she had been dating more than lived up to the promise of her pretty face.

After that they really enjoyed themselves. Reese had access to all the amenities offered from the various hotels she managed and she used them for the first time shamelessly. They parasailed, snorkeled, dined in and out, and used the spas. They enjoyed each other blatantly. Reese for the first time in all the years of managing was out and proud, the rumors that many had speculated about were true. She didn't care. She enjoyed Ariel and was proud of her. She wasn't ashamed of her relationship. Her work certainly didn't suffer. If anything, she was more relaxed and enjoyed it. The perks were finally something she could share with someone.

"My cousin Rita says she knows you," Ariel told her one night as they sat on terrace of one of their regular haunts.

Reese looked over her Mai Tai and raised her eyebrow in question.

"She keeps hinting at something, do you know what she means?" Ariel asked.

Reese finished her sip and put the glass down. Shrugging she asked, "Which one was your cousin Rita?"

Ariel laughed. She was kind of relieved since Rita had implied something vague but Ariel wasn't so sure. Rita was always causing trouble. They had both gone after the same type of women for years and Ariel was sure that Rita was just jealous because Reese was so attractive. "You remember our first night together?" she looked down a little as though she were suddenly shy.

Reese thought back to New Zealand and asked, "The first night we met?"

Ariel shook her head, "No I mean the first night we had sex together," she didn't say 'slept together' since they had technically slept together before that and she didn't say 'make love' since neither one of them had admitted to loving the other.

Reese nodded looking curiously at her lover wondering where this was going. She had had a long day and really had needed this drink to relax. She didn't want a heavy conversation.

"She was with my friends at that one club," Ariel explained watching Reese's reaction curiously.

Reese shrugged, "I meet a lot of people babe, I can't remember her, I'm sorry," she yawned from her long day and the alcohol she had consumed.

Ariel grinned acknowledging the point. People Reese never knew were always coming up to introduce themselves. Between her beauty, her position, and her charismatic ways she was popular. It could be intimidating but Ariel was confident in how this relationship was going that she wasn't going to lose Reese any time soon. Still, there was always that niggling doubt that lingered in the back of her mind that she just wasn't good enough for this beautiful woman.

They spent the night at Ariel's place. It was easier than the hotel with the knowing but respectful looks that Ariel got the next morning when she would leave Reese's suite. Not that she really cared but she felt Reese couldn't afford to lose the respect of her employees. It was nice to make breakfast together; they really had a routine down and quickly and efficiently made it. There was a knock on the door as they both headed to take a shower.

"I'll get it and catch up with you," Ariel told Reese knowing she had to get to work.

Reese was showered and putting on her make up when Ariel finally came into the bathroom looking a little pale. Looking at Ariel she asked alarmed, "Are you okay?"

Ariel looked back at her in the mirror and shook her head slightly.

Reese turned from the mirror and asked, "What happened? Bad news? Who was at the door?"

Ariel looked down for a moment to collect her thoughts before looking up with tear filled eyes, "Why didn't you tell me you had slept with Rita?"

Reese stared at her for a moment stunned at the question. "Slept with Rita? I don't even know Rita! Who says I slept with her?" She started to get angry.

Ariel took a deep breath; she was badly hurt and trying not to let her anger get the best of her. She didn't want to end up screaming or crying about this. She cared a lot more deeply than she had thought she did. She had fallen in love with Reese and her jealously at this moment was about to tear her apart. "Rita says she slept with you. She described your suite in exact details. She could only know that if she had been there." She waited to hear what Reese had to say to that.

Reese stared at her incredulously. "My suite isn't that much different than several others in the hote..." she started but was interrupted by Ariel.

"She described things in your bedroom that only someone who had been there could know." Ariel was feeling the hurt bubbling up her throat and strangling her. She wanted to lash out but squeezed her hands into fists to keep it inside.

Reese shook her head, "I don't know how she could know those things. Maybe she bribed a maid to go in and see but I swear to you, I don't know your cousin Rita!" She made a gesture to take Ariel into her arms but Ariel held up her hand to stop her.

"She's in the living room. She came to 'warn' me about you," she informed Reese.

Reese was angry. Whoever this Rita chick was she had a lot to answer for! She brushed past Ariel and stormed down the hallway to the living room where a dark haired woman sat, waiting expectantly. Reese stared. If these two were cousins, it didn't show. Reese realized she had met the woman before, the night they took the limo and went club hopping. She still had a vague feeling she knew her from somewhere else though but couldn't place her finger on it.

Ariel came in behind her and went around her so she could watch the two women's faces as they met. Reese looked angrier than anything Ariel had seen on her face since she had met her. Rita looked speculative. Ariel was sure that Rita was enjoying this way too much, she lived for drama.

"I understand you told Ariel we have slept together? Why would you tell her that lie?" Reese demanded angrily.

Rita stood up and tried to look Reese in the eye, she was way too short for that. She did however hide a grin, she was enjoying herself. "But I didn't lie, we have slept together. It was a pretty enjoyable night," she informed Reese without batting an eye.

"You're a liar," Reese told her, her American accent never more prominent than at this moment.

"I think you are lying to protect yourself. Ariel should know the truth. As her cousin I think I should tell her what I know."

Reese drew herself up to her full height, it was intimidating but Rita wasn't intimidated in the least. She was enjoying herself way too much for that. "I don't know what you're getting out of this, why you feel the need to hurt Ariel, but I don't know you. I met you for the first time a few months back."

Rita eyed her speculatively, "You don't remember do you? How many women *have you* slept with that you can't keep them straight?" she put that in for good measure enjoying the thunderous look on Reese's face.

"How dare you! I don't sleep around!" Reese spat at her angrily.

Ariel was watching them both closely. Rita's propensity for trouble was well known and Ariel was sure that Reese was telling the truth. She was getting ready to ask her trouble making cousin to leave when Rita answered Reese.

"You must have one-night stands all the time that you don't remember me," she looked down at her nails for affect before continuing with a shrug, "I would have thought I was more memorable than that," she looked back up before finishing with "But then if you do it all the time I guess not."

Reese was more angry than she could ever remember being. It was the one-night stand phrase though that joggled her memory. Eyeing Rita speculatively she remembered her vaguely now. She realized why at the club a few months back she had looked familiar. Rita could see when the comprehension dawned on Reese's face. Ariel could see it too.

Reese glanced at Ariel for a moment seeing the hurt on her face before saying tightly to Rita "I think you should go now."

Rita shrugged, mission accomplished. She couldn't help leaving with a parting shot, "I'd be more careful who you sleep with in the future cousin, this one is *way* out of your league," before she closed the front door with a satisfying clunk. She smiled as she walked down the sidewalk to her car. She had hurt her cousin and the beautiful blonde who had never called her, who probably thought she was too good for her. That was a bonus, two birds with one stone.

Ariel was staring at Reese incredulously. She couldn't believe her cousin's accusations were true. She would have bet her last pound that Rita had been lying but the look on Reese's face confirmed it. She waited for Reese to talk to her.

Reese felt embarrassed. She had totally forgotten that one night stand much less the brunette that had vaguely reminded her of Veronica that night. She looked nothing like her now that Reese had seen her in the light of day. She looked at the waiting Ariel and wondered how she could explain. She stood there a moment too long.

Ariel watched the play of emotions on Reese's face. Her own thoughts were hurt and confused. When the silence stretched out too long she finally gathered them together just enough to say, "Get out! Get your things and get out! Now! Right now, this instant!" her voice rising with each word as the hysteria bubbled up and threatened to run over.

Reese tried to talk to her, "Don't you want an explanation?" but Ariel was beyond reason and instead started shouting incoherently. Reese hurried back to the bedroom and bathroom and gathered the few things she kept there before heading out the back door to the car she had borrowed from the hotel. Driving back she had a heavy heart. What demonic need had Rita had to tell Ariel like that? Not that Reese wouldn't have told her if she had *even remembered* it but the way Rita had done it had soured things, possibly irreparably. Reese was only glad she hadn't told Ariel that she was falling in love with her. It would only have complicated things. This was better. They both would hurt for a while but since neither had loved the other perhaps they could at least be friends when it blew over. Reese doubted it but she had to hold out some hope.

Ariel watched as Reese drove away. She doesn't care! She thought angrily. She hadn't felt this hurt in a long long time. How dare Reese make *her* feel bad for *her* indiscretions! The anger and jealousy burned in her heart and made the love she felt for the leggy blonde a terrible thing. She felt like breaking things, she felt like revenge. Then she just felt awful and wanted to cry. She chose that course of action as she leaned against a wall and slowly sank to the floor sobbing incoherently at what had just happened and how she was feeling.

CHAPTER 65

Reese tried over the following weeks to talk to Ariel but she simply wouldn't take her calls. She even tried once to show up at the bungalow but Ariel shouted that she would call the police if she didn't leave and let her alone. Reese gave up after that with a heavy heart. She had tried, she had tried repeatedly. If Ariel didn't want to talk to her she couldn't apologize any more than she already had. She wouldn't leave lengthy messages on her voicemail and if Ariel didn't want to hear Reese couldn't make her. She had wanted to explain but apparently she wasn't going to get the chance.

Reese missed her friend. They had really enjoyed each other. It wasn't just the sex, although that had been fun as well, it was the time spent together doing things. The friendship and a myriad of other things they had enjoyed. It wasn't fair and for that Reese was angry. She wished she could hunt down Rita and give her a piece of her mind for the hurt that she had caused Ariel much less for how Reese felt.

Two months passed before a business function threw them together accidentally. It was inevitable with the contacts that Reese had sent Ariel's way that they would bump into each other eventually. Reese was required to attend certain functions to represent her hotels and resorts. Ariel too had to represent her firm. Finding each other at the same dinner wasn't too bad. They both caught each other sneaking looks from across the room.

She looks thinner, Ariel thought worriedly.

She isn't sleeping; Reese could see the circles from across the dinner tables.

God that dress makes her look incredible.

Look how hot she looks in that outfit.

They both survived the dinner without speaking to each other. A few of the other attendees knew of their former relationship and watched them curiously but no one thankfully commented to either of them. Their friends knew more of the details but no one needed to hear them now.

That was the first of a few dinners that threw them together however indirectly. As members of the tourism boards and other committees it was inevitable that they would actually be at the same table eventually. By then they had both had a chance to calm down and behave like adults. They were carefully cool to each other but only spoke as a necessity. None of the humor and warmth that had been the norm before entered their voices.

She hates me now.

I behaved like a child.

I miss her.

I wish I knew how to reach out to her.

Neither of them made the first move though.

CHAPTER 66

Mr. Morris looked up from the reports he was reading. Mrs. Morris grinned and gave Reese a wink. "Well Reese, I can't find anything to complain about. Revenues are up and I like what you've done with things. Well done. I didn't think I would like retirement but you've proven that with a good manager that we could enjoy ourselves worry free. I thank you on behalf of Mrs. Morris and myself," he finished with a grin himself.

Reese thanked him as Mrs. Morris handed Reese a pile of papers. Reese looked down at the contracts that would tie her to the resort for another few years. This was what she wanted wasn't it? She wasn't sure. She could feel the same old restlessness after she had accomplished her goals. She had proven not only to herself but to the people at these resorts that she could do the job. She certainly had enough money in the bank to last the rest of her life. Glancing at the figures in the contracts she realized she was well paid for her knowledge and expertise, very well paid. She had never seen this amount of money before. It was the result of years of hard work that she deserved. But did she want this?

"Thank you, I'll go over this and get it back to you shortly."

The Morris' smiled. Reese always did what she said she would do and for that they were grateful. No one they had worked with combined the skills she so effortlessly showed. They were pleased with the money that their resorts made for them and compensated their people accordingly. They too had never paid an employee this much money but with the increase of revenue due largely to Reese's efforts they couldn't help but keep her at all costs.

"We are going to go enjoy the amenities you've added," Mrs. Morris shared a laugh with Reese. Their fine shopping mall attached to the resort offered first class luxuries that their guests appreciated in many ways. There was enough that a middle class guest could enjoy and enough high end items that they occasionally indulged.

Their meeting concluded Reese took her contract and stopped in at her barrister's office so he could read it over for her. There was too much legalese for her to comprehend despite her fine mind. What would take her weeks to eke out he would immediately understand. Reese walked back along the stone path she had put in along their properties along the beach. It provided a beautiful walk to their guests who wanted to enjoy the beach without getting into the sand. It was especially popular in the evening as it wound back and forth around palm trees and strategically placed vegetation. As they owned several properties it stretched for quite a way and several other property owners had continued it onto their own stretches for the tourists after Reese had explained her proposal. As they used natural river rock instead of smooth concrete it tended to keep the skaters off of the path, it was way too bumpy for that.

Reese was deep in thought when she heard her name being called. She looked up and saw Ariel sitting on a beach chair at one of the other properties, not a Morris property. She stopped and waited for Ariel to approach her.

"Hello Reese," Ariel said quietly.

Reese had watched her tan body approach her, dressed in a bikini and sarong she looked lovely. "Hello Ariel, enjoying the sun?" she asked politely.

Ariel looked around the stretch of beach "Yes, I got a rare afternoon off and decided to relax here," she indicated her friends, some of whom Reese was acquainted with and watched the two of them unabashedly. Reese nodded hello to those she recognized.

"Well, I'm not actually dressed for the beach," Reese indicated her own business suit in linen, "So I should be getting back to the office."

"Could we talk sometime?" Ariel asked.

Reese looked down at her ex and could see the anxiety written on her face. Reese herself looked cool and confident, none of her own anxiety visible on her attractive face. "When?" Reese asked.

"Tonight? Dinner perhaps?"

Reese nodded. Since they had broken up she hadn't really socialized except through work.

"May I pick you up, say six?"

Reese could hear the hesitancy in Ariel's voice, she is so unsure of herself. "Would you like to eat in my apartment?" she asked before continuing, "That way we would have privacy," she indicated the people staring at them.

Ariel grinned, she had wanted that privacy as well, "That sounds like a fine idea. Six?"

Reese nodded again and looking warmly into her ex-friend's eyes said, "I'll see you then," before nodding to the others and heading off down the beach.

Ariel watched her until she was out of sight before heading back to her friends.

CHAPTER 67

The buzzer sounded at exactly six, Reese had arranged with the front desk to put Ariel in the private elevator for her. Reese laughed as she put the finishing touches on the dinner imagining Ariel arriving early and standing outside the door looking at her watch for the appointed hour. For once she had made the meal herself instead of having the kitchens send it up. It had been difficult but as it was mostly cool items like salad and chicken it didn't require cooking and she had purchased the items herself at the local market instead of using the hotel kitchens. The wines were chilled and the table set. She answered the door. Ariel stood there looking tanned and unsure of herself.

"Come on in," Reese invited.

Ariel looked around the familiar suite. It always amazed her that someone lived like this. Every need taken care of. She didn't have to clean her rooms, her laundry was even taken out, food was delivered, she noted the set table.

They chatted over dinner catching up but not really talking in depth. Reese didn't want to go there yet, she wasn't sure where Ariel was and she waited patiently for her to take them there. So far Ariel hadn't gotten around to talking about what she wanted. They talked with the same ease they had always had and enjoyed each other's conversation as they had for months before they broke up.

It had gotten fairly late before they ran out of things to talk about or so it seemed before Ariel finally said, "We probably should talk about what happened."

Reese looked over her wine glass that she was toying with. She hadn't drunk very much in anticipation of this but at the same time somehow they had managed to consume two bottles. She wondered briefly where it had gone before addressing Ariel's statement. "Yes we should, perhaps we should have months ago," she admonished lightly.

Ariel flushed slightly. She had behaved childishly cutting Reese out of her life. The repeated phone calls had fed her ego but she hadn't returned one of them and when they stopped she consoled herself with the thought that perhaps Reese had moved on. Apparently she hadn't. Ariel had been hurt but she had always felt Reese was too good for her and to have found out that she had slept with Rita, even for a one night stand that she didn't remember, had fed on her insecurities. "I owe you an apology. I should have let you explain but I was so hurt I behaved rather badly."

Reese nodded, "Do you want to hear it now?"

Ariel looked deep into the beautiful blonde's eyes. She had stared at her hungrily all night long. Somewhere along the line she noted that Reese had cut her hair, not short as she had seen in the pictures on her dresser, instead in layers that allowed the curls to bounce freely without the weight of her hair holding them into waves, as a result it was lush and rich looking and gave her beauty a new twist. It was a far cry from the short haired clean cut statuesque blonde who was in photos of old. "Yes if you don't mind," she answered holding her breath. Reese didn't owe her anything but she appreciated the effort she had gone to tonight, making their dinner, being the gracious host, she was a nice person and she deserved better than how Ariel had treated her.

"That night I met Rita was so long ago," Reese began, trying to remember the facts and how she had been feeling. She explained how lonely she had been feeling and almost how desperate. She had never done a one-night stand like that before and felt very ashamed that she hadn't even known Rita's name until Ariel introduced them. She had a long time to think about all this and while ashamed at her own behavior she didn't appreciate what Rita had done to them or how.

Ariel agreed with her about that. She was surprised to hear about Reese's insecurities and that a woman such as this could feel desperate. Her cousin had meant nothing to her. In fact she had nothing to do with her cousin these days and Rita had been going around telling people how jealous Ariel was that she had had the 'blonde hotel lady' first. None of their mutual friends appreciated it and Rita was slowly making enemies with her talk.

"So, I don't know what else I can say. It happened well before I met you and I am deeply ashamed by it. There was no way I could know she was your cousin though or that she would tell you like that. I certainly didn't remember her until this all came out."

That above all made Ariel feel better, that Reese didn't remember Rita, that the encounter was equally unmemorable. That she didn't have any feelings for Rita other than the obvious signs of disapproval for her actions. "I should have let you explain this months ago instead of letting it go on like this," she agreed. She felt ashamed. She had caused herself so much misery when it could have been resolved.

Reese felt bad, but at least now they could be friends again. The conversations this evening proved that. She leaned towards Ariel and took her hand, "That's why it's best to talk it out right away instead of letting it fester. I'm sorry you were hurt, that Rita went out of her way to hurt you. It wasn't intentional on my part," she assured her, "But it was stupid of me to have a casual encounter."

Ariel squeezed her hand. Reese had always been 'oh so polite' in all the time she had known her. The only time she let her reserve down was when they had been alone and intimate. She was a deeply passionate woman and Ariel counted herself lucky to have seen that side of her. It didn't mean they would get to that point again though, she had probably ruined it. "We are back to being friends then?" she asked.

Reese smiled, that had been what she had wanted for a while, "I hope so!"

They chatted a while longer before Ariel realized she should be going, it was getting late after all. They agreed to meet for lunch the following day.

Over the next few weeks they regained the friendship they had both lost. It didn't get intimate and perhaps that was a good thing, it didn't confuse things for either of them although both of them wondered if it would get to that point again. It wasn't that they didn't want it, in fact both of them did, and it just made sense to repair their friendship first.

They were out at a club one night enjoying each other's company when they both ran into Rita. If looks could kill they would have been dead on the spot. She tried to talk to them as though nothing had happened and they both turned on their heels and left her standing there with her mouth open.

"That was weird," Reese commented gauging Ariel's reaction.

Ariel had been watching Reese for the same reason. She laughed and said, "Do you want to dance?"

Reese smiled which caused Ariel to go weak at the knees, "You betcha."

They danced to a quick moving beat that changed to a slow moving tune. Wrapping their arms around each other they realized the chemistry was still there. Their bodies moving against each other brought on other thoughts.

Reese pulled back enough to look down into Ariel's eyes, what she saw there confirmed what she was feeling; she leaned down for a kiss.

It rapidly became heated as they both celebrated their victory over their fears, over their abstinence, over Rita.

"I thought we'd never get back to this," Ariel commented as they woke up together in Reese's suite.

Reese looked down at her from where she loomed over the woman she had just kissed awake. They were tangled up together in the sheets and she was very happy to see Ariel there. "I often wondered as well," she whispered in between the kisses that were immediately equally returned.

Breakfasting together on the balcony Ariel looked around and thought 'I could get used to this' as she looked at the luxurious room, the incredible view, and the beautiful woman sitting across from her in a satin robe with nothing beneath it which was obvious as the satin fit her like a second skin.

"What are you thinking?" Reese asked with a mischievous grin.

"How happy I am right now," Ariel answered with a grin of her own. Her bare foot began to caress Reese's leg.

Reese's grin turned into a smile as she asked, "And why are you so happy?"

Ariel set down her coffee cup and leaned forward, her own robe spilling open and giving Reese a fine view down it to Ariel's own naked body, "Because I am here, *with you,"* she answered simply.

Reese reached across the table to take Ariel's hand in her own and squeezed.

CHAPTER 68

"Something is wrong," Ariel confided in her friends as they sat around May's table drinking beer and eating chips and salsa. The house wasn't that much different than Ariel's own.

"I think it tastes fine," Guy answered looking at his food suspiciously.

"No dummy, I think she means her and Reese," May answered giving Guy a poke with her elbow.

Guy looked at Ariel expectantly as the others did too. May was the one who asked though "What's wrong?"

"Reese is watching me all the time, I'm afraid to ask what's it about," she answered with a shy little smile and then that left her face almost immediately.

"So what's wrong with her looking at you? I think you would like a woman like Reese looking at you?" Guy asked in bewilderment.

"What do you think it is honey?" May asked sitting and taking her friends hand.

Ariel leaned forward and answered, "I don't know but it's bothering me, I know she wants to say something and I'm afraid she might want to break up."

"Didn't you two just finally work all that out?" Guy asked sitting back and taking a swig of his beer.

"Yes, but I can't help thinking she just might want out, maybe she changed her mind." She looked miserable in her anxiety, "Do you know how hard it is to keep your eyes closed and your breathing even when you know someone is watching you?"

May laughed at her neurotic friend, "You're being paranoid. Reese Paulson loves you. You have never been so happy and why rock the boat. Be patient, if she has something she wants to say, she will eventually. Just enjoy her and quit looking for something to be wrong!" She patted her friends hand sympathetically.

Ariel nodded, she knew her friend was right but she couldn't help herself. "She's never told me she loves me..." she mused.

"Have you told her?" May asked astutely.

"Hey you," she smiled into the phone pleased to hear from Reese so unexpectedly during the day.

"Hi, what were our plans for tonight?" Reese asked distractedly. She had a million things on her desk and she had called Ariel almost absentmindedly, almost as though a habit.

Ariel laughed at how distracted Reese was as she explained that they were going over to May's place for dinner that evening. They couldn't spend *all* their time at Reese's or Ariel's place in bed…in fact, they rarely did which both of them were finding a bit frustrating but with Reese's intense work schedule it was difficult.

Reese had been pleased with how their relationship had come along despite the lack of intimacy. They had become good friends once again. It was as though the fight they had, had never occurred. They meshed into each other's lives very well. Reese's busy schedule often interfered but living at the hotel had its perks and Ariel benefited from waiting for Reese by taking advantage of spa treatments, the pool, or room service.

Reese enjoyed hanging out with the friends she had made through Ariel as well as at Ariel's bungalow. It gave her an escape from being at work *all* the time. They hosted barbeques, dinners, and an occasional beer party. Reese wasn't too thrilled with the beer parties, she felt she was getting too old for them but she was a good sport about it because Ariel and their friends enjoyed getting plastered now and then. She was beginning to feel out of place though when she was the only one not drunk at these. She enjoyed the hikes they took in the hills, getting far away from the high rise hotels and the beaches, seeing parts of nature that didn't come anywhere near the congestion of the beaches.

CHAPTER 69

The resorts threw a Grand Ball for their General Manager Reese Paulson to celebrate the five years she had been in charge and the fact that her contract had been renewed. The Morris' invited absolutely everyone they knew. It was an excuse to invite the creme de la creme, everyone who was anyone, and even a few 'mere' acquaintances from around the world to party down under. It was also an excuse to use the publicity to pull in a few more important people from around the world. It was held in the ballroom of one of their largest hotels and limo after limo dropped off the cream of the crop from all over Australia and Europe, the America's, Asia, and Africa, wherever there were important people that The Morris' knew, that Reese Paulson and her staff knew, they had all gotten an engraved invitation.

Reese knew it was just an excuse for people to party and an excellent reason to promote the Morris resorts but she was enjoying the challenge of arranging everything to the Morris' satisfaction to prove that she deserved this. The employees too liked Reese and wanted to make a good impression. She had won over most of them at one point or another and while a firm boss she was also fair and had been generous in her praise for the work they did as well as financially for quite a few of them as she implemented a bonus and merit increase for everyone from the lowliest maids, car hops, to the executives who managed the hotels under her. She accepted criticism without vindictiveness and also accepted suggestions without taking the credit for them. Many people felt they had risen in the ranks due to their own hard work as a result. She created a feeling of teamwork and camaraderie that other hotel owners admired and respected. It was hard to lure people away from the Morris chain of resorts but when successful the other owners were always pleased with the quality of the people they hired. Luring Reese Paulson away would be quite a coup for anyone who managed it but as far as anyone could see she was happy with the Morris chain.

The party was in full swing when Reese spotted Ariel and the other friends she had personally invited. She raised her glass in salute before turning her attention back to the group of people that always seemed to surround her at gatherings such as this. Her opinions were sought after and respected. She excused herself when she could do so without seeming rude and made her way to her friends to greet them.

"Quite a show," one of them greeted her.

"Congratulations," another one gave her a hug and a peck on the cheek.

"Good for you!" several others told her.

Ariel smiled and watched as their friends greeted Reese. She looked stunning as usual in an ice blue off the shoulder gown with diamonds surrounding her throat and matching earrings. Ariel was pretty certain that they were real, especially at a party such as this.

"Would you care to dance?" one of the guys asked knowing that Reese couldn't very well go out on the floor with Ariel or any of the other women unless it was a rock and roll song. As the live orchestra was playing traditional waltzes that seemed unlikely. Reese accepted graciously and they all watched how effortlessly she sailed away on Guy's arm. She was good at it too.

"Is there anything she doesn't do well?" one of the women sighed enviously.

Ariel grinned, she really doubted it but she didn't let that intimidate her anymore. She admired Reese too much to let it bother her. She was a good friend, hell she was a *great* friend, and Ariel was grateful she was back in her life. She wanted more though and didn't know how to ask for it, she wanted to tell Reese she loved her, and that chance hadn't come up either.

They all got their chance to dance together later when the orchestra took a well-deserved break and a DJ took over with his music. It was funny to see well mannered, cultured, and perfectly coiffured men and women who had previously only danced to waltzes and other highbrow dances get down and boogie with the masses in their tuxes and fine dresses. Reese was grateful she could dance with Ariel without anyone seeming to notice. She laughed when she saw the Morris' out on the floor getting down. It was a thoroughly delightful evening and she was enjoying herself immensely.

Dinner was buffet style at midnight and no one seemed to be leaving the gala early. They did justice to the slices of ham, turkey, beef, fish, the prawns and the shrimp seemed to be never-ending. Asparagus and other vegetables both cold and hot accompanied the main courses. Reese had enjoyed her third small plate when the deserts began to arrive and she acquitted herself quite well.

"I've never seen a woman eat so much and gain so little," Mrs. Morris laughed at their General Manager as they ate at the same table together.

Reese laughed with her; she knew she could pack it away. Not every day but this occasional feasting was nice. She knew with her large bones that she hid excess body fat very easily but with her work outs there was little extra.

In a gala this size it was inevitable that she didn't meet everyone. There had been a couple of people she glanced at that she wondered who they were but shrugged it off. She was sure there were quite a few gate crashers despite the intense security but she didn't mind, there was plenty and as long as there were no 'incidents' she didn't worry about it. She had even in her own mind thought she saw Veronica a time or two but that had happened to her for years, a superficial resemblance. She could go weeks now, sometimes months without thinking about Veronica and she thought that a good thing. They had both moved on with their lives.

It was as though she had conjured her though as Mrs. Morris walked up with a Veronica look-a-like in tow. Reese couldn't believe her eyes. She thought she was imagining things as Veronica walked towards her arm in arm with Mrs. Morris. The purple eyes still entranced her immediately as she took in and noted the changes that had occurred in Veronica. Pregnancy had obviously given her the curves she had but in a good way, she looked healthy, she had matured, life had aged her in a way that enhanced her looks, she was wearing make-up that made her look absolutely stunning and the gown she wore contributed to that. As the last time Reese had seen her she had been overwhelmingly pregnant this new and different Veronica astounded her. For a moment she didn't believe her own eyes. Veronica had matured and wow she had become quite the looker.

"Reese, I'd like to introduce Lady...." Mrs. Morris began but Reese interrupted her.

"Veronica!" she smiled, thrilled to see her and surprised that she was here.

Veronica smiled; she hadn't been sure how Reese would react but having met the Morris' while on vacation in St. Tropez and finding out that one Reese Paulson worked for them she had felt compelled to see her. Finagling an invitation hadn't been hard when she mentioned she would be visiting the Gold Coast. Reese looked great, her long blonde hair worn in a different style than what she had seen at the wedding made her look years younger than what she knew to be her real age, it suited her. As always Veronica found herself immediately attracted to the stunning blonde. "Hello, I wondered if you were the same Reese Paulson that the Morris' were bragging about to everyone. I'm not surprised though really."

Reese smiled at the brunette stunned to find her standing in the ballroom before her. "What are you doing in Australia?" she asked.

Mrs. Morris stared at her new friend curiously, how in the world did she *know* Reese Paulson? She hadn't mentioned it during their conversations. She recalled that Reese had worked in England years ago or so she remembered from their research all those years ago, she only really remembered that she had worked on the station in the Outback but then they had visited her there and gotten to know the brilliant blonde then.

"I thought it was about time I see a little more than Europe," Veronica told her with a grin. She was so happy to see Reese again.

"You knew Reese in England?" Mrs. Morris asked curiously watching them stare at each other intently.

"Yes, her daughter married a cousin of my husbands," Veronica told her absentmindedly.

"Oh we must show her all our resorts," Mrs. Morris entered back into the conversation enthusiastically.

Reese was momentarily startled; she had forgotten the existence of anyone else as she drank in Veronica, seeing only *her* in this crowded room. She looks good, she looks happy. "Yes, we must show her," she agreed with her employer.

Just then one of the security personnel whispered in Reese's ear and smiling with apologies she excused herself to follow the man. Veronica watched her intently as she walked away enjoying the cut of her dress on her tall body.

"She is a fantastic employee," Mrs. Morris commented as she watched her guest curiously.

Veronica blinked and getting a grip on herself she turned to her host and said, "Yes, she did incredible things for our estates in England."

"She worked for you as well?" she asked surprised.

"Yes, many years ago before she came down to Australia to run that station," Veronica informed her.

Mrs. Morris eyed her speculatively but never said a word as she vaguely remembered that about Reese.

The incident was minor, just some kids getting a little over zealous in their partying and security soon had it straightened out. A few well-placed taxis had these guests zipping away from the festivities so no one was the wiser. Reese returned to the ball but didn't see Veronica as she searched. What was she doing *here* after all this time?

"Who are you looking for?" Ariel asked at her elbow.

Reese turned to her in surprise, "Oh, a friend from long ago unexpectedly showed up and we were interrupted before we could really talk."

Ariel accepted that and then asked, "Would you like to dance?"

Reese shook her head which caused her blonde curls to dance, "Not really, this party has been long. I wonder how much longer I have to stay..." she mused.

"It is after all in honor of you..." Ariel said with a grin.

Reese smiled, "I know, I probably sound ungrateful, but it was a lot of work."

Ariel laughed, she of all people knew how much Reese worked since she didn't see her as much as she would like. She hadn't been able to address the sexual side of their relationship and she would really like to, she missed the intimacy, the foreplay, the beauty that they had had together. She also wanted to take it to another level but when had they had the time?

Reese looked around the still crowded ballroom. There were so many people. How was she to pick out Veronica in all this mass of humanity? Where was she? She spotted Mrs. Morris but Veronica wasn't still with her.

"Maybe I could come by later and help you relax?" Ariel was bold enough to ask.

Reese looked down at her friend and although she understood the innuendo she chose to ignore it. She just hadn't felt like becoming intimate as often as their friendship regained its former level, for her the friendship had become more important than the sex and she couldn't really explain it. There had been times that she had wanted Ariel desperately but this just wasn't one of them and now with Veronica in the room it almost felt dirty with Ariel hitting on her, however subtly. "Thank you for the offer, but I am sure I will be exhausted by the time this is all over. I'm going to take a few days off."

Ariel was surprised at this news as it was the first time she had heard it and they had spoken just the previous day. "Doing anything special?" she asked to hide her surprise and hoping she would want to do something together.

"Absolutely nothing, which is something I deserve." Reese grinned.

"You're right, you do deserve some time off, let me know if you'd like to do something together," Ariel gave her an out but at the same time felt a little hurt that Reese hadn't wanted to include her in her plans.

"I'll do that." Reese gave her a smile as she moved off.

Ariel watched the beautiful blonde as she greeted and chatted her way through the crowd.

"She's something else," Guy mentioned to her at her side.

Ariel glanced at him numbly.

"Can't you see she doesn't want you like that anymore?" he asked gently trying to break it to his friend. He had seen it for months, they had all seen it. Reese was willing to be her friend, had even wanted more occasionally, they indulged periodically, but the fates had decreed differently apparently. They never seemed to bridge that last hurdle to make it a regular thing despite both of them trying.

"That's a little cruel," Ariel answered trying not to agree with what she knew was the truth.

"No babe, it's honest," he looked at his friend sadly.

She sighed as she lost sight of Reese, "Yeah, I know."

He hugged her as he kissed her forehead and led her back to their friends. They all decided to leave soon afterwards and Reese never even knew.

Reese didn't find Veronica again that evening and she didn't feel right asking Mrs. Morris where she was. She checked the registry since she had access to all the computers and found that Veronica was registered under Lady Cavandish and not Lady Wilkins. This made Reese wonder what had happened in Veronica's world. She was also registered at the hotel where Reese lived, she wondered if this were a coincidence or not. She went home that evening with her thoughts full of Veronica. She wasn't alone in her thoughts.

CHAPTER 70

Gawd, I waited too long. She's even more beautiful than I remembered thought Veronica. I can't seem to get her out of my thoughts in all these years. Why did I jump at the chance to see her again? You know why you did, don't try to fool yourself. You have loved her for ten years; you know why you are here. You know you need to find out if she feels the same. You need her, you want her. Gawd, she did want her, seeing her tonight brought back memories and fantasies that she had buried over the last 10 years and yet they had been all she had despite making new ones.

She had seen the woman and men that Reese danced with, she didn't know if she was being extra sensitive but one of the woman seemed a little possessive and perhaps Reese danced with her a bit more than the others. There had to of been other women in the last ten years. That thought hurt but it was reality. A woman such as Reese couldn't possibly be alone for a decade. Veronica wondered what they had been like; did she even have a chance? Was she a fool for having come here?

CHAPTER 71

"She has the next few days off and she never said a word?" May exchanged a look with Guy as they listened to Ariel rant and rave on the ride home. They had dropped off the others of their party and the three of them were sharing the car that Reese had arranged for them to drop them at their homes.

Ariel shook her head and hung it. She had drunk more than she should have. Reese wasn't exclusively hers, she understood how important her job was, but this had really hurt to see her pull away at least in her own mind. The few times they had been intimate had been as terrific as before but still it wasn't as often or as convenient as before. It was like Reese didn't care to make the effort and only when she felt Ariel needed it that she let herself fall into bed with her. No, that wasn't fair, Reese was a busy woman. Ariel just wanted more than she was able to give. She had slept many times in the hotel suite with her but only to sleep. Room service had been nice but she had wanted the woman she had come to see, not just to sleep. It made her feel so needy, so alone, and it angered her that Reese was causing her to feel this way. Talking with their friends though didn't help; they had already told her that Reese wanted to be her friend, or worse: friends with benefits, nothing more.

CHAPTER 72

Should she seek her out? It was rather late after all. She should wait until the morning. She felt strangely awake despite the fatigue she was feeling from working all day and partying all night. She went over long buried memories, over and over as she got ready for bed. Her excellent staff would see to the clean-up and straightening of the ballrooms and the halls leading to it as well as anywhere else a guest had overflowed to. Parties such as these had people going to the oddest corners of an establishment but she understood, she had been one of those people occasionally who wanted a an out-of-the-way spot for a quiet conversation or a rendezvous.

Lying in bed she remembered working out in England, she remembered Veronica watching her, she wasn't always aware of her secretly watching her but when she did become aware of it she saw her, especially after they became intimate. Gawd, she had been Veronica's first! She wondered how Veronica felt about that, who she had known since, what was she doing here?

CHAPTER 73

As she lay in her own bed she remembered seeing Reese for the first time in that messy office. Her impression of her underlying strength, her beauty, she remembered being fascinated by her, admiring, and then attracted to her. She remembered how shy she had been, how afraid that Reese would reject her. That first kiss played over and over in her mind. Not constantly over the years but enough that she remembered it instantly, it didn't take much to recall the last ones either. She understood so much more than she had all those years ago. She understood what her brother had done for the sake of their family; she understood now what Reese had done. She herself had birthed three children to ensure the continuation of the Cavandish 'dynasty' as it were. Her children would inherit both the Cavandish as well as the Wilkin's estates. She had done her duty, she was still doing it. The children were off at school, she was allowed some 'free' time and this trip to Australia to visit an 'old friend' was all it was wasn't it? Who was she fooling? She was here to see Reese, what happened from seeing her would be up to fate.

CHAPTER 74

Reese slept soundly despite her thoughts, fatigue alone ensured that. It was short though as knowledge that Veronica was in the building somewhere awoke her fairly early. Staring at the clock angrily she got up and took a shower to wash the fog from her head and freshen herself. She quickly dried herself and used a hair dryer on her locks. Brushing on a minimum of makeup she knew she looked good despite her age. Quickly she dressed in deep cleavage t-shirt and put her long legs into shorts and her feet into sandals. She looked casual as she added earrings and a bracelet and slipped her room key, phone, and wallet into her pockets and was ready to go.

She got down to the restaurant wondering if she would see anyone she knew other than the employees that she nodded to but ignored as she looked for the one person she was seeking. Glancing around the restaurant she was disappointed not to see her anywhere. She was an early riser and Reese wondered with the time difference perhaps it was too early. She could go check the computer to see if breakfast had been ordered to be delivered to the room…

"Breakfast Ms. Paulson?" one of the waitresses asked courteously.

Reese smiled down at the gal; she had been prompt which spoke well for the service. She was tempted to say no and go back to her rooms but knew she had to eat, she had several days off and starting them without food wouldn't be a good idea. "Yes please," she answered back and was escorted to a quiet table where she could watch over the room without being noticed. She smiled at the gal, her preferences were known.

Reese had a nice meal of fruit and two pieces of dry toast. She was finishing up with passion fruit juice when she saw Veronica walk in. She smiled as she stood up to let her notice her. Veronica did so immediately and headed for her table.

"Good Morning," she said in a pleasant voice.

Reese nearly groaned at that voice, she had dreamt of it many times. She smiled in welcome, "Won't you join me?" She indicated the empty seat across from her own.

"Looks like you are finishing up?" Veronica grinned.

Reese nodded, "Yes I am but I will stay and keep you company."

Veronica's heart leapt at the positive response and she pulled out a chair to sit down. She didn't notice Reese signaling to the waitress who arrived promptly.

"May I get you some coffee ma'am?" she asked.

Veronica ordered juice and her meal instead.

"You should try this," Reese indicated the passion fruit.

"What is it?" she looked at the fruity concoction.

Reese lifted her glass and held it out to Veronica. "Passion fruit," she said.

Veronica didn't think twice about taking a sampling of her ex-lovers drink. "This is good!" she said delighted.

Reese ordered a carafe of the mix when the waitress returned with Veronica's order.

"So have you seen anything since you got here?" she asked Veronica to make conversation, she wanted to ask 'what are you doing here, did you come to see me?'

Veronica shook her head, "No, I really didn't have time, I needed to catch up with the time difference and then that party," she said admiredly. "That was something else!" she laughed.

Reese grinned which made Veronica's heart go pity-pat in remembrance. "So what are you plans while you are down under?" she tried to ask casually.

Veronica was not fooled and grinned in return as she accepted her food from the waitress. Reese poured them both some more juice from the carafe and Veronica bit into her toast. Swallowing she asked, "What do you recommend?"

Answering 'you in my bed' wouldn't have been proper social etiquette so Reese answered, "The beach of course!" instead.

Veronica nodded, "Am I dressed appropriately?" She indicated the shorts and t-shirt she was wearing.

Reese nodded admiring the body under the clothes and then mentally shook herself before answering, "Yes but if you want to get a tan you might want a bathing suit."

"With this skin?" Veronica teased; she was darker than most English women with her outdoor activities.

It did give Reese more of an opportunity to admire the body she was lusting after but pulling herself together and her hormones she asked, "Would you like a tour guide?"

"Can you get away?"

"I took a few days off after that party," she sounded relieved.

"Well, it will be as good as a native," she smiled.

"After all these years I feel like one," she answered honestly.

"You like it here?" wondering if she would ever leave. She felt her heart was hanging on this answer.

"Yes, it's beautiful here, warm, sometimes too warm, but the weather year round is very nice overall."

"You like your job?" Hoping she would say no.

"Of course, I just renewed my contract after all."

These answers didn't satisfy the underlying questions that Veronica was asking but if she wanted to know the truth, the whole truth she would have to ask outright and that wasn't her way. Agreeing to have Reese show her around she hoped by spending time with her that she would learn what she wanted to know.

CHAPTER 75

Reese took her up and down the coast staying at Morris properties with adjoining rooms. She found herself gone for longer than the few days she had planned to be off but she combined it with working so she really never took those few days. Veronica was amazed at the extent of Morris properties and realized how important Reese was to the running of the entire complex of hotels, resorts, and other properties. This was much more than the estates she had run for them back in England. She sort of got her answers though as they rode out on a boat to look at the Great Barrier Reef.

"I think though after this contract is up I'm going to retire," Reese confided in her.

"Will you really?" Veronica shouted over the noise of the boat and the wind as she held down the scarf holding back her hair.

Reese nodded as she looked out at the view. It had been difficult eating all their meals together and saying 'good night' as she escorted her to her room. She had used work as an excuse countless times to avoid a potentially embarrassing situation. She knew she wanted Veronica but she couldn't tell for sure if Veronica wanted her.

Snorkeling out over the reef their guide showed them wonderful displays of fish and fauna. The reef itself was a mixture of colors and incredible views. Reese had deliberately not gone with Jack's boat as she didn't want any awkwardness there. It was too hard and she had barely avoided Ariel and Veronica meeting when they returned to her home hotel. She didn't want to have to explain what she was doing with her ex-employer, her ex-friend, her ex-lover.

Veronica resumed their earlier conversation at dinner that evening, "What will you do when you retire?"

"Well Gillian has been threatening to make me a grandmother someday, maybe I'll just find a nice little cottage somewhere and play grandma," she laughed at the thought.

Veronica was shocked at the thought that this sexy woman would ever be a grandmother but then remembering Gillian's wedding she thought that could very well be. She just didn't think of her as the grandmotherly type. The thought of Reese in a 'little cottage' though made Veronica want to laugh but she asked knowingly, "How will you ever be able to take it easy though?"

Reese laughed; she wasn't exactly the slowing down type. She had done so much for so long that it was really hard to imagine taking it easy. Lord knew she could afford it now. "I have no idea, perhaps someone will have to tie me down."

Veronica laughed at the idea and yet inside the imagery of having her way with Reese's delightful body when she couldn't move from a bed slammed into her consciousness like a freight train. She swallowed and trying to get the idea off her mind asked, "So where do we go from here?"

"I was thinking I should go rent an airplane or a jet and take you inland. The mountains and the outback are beautiful. I could take you out to Wahbaing Station for a couple of days and before we come back make a sort of side trip and take you out to Ayer's Rock which I haven't seen myself."

"That sounds delightful, I will admit to being curious as to what Wahbaing Station looks like! Lady Emerson finally got around to showing me pictures and the brochure. You really did a lot for her and she brags about the amount they got for the place when she sold it! Her lawyers were certain you were ripping her off only to find the profits far exceeding the evaluation." She shook her head, "I only wish I could be as clever with the estates."

Reese had been careful in her conversations, asking very little and letting Veronica volunteer information as she saw fit. She had learned that her husband and she led very separate lives, that her children were off at school, and that David was near death and had a full time nurse. "You still manage everything yourself?" she asked.

Veronica nodded, "Although I hired a temporary manager to help me out so I could travel more." No one had gotten a more intense and short training. She didn't care what she came back to as long as she got this trip to see if Reese still loved her. She wasn't certain if she did, they hadn't gotten to that conversation and she wasn't sure enough of herself to initiate it. Just getting know Reese again had been thrilling, she was still the same beautiful and self-assured woman that Veronica had admired all those years ago but at the same time she had changed in a myriad of ways that intimidated Veronica to a degree.

"I hope they are qualified," Reese teased not knowing what thoughts were going on behind those amazing purple eyes.

Veronica smiled, causing Reese's breath to catch and asked, "You can fly a plane?"

Reese nodded and added, "Yes and a jet, the training was hard but very worth it. I don't use it much with driving up and down the coast but I kept my license current." She went on to explain about learning to fly out at Wahbaing Station and soon had Veronica laughing at her stories.

That night as Reese walked her to the elevator to escort her back to her room Veronica turned suddenly and said, "You know, I haven't seen your apartments; you did say you lived here in the hotel?"

Reese was startled and nodded, "Yes I live on one of the upper floors, part of my perks you know. You want to see them?"

Veronica nodded. It had taken a moment of bravery to manipulate the invite but she did want to see how Reese had been living here without her all these years. She wanted to go to Wahbaing Station, see some clue as to how she had managed without her.

Reese took out her manager key to the upper floor as the elevator opened to let some people off. She and Veronica got on the elevator together. Neither of them saw that they were being observed from across the lobby. Reese inserted her key into the elevator key box as the doors closed and punched the upper floor level that she lived on.

"All very high tech," Veronica commented and Reese nodded.

"Well most people can't just come up to my apartment without a key or an invitation," she grinned. She knew Veronica must be curious and hadn't really thought of inviting her before as she carefully kept her thoughts from lusting after her after all these years, the last week had been difficult knowing she was in the adjoining rooms and not taking advantage of that fact.

As they got off the elevator Reese unlocked the door to her suite. Veronica was amazed at how large the rooms were but then Reese wasn't just staying here, she *lived* here. Walking across the large room with its small kitchenette and bar she looked out on the balcony until Reese unlocked the door and slid it open. "Feel free," she murmured watching Veronica's expressions as she looked at Reese's home.

The view from the balcony was incredible. It wasn't so late that they couldn't see the beach far below or the people still taking advantage of the warm night air. The lights shone already lighting walkways but barely reached up so high to the apartment balcony.

"This is beautiful," Veronica breathed. Vacationing like this was one thing but *living* like this?

Reese shrugged, she was used to it. She kind of took it for granted with all her duties. This was her home, this is where she escaped her staff but even then she had a small office here in the apartment that she used to work late at night when she couldn't sleep.

Reese showed her the two bedrooms and the luxurious bathrooms attached. It was a lot for one person but someone of Reese's importance could have had more but in Reese's modest case she didn't need more.

"Do you spend much time here?" Veronica had seen how the various properties took up Reese's time.

"Not as much as I'd like but I travel a lot for the chain."

"Do you really think you could retire from this?"

They were walking toward the kitchenette as she asked and Reese pulled out a bottle of wine and indicated it to Veronica who nodded as Reese pulled out a cork screw and began applying it. "I don't honestly know. I've been so busy for so long and I'm certainly not ready to retire. I am however starting to feel that I shouldn't have signed another contract so soon."

"You aren't happy?"

Reese shrugged as Veronica looked around the room; there were few if any personal possessions. She had seen the same pictures with one or two new ones including one of Gillian in her wedding dress but other than that there was little that personalized the whole apartment. "I love it here, the weather is fantastic except for the rainy season when it comes down in sheets but even that is welcome. The people are pretty nice, but I don't know, I think I need a new challenge." She popped the wine bottle open and grabbed two wine glasses filling them effortlessly and handing one to Veronica.

"Let's go sit on the sofa," she indicated the two that were situated in the middle of the large room facing each other.

"Yes but what challenge next?" Veronica asked and barely missed Reese checking her out as she walked before her.

"I don't know, maybe I should go back to the States." Veronica's heart clutched at statement.

"What about Gillian?" she asked hoping to lead into a statement that would get Reese back to England.

"She doesn't need her dear old mom."

Veronica released a very unladylike snort at that statement, Reese was certainly not old!

"I don't know, I like it here, I know the job; I know the direction I want to take the resorts. Most of my hotel managers are easy to work with and know their jobs. It's the same though after all these years. The sameness is what is no longer a challenge."

They talked for a good hour as they discussed various topics and consumed the entire bottle of wine and started on another. Good friends who could never run out of conversation. They kept it fairly impersonal as they had during all of the tour of the various resorts, hotels, and properties that encompassed the Morris chain and that Reese managed for them. It was a huge enterprise that no longer interested the brilliant blonde.

Veronica hoped that this disinterest by Reese could possibly mean she was willing to come back to England. After all her only daughter was there. The good conversation, the delightful company, the wine all were having an effect on Veronica. She felt bold enough to make a pass at Reese.

Reese pulled back in surprise. In the time she had taken to show Veronica around she had been very careful not to touch her inappropriately, not lead her on, after all she was involved, sorta with Ariel. Although they weren't exclusive as far as she knew they had both been faithful. This could complicate things. She knew though that it had taken a super-human effort not to be the one to make a pass at Veronica. She knew her defenses were down, the wine, the good conversation, the woman who had occupied so much of her thoughts over the years; all were undermining her good intentions. She leaned back in to finish the kiss that Veronica had initiated.

It was like coming home. They both felt it. The instant feeling of satisfaction to be kissing this particular person in the world. Both leaned into the kiss and explored the flavors in each other's mouths.

She hasn't changed, she is still the best kisser ever.

She feels so good against me, I can't get close enough.

It didn't take long to find them both laying side by side on the sofa and straining against each other to feel the passion that each invoked in the other. They suited, they justified what they were doing as they both knew it was inevitable if they were together long enough. Both had been surprised to resist *this* long. There was none of the desperation on Veronica's part to be loved, she wasn't overly pregnant, she wasn't trying to prove anything. To Reese it was as familiar as it had been all those years ago. Other women didn't compare. This was *her* Veronica, she had taught her and no matter how many other partner's Veronica had in the meantime, she was *hers* for now.

Over and over they kissed deeply as their hungers grew out of proportion. There was no rush and yet each wanted what the other was offering.

"Come with me," Reese entreated rising from the couch to hold out her hand and pull her lover up.

Veronica felt dazed, the abrupt removal of Reese's body from her own had caused an ache and she wanted more, much, much more. She put her hand in Reese's unhesitatingly as she was led to the bedroom.

Reese stood there a moment looking down at the familiar face, seeing the years fade away as she began to kiss her and make love to her in earnest, removing pieces of clothing from her effortlessly.

Veronica felt anxious, she wanted a naked Reese against her and she wanted it *now*. Stripping Reese wasn't going nearly as fast as she wanted it to but not wanting to seem uncouth or hurried she mentally stopped herself from ripping the clothes off of her lover.

Soon they were both naked and standing against each other as they kissed passionately, lovingly. Grinding their bodies against one another they both realized it wouldn't be enough and slowly Reese maneuvered Veronica against the bed. Feeling the mattress against the backs of her legs she slowly sat down pulling Reese against her and burying her face into Reese's stomach. She could scent her arousal, she could feel her own. She wanted to bury her face between Reese's legs and inhale, taste, devour but she checked herself, there would be time for that later. Reese felt Veronica tremble and pulled her close as she looked down on her head. She wanted to ravage her, take her in ways she hadn't in the times they had been together in the past. The endless scenarios that had gone through her head over the years, the would haves, the could haves, and the should haves. She wanted them all, and she wanted them *now*. She deliberately pulled back to look down into those amazing violet eyes, so trusting, so aroused, so loving. She leaned down for a kiss only to lose herself in that kiss as she was pulled and she went willingly onto Veronica's lush body.

The weight on top of her felt so very welcome. A leg wrapped around Reese immediately pulling her closer as Veronica ground herself into her lover's body. Reese could feel the wetness from between Veronica's legs; the heat came from there as well, telling her that she was as aroused as Reese's own senses. Slowly Reese detached her lips from Veronica's and kissed her way into her neck, her senses were reeling at the scent of her, the familiar body smells that were driving her insane, she couldn't lick, kiss, or suck hard enough to get it all, to experience it all. She gentled her lips to honor the body beneath her, to worship it, adore it, and savor it.

Only Reese had ever made her feel like this. No one else in all these years could arouse her, could excite her. She had tried, a couple of times she had *tried* to find someone else. But no one measured up to Reese Paulson. No one excited her or engaged her body like this. Her husband disgusted her, the women she had tried to have relationships with hadn't suited her despite both she and them trying and not succeeding, and only Reese reached the depths inside of her that satisfied her.

As Reese kissed her way down the overheated body beneath her she stopped to worship and lavish her attention on the breasts that had grown considerably over the years. Three babies and a mature body and she was still as desirable as she had been before that. Her ample breasts delighted Reese; she licked hungrily at the engorged nipples, amazed at how hard she made them. Her hands were not idle as they memorized her lover's body, smoothed over curves that hadn't been there before, relearned the pleasure spots that had Veronica arching and curving into her palms in response.

Gawd, she felt so damn good against her, she knew, really knew how to make love to Veronica. The sighs and then gasps were heartfelt. To finally know her touch, really *know* her touch, soothed Veronica's soul in so many ways. As she reached the wetness between her legs she thought she had died and gone to heaven. The touch of her tongue on her engorged clit was nirvana. A small ripple went through her body as she squeezed reflexively on Reese's probing fingers.

Reese was surprised that three fingers fit inside her lover's body so readily and then remembering three babies had come out of this body she realized that it had probably stretched to accommodate them. She effortlessly found Veronica's G-spot and was thrilled to hear the gasp and then corresponding moans that incited as she licked and sucked at her clit. She could sense as a tremendous orgasm built inside her lover's body long before Veronica became aware of it. As her body began to tense in anticipation of the orgasm Veronica felt herself spiraling out of control and before she knew it she found herself wetting the bed and her body convulsing. She couldn't seem to stop herself and Reese didn't stop until she had wrung it all out of her body.

Veronica was ashamed, here she had wanted Reese so bad for so long and now she wet the bed? She sat up in embarrassment looking at the bedspread in horror, the large wet spot giving evidence of her lack of control. She didn't want to look at her lover, she was so embarrassed. She glanced at Reese and was shocked to see her grinning as she watched Veronica's reaction.

"When did you start squirting?" Reese asked quietly.

"Squirting?" Veronica asked alarmed.

Reese indicated the large wet spot mixed with a bit of white on the dark bedspread. Veronica stared at it without comprehension. All of her passion and the residual effects of a good orgasm had died within her. Reese looked at her lover and her grin died seeing that Veronica did not look happy. "You didn't know you squirted?"

Veronica shook her head and looked away. Despite her age and research on the subject she was still quite naïve.

Reese realized her dilemma and took pity on her. "Babe," she waited until Veronica looked at her again. When she did she continued, "That isn't pee, that's ejaculation. You squirted," she told her.

Veronica was confused, "Not pee?"

Reese shook her head delighted, "No babe, it's part of your body's reaction to our lovemaking," they both warmed at the word, love was in it. "It's odorless, and as you can see there is cum mixed in with it."

Veronica was relieved, she had thought she had done something wrong and the embarrassment of it would have killed her. She also suddenly realized they were both sitting there naked. She looked at Reese in consternation suddenly hungering for her naked body.

Reese smiled slowly seeing the passion that had been lurking but suppressed in her lover's eyes. "Here," she tugged Veronica further up the bed and away from the wet spot as they resumed making love to each other.

Veronica began kissing Reese, first in gratitude for what she was feeling, relief that she hadn't done anything wrong. In fact she had done something very very right and her lover was going to take advantage of it. Reese rolled her beneath her as she made love to her again, not able to get her out her psyche or soul for a couple of rounds before she took her own satisfaction. It was better than either remembered, even their fantasies didn't compare as they spent hours getting to know each other's bodies again. Veronica realized Reese still enjoyed her body despite the stretch marks and weight gained from having had children; Reese realized she desired Veronica just as much as she had five, even ten years ago.

"We do that so well," Reese breathed as they both took a break, having finally gotten under the covers and were falling off to sleep.

Veronica chuckled, she was satisfied, well-satisfied. Her body exhausted from the multitude of orgasms Reese had caused inside of her. She was amazed at how bold she had become even to the point of insisting that Reese sit on her face again, something she had wondered about for years after they had parted.

CHAPTER 76

"Let's order breakfast and then I'll call to rent a plane and make other arrangements. How long will it take you to pack?" Reese was full of boundless energy after having made love to Veronica in the shower they had shared.

Veronica laughed and smiled in return, "What should I take?"

Discussing what they wanted to do and where they wanted to go Veronica left with a kiss as she left Reese on the phone with her assistant Simone making arrangements for while she was gone.

Reese's cell phone rang; she could see by the caller I.D. that it was Ariel, "Hello?"

"Hi, how was your time off?" Ariel asked deliberately. She hadn't seen her since the party and last night with that brunette as she got on the elevator.

"I wish I knew, turned out that I had to show the properties to a friend of the Morris' so I didn't really get those days off I had anticipated." She didn't think she was lying after all Veronica was a friend of the Morris'.

Ariel felt suddenly relieved, with all the time away that Reese did for her job not once had she considered that she could be cheating on her. They didn't have that type of exclusive relationship at this point but still… "So are you going to take it after they leave?" She had almost said 'she' which would have given her away.

"I'm making plans now," Reese answered wondering if she would have to lie to Ariel after all. She couldn't very well tell her she was going away with her ex-girlfriend could she?

"Oh, anyplace special?" Ariel tried to ask innocently and at the same time wishing she could take off to go away with Reese and have her to herself.

Reese mentally sighed and shook her head, "No, but I have a million things to do here at work before I take any time away, you know how that is."

That was always the excuse, Reese had work to do. Ariel understood she was an important woman and the properties that Morris' owned extensive. It was hard to date such a woman but she was trying to get back to their former closeness and the blocks in the way that had been pushed aside in the past were not so easy this time around. She was feeling desperate as though Reese were slipping away from her. "Well give me a call when you get back then?" she tried to stay positive after all she had been wrong with her jealousy of seeing Reese walk into the elevator with the brunette.

"I'll do that," Reese answered dismissively wondering where her relationship with Veronica would take her *this time* and if she would ever call Ariel again. For a second it bothered her after all she had known Ariel for a while now and they had been working on repairing their relationship on several levels. Then thinking of the coming days with Veronica she buried whatever guilt that might have been rearing its ugly head.

Reese soon had things worked out for work to run smoothly while she was away, after all she had many competent managers working under her in the various properties and she was frequently gone inspecting and working with them. Her assistants could be in constant contact with her if they needed anything and they would but she hoped the cell towers would be able to reach her out at the station or further out at Ayers Rock. She called the station to make arrangements for a visit and was surprised at Jeremiah answering the phone and taking her reservation. He assured her that he would have a room for her ready and waiting. Next she called a company that rented out planes to licensed pilots and made arrangements to have a Cessna for the next week for their trip.

All of this took several hours and she packed as she sat on the phone making the arrangements. She was excited, she wondered if this meant anything with Veronica beyond what she wanted to read into it. She knew she had loved her, they have loved hard, but she didn't know exactly how she felt right now. She was confused but at the same time she wanted to spend whatever time she did have with Veronica while she could.

"Ready to go?" she asked as she rolled a large suitcase behind her and Veronica answered the bell to her suite.

"I think so, I wasn't sure what I would need so I packed it all again!" Veronica gestured at the two large suitcases she had brought with her from England.

Reese laughed at her but shrugged and called down for a bellboy to come and take the cases to a hotel limo that would take them to the small airport where their Cessna was gassed up and awaiting their trip.

"Are you sure you can fly this?" Veronica asked nervously as the driver lifted their cases into the back of the plane and Reese inspected it doing a mental check off list before taking off in it.

Reese laughed and said, "We will soon find out won't we?" which alarmed Veronica until she saw the glimmer in her lover's eye.

Veronica was amazed at the little plane and how competently Reese handled it. Take off had plunged Veronica's stomach like a roller coaster ride but she was loving the scenery as Reese pointed out landmarks and then as the hours went by and she became more familiar with the territory she pointed out places she had visited when she lived out in the outback. Flying into Wahbaing Station Veronica was surprised at how 'modern' it looked, there was asphalt on the runway and while dust did billow up behind them a practically new Jeep was waiting for them after Reese parked the plane.

"Missus!" an aborigine man welcomed Reese exuberantly and gave her a big hug which she returned wholeheartedly knocking off her sunglasses.

"Jeremiah! When did you get all grown up?" she asked in return delighted to see her old friend.

He smiled showing off perfectly white teeth against his dark skin. "Ah time does that to all of us except you!"

"Veronica, let me introduce you to someone," she called as she saw Veronica hesitatingly standing next to the plane.

"This is Jeremiah, he was just a youth when I worked here and now I understand he is the assistant manager here on the station!" she had done her research and looked up the station while she made her plans after making her call to get a room for a few days.

Veronica played the upper crust Brit very well at that moment and Reese was reminded of some of the prejudices she hadn't seen in a long time as her lover barely shook the man's hand. Jeremiah shrugged it off as though he didn't notice as other guests had behaved the same way periodically. He quickly had their luggage in the back of the Jeep and his guests on their way back to the station house.

"I've put you in the main house, we is full up missus," he addressed Reese who was sitting in the front seat while Veronica sat in the back holding on to her seat strap on the bumpy road.

"That's great, so the new company is treating you well?" she asked genuinely interested.

"Yes and no Missus, they expect profits but don't spend it on improvements," he mentioned as they went over a particularly big bump in the road.

"Jeezus Jeremiah, where is the bulldozer so you can level this out!" Reese asked as they bounced around madly in the SUV.

"No time Missus with all the work I do now," he said with a grin.

They were soon at the station house and it looked as beautiful as ever. Reese recognized several of the employees she had known in the past, all older, and looking good as she greeted them. She didn't introduce them to Veronica having noticed her distaste for meeting the Aborigines. She was surprised as they put her in one of the master suites with a new connecting door to the next room where they put Veronica. Both rooms were luxurious but Reese's was definitely superior.

She wondered what had become of Sheila but didn't ask since she knew she had left the station years ago. She recommended they change and she would show Veronica around the home paddock. Veronica while apparently prejudiced against anyone with darker skin than her own did however greet and meet anyone that Reese introduced her to who was white. She found their Australian accents charming. They ended their tour after a hot and dusty afternoon at the pool to refresh themselves before dressing for dinner and meeting several of the other guests.

That night Veronica came to her room and she and Reese enjoyed themselves immensely. Learning each other again, trying things each had only imagined after the end of their affair all those years ago, they learned new things about one another. As Reese rolled around in the sheets with Veronica she remembered her lover's reaction to the Aborigines on the station and knew she could never tell her about Sheila, she wouldn't understand. Thoughts of Sheila and what she had done in this very room with her made her wonder if she was disturbed to be taking another lover in the same room?

The next day they took horses out on a trail ride looking at the ponds that had been formed in Reese's time on the station and that now looked natural and a part of the landscape. Reese took along a rifle which a cheeky grinning Jeremiah handed to her before she left. He glanced at the old familiar red hat she had unearthed and nearly laughed aloud upon seeing it. Reese grinned in return knowing the flack she had taken over the years for wearing it.

"What on Earth is that for?" Veronica asked alarmed as Reese shoved the rifle into the boot attached to her saddle.

"It's 'in case,' this isn't a nature preserve but an actual working station, there are wild animals here," Reese told her amused.

The scenery was as lovely as Reese remembered and she took Veronica on a tour that normal tourists never saw. She knew paths and draws and hilltops that commanded an excellent view. They stopped to rest under some trees to eat their lunch and give their horses a well-deserved rest but only after Reese swept the area making sure there were no snakes or animals to disturb their picnic the new housekeeper had packed into saddle bags for them.

"This is lovely Reese," Veronica commented as she lay on her side looking out at the view and popping grapes into her mouth.

"Yes it is," Reese responded but her view encompassed a slightly perspiring Veronica and not mother nature.

Veronica blushed at the compliment and then her thoughts. She couldn't ever remember being this randy and ready to make love before, was it because she was older or because she wasn't sure how much time together they had? She didn't care as Reese carefully put aside the food they hadn't eaten and took her jaw tenderly in her hands to kiss her deeply. All either cared about was the moment, the lovemaking they were able to fit in the time allotted to them.

They spent four days on the station and didn't see half of it, they were luckier than some tourists though as Reese took them up in the Cessna and flew over the vast acreage pointing out different areas and explaining them to Veronica. Veronica hadn't realized how extensive stations were in the outback and she was impressed as Reese explained what different things were for and how they affected the running of the successful station, she showed her some of the things she had implemented and noted the changes that the corporation who now owned it had done. She even took a few hours to show Veronica how to run a bulldozer as she smoothed out a couple of rain bitten roads that led up to the station to help out. Veronica had laughed delightedly at the different things she was learning about Reese; she always managed to surprise her. She remembered her running a bulldozer back in England and this led to a lot of remembrances for both of them as they waxed nostalgic.

It was a bittersweet leaving of the station for Reese, she had loved 'coming home' but it had changed. Having Veronica there had been odd when she was looking to see Sheila who she didn't find anything out about. She smiled and shook as many of her 'old' employees and friends hands as she could before she left with a wave. Jeremiah himself drove them to their plane that he had gassed up and checked for 'Misses' and waved as they took off. Reese headed Southwest towards where they wanted to go to see Ayer's Rock. Flying over a few other stations that she remembered she shared stories with Veronica to pass the time. Veronica was amazed at the sheer size of the stations, many even bigger than the one they had just left.

CHAPTER 77

Landing in a small dusty red earthed airport near the Ayers Rock they were able to rent camping gear and a Jeep that Reese gamely drove out toward the massive tourist destination. She laughed at Veronica when she became the prissy Brit and had her laughing at herself in no time as they found their campsite near the monstrous rock.

The next day they joined tourists who hiked around the ancient sandstone monolith listening to their tour guides which all seemed to be Aborigine. Reese was surprised that Veronica managed to remain civil and actually seemed interested as they relayed stories and explained the importance of the tourist attraction to their history. She realized as long as Veronica didn't have to 'touch' these darker skinned people she was fine with them 'working' around her. It was an insight she didn't appreciate in her friend but she accepted her foibles and faults despite not agreeing with them. Ayers Rock was known as Uluru in the Aboriginal language of Anangu. It was located in Uluru-Kata Tjuta National Park in the Northern Terriotry of central Australia. They both found it fascinating, the springs, wterholes, rock caves, and ancient paintings.

Camping in a tent with Veronica was amusing. She wasn't the most 'outdoorsy' woman and Reese covered a lot of her annoyances with humor. From burning too much of their supply of wood to making charcoal out of their food it was an experience. Veronica however was game to try and insisted she had camped out before although Reese doubted it. Seeing people with travel trailers Reese realized she should have rented one of these for her snobbish friend but she respected Veronica for trying. Sleeping on an air mattress together and silently making love under the stars though made up for a lot of inconveniences. They were closer than ever, certain subjects were not brought up, like past lovers or when this would all end.

Reese checked in daily with her offices but nothing came up out of the ordinary that she couldn't handle by phone. A few times she did not have service and had to find a landline but it all worked out well for their vacation. All too soon they were flying back and heading towards the coast.

"That was a delightful trip!" Veronica enthused covering up her panicky feeling as they hadn't discussed a future, nothing about her departure. She knew she couldn't stay much longer without raising serious concerns back home.

"Yes I'm glad we came," Reese answered as she glanced over, her eyes hidden behind the sunglasses she wore, her own heart constricting knowing that their time together just might be limited after all.

They chatted and talked about nothing in particular as the plane slowly made its way across the vast outback of Australia. Reese was tired when they finally set down at the airport where she had rented the plane. She had called the hotel to arrange a car and it was waiting to unload their luggage and take them back to the hotel. She hadn't bothered making a reservation for Lady Cavandish as Veronica would be staying with her and she wasn't going to hide that fact.

They collapsed into bed and slept the night through to find that Reese's efficient staff had washed and pressed all the clothes in their suitcases which was good since a fine coating of red dust had gotten into everything on their trip. They had brought a lot of thc outback back with them.

"Veronica?" Reese asked as they shared breakfast on her balcony.

Veronica looked up from the newspaper she was reading, news here in Australia was much different than back home in England and she found it fascinating and odd. The peculiar names, both Aborigine and British or a combination of both were amusing and a learning experience at the same time.

"Why are you going by Cavandish instead of Wilkins?" she asked, bringing up an issue that was a bit personal, something they had avoided in their many conversations the past two weeks together.

Veronica was surprised it had taken this long to ask. Reese had asked nothing of David, her children, or her husband. "I'm entitled either way since David is my brother and his titles will be passed on to my son."

"Yes but why are you using it instead of your husband's name?" Reese persisted.

Veronica shrugged and then looked up, they had avoided certain personal issues for a reason, and maybe it was time to air some of them. "I have no respect for my husband so I prefer not to be associated with him," she told her lover honestly.

Reese was surprised to hear Veronica openly admit it but she had suspected something like that as she sensed Veronica was not happy with Oscar Wilkins. Perhaps now that they were back she should start asking some of the hard questions. "Why aren't you happy with him?" She looked Veronica straight in the eye.

Veronica suddenly looked a bit bitter and shrugged. Looking down nervously at her hands she answered quietly, "He's a drunkard and a cheat," she said almost defiantly.

Reese wondered if there was more and was certain there was much more. "So what was this trip about, you wanted to cheat on your husband?"

Veronica's head reared up in anger, "No, I just…" she gulped. "I wanted to see you," she said quietly.

"And now that you have seen me, now what?" Reese asked knowing it was time to find out more about each other.

"I know I love you, I always have," she answered just as quietly if not more so, almost the Veronica of old, afraid of her own shadow. She was afraid though, afraid of where this conversation that they had avoided for so long and the answers it would give them.

"I love you too, you know that though," Reese answered just as quietly. During all their lovemaking she had never heard Veronica say it, she hadn't said it either, she had sensed it, seen it in her eyes but not said a word as they both took their pleasure in the time allotted them.

Veronica leaned forward and took Reese's hand, "Then come back with me, come back to England, be with me," she almost pleaded.

Reese wasn't startled; she had wondered if this were what the whole trip was about. She had been surprised that it had taken this long to bring it up. She sighed. She had thought briefly about Ariel but she knew what she had with Veronica was a lot different from what she had every had with Ariel. "I don't know that I can…" she began to be interrupted by Veronica.

"You would be nearer Gillian, she has been talking about having grandchildren you said," she said it as though to entice Reese to convince her.

Reese realized she did want to go to England but at the same time she had obligations to herself. She had just signed a contract with Morris Corporation and while she hadn't tied herself in for a five year deal the two years she had agreed to had just begun. As tempting as Veronica was, as much as Reese loved her, she was still married, David was alive, how would all that look if Reese Paulson came back and managed the estates of both Cavandish as well as the Wilkins? She knew from things Veronica had let slip that she was tired of doing it all, it was all she did anymore, she didn't enjoy life except where her children were concerned. As a parent herself she knew devoting herself to her children was what Veronica should be doing, not bringing in a stranger to upset the balance of things. Reese knew the balance would be upset by her meere presence in their lives and who knew how Oscar would react. Before she could voice her concerns though her phone rang on the desk. Rising apologetically Reese went inside to answer it.

"Hello?" she answered pleasantly expecting her office downstairs to have some minor thing for her to straighten out.

"Ms. Paulson we have an international call for Lady Cavandish, do you happen to know where we can reach her?" the front desk intoned. Reese knew they had worded it like that knowing that Lady Cavandish was staying in her suite. The laundry alone would have told someone of the extra clothing that had to be washed after their trip if not the room service who had delivered the extra food for their breakfast.

"Just a moment please," she said formally knowing her cold business like voice would keep the gossip to a minimum. Reese Paulson was a good boss and no one wanted to cross her, she had made things very pleasant for those employed at her resorts and hotels.

"Veronica? Phone is for you," she said wondering who could be calling her. She sat down on the couch as Veronica came in from the balcony and took up the phone.

From Reese's end she could hear that Veronica did a lot of listening before asking very little. "He's where?" followed by, "How long?" and, "I'll be there." She hung up the phone in a daze.

"Are you okay?" Reese asked her concerned seeing how pale she had become despite the tan she had acquired on the beaches and in the outback.

"My son Clinton apparently broke his arm at school, I have to go home…" she said in despair realizing her trip had ended far too soon and with nothing resolved. Her worry over Clinton and her desperation over Reese had her blurting out, "Come with me, come back to England!"

Reese took her into her arms; the wetness she could see in those beautiful purple eyes was too much to bear. It was breaking her heart and if she could, she would take the worry and despair from her. She let Veronica cry it out in her arms, her worry over several things coming out in the sobs. When it went on a little too long Reese pulled back slightly and teased, “You are soaking my shirt.”

Veronica chuckled a wet and throaty chuckle as she sniffed like a child and pulled back. Reese handed her a tissue and watched as Veronica pulled herself together.

“Are you going to be okay? Is Clinton badly hurt?” she asked concerned at the amount of sobbing Veronica had engaged in.

“He will probably be fine and have a cast to show off to his friends,” she said with a laugh and shook her head as she blew her nose. “I’m just being silly. I hadn’t planned on leaving so soon but I guess I have to,” she didn’t sound convinced.

Reese felt bad for her but she wasn’t ready to commit to going to England in fact she knew she wouldn’t. She had thought about this a few times over Veronica’s stay here in Australia and realized she had to fulfill her contract with the Morris’ and she needed to resolve things with Ariel even if they had been just friends for a long time, it was only fair.

Veronica took a deep breath recovering her equilibrium and asked quietly, “Will you come back to England with me?”

Reese shook her head sadly knowing she would be hurting Veronica to answer her now but knowing she had to. It wasn’t right, it wasn’t fair, and she knew it as she answered, “No, I can’t, I have obligations here.”

Veronica held her hands out as she entreated to her lover, the one woman who had never been far from her thoughts over the years, “You can get out of that contract, I’m sure you can, what else do you have to keep you here?”

Reese knew she could get out of the contract too but part of her didn’t want to. She had never reneged on an agreement. Besides Veronica had David and Oscar, how would that look? Her children would lose respect for her. Didn’t Veronica realize any of that? Taking a deep breath she tried to explain herself only to have a hurt look come into Veronica’s eyes and begin to tear up again. This angered Reese that she would use tears to try to convince Reese.

“You said so yourself you were ready to retire!”

“I know what I said but I just signed the new contract, I have an obligation to them! I have an obligation to myself. With David and Oscar there as well as your three children you have an obligation to them!" she said angrily in return reminding Veronica of her own obligations.

"I've given them years of my life, how much more must I keep sacrificing until I get what I want?" she answered heatedly.

"Your whole life now that you have children involved!" she answered equally angry.

"I know I have children involved, you don't have to keep reminding me!" she said becoming furious at Reese's stubbornness.

"Look, we haven't discussed this, you have to go home, I have to stay here, it's that simple!"

"No it's not that simple, I love you dammit!"

"I love you too," she answered gentler; her anger fading as she realized their anger had heightened as they both were passionate about their stances. "But you have to go, this won't work," she said sadly.

Veronica stared at her as her anger faded, she knew this would be the last time she would try to change Reese's mind. As much as she wanted her to go Reese wouldn't change her mind. She felt so hurt by that but Reese was right. She did have obligations to her children. She could ignore both David and Oscar and frequently did but her children had to come first. She got up suddenly, "I need to get a plane," she said and then asked, "Could you arrange that for me? While I get showered and changed?"

Reese nodded as she watched Veronica take some clothes from the piles that had been returned to them. As she headed into Reese's bathroom it took only minutes to arrange a car for her and a flight back to England. Reese packed her things for her until she returned to the living room.

"You packed for me? You must really want me to leave," she said petulantly.

Reese looked up from where she was lovingly putting Veronica's clothes in the large suitcase, the other one was already packed and waiting by the door. She could see the hurt on her lover's face and it tore at her heart. She hardened herself as she straightened up and answered, "No, I'm helping you get ready, your plane is in three hours and the commute is a bit long so I've arranged for a car to take you."

"I don't want to go," she answered her eyes beginning to tear up.

"I know baby, I know," Reese answered as she went to take her in her arms. Holding her close she felt her tremble. This wasn't how either had envisioned their time together to come to an end but life had a tendency to get in the way of any plans they made.

Reese helped her pack the rest of her things in the second large suitcase and making sure she had her passport and other identification she gave her a big hug.

"Is there no way I can change your mind?" she asked one last time.

Reese shook her head and held her tighter. "I'm sorry Veronica, I truly am, I've loved you forever it seems but it never works out for us. Maybe that's just our fate. To take our pleasure where we could," she answered sadly.

Veronica had to mentally agree as she took a step back and memorized Reese's face. She had dressed in a casual set of capris and gypsy like blouse, her natural blonde beauty wasn't enhanced by makeup and despite the age she knew her to be she looked youthful and beautiful. She loved this woman more than life itself. She would be brave and let her go. She had no choice.

Reese accompanied her down in the elevator; each of them had a firm grip on one of the huge suitcases and walked out to the waiting car where the chauffer leapt out to wrestle the suitcases into the trunk. One last hug and Veronica got in the back of the town car hiding her teary eyes behind dark sunglasses.

"Danny here will make sure you get to the international terminal on time," Reese assured her nodding towards the chauffer as he got behind the wheel.

Veronica nodded as she sat back in the car looking at Reese from behind her glasses. Reese waved her hand in goodbye and turned away sadly as they pulled away from the curb.

"Reese!" she heard herself being called and turned in time to get an exuberant hug from Ariel. "God I've missed you," she said happily and Reese had to switch gears as she glanced at the car that had pulled away.

Veronica looked back once more and saw Reese being hugged by another woman. "Danny?" she asked curiously, "Who is that woman hugging Reese?"

He glanced back in his rearview mirrors on the side and as an employee of the hotel realized who the head honcho was hugging. Not even thinking about the repercussions he answered the client honestly, "Oh, that's Ms. Paulson's girlfriend."

Veronica sat there stunned. Not once had Reese mentioned having a girlfriend. They had been together for two weeks, not once had she come up. Veronica had assumed there had been someone over the years but since she wasn't mentioned she guessed that there had been no one important. What kind of woman would go from her girlfriend's bed to an ex-lover's bed? She glanced back once more but foliage now hid her view of Reese and the other woman. She was devastated. She had never known Reese after all. What had the last two weeks been about? While they certainly hadn't been lovers the whole two weeks at some point wasn't Reese obligated to of told her about this other woman? Her tears were no longer for the fact that Reese wouldn't come with her back to England or for her son who had broken his arm but for herself and her stupidity at not realizing what kind of woman Reese Paulson was.

CHAPTER 78

Reese wasn't the same woman that Ariel had known before the party. There was a listlessness there, almost as though someone or something had died. Ariel tried to ignore it but as the months went by she couldn't. They hadn't been intimate in so long she wondered why she bothered. She realized Reese was a busy and important woman but her moodiness was taking a toll on their relationship. Ariel was getting fed up with their lack of sex, their lack of everything. What had happened to the Reese Paulson she had fallen in love with back in New Zealand?

Reese did her usual excellent job for the hotels and resort. She threw herself into expansion acquiring a few key smaller hotels for their chain and demolishing them in order expand what they already had, providing better and superior service for their guests at reasonable rates to bring them back time and time again. She found herself walking on the beach a lot, a lonely figure on deserted beaches wondering if she had made a mistake by not going with Veronica when she left. She wasn't surprised she had heard nothing from her lover since she had left but as the months went by she was a little concerned and then decided that Veronica had wanted the clean break this time. It was her turn to be an adult and sever all ties. This saddened Reese and didn't make her a pleasure to be around so she avoided everyone in her off time including Ariel.

Eight months had gone by when Reese received a phone call. "Mom, you are going to be a grandmother!" Gillian enthused across the miles that separated them.

"Oh baby, that's terrific, how are you feeling?" she could fake her enthusiasm with her daughter as she didn't see her face and the miles tended to allow for a bit of distortion in the lines.

"It's awful, I can't shake the morning sickness but we are thrilled!"

Reese smiled what was probably the first real smile she had had in months as she heard how happy her daughter was. "Do you want a boy or a girl?" thinking that all English nobility wanted a boy to carry on the family name and inherit although rights of inheritance had changed over the years.

"I just want it to be healthy," Gillian answered and then said, "Hang on!"

Reese could hear the sounds of retching in the background that Gillian had failed to muffle. It took her back more years than she cared to admit to her own pregnancy, many things she had thought she had forgotten.

"Mom, you there?" Gillian came back on the phone.

"I'm here," Reese answered.

"I've got to go, this nausea will pass the doctor assures me but I wanted you to know."

"When are you due?" Reese asked before she could go.

"Six months," Gillian answered quickly, "I've got to go, I'll email you, love you Mom," and the phone went dead before Reese could answer back.

Well she had threated for years to make Reese a grandmother and she was about to make good on that promise. Reese sat back to realize she was going to be a grandmother in six months! Wow, where had the time gone. It seemed like yesterday that her daughter was in pig-tails and riding her tricycle in her parent's driveway. So many years had passed, where had the time gone?

Over the next few months Reese's disposition improved and Ariel saw it as a good sign. They still hung out but only as friends. Ariel wanted more but any sign of that and Reese seemed to turn away. Ariel was disgusted over the idea that someone as hot as Reese was going to be a grandmother but she hid her annoyance well and discounted it since Gillian was so far away, she had never met her, and it didn't interfere with their lives.

Reese wanted to share the pictures of the ultra-sound and the emails she got from her daughter and she could sense that Ariel wasn't too enthused. Her other friends while polite about it were actually Ariel's friends and now that their relationship was only friendship several of them found themselves taking sides to the obviously strung along Ariel, after all she had been loyal and faithful for so long.

Reese didn't realize it but several people had withdrawn from being too friendly with the tall blonde. She was busy as ever with the hotels and resort but her preoccupation with a distant grandchild that wasn't even born yet didn't interest the younger crowd.

Slowly it occurred to Reese that now she had an excuse to return back to England. She knew without a shadow of a doubt though that the silence from Veronica meant they were probably over, forever. She was deeply saddened by that and had mourned the loss of not only their friendship but the possibilities of that friendship. She knew she had been right not to go with her but perhaps she could have left the door open to some distant future. It wasn't like when they had been silent for years before, now she could actually feel the silence between them, this time *was* different. Those two weeks together had been idealic. They had learned so much about the older selves they had become. The love was as strong as ever but it hadn't been enough after all this time. Now she was seriously thinking of having a life once again in England and there would be no chance of reconciliation.

She returned to England for the week prior to Gillian's giving birth, scheduling the trip carefully. She had the baby boy and girl right on time according to the doctor. The second child hadn't been seen on any of the scans and their surprise over the twins had them seriously doubting the conception date versus the due date since twins normally came early. No one minded though as they were happy and healthy and a good mix to their parents. Their other grandparents generously shared with Reese as they all took turns holding the small bundles. The two weeks Reese spent with the couple and their newborns was beautiful and while she rocked her new grandchildren she wondered how close and yet how far away Veronica was. She was only across a few sets of hills if Reese wanted to drive over. She was tempted but at the same time, she knew she couldn't go. She returned to Australia without ever seeing Veronica.

Veronica got the notice of the new heirs to the Cantwell estates and her thoughts immediately turned to Reese, wondering if she had come for the baptism or births. She glanced up to her own set of hills and wondered how far away the couple lived from their own estates. She wouldn't be attending as she had no idea where Oscar was these days and David needed her near home. Her time down in Australia had been noted, he didn't approve. He had taken her to task over her absence that somehow allowed Clinton to break his arm at school. It was totally unjustified the attack as she bore it stoically. David's mind was not very good these days but sometimes he remembered a little too much, saw way too much, and misinterpreted it all in the confusion of his illness.

CHAPTER 79

Reese returned with a new spring in her step. She had less than ten months left on her contract and she intended to work it out. She had decided to move back to England. Veronica or not she wanted to be closer to her new grandchildren. Family was what it was all about after all. Gillian had shown her that as she labored to bring forth the next generation of Cantwells. They were Cantwells through and through but they were also a part of Reese Paulson and only Reese could show them that. Living half a world away was pointless anymore. While they were still newborns they wouldn't realize that their grams was out of their life but she intended to be a part, a very big part of their future lives. Gillian hadn't 'needed' her in years, since college, but Reese needed these grandchildren and intended to be there for them.

Six months before her contract expired with the Morris' she handed in her resignation. This would allow them time to find someone and allow her to train her replacement. They were very reluctant to let her go offering her an even more lavish contract than her previous one but she was adamant that she would be leaving. They understood the draw of grandchildren, their own stayed frequently in the many hotels and resorts they now owned. They had caused frequent headaches for staff and especially Reese over the years but she thought of it as all part of the job.

Ariel though was a harder part of her decision. "What do you mean you are moving back to England? Did you get a job offer there?" she asked incredulous. She had waited, patiently for a very long time to be with Reese and now she was leaving? That wasn't fair!

Reese shook her head from where she was sitting on her couch sharing a bottle of wine with Ariel, it was the first time in a long time she had thought to invite her up but she had been a little self-absorbed and not thought of inviting her 'friend' up. Ariel had thought she would finally 'get lucky' after all this time, she had been so patient. "No, I told you, I want a relationship with my grandchildren. My contract is up soon so I put in my notice."

"But what about us?" Ariel asked suddenly angry.

Reese looked at her in surprise. There was no 'us' and hadn't been in a long time. "I thought we were friends," she began hesitantly only to be interrupted by Ariel.

"We were more than that!" she retorted.

Reese nodded looking at her and misunderstanding, trying to downplay her anger she said, "Yes we were at one time but I thought you understood that we were just friends?"

Ariel stared at her incredulously and her anger spilled over as she lunged at Reese from across the couch "I was once the woman you wanted to be with, is there someone else?" she nearly spat into Reese's face.

She found the situation distasteful as Ariel got right into her face, "At one time we talked like that but that was long ago, I thought you understood?"

"I've waited for you, months! Hell over a year!" she said angrily, "What about me?"

Her own anger spilled over, "Christ Ariel, I made no promises. I thought things had cooled between us. I had no idea you were waiting for me." Reese cringed inside, she had known even if superficially that Ariel still wanted her.

"Well I did!" Ariel said ungraciously and pulled back as suddenly as she had lunged forward. "What a friggin' waste of my time!" She got up and looked angrily at Reese. "I've waited patiently for you only for you to dump me like this?"

"Dump you?" Reese parroted weakly. "I didn't dump you, we just drifted apart. I thought we were friends?"

"Friends? Friends with benefits more like it!" she spat out as she angrily looked around the room as though looking for words that wouldn't come.

"I'm sorry Ariel; I thought you understood I wasn't interested in you like that anymore, I thought we had come to some mutual unspoken agreement?"

Ariel looked back at Reese stunned once more by her striking good looks and weeping inside for the loss she was experiencing. "You know, you are going to regret someday for stringing me along. Someday somewhere someone will make you pay!" she threatened.

Reese was extremely uncomfortable. The conversation was definitely distasteful. "I think you should leave before this gets ugly," she advised and stood up to escort Ariel out.

Ariel knew she had to leave; she wanted to say so much, she wanted to plead but knew that a woman like Reese would only pity her. She was hurt, she was angry, and she wanted revenge now. She brushed by Reese and swept out the door.

Reese watched her go and felt bad about the whole situation. She wondered if she had misunderstood something and then thinking back she realized she had been aware of Ariel's hope that they would re-connect. They hadn't been intimate since before that party that the Morris' had thrown to celebrate all her years of employment as well as the renewal of her contract. The party that had brought Veronica back into her life. It was Veronica that had finished it for them though, whether she admitted it not. Ariel's love couldn't compare to the love she felt for Veronica. What she had felt for Ariel had been love, but it had lessened over time and since she hadn't tended it, nurtured it; it had become a friendly love and not a passionate one. She thought for the most part that Ariel had understood she now realized she had been horribly wrong.

Reese called down to the desk to make a distasteful order letting everyone know that Ariel was no longer allowed free access through the hotel or resorts. As she had never made such an edict before the gossip spread quickly that she had dumped Ariel.

Reese spent a lot of time on the deserted beaches early in the mornings before the tourist and locals crowded them. A lot of introspection. She missed her friends but no one had contacted her after Ariel had left. She missed Ariel but understood her anger. She was lonely in the final months of her work at the hotels as she inspected things one last time in preparation for turning it all over to the Morris' nephew who had been brought up to run their properties for them. Their children weren't interested and a relative was a good choice. Reese was just grateful that not only was he qualified he was enthusiastically looking forward to taking the reins from her. He had thought he would have to wait years for Reese to retire and been surprised when his Uncle informed him of her resignation. He absorbed everything she showed and told him and noting the direction she had been taking the organization agreed with most of her decisions.

It didn't take long to pack up the few belongings she kept around her and ship them to England. Most of it was clothes and she wondered how much of it she would ever wear again as England wasn't nearly as warm as Australia. As it was she had gone through a lot of her clothing and donated it to charity. Still there was years of accumulation to go through and sort.

The Morris' were appreciative how professional she was to the end. Their nephew was well set up and happy with the arrangement they had made with him. They could still enjoy their retirement and have things taken care of. They were sorry to see her go but understood her desire to enjoy her grandchildren while she was still young enough to do so.

Reese arranged for her storage unit in Connecticut to be emptied and shipped to England, she didn't remember after all these years what exactly they had stored there but she could afford to have it shipped in its entirety to her new home. Gillian said she could stay with them until she found a house and was looking forward to shopping for one with her mom. She had several places nearby already in mind for her.

Reese said goodbye to her various employees as she showed around the Morris' nephew Carter as they would not be invited to the small party that would be held to wish her goodbye at the hotel she had lived in for years. It was by no means as large as the gala a few years back but enough people had worked with Reese on various levels that there were a lot of tearful goodbyes. If anyone doubted that Reese was beloved by most of her employees they were no longer in doubt after the party. There were of course a few people who would be glad to see the last of her but they were few and far between.

Two days later Reese waved a last goodbye from the town car speeding toward the airport that would connect her with an international flight and then on to London. The hours on the plane she planned to sleep, or she hoped to. She was exhausted. Teaching Carter and saying goodbye to so many people had drained her. A couple of days before she had been so tired she nearly got hit by a car. She had jumped back in time to recognize Ariel's Miata and see her looking back in the mirror scowling that she had missed. Alarmed Reese had been much more careful the final days she was at the hotel. Now in the car taking her to the airport she looked around cautiously wondering if Ariel would really have hit her or was it just a scare tactic?

Even on the smaller plane taking her to Sydney to the international one she wondered at Ariel's behavior. She was sorry that they couldn't have had more but she didn't think she had led the younger woman on.

Looking forward to England and her new life she wondered if she should look up Veronica or not and decided she really shouldn't. It wasn't fair. They had had so many chances and none of them had been good timing. It just wasn't meant to be. It had been a final break two years ago; she hadn't heard a word from Veronica since she had left. She was going to England to be with her daughter and grandchildren and that was the end of it. At least that's what she kept telling herself.

CHAPTER 80

"So what do you do?" the little boy asked her as he looked her over.

"I'm a manager," she answered simply.

"What does that mean?"

"I manage things for people, big things like hotels, resorts, estates," she expanded wondering where this line of questioning was going and hoping it appeased his curiosity, it had been a long time since she had to deal with a child.

He thought for a moment and then replied importantly to her statement, "Yeah, I didn't know what I wanted to do when I grew up either."

She looked at the little boy incredulously and wondered if her own grandchildren would be as precocious. The thought made her grin, probably, especially if they were related to her.

Sitting next to the little boy for most of the flight back to London she got to hear all about his life when he wasn't napping. She tried to sleep too but she was too churned up. She knew a lot of it would work itself out when she got there but it was a long flight between Sydney and London. Flying first class as she usually did she had been surprised to find the little boy next to her but he was going to spend time with his father who lived in England. Flying alone on an international flight she wondered if she would have been as brave as a youngster, probably not.

She told him about her daughter but when he realized her daughter was a grown-up he had only shown enthusiasm when she mentioned her grandchildren until her realized they were 'mere' babies. At his age and she guessed he was about nine it was more important to be more of a kid around his age than a baby or a grown-up. She was vastly amused and the stewardess was relieved that she wasn't bothered by their little first class guest.

CHAPTER 81

Gillian was thrilled to have her mother indefinitely in her home. The twins were old enough to be quite a handful and she didn't like turning them over to the nannies that had been hired by her in-laws to help with the heirs. She preferred to do as much of the work as she could herself. Reese enjoyed helping her to a point; it had been a long time since she had been around babies. Diapers and spitting up were a lifetime ago, that point did not thrill her. Gillian seemed reluctant to let her find her own home too, not finding time to go with her and point out the areas she should or shouldn't look.

Steffan had gotten a position not that far from his parent's holdings and they had generously given the couple this home to stay in indefinitely. It wasn't far from Cavandish and as Reese was staying with them she couldn't help but look at the hills separating them and wonder, think of Veronica.

Reese was tempted to go see Veronica but knew it wouldn't be fair after they had left things the last time they saw each other. She kept telling herself, it just wasn't meant to be, it wasn't their time.

Reese was in her old familiar town of Cavandish, she just had to visit and shop there after all this time when she ran into Audrey.

"Reese? Oh my gawd, Reese Paulson?" she said grabbing her arm in the store she had gone into.

"Audrey!" she answered delighted, she should have thought of her, called her but in the whole moving hoopla and dealing with Gillian and the twins she had forgotten.

"What are you doing here?" she asked delighted and then thinking about it she quickly asked, "Does she know you're here?"

Reese knew immediately who she meant and shook her head. "No, she doesn't know I'm back…"

"Back, as in you live here?" she gestured around the store but meant the town.

Reese nodded and shrugged, "Well you know my daughter Gillian had twins, I came to help her and see them."

"You left Australia to play nursemaid?" Audrey was astounded and wondered how Veronica would deal with this news or had she dealt with it? She hadn't seen her in a while.

Reese chuckled and gestured at her outfit which consisted of a smart day suit and asked, "Do I look like your typical nursemaid?"

Audrey laughed with her and said, "We have *got* to catch up, may I ask you to tea?" she glanced at her watch to be sure she had the right hour of the day for it.

Reese was delighted at the idea and the company, she hadn't gotten out nearly as much as she would have liked since she moved back and Gillian was starting to get on her nerves as well as the children. She had gone out to see for herself what was available to buy, a place of her own. She was looking forward to gardening and having her own little place. Nothing too large but something that was uniquely hers, she hadn't really had a place of her own since her parents place and was looking forward to it, or so she told herself so she wouldn't get bored.

They chose the old familiar pub they had gone to many times years ago, danced in, and drank together with Veronica. It didn't hurt to think of Veronica and Reese wished her well, mentally. She didn't mention her to Audrey and Audrey, used to keeping secrets from the other didn't bring her up. She did have a lot of other gossip and information about the locals and they were enjoying their visit immensely. Suddenly Audrey stiffened up and looked at the entranceway which was behind Reese. Reese, seeing her reaction looked over her shoulder and saw an equally shocked Veronica standing there. Seeing Reese her eyes opened wider. Reese slowly stood up to stand by the booth they had been sitting in. Reese took in what looked like a haggard appearance. Veronica hadn't aged well in the last two years.

Veronica forced a smile onto her shocked face and headed for her two former friends. "What in the world are you doing here?" she asked Reece in surprise.

"Won't you join us?" Reese asked respectfully.

Veronica debated, she wanted to and yet, *she didn't*. She glanced at Audrey who nodded imperceptibly and chose to take the side of the booth on Audrey's side rather than Reese's. Everyone at the table noticed her decision and realized why she chose it.

"What are you doing here?" she said forcibly bright and cheery as though it wasn't awkward for any of them.

"I came back," Reese answered her awkwardly, "For Gillian," she added.

Veronica was nearly squirming in her seat but for another far different reason. "I am so surprised to see you here," she answered. "I suppose having twins was awkward and a bit much for her?"

Reese was gaining her equilibrium back, "Well she has two nannies, that should make it easier," she answered dryly.

Veronica laughed and nodded, "It should but it's amazing how much work children can be."

"Well with your new…" Audrey stopped abruptly when Veronica stepped on her foot. "Ouch," she finished and glared at her friend.

"You okay?" Reese asked having not noticed the by-play or the looks between the two friends.

"Yeah, cramp in my foot," Audrey lied ruefully.

They chatted about non-essentials for a while as they were brought their tea. Veronica had had the same idea as Reese to get out of the house and shop today so it was just by chance that they had run into each other. Reese explained about running into Audrey. They enjoyed tea together as they prolonged it with conversation. Only Audrey seemed to catch the longing looks between the two when the other wasn't looking.

Then Reese asked, "How is David?"

The devastated look on Veronica's face told its own tale. "Oh no, when did he pass?" she asked in concern reaching out to touch the back of Veronica's hand in sympathy. Veronica pulled her hand back as though it had been burned and placed it in her lap. The gesture didn't go unnoticed by any of them at the table.

"A little over a year ago," Veronica said in a strained voice.

Reese's heart constricted for her friend, she had loved her brother, done so much for him. She herself held some affection for her old employer.

Veronica made a show of looking at her watch, "Well will you look at the time, I'm sorry, I never intended to spend so much time away, I have to get back to the house." She stood up and looked at Reese regretfully, "I'm so happy to hear you are back *for Gillian*," did she perhaps stress that a little too much? "I hope we can be friends again," she added insincerely. "I'll see you both soon," she said before giving either of the other two a chance to say anything and she walked out.

"Is she that torn up about David's passing? She's known he could go at any time for years!" Reese asked Audrey.

Audrey looked at her oddly debating whether to tell her the truth or not and then deciding that Reese deserved to know, needed to know if those two ever stood a chance of making a go of it she took a deep breath. "It wasn't a matter of expecting him to go, it was how he went."

Reese looked at her uncomprehending wondering what she meant but waiting patiently for her to continue.

"Oscar managed to convince David to get into his car one day to view the estates, he wanted to show David what a rotten job Veronica had been doing. No one knows to this day how they managed it; David needed almost total care at that point, and where his nurse was is anyone's guess. Anyway, Oscar got him down into his car and drove them into a tree. He was so drunk that he didn't know what had happened. He had been determined evidently to make Veronica see reason and as David had sided with him in the past he thought that David could help him again or so he reasoned in his drunken state. Veronica didn't 'obey' him. He was overheard talking to David." She stopped for a moment to take a sip of the water on the table. "David was killed instantly, Oscar lingered for a month or more before Veronica made the decision to pull the plugs. She had to hire an attorney but she finally got a court order that he wouldn't have wanted to be kept alive on machines, he hadn't woken but in a drugged stupor for weeks. The courts tried to fight pretty hard against it but how do you fight a Cavandish and especially a grieving wife?"

Reese was shocked and saddened by what Veronica had gone through, she must have been devastated. How awful. To lose David, that had been expected, to lose him in such a brutal fashion, that had to have hurt and by her own husband. "How has she been?" she asked concerned.

Audrey shrugged, "She has pretty much become a recluse except for the children and the estates. She was pregnant at the time of the accident. She nearly lost her little boy."

Reese was reeling. She was pregnant? How could she have gone back to her drunkard of a husband, a man she has assured Reese she detested to get pregnant? She was sure she had been told that he had never touched her, that they had used invitro-fertilization, that the third child was going to be her *last* child. Unless he raped her? No, Reese remembered the story a very pregnant Veronica had told her of defending herself against him. What had happened in the nearly two years since she had last seen Veronica? "So she has four children now?" she asked to make conversation.

Audrey nodded watching Reese closely; she could see the concern and the endless questions in her friend's eyes. She didn't know if her two friends could heal the rift between them but she had hopes, Veronica had been miserable for far too long.

Reese sat there a long long time, just thinking. She wished there was a long stretch of Australian beach that she had used for the last two years to go take a walk on and think. Sitting in a darkened pub was not the kind of thinking she wanted to do. She had more questions than answers but was she entitled to either the answers or to even ask those questions?

Audrey sat there companionably as she sipped her water. She had stopped drinking in anticipation of driving someone home but there was no way Reese had too much to drink and Veronica had left very sober.

"Do you think she will see me if I go up to the house?" Reese finally asked her as her eyes focused on Audrey.

Audrey shrugged, "I don't know, she's changed a lot over the years, she's gotten harder. I think her grief and what Oscar put her through has aged her."

"Do you think he raped her?" she asked remembering the long ago estate agent and what he had done to Veronica, had Oscar repeated the cycle?

Audrey immediately shook her head. "No, she wouldn't let Oscar near her, he totally repulsed after he began drinking so heavily and taking lovers so openly."

Reese's heart clutched at her for Veronica's sake. "Then how…?" she asked the obvious question and remembering the invitro the question turned to 'Then *why*?' in her mind.

Audrey knew but it wasn't her place to say, "You will have to ask her, I was totally shocked when she got pregnant the last time. It was after she came back from Australia," she offered, she hoped helpfully, wondering what had happened down under. Veronica certainly hadn't been too happy when she got back. "I thought when her youngest David was old enough to go to school she was done and then a few months after she got back she announced she was pregnant again. Oscar was strutting around as though he had birthed all the children, it was really nauseating."

Reese could well imagine, the little she had seen of him at the wedding didn't bode well. He was disgusting. That he had touched Veronica, *her* Veronica, repulsed her.

Reese left Audrey with a lot to think about. Going back to Gillian's she had to really concentrate on her driving. The dark roads and some of them unfamiliar she had to forget about thinking of Veronica, she had so much to think about that it was almost overwhelming. She wasn't happy when Gillian tried to foist her children off onto her and insisted that the nannies do their jobs and leave her alone that evening. She claimed a headache and went to bed early only to lay there and think about Veronica for hours before falling into an uneasy sleep.

Many miles away Veronica too was restless. She was thinking over the shock of running into Reese in the pub where they has spent so many pleasant hours together years ago. Where her infatuation with the more sophisticated Reese had run its full course. Again, bad timing. Would Reese come to see her? Should she go see Reese? There was nothing to keep them apart now? Then she realized there was a lot to keep them apart. Time alone had changed them both. What they had once felt, what they had tried to get back had never worked. None of the times had been right. She was a mother now, she had four children to look after and while three of them were off at school most of the time she frequently had them home for weekends, sometimes with friends, and she insisted they come home for every holiday. She couldn't go gallivanting after an American who didn't even want her.

CHAPTER 82

Reese dressed carefully the next day in a black suit. Her garters held up her light black stockings on her long legs. They were still good legs despite her age. The short skirt came down mid-thigh, appropriate for a woman her age who still could show off a body that a woman years younger would envy. The suit jacket crossed comfortably holding her breasts up in the right way with the push up bra making them spill nicely against the material. She borrowed her son-in-laws extra car once again and thought for the umpteenth time that she should buy a car of her own. Heading over those hills that separated Gillian's home from the Cavandish estates she drove on familiar roads, some she had helped to improve even, up to the grand house. Its pinkish brick exterior looked in fine shape, much better than when she had seen it all those years ago in disrepair. Evidence of a lack of an estate manager and owners who didn't or couldn't cope, then. Now it looked important, grand, and the driveway raked and clean. She pulled up as though in the years of old and got out of the car to look around. She saw no one about and wondered if Veronica had run away and taken the servants with her. Shaking her head at her silly thought she rang the doorbell remembering a time when she would have just walked in.

"Ms. Paulson!" Frank the driver for the estate answered the door.

Reese was equally surprised having expected someone else to answer the door. She smiled and Frank again was struck at how beautiful she was. He went back a dozen years remembering having met her at the airport. "Hello Frank is Lady Cavandish in?" she asked formally.

"Oh yes, of course," he heard the note of authority in her voice and being a creature of habit he gestured her in, "She is in the library," he informed her helpfully.

Reese nodded and headed for the double doors, she knew her way well. She noticed how nice the house looked, a far cry from what she had encountered all those years ago when it hadn't been kept on top of. The familiar grandfather clock ticking ominously in the hall as she passed it. She opened the library door and walked in closing it behind her, locking it as she leaned against it.

Frank hurried back to the kitchen and hissed, "She's back!" to the others.

"Who is back?" Mrs. Gunderson asked wondering who had been at the door and wondering if she was expected to serve more for lunch. Lady Cavandish hadn't said anything about guests.

"Reese Paulson, she's back," he said delightedly pleased to be the one to share the news.

Mrs. Gunderson and her sister Mrs. Anderson stood there in stunned silence wondering what *that* meant?

"Reese," Veronica said in surprise as she rose up from behind the desk that had been her brothers, "I didn't know we had an appointment?" Knowing full well that they didn't but deciding to be formal.

Reese grinned and shook her head, "No, we didn't did we?"

"Then what are you doing here?" Veronica's heart was beating hard inside her chest. She hadn't been prepared for this confrontation and she really didn't want it. She walked out from behind thc desk intending to confront her ex-lover.

"I came here for you, I think you know that," Reese told her quietly as she stood there tall, blonde, and beautiful in her black suit. The tan she had acquired from living in Australia all those years hadn't quite faded. She looked healthy and sexy as hell.

"For me what?" Veronica asked confused.

"I came here to get you, for you, to make love to you, to be with you," Reese said, each statement she took a step further into the room stalking Veronica.

"Now wait a moment, don't I have something to say about this?" Veronica asked indignantly as she sat down on a settee in consternation.

Reese nodded as she stopped halfway across the room and began to unbutton her suit jacket which revealed that she only had a bra on underneath it when she should have had a camisole. She stood with her legs apart defiantly as she began to undress in front of Veronica who stared in rapt attention. "Yes, it's totally up to you, but I don't think you want me to leave do you?"

Stupidly Veronica shook her head in the negative as she watched the suit jacket fall to the floor revealing the tan of Reese's strong shoulders, a black bra, and the short skirt that was rising up from Reese's stance in the middle of the room. "What are you…" she stuttered as Reese's intent suddenly dawned on her. Feeling unattractive, depressed, and despondent for months Veronica didn't know how to fight against the lust she suddenly felt for the attractive blonde.

Reese hadn't know how she would convince Veronica, she had never used sex as a weapon but for some reason today she felt the need to feel sexy, to look stunning, and all for this woman, this love that she had loved for so long she couldn't imagine any other woman in her life. Not Sheila, not the random women she had met, not Ariel even. No other woman had aroused in her the need to protect, to love, and cherish that this one woman did in her. As she seduced her, as she made love to her on the settee, she felt no bought of conscience as Veronica capitulated and melted in her arms. The settee had never been used for this kind of physical activity but it was well used by the time Reese finished with her.

Much later, much, *much* later Reese and Veronica ended up on the fine Oriental rug that now covered the wooden floors of the library. Their breath coming in gasps each held the other firmly.

"I love you, don't ever leave me," Veronica cried into Reese's neck sobbing incoherently for so many things. She was feeling very vulnerable.

"Never my love, never, I'm here for you, always, and forever," Reese comforted her lover whose cries she had muffled a short time before as she orgasmed repeatedly and cried out from what Reese generated in her body. Only Reese, no one else had ever caused this in her.

CHAPTER 83

They did have to have Mrs. Gunderson set an extra plate to a late lunch for Reese. Reese was welcomed back by the staff with smiles and a few hugs. She was remembered well and many remarked that she hadn't aged a day from that day long ago when she arrived at the estate. As Veronica showed her around the house, nothing really had changed but then on these estates they both knew it took time for change, unless they were approached with someone like Reese Paulson determined to improve what was there.

"I have something to tell you," Veronica told her; the pain could be heard in her voice as they walked hand and hand on the land surrounding the house.

"Audrey told me about David and Oscar," she answered to alleviate some of the pain, she hoped.

Veronica nodded and said, "Yes, that accident, that horrible accident. Oscar should have died then too," she said bitterly.

Reese nodded wondering what else she had to tell as Veronica went on.

"Well I was pregnant at the time."

Reese nodded again and stopped to turn at look at Veronica, not wanting any more misunderstandings between them as she was here now; it was their time together, finally. It was time for them to have a little happiness.

"I had a boy a while later, he was nearly premature because of all the stress I was under."

Reese nodded again wishing she could have taken some of the pain away from Veronica and knowing she couldn't. She had survived though.

"I named him Reece," Veronica said quietly and waited with baited breath to see Reese's reaction.

Reese stared at her incredulously and frowned, "You named your son after me?"

Veronica nodded, and waited.

Reese felt warm suddenly. That after all they had been through, it was obvious Veronica had still loved her, after all that time. But she had come home and gotten pregnant by her then husband, that bastard Oscar. That poor bastard. "But why?" she asked, her thoughts racing, her heart constricting at the thought of Oscar touching her.

"I thought if I couldn't have you, I could have a part of you." She shook her head, she knew it didn't make sense but coming back from Australia she had been devastated that once again they hadn't been able to be together, that somehow with this baby she could have a part of this woman in her life. A reminder forever, one that was totally and absolutely her own. She knew it wasn't logical but she hadn't exactly been thinking clearly at the time.

"But Oscar?" Reese asked not sure what Veronica was trying to share. "You let him touch you after what you told me…"

Veronica realized then she had forgotten to tell Reese a very important small detail. She smiled in understanding, "Oscar never touched me, I couldn't let him, never," she smiled even more as she realized Reese had been jealous over the thought of him touching her intimately. "He donated his sperm years ago. Remember? I told you, it was just waiting there for me to use when I wanted a child."

The relief was obvious on Reese's face. She took Veronica in her arms. "I'm so grateful he never touched you," she said softly and then as the impact of realizing she had a child with Veronica, one she could help raise, one named after her, even if she hadn't been part of its conception or gestation, it was a part of her, a part of her lovely Veronica. Kissing her softly in gratitude they continued on with their walk through the immense fields that surrounded the estate admiring the horses that were out in the fields.

Veronica explained how she had ruthlessly gotten rid of dozens of horses that Oscar had foolishly purchased. There were a few that showed promised but the vast majority he had paid too much for. If she broke even on the deal she counted herself lucky.

During the course of their conversation they held nothing back, not the years, not the previously unspoken details they never got around to in Australia. Clean start. Reese finally asked, "So who else has been in your life all these years?"

Veronica stopped them and shook her head, "No one," she said softly.

Reese frowned and looked at her in surprise, "What do you mean, *no one*?"

Veronica shook her head again and said, "No one, only you. It was always you."

Reese couldn't believe her ears, "You mean you haven't ever been intimate with anyone else since…?"

Veronica nodded as it began to sink in. "I tried, I even met one or two women over the years but they paled in comparison to you and my heart wasn't it."

Reese was overwhelmed. Considering how much passion they both expended when they were together she was astounded. She had been sure that Veronica had known someone, someone who had taught her the things she knew when they were finally together again after so long. "Then how…?"

Veronica instantly understood and interrupted, "A good imagination and regrets for things we hadn't tried as I read up on the subject. I fantasized about you forever…" she admitted shyly.

Reese couldn't believe what she was hearing but at the same time she felt so grateful for this woman who had waited for her, for a time that might never have come if fate hadn't intervened. For the timing to be right between them.

"What about you?" Veronica turned it around on her raising an eyebrow in question and knowing the answer before she asked the question. She had seen the woman in Australia hugging Reese exuberantly.

Reese suddenly felt a little uncomfortable. Here Veronica had waited all these years for her but she had moved on, not knowing she would end up where they had started, together. But if they were to continue together she had to be totally honest. "Three," she answered knowing that was an accurate accounting. She had only been sexual with three of the women over the years although she had tried to date a few others.

Veronica was surprised at the low number having expected it to be in the double digits at least. "Why, what is wrong with those Australian women, how could they let you slip through their fingers and why aren't there more?"

"Are you saying you are more upset that I didn't sleep with more women or that no one tried harder to win me?" Reese looked at her puzzled.

Veronica laughed, she felt so happy. Sobering she asked instead, "Did you love them?" feeling a little kernel of doubt in her confidence.

Reese smiled and nodded, "Yes, two of them I loved and it just never worked out. You were always there in my mind over the years. Seeing you, being with you, it was never the same with anyone else. I loved *you*, I wanted *you*."

"But you loved two other women....?" The confidence was definitely slipping.

Reese nodded knowing she would never tell Veronica that Sheila had been part Aborigine; she had seen her prejudice and understood it. It wasn't right but it was how she was raised. It was ingrained. All she could do was see that the children didn't become like that. She realized she had four children to help raise with Veronica now and she was looking forward to it. Her two grandchildren were nearby and she would be there for them as well. "Yes, it took me a while to even see the first one because I was mourning the loss of you, but eventually I had to move on. She let me go," Reese choked up remembering Sheila; she had always known their romance was temporary, that had taken years to understand. "And then on vacation in New Zealand I met another woman, we had ended it, fallen out of love, when you showed up in Australia for that party."

Veronica was amazed. Reese had been with so few women and could have had as many as she wanted. It wasn't the total abstinence such as she had done but she said she had loved them. She had to ask though, "Who was that woman hugging you when I left?"

She had to think for a moment and then asked, "You saw that?" Reese was surprised. At Veronica's nod, she answered truthfully, "That was Ariel; she had come to see me and surprised me. Nothing happened again with us other than as friends." She winced inside remembering how angry and hurt Ariel had been when they truly ended it. She had been blind on some levels. But it wasn't meant to be. They had their time and it had ended long before she told Ariel she was leaving.

"So you've been as lonely as I," Veronica asked as she realized the number of years they had been apart.

Reese nodded holding her closer and saying, "It wasn't our time. Fate or whatever you want to call it played us a bad hand, but it kept reminding us that we still loved each other. I promise to stay this time, for us, for you, for the family we now have. I love you Veronica so much if it were legal I'd marry you."

Veronica nearly started crying her big eyes drawing Reese in, not for the first time, and now, not for the last. "I love you too Reese, it's our time now isn't it?"

"Yes m'love, it's our time," Reese answered as she leaned down to kiss her sealing the bargain.

~THE END~

If you have enjoyed *TIMED ROMANCE* you'll look forward to another of K'Anne Meinel's splendid and unforgettable novels:

Long Distance Romance

In print and E-book and available at fine retailers.

Long Distance Romance

Eliza was hanging signs up about 16' in the air when she heard the melodic voice ask her friend in German "Do you think they have these in German" and they shared a laugh.

Eliza answered without even thinking "Ja, wir kann machen alles auf Deutsch" and continued hanging the few she had left to hang. She was up on a platform that raised her to the level she needed since she had an entire wall of signs to hang. Finishing the few she had left Eliza began to lower the machine its beeps could be heard throughout her little store. The astonished women that she had answered without thinking came into her view as the machine rested at the four foot level. She unbelted herself and using the little gate at one end of the machine she climbed adroitly down the ladder to the floor ending with a little bounce. Smiling at the two women who had unknowingly walked into her store today she wanted to laugh at the astonished looks that still were on their faces. Instead she greeted them "Guten Tag, kann ich helfen sie?" Good day, can I help you?

"Du sprichts Deutsch?" You speak German the pretty curly haired blonde one asked astounded.

Nodding at the obvious Eliza's grin threatened to turn into a laugh as she answered "Ja, Ich spreche eine bisschen Deutsch" Yes, I speak a little German "aber nicht sehr gute and nicht sehr schnell" Not so good and not very fast. Might as well warn them ahead of time.

Switching to English the blonde smiled in return "impressive."

Looking at the store with over 1000 signs hung Eliza had to agree, it was impressive and she nodded. She didn't realize the blonde was admiring her and not the store. Eliza wore Levi's and a polo shirt that read 'ask me about a sign' on one side and 'hey, what's your sign' on the front. The back was taken up by a screen printed crossing sign that read 'Sign Crew.'

"Are you looking for anything in particular?" Eliza asked, her gaze returning to the two women. "We do have German Parking Only signs" she laughed.

They joined in with her laugh. "Actually, if you have two of them we will take them" the curly blonde replied.

Going to one of the bins at the back of this section of the store Eliza perused until she came through the G bin and fingering the signs pulled out two German Parking Only signs. Putting them on the counter she asked "is there anything else you would like or would you like to look around for a while?"

The platinum blonde with the pin straight hair looked ready to go but the curly blonde walked up to the counter to pay the $30 that Eliza rang up on the register. "It's not often we find someone who understands us when we speak in German" she offered hesitantly almost apologetically.

"Then you have to be careful what you say?" She laughed to show she was teasing "I studied German way back in high school, so what I know is a little out of date and probably I have forgotten more than I remembered." Eliza took the $50 and made change.

"Is this your store?"

Nodding Eliza looked around. There were still a lot of open spaces but she had been filling those steadily but surely for days.

"Yes we just opened, I've been wanting to do this for years" she answered proudly.

"Why now?" the blonde asked curiously.

"Well, I finally qualified for a loan" Eliza admitted sheepishly. "I've been making these signs for like 20 years" she added.

"You make them?" the beautifully plucked eyebrows on the blonde raised high in astonishment "yourself?"

Nodding Eliza looked around the store with pride. She had been working towards this for a long time. She had tried having a store before but had been too sick to really make a go of it before; she was ready now, 10 years ready! There was still a lot to do and she intended to do it!

"Wow, you really have done a wonderful thing, these are so clever!" the blonde was looking admiredly at Eliza but she was oblivious as she looked around her store.

"Thank you" she answered absentmindedly. Then she looked, really looked at the blonde. Tall with aristocratic features, fine bones and very very pretty. She wore expensive clothes despite the summer heat. Very well put together. Already Eliza could spot the 'types' of tourists who visited this tourist town in Wisconsin. Wisconsin Dells was a mecca for tourist shops and the tourists loved to vacation there for the water, the waterparks, the beautiful scenic trails, the incredible cliffs, and just the whole vacation theme of the town. Nearby Lake Delton was the same, in fact the two towns seemed to be just one continuous town to the unknowing.

Eliza realized the look the woman was giving her was a little speculative and she couldn't help but wonder herself. When a woman this attractive was checking her out shc had to wonder if perhaps she was reading the 'signs' correctly. Smiling hopefully she held out her hand and said "Hi, I'm Eliza Schmidt, and this is my store."

The beautiful blonde shook her hand warmly squeezing it slightly in response to the warm 'American' styled welcome. "Ich bin Grafin Krystal Von Der Konigin" not even realizing she was speaking in German it was so automatic.

"Grafin?" Eliza asked not sure of the word.

Nodding Krystal waited for something, apparently waiting for a comment, but when Eliza didn't ask anything more she turned and beckoned the second woman, a platinum blonde and said "Das ist Aarika Schultz mein guter freund."

Eliza shook Aarika's hand as well. She looked between the two women wondering at their friendship and how good a friend Aarika really was. She didn't realize that Krystal was watching her amused. "So how long are you two in town for?"

"Oh I don't know it depends on what amuses us. We found out about the Dells only recently when we were in Chicago visiting friends." Krystal switched to English effortlessly. Her accent was enchanting.

"Ah, then you should go ride the Ducks" Eliza told her with a grin. By the looks she got from both of her guests she had to laugh knowing they had totally misunderstood her. She wasn't going to elaborate though, she was enjoying this too much.

"Are there any good clubs here in town?" Aarika thought to ask. She was eyeing Krystal and she noted the interest that she was showing on this store owner.

"Well it depends on what you are looking for but yes there are several." Guessing at the age of her guests she made a suggestion "there is a nice 80's club called Culture."

"Culture?" asked Aarika frowning.

"Yes as in Culture Club, do you remember Boy George and his music?" Eliza waited for a telltale sign from either of them.

Krystal's face lit up at the double entendre that had been thrown to them. "Yes, I enjoyed his music immensely. Do you go there often?"

Eliza grinned and shook her head. "No, I haven't had time with the moving of my businesses down here and opening the store. But I hear it's a good club if you like to dance."

Krystal smiled and answered "I love to dance."

Eliza grinned "Well, maybe I'll see you there sometime; I'm due for some time off. All work and no play makes me very dull."

Krystal liked that answer. "Yes, maybe we will see you there. Perhaps tonight we will go there."

Aarika was done with their conversational play on words. She started heading for the door under the guise of looking at more of the signs on her way out. Krystal hesitated for only a moment as she gathered the bag Eliza had thoughtfully put her signs in as well as a business card.

"Thank you! Have a nice day." Eliza grinned one last time. She watched Krystal the whole length of the store as she walked out and was caught as Krystal turned one last time to look back. Blushing she pretended to be looking through another carton of signs.

Another woman emerged from behind the wall at the back of the store that contained horizontal files on their sides which were full of signs. "Ah, we had a customer I see" she smiled.

Nodding absentmindedly Eliza shook herself and looked at Lynn. "Yes, that makes two today. I guess opening and unlocking the doors was a good idea even if we aren't all set-up."

Lynn laughed. Eliza had worked like crazy to get moved in and set up in just under a week. She had moved her entire warehouse from Wausau, Wisconsin into this store and divided it so that the production was done at the back and the front held stock and showcased what they made and sold. Her entire business had been primarily wholesale but she found she needed the input of the retail scene to keep growing and maintain a variety of products. She already made over 5000 different signs and was contemplating adding stickers and magnets. She wanted to make them herself though and the machinery to do it like she wanted cost more than her start up for this store so she was holding off to see how this went. She wanted to give it a year, maybe two to see how well it was received. If she got an offer to sell it all though she was prepared to move on as well. She was so excited about the prospect though, this had been a real achievement and a hell of a gamble on her part. No one believed she could do it but she knew her product, had done every aspect of her business at one time or another and was now ready to prove it to herself, the hell with the naysayers and there were a lot of them in the form of her family members.

Lynn was a good friend who was fed up with factory work. Carpal tunnel syndrome had caught up with her and she had jumped at the chance of moving out of Fairfield and working with Eliza. They had known each other since their college days. Eliza had thrown into the deal an apartment that Lynn was fixing up upstairs for part of her pay. The insurance and the benefits made it a sweet deal for her. Eliza was just grateful to have someone she could trust who believed in what she was doing. They would have to eventually hire another person or two as summer progressed but this town was full of people looking for work.

The fax machine went off as they were putting more stock on the shelves. Pulling the paper from the machine Eliza sighed in genuine regret. She had taken out several ads in several trade magazines and this was another request for a catalog. Everyone wanted a 'free' catalog but it was expensive to print as well as mail them out. With over 5000 signs people didn't realize it. It was the wholesale side of her business though and she couldn't gripe, it made a lot of money for her despite the economy. Quickly typing the name into the computer she printed out an address label and attached it to the pre-printed oversized envelope she had ready. She had collated many catalogs in advance of these requests and pulled one to put in the envelope as well as price sheets and terms and conditions. Sticking a printed stamp on the envelope she dropped it into an oversized mailbox they had by the doorway for the mailman. With so much going on at least the poor mailperson knew where to pick up and drop off the mail in this establishment.

The day grew busier as tourists vacated their hotels and began shopping or taking advantage of the various amusements the town had to offer. There were so many that a one day trip wasn't sensible unless you lived within a few hours distance. The hotels were already doing a booming business and Eliza had wanted to start her summer off right. She had gotten the loan and a week later had driven to the Dells to look at properties. It was fortunate that she had been persistent as this one barely had become vacant and she snatched it up immediately. The ensuing move had been achieved in two stages, first the business, then her personal items. She had hired big strong guys who wanted a quick buck but knew her through friends and were willing to lift all the heavy stuff for her. And there was a lot of heavy stuff! Aluminum was not light, especially in mass quantities.

Finding a place to live hadn't been easy but she had driven around looking for 'for rent' signs. Most were for 'vacation' rentals and were overpriced but she found one that was a 'rent to own' and intrigued had pursued it. The little old lady who owned the property was thrilled that Eliza appreciated her little gem and had allowed her to sign a one year lease nearly on the spot. Eliza was thrilled with the three bedroom bungalow she had to live in. She had been considering the apartment upstairs but had been happy to give that to Lynn to sweeten their deal. She hadn't relished the idea of living on the premises anyway; she would never have gone home at night. She needed the definite break from home and work.

All day in between helping customers Eliza hung signs. The beeping of her lift could be heard and it was driving Lynn nuts but the signs had to be hung and neither of them could have been on a ladder that tall. Eliza had acquired a really cool extendible bar that could unhang up to 12' but the lift was necessary to the 16' and 20' heights. Eliza hadn't hung any signs above the 16' height instead leaving that for banners and promotional items. Finally though by the end of the day all the top signs were hung and she could put away the lift in its corner. It was available if they really needed to remove a sign from the high walls she had hung with grid wall.

By seven they were both exhausted and ready to call it a day. All day long though Eliza had thought about the interesting German woman she had met that morning and wondered if she was too tired to go to the club. She hadn't socialized in years and knew she was due for some fun. With only her and Lynn though she couldn't afford to be tired all the time. Debating it back and forth all day she decided not to go. Heading home that night she was all set to put away her car and crawl into bed when she thought, ah what the heck. What's the difference if I sit in bed for a few hours watching TV or reading a book or go to Culture for a few hours? She knew deep down though the real reason she was going was her interest in the German blonde.

She quickly showered being careful not to get her hair wet. Pulling out the pins that held it back in its long pony tail she brushed it out enjoying its beautiful length, her pride and joy. She knew her hair made her look beautiful, noticeable but she also knew the hard work it made for her. She figured a couple of more years and she would have to keep it short as she would have enough gray then that it would look gross. Meanwhile she enjoyed the attention it garnered. It had a lovely red brown hugh with blonde highlights and its natural curl made it look lovely. Few people probably believed any of it was natural but she had it this way for thirty years and no one could color it or curl it that convincingly.

She quickly shaved and primped freshening her makeup and putting on perfume before dressing in a little black dress with a matching shawl. Putting on some jewelry she took one last look in the mirror and was pleased with what she saw. As she had gotten older her looks had matured. She had been a plain Jane for as long as she remembered but the last few years something had changed. Perhaps it was maturity, perhaps she had grown into her looks, maybe it was confidence but suddenly and surprising she was now beautiful. A new exercise program this last year and changing her eating habits had slimmed down her figure that now she got second looks where before that was maybe only a first look. She knew that she was in her prime now and was enjoying her body and looks for the first time in her life. Not conceited in any way she took pleasure in knowing that she felt and looked good.

With all that in mind she was at the club by 9. Paying her entrance fee she began to weave her way through the crowd. She was surprised that it was crowded at 9 already but then this was the Midwest, it wasn't like the coasts where partying started at midnight and went until 5am. They still rolled up the sidewalks in places at 9 here! Too funny. Looking around she began checking out the bars and finding one that was fairly centrally located she ordered a sloe screw. As she would be driving later she sipped this as she people watched. Two guys asked her to dance and she thanked both of them but declined. It was nearly 10 before she spotted Aarika dancing on the floor with one of the men she had turned down! She immediately began looking around for Krystal but didn't see her. Had she misinterpreted the interest that was so transparent? She hoped not! Just then she felt a tap on her shoulder and she turned.

Staring her right in the face was the aristocratic beauty she had thought about all day. Wow was she dressed hot! She had put her hair up and the lines of her neck reminded Eliza of a beautiful Arabian horse. She was so clean cut and sleek! Taking all this in at a glance Eliza grinned and said "Guten Abend!"

Krystal smiled at Eliza's use of German "Guten Abend" she answered in her smooth lilting voice. "So you came?" she asked in English.

"Yes, I couldn't pass up a chance to have some fun" Eliza answered as she admired the beauty before her.

"I thought perhaps you would be too tired?"

Nodding Eliza had to agree with her, she was tired, she was exhausted but she was also interested in this woman before her and couldn't pass up the chance to get to know her better. "I am tired, I'm exhausted really, but I guess I'll sleep when I'm dead." She answered quoting a popular song.

"Well then we will have to make sure you have that fun you were looking for" Krystal smiled again as she admired what Eliza was wearing. She had incredible legs that had been hidden under the jeans she had been wearing in the store this morning. Now in her little black dress she looked very inviting. Krystal could look right down it with her heels and additional height and it wanted or screamed 'look at me' and Eliza filled it out in all the right places. Krystal loved the way her hair looked she wanted to run her fingers through it, imagining how soft it would feel in her hands. She reached out her hand to take Eliza's in her own "come on, let's dance!"

Eliza tossed off the rest of her drink and left the glass on the bar before allowing Krystal to pull her towards the dance floor. She really should have eaten something earlier the drink was already relaxing her way too much but she was feeling good and she definitely wanted to dance with Krystal. As they both began to rock to the beat she admired the way Krystal moved. She was a pretty good dancer herself and enjoyed swaying to the music in front of the woman she found so interesting. The next song was a slow dance and Krystal never hesitated as she gathered Eliza into her arms to move right against her. Eliza thought really hard about the fact that she should have eaten something this was happening way too fast and she was too relaxed already. Having this sexy woman in her arms already was giving her ideas that were at least a couple of dates away. She was enjoying it though and she could smell the wonderful perfume that Krystal was wearing as she held her close.

Krystal couldn't believe how receptive Eliza was to her advances already. Given she was an American and probably thought Krystal was just having a holiday fling she was used to women giving off certain signs and Eliza wasn't a quick lay. She had tried pushing the limit with the slow dance sure that she would object but instead she not only found Eliza willing but compliant. They danced wonderfully together. She caught Aarika's eye as she danced chastely with some guy and grinned. Aarika gave her 'I can't believe you' look shaking her head. Krystal found herself dancing a little more closely than she would have normally and perhaps brushing suggestively. Eliza didn't object and Krystal heard her despite the loud music change her breathing.

Eliza pulled back enough to ask "are you trying to drive me insane?"

Doing her best to look innocent and failing miserably Krystal asked "what? Who me?" But she did back off a fraction.

Grinning Eliza was a little tipped but not drunk and certainly not unaware of what Krystal had been doing already. Although it was a little soon and they didn't know each other well enough she was becoming aroused by this beautiful woman in her arms. She tried at least to maintain her dignity while still welcoming the body language the woman was giving her. It had been so long since she had been with anyone but the instant attraction she had felt towards Krystal surprised her. She knew for Krystal it would just be a fling and no big deal but Eliza wasn't built that way. She didn't do one night stands. She had more respect for her body. It was fun though playing the game and she hoped harmless.

Krystal tried to pull Eliza closer if that was possible. When her hand at Eliza's back dipped a little low though Eliza pulled back with a look that said Krystal had gone too far and she let her go, for now. Krystal began telling Eliza about their trip that had started in New York and then gone on to Chicago. How friends had mentioned the Dells and on impulse she and Aarika had come up to see the sights. Eliza was surprised that they weren't German but Austrian, but then it was a natural assumption since Austrian's spoke German.

Eliza began telling Krystal about her move into the store and a little about her business. Krystal was surprised to find she had been making signs for over 20 years for herself and a couple of years for someone else. She had quite a work ethic and despite the bad economy it had raised her family on the profits. Krystal was also surprised when Eliza told her she had two sons in college, she didn't look that old but when Eliza confided she had started young Krystal assumed that was why because Eliza didn't look very old. She guessed her to be at the most 36 to her own 37 which would mean she started at least at 16 maybe if her sons were just in college.

They couldn't talk during the disco songs but they did dance five straight before they sat out and chatted finding more and more in common and intrigued about the other. Krystal found herself very attracted by the sheen of sweat on Eliza's brow, Eliza found Krystal and the things she had done to be fascinating as they talked and talked. Eliza didn't realize the passage of time until she looked at her phone and realized it was nearly midnight.

"I'm sorry to say I'm going to have to be going" she told Krystal reluctantly. She had really enjoyed herself and regretted having to leave but she had to get some sleep before her full day tomorrow and she desperately needed her sleep!

"I'm sorry as well, can I come with you?" Krystal asked on impulse.

Turning her head slightly Eliza looked at her looking for hidden meanings. They had enjoyed their witty repartee for the most part and she didn't know if it was fatigue or what she wasn't sure how to take the question. "Krystal, I really like you but are you asking if I will take you home?" She didn't do that!

Krystal wasn't sure if she had scared this intriguing American off. Eliza had surprised her with the amount of sophistication she showed. She was articulate, well read, and very intelligent. She did want to get to know her better and calling their evening short was not what she wanted in the least. "I don't necessarily mean it like that, unless you'd like to and then we could at least discuss it, but I really like you too and want to get to know you better."

"I don't take strangers home and have one night stands" Eliza told her stiffly.

"No, no, it's not like that. I swear. I don't do that either." Here Krystal paused not sure how to articulate what she meant, she only knew that she hadn't enough time to get to know this woman and she hadn't enjoyed herself like this in a long long time. Her life was full of opportunities for one night stands and she hadn't been one to take anyone up on that offer, ever. Her world was full of casual sex and that wasn't what she wanted at all. "I want to just get to know you better" she finished lamely.

Eliza understood, or rather she thought she did. She thought quickly, getting to know this lovely woman better and losing precious sleep that she needed badly or going home alone and knowing she might not get that precious sleep because of thinking about this woman. Deciding that life offered few chances she could make up her sleep another time and nodded "yes, if you would like to come home with me, I'd like that."

They discussed that Eliza would drive Krystal back in the morning before she opened the store. That they might 'sleep' together but both understood that it was going to be sleep and not sex that was implied. As they both made it clear it relaxed the situation that they had unintentionally made tense. Aarika had come and gone from their table periodically during the night and just then she walked up again.

"Aarika, Eliza is going to take me home so we can talk the night away" Krystal grinned. "She will bring me back to the hotel in the morning."

"Are you crazy? You barely know this woman!" Aarika glared at the two of them as she made herself heard over the rock beat.

"No no, it's not like that!" Krystal tried to reassure her friend "we don't want the evening to end and we do want to chat."

Aarika didn't believe her friend and let her know in no uncertain terms that she didn't believe the 'chat' part at all.

"Aarika, we just want to get to know one another better, relax, I'm a big girl!"

Eliza butted in at that point "Aarika, It's not that far from my store where I live" with that she took out a business card from her purse and turning it over she grabbed a pen and wrote some things on the back. "Here is my business card and my address and phone number on the back. You can even call it now to see that my cell picks up. I am an honest person and no harm will come to Krystal."

Aarika was surprised as she read the card. She went to object and Eliza beat her to it.

"Yes, I could have made up the address but not the cell number and you can phone it now."

Krystal grinned at her friend. How much more fair could Eliza be? Yes they barely knew each other but Eliza was being forthright and honest and providing Aarika with the information she needed to get a hold of both of them if something should come up, which it shouldn't. Krystal sensed, she knew, that Eliza wasn't an ax murderer and she hoped to get to know her better, that wasn't a crime.

Aarika finished examining the card and looked up at Krystal. Studying her friends face for a moment she nodded and said "ok, I'll catch a taxi when I'm ready to go back to the hotel."

Krystal hugged her friend and turned to Eliza "ok, let's go."

Eliza nodded to Aarika and gave her a small grin as she and Krystal left the club.

Krystal was pleasantly surprised at the Mitsubishi Spider convertible that Eliza was driving. It was a cute little car and Eliza didn't bother putting the top down as she drove it expertly away from the club. Going over the bridge through town which was now very quiet she headed for a more residential area off the strip and was soon pulling into a quiet neighborhood. She explained to Krystal how lucky she had been to find this little bungalow and Krystal was enchanted as they pulled into the driveway. It was a neat little find with welcoming windows and white trim on a powder blue house. Eliza explained it had three bedrooms, two upstairs one downstairs that she had converted into a den/office. Unlocking the door she showed Krystal the efficient little kitchen, the living room, and the den before taking her upstairs and showing her the large master bedroom and the smaller guest room.

"Would you like to use the bathroom up here, I can lend you some night clothes?" Eliza asked.

Nodding Krystal headed for the bathroom as Eliza handed her some satin pajamas from her dresser. Taking out some satin ones for herself she waited until Krystal had closed the bathroom door and quickly stripped off her dress, slip, underwear, and pantyhose. Pulling on the pajamas she quickly put her clothes in the hamper by her door. Slipping back downstairs she quickly removed her makeup with soap and water and used the brush she kept there to brush out her long hair. She felt she looked very plain at the moment but oh well. She heard the water from upstairs and quickly washed herself and brushed her teeth. Heading back up the narrow bungalow steps she met Krystal as she came out of the bathroom. Looking at her she was surprised to see Krystal without her own makeup and pleased how pretty she still looked with a sprinkling of freckles across the bridge of her nose. Krystal was surprised to see Eliza without her own makeup and in satin pajamas already. She had hurried since she thought Eliza was waiting to use the bathroom.

Eliza felt a little awkward. Although they had agreed to 'sleep' together it wasn't like a sleep over from grade school days and she wasn't certain what to do with this grown woman in her room. Although she had been with women before, never one on such short acquaintance. Krystal solved her moment of awkwardness by coming across the room and taking her in her arms as though they were going to dance. They did in fact sway there to some unspoken music and Eliza liked the feel of this woman in her arms. They both must have felt the moment as they kissed. Eliza was surprised at how good that kiss felt and quickly opened her mouth to deepen it. Krystal was surprised at how good a kisser Eliza was and enjoyed the fact that Eliza quickly deepened it. Krystal got her earlier wish as her hands delved into Eliza's long hair. Eliza cupped Krystal's head to hold it in place so her mouth could play with Krystal's lips. They both enjoyed their first kiss together so much that it continued into a second and third before they even realized it. Finally though they pulled back in amazement and looked deeply into each other's faces to read what was unspoken there.

Krystal was the first to break the silence "I don't know what it is about you but I've been drawn to you from the moment I met you in your store. I don't want you to think I do this regularly, getting into strange women's beds."

Shaking her head Eliza answered honestly "No, I don't think that at all, I too have felt strangely drawn to you. I haven't slept with a woman in two years and I worried that it was just sexual that I was feeling towards you, but I am so very attracted to you its almost painful."

Krystal hesitated and then asked "how many partners have you had?" She was still holding Eliza in her arms and they were about six inches apart. Her hands were gently caressing Eliza's shoulders and arms as she looked into her face as they talked.

"Two, only two, ever. That is women. I've been with two men before that and one was my ex-husband who gave me my two sons." Eliza answered and then asked "and how many partners have you had?" Her own hands were caressing Krystal's back using her fingertips and short nails to good effect.

"I've been with four women in my life and those were fairly long commitments but I haven't been with anyone in nearly a year" Krystal admitted almost sheepishly.

"Why not? You're a beautiful woman, what's wrong with you?" Eliza asked in a teasing manner but was genuinely surprised. Krystal was a catch, anyone would be grateful to be with her.

Smiling at the compliment Krystal thought and then answered "I'm fairly picky, I don't do casual. The first one was my 'experiment' and then I realized I really was a lesbian and we enjoyed learning with each other but then after a year realized neither of us was ready for a commitment and we went our separate ways, amicably. That was when I was 18. I dated some men but not one of them have I ever wanted to sleep with. I tried but couldn't make myself have sex with any of them. Kissing and caressing by them felt invasive and I finally stopped trying that after a few years." She grinned ruefully, acknowledging she had at least tried.

"If you have never been with a man then what about the daughter you mentioned earlier?" Eliza asked naively.

"Oh, that was my third girlfriend and my idea. We thought it would be terrific if we had a child together, we planned to get married but by the time I got pregnant she lost interest. It was kind of sad but there you have it and once I was pregnant I certainly wasn't going to get rid of it and I love my daughter, she is terrific, her name is Selena."

Enjoying children Eliza asked "how old is she?" she could see the genuine pride in Krystal's voice as they talked.

"Ah, she is two now" she said with a smile.

Thinking quickly Eliza she mentally counted off on her fingers and asked "wait, you said you had four relationships, one is missing?"

"Ah, three were just relationships, one was a marriage. I married a wonderful woman several years back but she died" at this revelation Krystal hung her head a little, Eliza could see the genuine regret when she continued "I don't consider her 'just' a relationship, I loved her incredibly and she was taken from me."

Softly Eliza asked "how did she die?"

"It was a freak avalanche in the Alps where we were skiing. She got caught and I was rescued. Sometimes I wonder if I should have died there." Eliza could hear the catch in Krystal's voice and pulled her close for a hug. She didn't want their conversation to cause her pain.

"I'm sorry, you obviously loved her very much, I didn't mean to hurt you by my questions." Eliza told her sadly.

Pulling back Krystal looked at her to see the genuine sorrow for her and appreciated her understanding. It still hurt, it would always hurt. This wasn't the time or the place though. "Her name was Selena; I named my daughter after her in her honor. My little Selena is nothing like the woman I married." She laughed ruefully. "In fact, she would be angry with me for naming my daughter after her but she would also find it wonderfully ironic." She smiled remembering the woman who was long gone, who she sometimes had trouble visualizing anymore, who's picture was all she had left of her besides her memories.

Gently Eliza kissed her. This sweet action more than anything else melted Krystal on the spot. Her knees began to buckle as the kiss deepened. Firmly she changed her thoughts. Pulling back slightly she asked "what about you? Why two men, why two women? What happened?"

"Ah for that we should sit down." Eliza pulled from Krystal's embrace to pull down the bedspread and then the blanket. Reaching across she flicked the blanket and cover sheet down on Krystal's side and invited playfully with a pat on that side. Krystal got into the bed and pulled the cover sheet up to her waist. Leaning back against two comfy pillows she waited for Eliza to continue her story. Eliza got in on the left side of the bed and pulled the cover sheet up as well. Using the sheet as a distraction she began her own recital "I was with my first man at 19. I was feeling depressed and down and very unsure of my teenage body. Men weren't attracted to me and I never had considered a woman." Her eyes flicked up to look at Krystal at that moment. "A friend introduced me to this man through her own boyfriend one day and we disliked each other at first sight. I don't remember to this day how it happened but I allowed him to have sex with me that night and take my virginity. It was a mess; I bled for several days after that. My friend said the bed looked like someone had been murdered. Needless to say it was not a good first experience." Swallowing Eliza continued. "A year later I met my husband. He seemed like a good man, young but hard working. I was wrong on several accounts. Being naive and hoping to love someone who would take care of me, provide for me, and give me a happily ever after I put my trust in the wrong man. He took advantage of my naiveté and got me pregnant so I would have to marry him. He seemed to resent that he wasn't my 'first' and that I wasn't a virgin when he met me. He then proceeded to abuse me until I had no self-esteem left. Once he had me with the two children his abuse continued until finally I had to get out and I took the children and ran to protective services. The ensuing divorce was nasty but what he didn't know is that I had written down in my diaries what he had done and when, there was a carefully kept log of all his abuses and the worst of them corresponded with hospital visits. He was lucky not to be arrested. I was lucky that he didn't want visitation rights once his abuse became public knowledge and his reputation ruined in our little town. Man, was he angry, I thought I was going to die. Once the divorce was final I gathered what I had left and moved across the state to start over." She stopped for a moment to let the bad memories pass before continuing.

Krystal leaned over and gently caressed her cheek, to remind her that it was over, she was with someone else now, or for the moment, and to offer her support. Eliza reached up and held the hand to her cheek for a moment before continuing.

"I was working with a sign company when I left him and I started making my own signs out of my garage when I moved. The company I had worked for went under and I began soliciting their accounts. The people who remembered me started to order and I began to grow, slowly but surely. My children started school and I found myself getting lonely. I didn't really fit in with the other mothers but one stood out and we began to become friends. I found myself attracted to her but I was surprised to find she felt the same. Neither of us had been with another woman. We fell in love and discovered what each of us liked, what worked for us, we shared a house together until her daughter and my two sons were teenagers. We were gossiped about all around town and it became awkward for our children. Her daughter began a campaign to break us up and eventually it succeeded. Marg couldn't take the stress and eventually she had to move out, she told me she wanted to be with men now and she proceeded to marry the first one that came along. They were married three months after she broke up with me. That was hurtful and we haven't spoken since."

"That's terrible, you couldn't reason with her?" Krystal asked.

Shaking her head Eliza had been watching Krystal's kind face as she told her story. "I was so lonely and I realized I needed to be happy with me, one day I met a woman off the internet and we ended up going to lunch, that night I ended up in her bed but I wasn't attracted to her, I was very lonely though. She and I ended up having awful sex. We tried dating for a while but she was more screwed up than me. I decided at that point that I wasn't ever going to try casual sex again and to concentrate on my boys and business." She grinned at Krystal "and then today in walks a beautiful woman who blew all my good intentions out the window with her smile" she leaned forward for a kiss "and I find myself wondering how someone I am so attracted to, could wind up in my bed to just 'talk?'"

Krystal laughed, she had been wondering the same, if she were insane to agree to come home with this woman, if she were insane 'just to talk' when she really wondered about that body under the satin pajamas. Pulling Eliza close she just held her and caressed that wonderful hair. It really felt wonderful holding her and winding her fingers through the silky hair. "I think perhaps fate is laughing at us and wondering if temptation might be good for our soul?"

Eliza grinned at the deliciously accented Austrian she was holding. Whatever perfume Krystal used it clung to her or her hair and smelled breathtaking. Eliza wondered if she would get any sleep and really didn't care if they stayed up all night talking. They did indeed talk until the early morning hours, getting to know one another; it was nice for both of them. Eliza finally couldn't keep her eyes open any longer, she had been working too hard for too many weeks and sleep was precious, she drifted off in the middle of her conversation with Krystal telling her about her sons. Krystal laughed softly as she watched this beautiful and incredibly interesting American fall asleep.

Since Krystal was from Europe, the time difference, and her own night owl activities, she could sleep in catnaps and be fine for days. This trip with Aarika was just a diversion in an endlessly long line of diversions. She was tired of the nightlife, she was tired of the same people, the same dramas, the change in scenery had done her good, she enjoyed traveling but she was bored. Eliza had proven to be an interesting person for her to know, she really had enjoyed herself, and she looked forward to getting to know her better. She too drifted off for a few hours.

~End of Chapter 1~

About the Author

K'Anne Meinel is the BEST SELLING author of REPRESENTED and several other books including her first SHIPS which was written in 2003 over the course of two weeks. She then played with it for several years before publishing it as an e-book and then was approached to publish it in book form. After that it was published on other sites as an e-book. In the meantime she published some 50 short stories, novellas, and novels of various genres. Originally from Wisconsin many of her stories have taken on locations from and around the state. A gypsy at heart she has lived in many locations and plans to continue doing that. Her fans have compared her to some of the great authors of our times including Danielle Steel and Dean Koontz. Videos of several of her books are available on You Tube outlining some of the locations of her books and telling a little bit more…giving the readers insight into her mind as she created these wonderful stories.

SHIPS
CompanionSHIP, FriendSHIP, RelationSHIP

Have you ever met a person that you just were so in synch with? You knew immediately that they were someone special for you? Would you know how lucky you were? Would you know they were the one?

What do you do when you fall in love with a woman? When you yourself thought you were straight? Dealing with this unusual relationship brings a lot of 'firsts' to Joans life.

Joan is a world renowned artist who is straight, has three children, and is content with her life when she meets Grace, a respected psychiatrist who also happens to be a lesbian. Joan is conflicted and has to deal with her feelings, the incredible woman she finds herself in love with, and the relationship that occurs over the next 20 years.

If you have enjoyed this book and the others listed here Shadoe Publishing is always looking for first, second, or third time authors. Please check out our website @ www.shadoepublishing.com for information or contact us at shadoepublishing@gmail.com.

We may be able to help you make your dreams of becoming a published author come true.

Made in the USA
San Bernardino, CA
12 December 2013